Distributed Database Systems

INTERNATIONAL COMPUTER SCIENCE SERIES

SELECTED TITLES IN THE SERIES

Data Models, Database Languages and Database Management Systems *Gottfried Vossen*

The Theory of Computability: Programs, Machines, Effectiveness and Feasibility *R Sommerhalder and S C van Westrhenen*

Clausal Form Logic: An Introduction to the Logic of Computer Reasoning *T Richards*

Software Engineering (4th Edn) *I Sommerville*

Programming in Ada (3rd Edn) *J G P Barnes*

Elements of Functional Programming *C Reade*

Interactive Computer Graphics: Functional, Procedural and Device-Level Methods *P Burger and D Gillies*

Common Lisp Programming for Artificial Intelligence *T Hasemer and J Domingue*

Program Derivation: The Development of Programs from Specifications *R G Dromey*

Object-Oriented Programming with Simula *B Kirkerud*

Programming for Artificial Intelligence: Methods, Tools and Applications *W Kreutzer and B J McKenzie*

Program Design with Modula-2 *S Eisenbach and C Sadler*

Parallel Processing: Principles and Practice *E V Krishnamurthy*

Real Time Systems and Their Programming Languages *A Burns and A Wellings*

Fortran 77 Programming: With an Introduction to the Fortan 90 Standard (2nd Edn) *T M R Ellis*

Prolog Programming for Artificial Intelligence (2nd Edn) *I Bratko*

Introduction to Expert Systems (2nd Edn) *P Jackson*

Logic For Computer Science *S Reeves and M Clarke*

The Programming Process: An Introduction using VDM and Pascal *J T Latham, V J Bush and D Cottam*

Analysis of Algorithms and Data Structures *L Banachowski, A Kreczmar and W Rytter*

Handbook of Algorithms and Data Structures (2nd Edn) *G Gonnet and R Baeza-Yates*

Distributed Database Systems

David Bell
University of Ulster

Jane Grimson
Trinity College, Dublin

ADDISON-WESLEY
PUBLISHING
COMPANY

Wokingham, England · Reading, Massachusetts · Menlo Park, California · New York
Don Mills, Ontario · Amsterdam · Bonn · Sydney · Singapore
Tokyo · Madrid · San Juan · Milan · Paris · Mexico City · Seoul · Taipei

Cover designed by Chris Eley.
and printed by The Riverside Printing Co. (Reading) Ltd.
Printed in Great Britain by T.J. Press (Padstow) Ltd, Padstow, Cornwall.

First printed in 1992. Reprinted 1992 and 1994.

British Library Cataloguing-in-Publication Data
A catalogue record for this book is available from the British library.

Library of Congress Cataloging-in-Publication Data
Available from the publisher

ISBN 0–201–54400–8

Preface

Overall objectives

For many types of organization, the ultimate information handling aspiration is to have an integrated database system so that common files can be consulted by various sections of the organization, in an efficient and effective manner. However, database systems are not just pertinent to organizations or even large sections of enterprises. Many users of personal computers now accept a database management system (DBMS) as an integral part of their computing software almost as important as an operating system. Databases are no longer confined to the province of large-scale users.

The addition of communications facilities to a database system can take it from a centralized concept to a decentralized concept. The reservoir of data need not all be situated at a single site on a single computing facility. Neither does the database have to be confined within the boundaries of a single organization or corporation.

Now this has caused some debate among commentators on technology. For a long time, even predating the advent of electronic computers, the notion has been around that computers will start to 'take over' and control the destiny of *homo sapiens*. This has recently been countered by pointing to the wide availability of personal computers and the possibility of linking them through increasingly sophisticated communications facilities. A message of great freedom and decentralization is now being preached in some quarters. The other side can of course argue back.

We do not wish to contribute directly to this debate. On the other hand, we do wish to present the core knowledge of one particular aspect – the data-handling aspect – of distributed computing which impacts on both of the views stated above.

The idea of writing this book dates back to a St Patrick's Day in the mid-1980s when we were in Rome to plan the third phase of an EC project on distributed databases (DDBs). The motivation was that we could share with others our findings on that project. It has taken longer than expected to get round to writing, and our goal has widened a little in the interim. We are interested in presenting the details of a new tool for information handling to help cope with the bulk of information that is in existence at present or being accumulated in the modern world. In particular we are interested in showing that generalized data management which is integrated but decentralized is already here.

So we make the implicit assumption that this is desirable, at least in some computer applications, for reasons of increasing robustness, efficiency, and local autonomy. It could of course be argued that we therefore favour the second of the two viewpoints above – that we are backing the optimistic notion of greater openness and availability, but we are very aware that the same technology could be used for negative purposes. Our view as technical researchers is that this is really a perennial problem with technological advance. Social and moral considerations have to be taken into account before the use of any powerful tool is contemplated. Widening the data landscape will not of itself make the world a better place. Knives and telephones have negative potential as well as positive – but few would say that it would be better if they had not been invented.

Information is in many ways an unusual commodity. For one thing it is one of the world's few increasing resources. The essential features of an information bank are that the information can be lodged in it, saved indefinitely without deterioration, and withdrawn as desired. Books and other media have served the purposes of previous generations admirably but cannot cope effectively with the bulk of information generated in a space-age, post-industrial society. Computers emerged at just the right time as tools to manage the mountains of data accumulated and encountered in many walks of life. Networks of computers and cheap stores and processors mean that the systems need no longer be centralized. Huge collections of information can be made available at arm's length, and telecommuting and electronic cottages are being talked about. Some observers have even said that there are enough electronic storage devices, or quickly could be, to hold all the recorded information presently in the world (estimated to be of the order of less than 10^{20} bytes).

Again, we are not in the business of commenting on the desirability or otherwise of such developments. We simply recognize that distributed database systems are needed as tools if even the more modest dreams for distributed information handling are to become a reality.

However, many difficulties are encountered when we attempt to make a diverse collection of data stores appear as a single unit to the user. Not only do we have the problem of providing a common interrogation interface to the data, but we are also faced with problems of efficiency, harmonization and representation as we develop distributed database systems. Not all of the problems have been satisfactorily solved yet, but there are now some systems available commercially to provide some of the required functionality. This book is intended as a basic treatment of most of these problems.

Rationale

Our approach to the book derives from accumulated experience in course design. When designing degree courses in disciplines which have a strong vocational character, we believe we should address four aspects of the subject. First we should ensure that on completion of the course the student should have a good grasp of the 'timeless' aspects of the subject. As computing matures an increasing body of theoretical underpinning is being built up. We believe that students should acquire this knowledge. Now, this is not a theoretical book, but its primary objective is to acquaint the reader with the most significant results of research and development relevant to DDB systems at an appropriate level. So we have to make sure that this aspect is recognized and acknowledged at appropriate places and it is the foundation for the second objective of course design. This is that the students should acquire a knowledge of the product-related state of the art of the topics considered, so that they have an awareness of the differences between research ideas and what is available to the practitioner. It is, of course, impossible, using a static medium such as a book, to ensure that the necessarily incomplete snapshot of today's situation is kept up-to-date. The representation of any supplier's wares must be verified and supplemented by anyone seriously surveying the market in connection with a particular application. Nevertheless, an appreciation of the broad view can be imparted.

The remaining two objectives of course design are exceedingly important for students. They are that the students should have skills to sell – a very important aspect for a vocational course – and (a not entirely orthogonal objective) that they should have a systematic approach to problem solving. Now while these two facets of course design are really outside the scope of this book, we have endeavoured to ensure that the presentation is compatible with the tutorial/practical aspects of courses for which the book is a suitable text. This particular aspect of our philosophy is reflected in the worked examples and the exercises for the reader in each chapter of the book.

Outline of the book

The text begins with introductory material in Chapters 1–3. After the introduction in Chapter 1, Chapter 2 presents the basic concepts of databases and computer networks needed to make the book a self-contained volume. The terminology and notation used in the book are introduced in this chapter. Most of this material will be familiar to many students of computer science who have completed early undergraduate courses. However, it is recommended that all readers take some time to look at this chapter, at least briefly, to avoid the ubiquitous terminology problems of computing.

Chapter 3 is considered to be an essential ingredient of a book like this. As indicated by our rationale discussed earlier, an appreciation of the gap between the products currently available in the market place and the ideas emanating from research laboratories is essential for an appreciation of computing technology. Nowhere is this more apparent than in DDB systems where some ideas have been around for well over a decade but are, as yet, not available in any product. Experience has shown that the picture customers perceive of what is available in products for data-handling errs significantly on the side of rosiness. We hope that this chapter goes some way to redressing the balance, although we are aware that this situation can change very rapidly.

Chapters 4–9 deal with technical aspects of DDBs. Our treatment reflects our focus on an evolutionary approach to providing basic functionality for accessing data in pre-existing, diverse collections. We also aim to give the reader an appreciation of the more general issues being addressed in each area.

Chapter 4 deals with two important issues of distributed data. When it is possible to decide where in a network of data stores to place particular data items it is critical, for performance reasons, to make the decisions sensibly. So the first part of this chapter deals with the problem of finding 'good' allocations of data to devices in a computer network. The goodness depends on the profiles of the transactions which arise at different sites, and the capacities of the stores at the sites. Some particular strategies for data and file allocation are presented. The other issue is that of harmonizing data collections at different sites, in the case where the data collections can vary with respect to such things as the data model used, the query language and even syntactic issues like the units used for the data values. For example, one site could use miles and pounds as the units of some data items, while another uses kilometres and kilogrammes. Dealing with heterogeneous data is a very difficult problem, and we cannot hope to cover all its aspects in half a chapter, but we do deal with approaches to the central difficulty of mapping between different data models.

Data placement or allocation as dealt with in Chapter 4 is really a performance-related issue. Chapter 5 also deals with a performance problem, that of ensuring that, having placed the data, we use the most efficient methods and strategies to navigate through the distributed data in order to service any particular query. We have to remember that a database is a shared system, and so there must be compromises between the needs of different transactions. The placement of data will be the result of compromises between competing transactions, so care must be taken when servicing any particular query. The order in which we access the data items, move data around the network and carry out operations greatly influences the responsiveness and cost of servicing queries. The language in which the queries are expressed is high level in the sense that the users need not specify the path of access to the data items. But the system has to do this, and the query optimizer is the system module responsible for this.

Chapters 6 and 7 deal with transaction management. Transactions on a database are 'collections of actions which comprise a consistent transformation of the state of a system', invoked on the objects in the database. Transformations are changes to the data records and devices. In many applications a halt in the operation of the computer due to transaction or other system failure is unacceptable. For example, backup or replica database systems are often used to track the state of a primary database system. These take over transaction processing in the event of disaster in the main system. This is an example of database recovery. The difficulties of ensuring that database recovery is effective and efficient in distributed computer systems are addressed in Chapter 7.

Having multiple versions of data in distributed sites can increase concurrency as well as supporting failure recovery. This is possible because out-of-order requests to read data can be processed by reading suitable older versions of data. More generally, it is important for transaction management that such out-of-order operations do not interfere with the operation of other transactions addressed to the system at the same time. For example, it is possible to lose updates if the operations within different transactions are out of sequence. Various techniques for enforcing a correct sequence of operations within and between transactions are discussed in Chapter 6. Efficiency is important because the enforcement of good 'schedules' can result in indefinite blocking leading to long delays, especially in distributed systems.

Some potential users of distributed systems are put off by the perceived lack of control they have if their data is scattered over several computers linked by telecommunications lines which are vulnerable to unauthorized access or accidental corruption and failure. Chapter 8 deals with these problems. Another major drawback of distributed databases is due to the problems of database design and management, and these are discussed in Chapter 9.

Given our course design philosophy expressed above, it would be unforgivable to treat all of these topics in isolation from an example of the sort of applications which might be expected to use DDBs. So Chapter 10 is devoted to an introduction of a case study based on a project we jointly worked on for several years in health care. The idea is not to look at the details of the DDB components already addressed by this point in the book, but to provide the basis for a practical case study which readers can use to appreciate the value of the DDB approach in applications, and the difficulties that can be expected to arise.

Chapter 11 presents our views on the areas related to DDB technology which we expect to be of increasing importance in the next decade or so. In particular the expected impacts of artificial intelligence, multimedia and object-orientation on distributed data systems are discussed.

Each chapter contains practical exercises whose solutions are given at the end of chapters.

Audience

The text should be useful for a variety of readers. We have focused our attention on the needs of students doing a third or fourth year undergraduate course on computing, but we have also tried to make it suitable as a management information system text. Some engineering courses may find it useful as well. We believe that it will be suitable for introductory postgraduate readings. We have also tried to ensure that it is readable by managers and professionals who simply want to keep abreast of the changing technology and the challenges they can expect in the near future.

By limiting the coverage to key issues and to basic aspects of various topics, supplemented by pointers to the research literature for more advanced readers, we believe that the material can be covered in a two-semester course. This would permit coverage in detail of the algorithms in the book and allow a substantial case study to be carried out.

Acknowledgements

The material for this book was drawn from our notes for lectures and research projects, and these were accumulated over a fairly long period. There were several key contributors to this knowledge, and also to our way of presenting it, and while we have not attempted to make a comprehensive list of these, we hope it will be clear from the references at the ends of the chapters who were the most influential. We ask to be forgiven if we have underemphasized or misrepresented any individual's work.

All our friends who worked with us on the Multistar project had an impact on our approach to DDBs. We are also grateful to all our postgraduate students and research staff who contributed to our database projects over the years.

We would like to thank colleagues who were inveigled into reading drafts of the various chapters and whose comments have undoubtedly improved the quality of the book. Also thanks to Rita whose assistance in the preparation of the manuscript was invaluable and to Simon Plumtree and Stephen Bishop of Addison-Wesley, and Mary Matthews of Keyword Publishing Services for all their help and advice.

Finally, to our families – Sheelagh, Michael and Allistair, Bill, Andrew and Sarah – go special thanks for patience, forebearance and the "Colle Umberto" spirit during this project.

David Bell, Jane Grimson *January 1992*

Contents

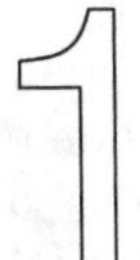

Introduction

1.1 Introduction

At no previous time in the history of computing have there been so many challenging innovations vying for the attention of information systems engineers as there are at present. Technologically, advances are continually being made in hardware, software and 'methodologies'. Improving speeds of, possibly parallel, action and the increased size of rapid access stores available, along with new announcements of products and new ideas from researchers bring with them demands from the user population for their exploitation. For applications, even if users are not aware of particular developments relevant to their operations, there is a perpetual demand for more functionality, service, flexibility and performance. So the information engineer designing a new information system, or prolonging the life of an old one, must always be seeking ways of linking solutions offered by the technologists to the needs of users' applications. One area in which solutions are becoming increasingly viable is in distributed information systems. These are concerned with managing data stored in computing facilities at many nodes linked by communications networks. Systems specifically aimed at the management of distributed databases were first seriously discussed in the mid-1970s. Schemes for architectures really started to appear at the end of that decade.

1.2 The pressure to distribute data

1.2.1 User pressure

Large databases manage data relevant to at least part of the operation of organizations like health service networks, industrial corporations or banks. By collecting all the data into a single 'reservoir', as in Figure 1.1, the original dream was that all data access could be integrated using a kit of database tools, such as data description languages, data manipulation languages, access mechanisms, constraint checkers and very high level languages. However after some experience with the database approach, many enterprises found that the package was to some extent satisfactory for a reasonable number of users, but that few of them got anything like optimal service. 'Owners' of particular data collections found that they had lost control of them and that they were no longer stored at their workplaces. Where they were used, dynamic tailoring of the data structures and details to fit individual needs was almost impossible (Figure 1.2). And yet most accesses to data were, and are, to 'local' data only. Experience has shown that over 90% of input and output data operations are local.

As companies grow user frustration can be expected if data remains centralized. In many organizations users 'voted with their feet' and opted for *de facto* decentralization by acquiring local departmental database systems. Difficulties then began to be manifested in maintaining consistency between the central and local systems and there were operational difficulties in transferring data between them. For example, this was done in some cases by keying in data from reports. So pressure started to grow

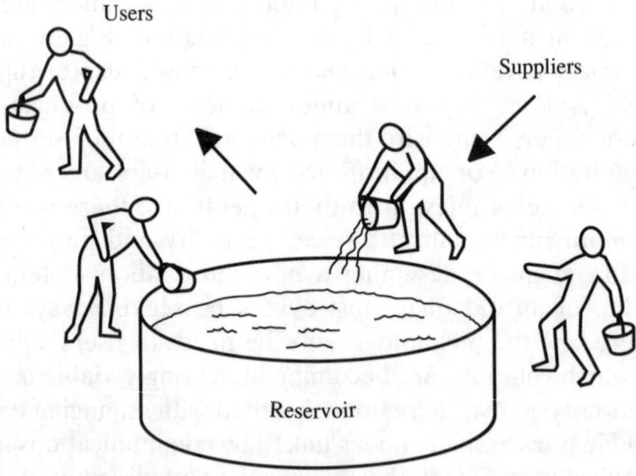

Figure 1.1 Database as a data reservoir.

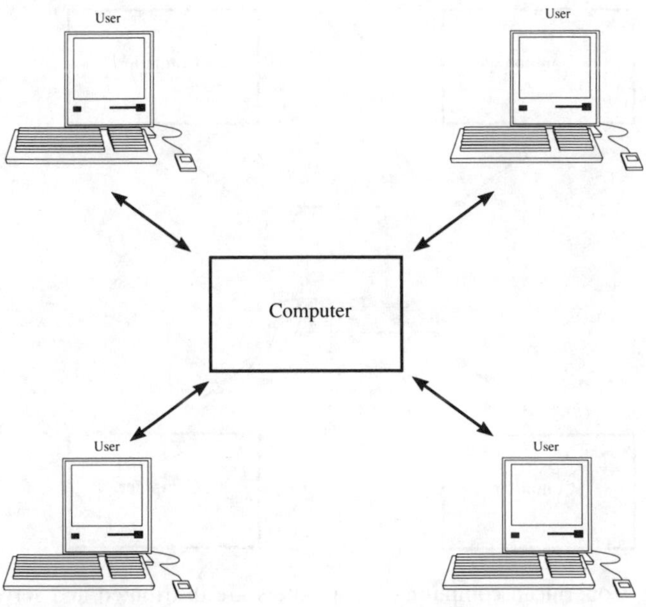

Figure 1.2 Ptolemic computing – users 'fitting in' with a centralized computer.

for the formal decentralization of databases and database functions (Figure 1.3) while maintaining integration and perhaps some centralized control.

Other evolutionary forces for distribution arose for security reasons and because of difficulties in capacity planning and maintenance problems. For backup purposes (e.g. for recovering from disaster) it is clear that having data and processing at various locations is desirable. If files are very large it might be desirable to partition them so that maintenance of a partition can be carried out in isolation from other partitions.

1.2.2 Technology pressure

To accompany this user pull there is a technology push (Figure 1.4). There are very good technical reasons for distributing data, even if we ignore the relatively infrequent cases where multiple computer complexes are needed because of disk I/O overloads and similar phenomena which occur when connections between devices are not up to scratch. The technical pressure to decentralize has been around for some time. 'Grosch's Law', which states that the power of a computer is proportional to the square of its cost, was quoted in support of centralization in the past because of the economies of scale at the time it was formulated. But this 'law' has been repealed by the onward march of technology. Competent and affordable communications network facilities open the door

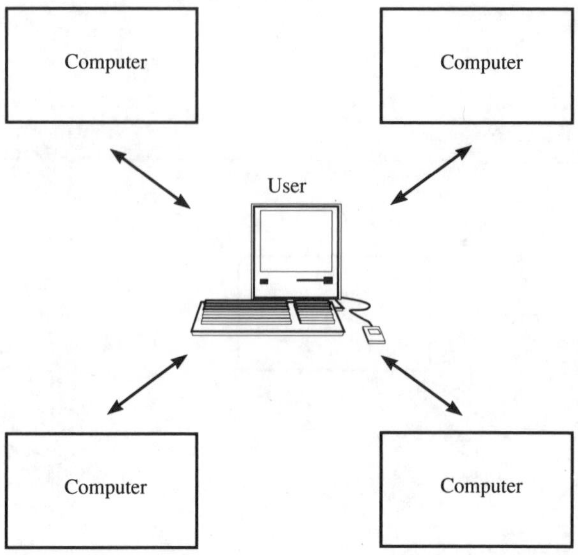

Figure 1.3 Copernican computing – computers are distributed and services are tailored to users' needs.

to distribution. The turn-around of attitudes to distribution of computing can be dated back to the mid-1970s, but it gained momentum in the 1980s.

The major advantages offered by modern technology lead to the following reasons for decentralization of data:

- To provide for systems evolution or changes in user requirements and allow local autonomy;
- To provide a simple, fault-tolerant and flexible system architecture;
- To give good performance.

A related methodological influence is the better understanding of how it is possible to decouple computer applications systems through work done on strategic information system planning studies in the 1980s.

At the same time as this pressure for distribution was mounting, a quite different pressure was being experienced – to use the new technology to integrate, with as little disturbance as possible of users' lifestyles, data systems that were already distributed (and perhaps incompatible).

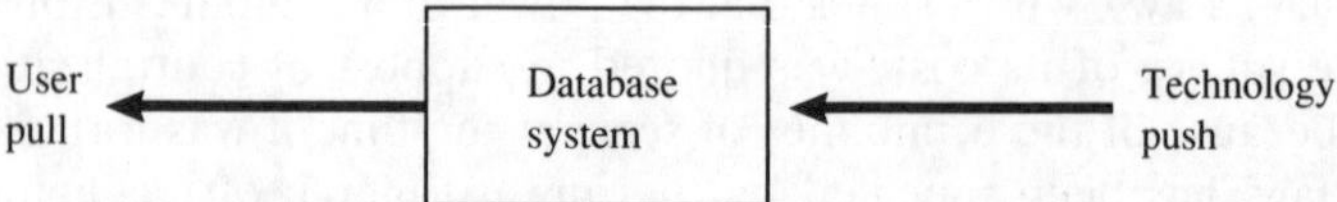

Figure 1.4 Evolutionary forces on database systems.

1.2.3 Difficulties

A number of objections can be raised to counterbalance these advantages. Some technological and user-related difficulties still hinder the take-up of distributed information systems ideas, although these difficulties are being energetically addressed by researchers and developers.

Technological problems occupying the attention of researchers worldwide include

- Ensuring that intersite accessing and processing is carried out efficiently – perhaps even optimally;
- Transforming data and integrating processing between nodes/sites;
- Distributing data around the dispersed sites of a network in an optimal manner;
- Controlling access (e.g. by complex password control) to computerized information linked by communications networks;
- Supporting recovery from failure of systems modules (hardware or software) efficiently and safely;
- Ensuring that the local and global systems remain a true reflection of the real world under consideration by avoiding destructive interference between different 'transactions' against the system.

Some user and organizational problems are

- Developing models for estimating capacity and other capability requirements, and the expected traffic against distributed systems;
- Supporting the design of distributed information systems (e.g. to assist with decisions such as where a particular data object is to be stored or a particular program is to be run);
- Coping with competition for resources between nodes/sites.

While it is important to recognize and address these difficulties, the basic advantages of decentralization give it a decided edge for large scale information processing in present and expected future environments.

1.3 Heterogeneity and the pressure to integrate data

1.3.1 User pressure

So decentralization of data systems and the advent of distributed systems is well justified. But arguments for this would have much less force if the required integration of the *non-local* processing requirements of organizations is not addressed (Figure 1.5). Distributed database (DDB) systems developers address the issue of stitching together disparate, dispersed data systems which predate the DDB, as well as that of supporting the 'purer' distribution scenario, where the data architect has a completely free hand as to the sites and characteristics of local data collections.

Data may be stored at many sites of an enterprise for historical reasons. Yet there are many situations where remote access to that data is required. One example is where managers at regional, national or enterprise level (i.e. at headquarters) require summary data from local (branch) sites. Another example is where the automatic teller systems of several banks are integrated to provide an improved service to customers. Perhaps the systems were designed in ignorance of one another, to serve a single organization, but business opportunities based on evolving technology have altered the perspective.

Also interesting is the fact that there is often a driving need for integration to handle *change*. Applications are continually being developed due to corporate reorganization, changes in local or global standards, new government regulations, evolution of product types or simply to tune their performance. Therefore management of change is of central importance in database systems.

A revealing example of a situation where heterogeneity arises for user-oriented reasons is in organizational changes, such as corporate mergers or acquisitions. These enterprise adaptations often lead to conversion or integration of database systems. The economic climate can sometimes mean that this type of movement is exceptionally prominent, as was the case in the mid-1980s. A conspicuous example is in banking, where mergers are triggered by the desire to expand customer bases and compete on a broader front in the financial services markets. For banks and other merger-prone organizations such as oil companies, the merger of information processing systems is normally given top priority. There is tremendous potential for conflicts within and between these systems and

Figure 1.5 Problems of singing out of different hymn-books.

good analysis, planning and change-over management, accompanied by clear directives and a willingness to compromise, are essential ingredients of a smooth transition.

The cost of file and database conversion is often claimed to be a major factor in information systems mergers. Companies which frequently participate in mergers have found it prudent over the years to develop standard conversion kits and procedures for this purpose. Techniques for integrating pre-existing heterogeneous data collections and systems are useful here, even if only as an intermediate solution.

1.3.2 Technological pressure

A database may have to be converted from one logical data model to another, or several databases using a variety of logical data models may have to be integrated for any of a number of technology-related reasons. Very significant forces for such change and hence heterogeneity are generated by the following trends:

- Evolving database-related technology,
- The desire to get a better match from among the available database management systems packages for a given application profile,
- The requirement for greater flexibility or sophistication of services from software packages.

These compound and supplement the user pull experienced as a result of organizational adjustments such as mergers of organizations with different systems, as discussed earlier.

Organizations opting for the database approach to support their information handling do so in the expectation of a high level of flexibility of data access, cost effectiveness of applications development, integration of applications systems in an efficient manner and user-to-program and program-to-data harmony and even independence. Yet it is rare for all of these expectations to be realized in practice and this is confirmed by the fact that methods for bridging the gaps between expectations and reality are the subject of continual and diligent research and development effort. Activity in this area provides a basis for hope that database systems which provide the envisaged benefits will eventually materialize. Some conspicuous and promising areas of investigation will be treated in Chapter 11.

Managers who control installations where there is a commitment to the currently available, albeit imperfect, database systems must face up to the problem of coping with upgrades when existing systems become technically obsolete. Typically, large organizations find it necessary to upgrade to a 'better' database management system (DBMS) every few years. Other prominent systems components are also replaced from time to time. At least during the changeover period, integration is usually required between these and the previous systems. For those managing the database systems in such organizations, converting to a new operating system, hardware or DBMS is a traumatic experience. The frightening 'war stories' and disastrous case histories of others' attempts to convert to a new database strongly influence management in many companies to make a decision, based on insubstantial technological or operational reasons, not to change their systems. A system to cope with distributed heterogeneous data systems holds the promise of easing the pain associated with these experiences.

1.3.3 Difficulties caused by heterogeneity

Making use of communications networks linking computing facilities is not by any means a complete answer to users' problems. Programmers and other users who want to make an enquiry on a set of interconnected databases must be aware of the location and format of the data they wish to access; split the question up into bits that can be addressed in single individual nodes; resolve, where necessary, any inconsistencies between the styles, units, and structures; arrange for the partial results of the single-site queries to be accumulated at the site issuing the query; and extract the details required. When it is considered that data must also be kept current and consistent and that failures in communication links must be detected and corrected, it is clear that the programmer would appreciate system support. For several years the issues raised when attempting to supply this sort of service have been the focus of attention of many researchers and system developers in the database community.

The removal of these difficulties is precisely the objective of data management systems for the integration of heterogeneous component systems.

1.4 Integrating other kinds of information system

It is important to avoid the mistake of treating the distribution of databases as promising to provide the ultimate answer, in any sense, to professional, business and technical data handling problems. The systems introduced in this book must be seen as being just one area in future information handling provision (Figure 1.6).

Historically, different generic classes of information systems have evolved largely in mutual isolation. For example, there is a traditional class called information retrieval systems, another called knowledge based systems, and another called database systems. The reader's attention is drawn to the references at the end of this chapter for introductory material

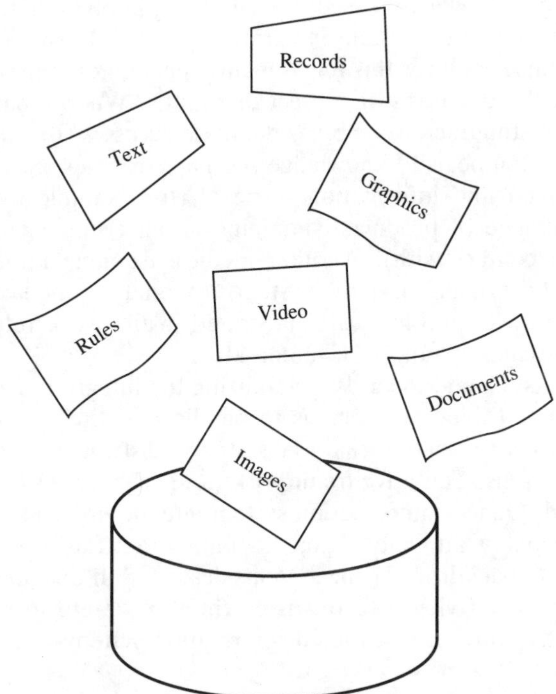

Figure 1.6 The diversity of information.

on these subjects. Each of these has generated its own propaganda, and it is frequently found that a single concept appears under different names in different classes. The forces for distribution have led to the development of corresponding distributed architectures in all of the classes, and it is advisable to keep some perspective on the current state of this evolution.

For example, it is possible to consider the information retrieval systems class as having been generalized to cover multimedia data generally, including voice, graphics and video as well as text. An example of a generalized system developed for this purpose is a distributed multimedia database system called KALEID. Distributed expert systems prototypes are also beginning to appear. An example is the HECODES heterogeneous expert system framework which has been demonstrated on a widely distributed computer network. The results of this development pattern is a collection of distributed but discrete, individually-limited systems, each very imperfectly representing the world and hard to link up to the others. There is, as could be expected from previous experience, a user pull to permit these heterogeneous classes to co-exist, conveniently, in a single system.

Pairwise integration has been taking place for a considerable time. Knowledge based system–database system integration, information retrieval system–knowledge based system integration and information retrieval system–database system integration have all been tackled. One example of the user pull for this functionality, encountered in the medical world, was for the diagnosis of contact dermatitis. When a patient has a rare skin disease the doctor combines database accesses (for the patient's standard details), appeals to knowledge (perhaps from a specialist conference proceedings) and information retrieval (for example by browsing through a catalogue of products containing an allergen that the patient could come in contact with). Another medical example requiring integration is that of using Expert Systems to analyse medical images. Approaches to these problems are illustrated in the work referenced at the end of this chapter, and in Chapter 11.

So there is a trend towards generalizing the integration approaches used in distributed database systems to handle the stitching together of heterogeneous classes of information systems, distributed over various geographic locations. Tentative frameworks for such systems have already been presented. Generic information system integration gives us a worthwhile, and probably attainable, goal to pursue for future systems and provides a useful backdrop for the systems described in this book. Having a global, wide-angled view like this is essential if we are to make sense of the evolving nature of distributed information systems.

SUMMARY

The pressure to distribute data comes from both user pull and technology push. User pull is prompted by the growth of information systems and by the need for security and consistency and for maintenance and local autonomy reasons. Technology push is because, on the processor side, Grosch's Law has been repealed, and this is complemented by the fact that communications networks are continually being enhanced.

The difficulties that this brings also come from users and technology. We are convinced that these are secondary, but it must be said that by no means everyone agrees that the virtues outweigh the difficulties. We will discuss this further at various points in this book. Users need to have applications and development tool kits appropriate for distribution; conflicts between users can also be expected. Technology brings difficulties in optimizing the evaluation of queries, harmonizing the processing of diverse nodal contributers to solutions, allocating data around the nodes in a sensible way, controlling access to the data, facilitating recovery from failure of system components and maintaining the fidelity of the model of the real world represented by the distributed data collections.

Integration is needed for user and technology reasons. It is needed for users in that for historical reasons data may be scattered over many sites, but new applications could all require its integration; corporate evolution and change often needs integration of computing systems. It is needed for technology reasons because database and other computing system technology is changing all the time, and applications tend to follow these developments; there is a challenge for applications developers to match changing requirements to the appropriate technology.

Difficulties are posed for applications programmers whose job is to access heterogeneous, distributed data collections. System support is sought for this.

Integrating 'structured text' as found in conventional database systems is only part of the (distributed) information handling picture. Accessing other kinds of data and 'knowledge' is also required, and this adds an additional dimension to the problem.

EXERCISES

1.1 Discuss three important technological reasons for distributing data.

1.2 Discuss three important user-related issues which suggest that data should be distributed.

1.3 State Grosch's Law. On what grounds is it claimed that this 'law' has been repealed?

1.4 A department in a manufacturing company has installed a centralized relational database holding all its corporate data. What problems can be expected if a move to a distributed database is contemplated?

1.5 'No chief information executive in his right mind would allow heterogeneous data collections to arise in his organization!' Discuss the ways in which data collections conforming to many styles and data models and using many different types of computers and programming languages can evolve in a large organization (such as a hospital).

1.6 In a hospital the medical clinicians wish to access 'structured' data records describing their patients (holding, for example, date of birth, address, profession and previous illnesses and treatment episodes). From time to time they all wish to access various non-text and non-structured data collections for their work. Identify examples of some of the additional types of information they might require access to, and suggest how communications networks and other computer system support can help in meeting their needs.

1.7 Suggest how pressure to decentralize data handling could arise from problems in capacity planning and maintenance.

Bibliography

Abul-Huda B. and Bell D.A. An overview of a distributed multi-media database management system (KALEID). In *Proc. 1st European Conf. on IT for Organisational Systems*, Athens, Greece, May 1988

KALEID is an attempt to adopt the principles of multidatabase systems (see Chapter 2) for application to multimedia data systems. It is a generalization to cover not only multisite data but also multimedia data.

Bell D.A. (1985). An architecture for integrating data, knowledge, and information bases. *Proc. ASLIB Informatics 8 Conf.*, Oxford, England

Many of the concepts described in Section 1.4 are considered in this paper. An extension of the multidatabase approach to the retrieval of structured text data to allow integration of multimedia information, structured text and rules is proposed.

Bell D.A. and O'Hare G.M. (1985). The coexistence approach to knowledge representation. *Expert Systems J.*, **2**(4), 230–238

This is a short but interesting case study where a network database structure is used to handle some aspects of medical diagnosis which would normally be expected to require artificial intelligence techniques.

Brodie M.L. and Myopoulus J. (1986). Knowledge bases and databases: semantic versus computational theories of information. In *New Directions for Database Systems* (Ariav G. and Clifford J. eds.), pp. 186–218, New Jersey: Ablex Publishing Co.

Knowledge based systems are one of the three classes of information systems which have evolved largely in isolation from each other. This paper is one example of a useful introduction, vintage 1982, to this subject.

Ein-Dor P. (1977). Grosch's Law revisited. *Datamation*, June, 103–108

Grosch's 'Law' – really a very rough rule of thumb – stated that the returns on an investment in terms of computer power increased as the square of the investment. However the more recent studies reported here have shown that this is no longer the case, and that returns are now about linear to the investment.

Mostardi T. and Staniszkis W. (1989). Multidatabase system design methodology. *Database Technology J.*, **1**(3), 27–37

There are few papers treating the subject of distributed database design. CASE tools are not yet distributed. This paper takes a step in the right direction by addressing the multidatabase design issue.

Otten A.M. (1989). The influence of data distribution on the systems development life cycle. *Database Technology J.*, **1**(3), 39–46

A hard-headed look at the practical importance of distributed database systems on systems design, building and operation.

Pavlovic-Lazetic G. and Wong E. (1985). Managing text as data. *Proc. 11th Conf. on VLDB*, Tokyo, Japan

The integration of database and information retrieval systems is considered here.

Salton G. and McGill M.J. (1983). *Introduction to Modern Information Retrieval*. Tokyo: McGraw-Hill

This is one of the many excellent books that are available as introductions to the subject of textual data access, or information retrieval, as mentioned in Section 1.4.

Ullman J.D. (1982). *Principles of Database Systems*. Rockville MD: Computer Science Press

One of the best introductions to databases around.

Wagner F.V. (1976). Is decentralisation inevitable? *Datamation*, Nov, 86–97

In 1976 Wagner proposed a 'Principle of decentralization' which supported distribution of reasonably sized data sets to users' sites when the access traffic passed a threshold, so that 'autonomy' could be supported.

Warner H.R. and Haug P. (1983). Medical data acquisition using an intelligent machine. *Proc. MEDINFO Conf.*, Amsterdam, Holland

A very interesting medical system which permits knowledge based techniques to be applied to the accessing of hospital information which would normally be dealt with solely by a database system is described here.

Zarri G.P. (1983). A fifth generation approach to intelligent information retrieval. *Proc. 1984 Annual ACM Conf.*, New York

This paper shows how information retrieval and artificial intelligence techniques can be mutually beneficial.

Zhang C. and Bell D.A. (1991). HECODES: a framework for heterogeneous cooperative distributed expert systems. *Data and Knowledge Engineering J.*, **6**(3), 251–273

Human experts often collaborate on a problem by pooling their individual expertise. An example is in medicine where doctors from different specialisms confer on a complex case. HECODES is a framework which has been used to implement a prototype system, in Common LISP, for integrating heterogeneous (in terms of knowledge representation, language, inexact reasoning method, etc.) expert systems to enable them to collaborate in solving a problem. It works on networked systems as far as 80 miles apart.

2 Overview of Databases and Computer Networks

2.1 Introduction

Distributed database technology involves the merging of two divergent concepts, namely **integration** through the database element and **distribution** through the networking element, as shown in Figure 2.1. This chapter gives a short overview of database technology, followed by an introduction to computer networks, a basic understanding of which is necessary to many of the issues involving distributed databases addressed in the rest of the book. The final section of the chapter is devoted to an introduction to distributed databases.

2.2 Database technology

Database management systems first emerged on the marketplace at the end of the 1960s and are now sufficiently mature that a powerful database management system (DBMS) underlies virtually all information systems today. The aim of the DBMS is to provide powerful tools for managing

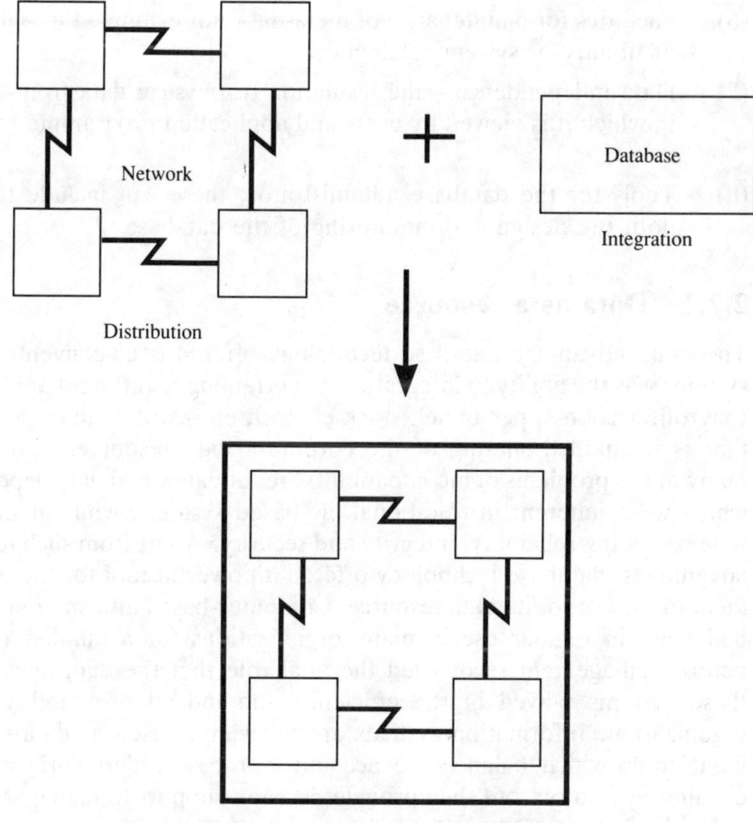

Figure 2.1 The distributed database concept.

a database, where a database is defined as an **integrated collection of shared data**, a reservoir of data. A typical DBMS is expected to provide a number of specific functions:

(1) Maintenance of physical data structures (files, indexes, etc.);
(2) Languages for storage retrieval and update of the data; these come in many forms from conventional third generation programming languages (3GLs) such as COBOL, higher level query languages such as SQL and more recently 4GLs such as FOCUS, NOMAD and RAMIS;
(3) Facilities for ensuring data integrity and security;
(4) Support for multi-user access including users who are 'simultaneously' updating the database (concurrent update);
(5) Backup and recovery measures;

(6) Facilities for maintenance of meta-data, for example through a data dictionary or system catalogue;

(7) Data independence – the insulation of physical data from the way in which it is viewed by users and application programmers (logical view);

(8) Tools for the database administrator; these can include tools for both the design and monitoring of the database.

2.2.1 Data as a resource

The main advantage database technology offered over conventional file systems was the ability to integrate data pertaining to different applications (payroll, accounts, personnel, stock control, etc.) within an organization, that is it enabled sharing of the corporate data resource. It overcame many of the problems of incompatibility, redundancy and data dependency which were inherent in traditional file-based systems, while at the same time providing reliability, integrity and security. Apart from such technical advantages, database technology offered a powerful tool for the management of the corporate data resource. Computer-based information systems had been in regular use in many organizations for a number of years before management recognized the vital role that the data managed by these systems played in the efficiency and indeed profitability of the organization. Information systems are not simply used as data management tools which balance the accounts, process orders, print the pay cheques and so on, but they provide decision support to management for strategic planning. Data came to be regarded as a resource which is just as critical as plant and personnel. Database technology provided a practical approach to controlling and managing the data resource.

2.2.2 DBMS architecture

The majority of commercial DBMSs available today are based on the so-called ANSI–SPARC architecture which divides the system into three levels – internal, conceptual and external, as shown in Figure 2.2.

The conceptual level represents the community user view of the data in the DB, namely a global logical view. It does not take into account how individual applications will view the data or how it is stored. The conceptual view is defined in the conceptual schema and its production is the first phase of database design.

Users, including application programmers, view the data through an external schema defined at the external level. The external (user) view provides a window on the conceptual view which allows users to see only the data of interest to them and shields them from other data in the DB. Any number of external schemas can be defined and they can overlap with each other. Finally the conceptual schema is mapped onto an internal

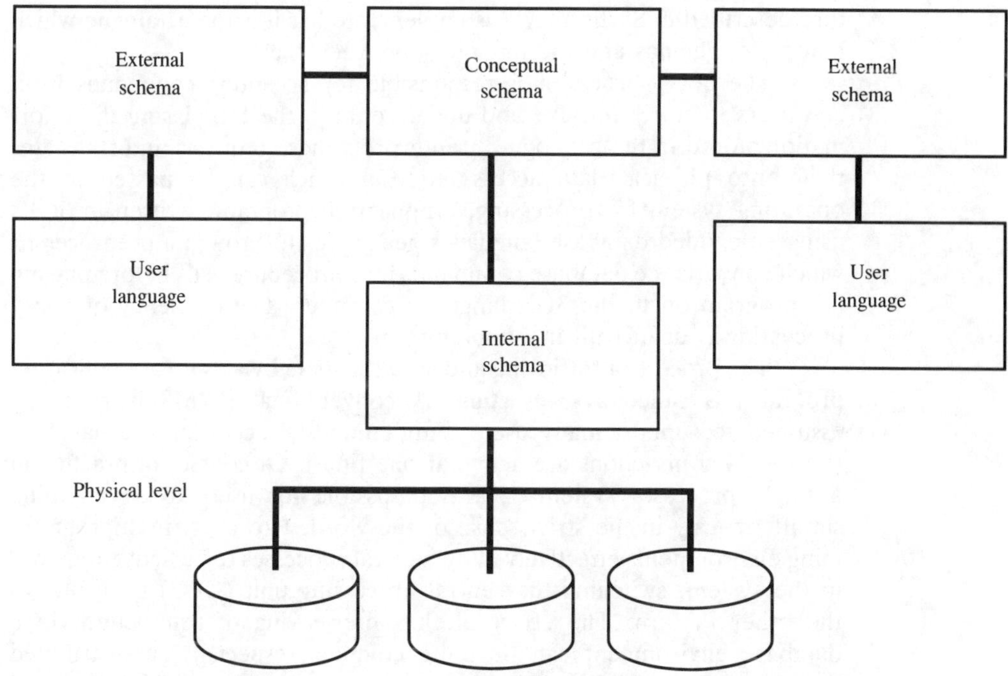

Figure 2.2 The ANSI–SPARC three-level architecture.

schema at the internal level, which is a low-level description of the data in the database; it provides the interface to the operating system's file system, which is usually responsible for accessing the database. The internal level therefore is concerned with specifying what data items are to be indexed, what file organization technique(s) to use, how the data is to be clustered on disk to improve performance and so on.

2.2.3 Components of a DBMS

DBMSs are highly complex, sophisticated pieces of software which aim to provide reliable management of shared data. Databases can range in size from kilobytes to gigabytes. It is not possible to generalize the component structure of a DBMS since this will vary considerably from system to system. However, it is possible to identify a number of key functions which are common to all DBMSs and these will be discussed below.

At the heart of the DBMS lies the **system catalogue** or data dictionary, with which virtually all other components of the system interact. The catalogue contains all the meta-data for the system, that is, a description of all the data items (type, length, allowable values, etc.), access permissions, views and so on. It is through the catalogue that the three-level architecture described in Section 2.2.2 is implemented as it is the catalogue which holds the schemas and the mappings between them.

The **query processor** is responsible for accepting commands from end-users to store, retrieve and update data in the DB. Using the information stored in the catalogue, it interprets these requests and translates them into physical data access requests which can be passed to the operating system for processing. Application programs written in 3GLs using embedded database languages generally go through a preprocessor which converts the database commands into procedure calls before passing the program on to the 3GL language compiler. The efficiency of query processing is dealt with in Chapter 5.

The process of retrieving and updating data by a user (or application program) is called a **transaction**. A conventional DBMS is generally assumed to support many users 'simultaneously' accessing the database (i.e. many transactions are active at one time). Of course, in practice in a single processor system, it is not possible for users to do anything simultaneously in the strict sense of the word. However, multiprogramming environments effectively allow several processes to be active together in the system, switching the central processing unit (CPU) from one to the other in turn. The effect of this interleaving of transactions in a database environment can be quite complex, especially in distributed databases where both interleaving (at one site) and parallel (at several sites) processing takes place. It is the responsibility of the **transaction manager** of the DBMS to ensure that transactions do not interfere with one another and corrupt the database. Transactions and the problems associated with controlling concurrency in a distributed database are discussed in detail in Chapter 6.

One of the most important aims of database technology was to provide better backup and recovery facilities than were provided by the traditional file processing systems which they replaced. Nothing is ever 100% reliable; systems must be designed to tolerate failures and recover from them correctly and reliably. It is the role of the **recovery manager** of the DBMS to minimize the effects of failures on the database. There are many different causes of failure in a database environment from application program errors (e.g. trying to divide by zero) to disk head crashes, power failures and operator error. The objective of the recovery manager is principally to restore the database to a state known to be consistent. Because of the numerous causes of failures and the complexity of database processing, the recovery manager's job is quite difficult and can account for 10% or more of the code of the DBMS. Recovery issues are discussed in detail in Chapter 7.

2.2.4 Relational databases

DBMSs are generally classified according to how data is represented in the conceptual schema (i.e. the conceptual data model). There are three main approaches:

(1) relational
(2) network
(3) hierarchical.

By far the most important is the relational model and since it is used to illustrate concepts throughout this book, the discussion here will concentrate on relational systems. A brief introduction to network and hierarchical systems will be given in Section 2.2.5.

Relational database technology is attractive both for its simplicity and for the fact that it has a sound theoretical basis in mathematical relational theory. In a relational database, data is viewed through two-dimensional structures known as **tables** or **relations**. When describing a DBMS as **relational**, we mean that it supports relations at the conceptual and external levels; at the internal level there are no restrictions. Each table has a fixed number of columns called **attributes**, and a variable number of rows called **tuples**. An example of a relational table is given in Table 2.1. Relations always have one attribute, or group of attributes, designated as the **primary key**, which uniquely identifies the tuples in the relation; hence duplicate tuples are not allowed. For convenience, relations are generally written in the following form with the primary key underlined:

```
INPATIENT (patient#, name, date_of_birth, address,
           sex, gp)
```

Attributes in a relation are defined over a **domain**; which corresponds to the range of values which the particular attribute can hold. For example, the range of values for 'sex' is simply M or F, the range of values for 'date_of_birth' would be less than or equal to the present day.

An important feature of the relational approach to DBMS is the fact that all physical implementation details are hidden from the user. In particular, this means that no pointers are visible. In network and hierarchical systems, users must navigate across the DB following pointers

Table 2.1 Sample INPATIENT relation.

INPATIENT

patient#	name	date_of_birth	address	sex	gp
01432	John Murphy	14.02.79	Dublin	M	Dr Haughey
09686	Patrick Delaney	28.08.85	Sligo	M	Dr Murphy
41268	Mary Geraghty	12.09.35	Cork	F	Dr Corrigan
19743	Ann Mahon	08.12.89	Belfast	F	Dr White
97231	Joseph McArdle	05.12.49	Donegal	M	Dr Jones
80233	Patricia Farrell	01.03.25	Dublin	F	Dr Browne

from one record to the next. In relational DBs (RDBs) relationships between tuples are represented purely by the fact that they contain attributes which are drawn from a common domain.

Consider a second relation, LABREQ

LABREQ (<u>patient#</u>, <u>test_type</u>, date, reqdr)

as shown in Table 2.2, which records requisitions for laboratory tests for patients. There is a relationship between row 3 of the INPATIENT relation (for patient Mary Geraghty) and rows 1 and 2 of the LABREQ relation, as all three rows share the same patient# (41268). Similarly row 5 of INPATIENT is related to row 3 of LABREQ (patient# 97231) and the last rows in the two relations are also related (patient# 80233).

This example serves to illustrate another important concept in relational DBs, namely **foreign keys**. Patient# in LABREQ is a foreign key referencing INPATIENT. This means that the values of patient# in LABREQ are constrained to a subset of the values of patient# in the INPATIENT relation. In practical terms, this rule means that it is not possible to requisition laboratory test results (insert a tuple into the LABREQ relation) for a non-existent patient (a patient for whom there is no corresponding tuple in the INPATIENT relation).

Both primary keys and foreign keys express **integrity constraints** on the database, that is they constrain the allowable values of attributes. In the case of primary keys, duplicate values are forbidden and no part of the primary key may be null, and in the case of foreign keys, the value must already exist in some other relation in the DB. DBs generally reflect a real-world situation – they represent physical data and events. For example, Mary Geraghty is an actual patient in the hospital for whom Dr Keogh has ordered two laboratory tests. Ensuring the integrity of the DB is mainly concerned with making sure that the DB obeys the rules of the outside world it is modelling. This is a complex issue and will be discussed in more detail in Chapter 8.

An integral part of the relational approach is the relational algebra, which consists of two groups of operators, enabling users to operate on an entire relation. Non-relational systems by contrast generally only support

Table 2.2 The LABREQ relation.

LABREQ

patient#	test_type	date	reqdr
41268	FT4	30.11.90	Dr Keogh
41268	TT3	30.11.90	Dr Keogh
97231	TSH-RIA	28.11.90	Dr Smith
80233	FT1	01.12.90	Dr Mayhew

languages which operate on the database one record at a time. The operators listed below are those which are most commonly used; other operators are possible in addition to those defined below, but are not included here. The interested reader is referred to Merrett (1978). The result of any of these operators is always a relation with zero, one or more tuples in it.

The first group of operators corresponds to the conventional **set operations** of union, intersect, difference and Cartesian product. With the exception of Cartesian product, these operations can only be performed on **union compatible** relations (i.e. those whose attributes are drawn from the same domains). They are particularly useful in distributed databases. For example, data on in-patients and out-patients might be stored in different relations or even at different sites, as shown in Table 2.3. Note that some tuples are common to both relations.

The **union** of two relations, A and B, is the set of all tuples belonging to either A or B (duplicates eliminated). Thus

```
INPATIENT UNION OUTPATIENT
```

would return the relation shown in Table 2.4(a).

The **intersection** (INTERSECT) of two relations, A and B, is the set of all tuples belonging to both A and B. The result of

Table 2.3 Sample INPATIENT and OUTPATIENT relations.

INPATIENT

patient#	name	date_of_birth	address	sex	gp
01432	John Murphy	14.02.79	Dublin	M	Dr Haughey
09686	Patrick Delaney	28.08.85	Sligo	M	Dr Murphy
41268	Mary Geraghty	12.09.35	Cork	F	Dr Corrigan
19743	Ann Mahon	08.12.89	Belfast	F	Dr White
97231	Joseph McArdle	05.12.49	DonegalDublin	M	Dr Jones
80233	Patricia Farrell	01.03.25		F	Dr Browne

OUTPATIENT

patient#	name	date_of_birth	address	sex	gp
01432	John Murphy	14.02.79	Dublin	M	Dr Haughey
19743	Ann Mahon	08.12.89	Belfast	F	Dr White
63412	Michael Brennan	13.06.42	Limerick	M	Dr O'Donnell
39762	Patrick White	19.08.76	Sligo	M	Dr Murphy
80233	Patricia Farrell	01.03.25	Dublin	F	Dr Browne
45307	Mary Anderson	14.06.42	Belfast	F	Dr Robertson
96658	Anthony O'Grady	30.04.85	Dublin	M	Dr O'Mahony
41326	Thomas Robinson	28.02.87	Donegal	M	Dr Jones

Table 2.4 (a) The UNION operator. (b) The INTERSECT operator. (c) The DIFFERENCE (MINUS) operator.

INPATIENT UNION OUTPATIENT

patient#	name	date_of_birth	address	sex	gp
01432	John Murphy	14.02.79	Dublin	M	Dr Haughey
09686	Patrick Delaney	28.08.85	Sligo	M	Dr Murphy
41268	Mary Geraghty	12.09.35	Cork	F	Dr Corrigan
19743	Ann Mahon	08.12.89	Belfast	F	Dr White
97231	Joseph McArdle	05.12.49	Donegal	M	Dr Jones
80233	Patricia Farrell	01.03.25	Dublin	F	Dr Browne
63412	Michael Brennan	13.06.42	Limerick	M	Dr O'Donnell
39762	Patrick White	19.08.76	Sligo	M	Dr Murphy
45307	Mary Anderson	14.06.42	Belfast	F	Dr Robertson
96658	Anthony O'Grady	30.04.85	Dublin	M	Dr O'Mahony
41326	Thomas Robinson	28.02.87	Donegal	M	Dr Jones

(a)

OUTPATIENT INTERSECT INPATIENT

patient#	name	date_of_birth	address	sex	gp
01432	John Murphy	14.02.79	Dublin	M	Dr Haughey
19743	Ann Mahon	08.12.89	Belfast	F	Dr White
80233	Patricia Farrell	01.03.25	Dublin	F	Dr Browne

(b)

INPATIENT MINUS OUTPATIENT

patient#	name	date_of_birth	address	sex	gp
09686	Patrick Delaney	28.08.85	Sligo	M	Dr Murphy
41268	Mary Geraghty	12.09.35	Cork	F	Dr Corrigan
97231	Joseph McArdle	05.12.49	Donegal	M	Dr Jones

(c)

```
INPATIENT INTERSECT OUTPATIENT
```

is shown in Table 2.4(b).

The **difference** (MINUS) between two relations, A and B, is the set of all tuples belonging to A but not B, which in the case of

```
INPATIENT MINUS OUTPATIENT
```

would give the relation shown in Table 2.4(c).

The **Cartesian product** (PRODUCT) of two relations A and B concatenates every tuple in A with every tuple in B. Thus the Cartesian product of INPATIENT and LABREQ

```
INPATIENT PRODUCT LABREQ
```

would be as shown in Table 2.5.

The second group of operators are the **relational operators**. There are two **unary** relational operators, that is those which operate on a single relation, namely **select** and **project**, and one **binary** operator which operates on a pair of relations, **join**. The SELECT operator takes a **horizontal** subset from a relation, that is it selects those tuples from the relation which satisfy a certain constraint. For example,

```
SELECT FROM INPATIENT WHERE sex = 'F'
```

would produce the relation shown in Table 2.6(a). Selects are denoted by $\sigma_{\text{condition}}$ so the above select would be written $\sigma_{\text{sex='F'}}$INPATIENT.

The PROJECT operator takes a **vertical** subset from a relation, that is it selects particular columns from a relation, eliminating duplicates. The effect of

```
PROJECT OUTPATIENT OVER address
```

would be to produce the relation shown in Table 2.6(b). The project operator is denoted $\pi_{\text{attributes}}$ so the above projection would be written π_{address}OUTPATIENT.

Two relations may be **join**ed if they each have an attribute drawn from a common domain, the resulting relation then contains a set of tuples, each of which is formed by the concatenation of a tuple from one relation with a tuple from the other relation such that they have the same value in the common domain. For example, the relations LABREQ and INPATIENT can be joined over patient#

```
JOIN LABREQ AND PATIENT OVER patient#
```

giving the relation shown in Table 2.6(c). The JOIN operator is denoted

$$\bowtie_{a=b}$$

Using this notation, the above JOIN would be written

$$\text{PATIENT} \bowtie_{\text{PATIENT.patient\#=LABREQ.patient\#}} \text{LABREQ}$$

There are a number of different types of joins (natural join, equi-join, outer-join, semi-join, etc.) but it is beyond the scope of this book

Table 2.5 The Cartesian product operator.

INPATIENT PRODUCT LABREQ

patient#	name	date_of_birth	address	sex	gp	patient#	test_type	date	reqdr
01432	John Murphy	14.02.79	Dublin	M	Dr Haughey	41268	FT4	30.11.90	Dr Keogh
01432	John Murphy	14.02.79	Dublin	M	Dr Haughey	41268	TT3	30.11.90	Dr Keogh
01432	John Murphy	14.02.79	Dublin	M	Dr Haughey	97231	TSH-RIA	28.11.90	Dr Smith
01432	John Murphy	14.02.79	Dublin	M	Dr Haughey	80233	FT1	01.12.90	Dr Mayhew
09686	Patrick Delaney	28.08.85	Sligo	M	Dr Murphy	41268	FT4	30.11.90	Dr Keogh
09686	Patrick Delaney	28.08.85	Sligo	M	Dr Murphy	41268	TT3	30.11.90	Dr Keogh
09686	Patrick Delaney	28.08.85	Sligo	M	Dr Murphy	97231	TSH-RIA	28.11.90	Dr Smith
09686	Patrick Delaney	28.08.85	Sligo	M	Dr Murphy	80233	FT1	01.12.90	Dr Mayhew
41268	Mary Geraghty	12.09.35	Cork	F	Dr Corrigan	41268	FT4	30.11.90	Dr Keogh
41268	Mary Geraghty	12.09.35	Cork	F	Dr Corrigan	41268	TT3	30.11.90	Dr Keogh
41268	Mary Geraghty	12.09.35	Cork	F	Dr Corrigan	97231	TSH-RIA	28.11.90	Dr Smith
41268	Mary Geraghty	12.09.35	Cork	F	Dr Corrigan	80233	FT1	01.12.90	Dr Mayhew
19743	Ann Mahon	08.12.89	Belfast	F	Dr White	41268	FT4	30.11.90	Dr Keogh
19743	Ann Mahon	08.12.89	Belfast	F	Dr White	41268	TT3	30.11.90	Dr Keogh
19743	Ann Mahon	08.12.89	Belfast	FF	Dr White	97231	TSH-RIA	28.11.90	Dr Smith
19743	Ann Mahon	08.12.89	Belfast		Dr White	80233	FT1	01.12.90	Dr Mayhew
97231	Joseph McArdle	05.12.49	Donegal	M	Dr Jones	41268	FT4	30.11.90	Dr Keogh
97231	Joseph McArdle	05.12.49	Donegal	M	Dr Jones	41268	TT3	30.11.90	Dr Keogh
97231	Joseph McArdle	05.12.49	Donegal	M	Dr Jones	97231	TSH-RIA	28.11.90	Dr Smith
97231	Joseph McArdle	05.12.49	Donegal	M	Dr Jones	80233	FT1	01.12.90	Dr Mayhew
80233	Patricia Farrell	01.03.25	Dublin	F	Dr Browne	41268	FT4	30.11.90	Dr Keogh
80233	Patricia Farrell	01.03.25	Dublin	F	Dr Browne	41268	TT3	30.11.90	Dr Keogh
80233	Patricia Farrell	01.03.25	Dublin	F	Dr Browne	97231	TSH-RIA	28.11.90	Dr Smith
80233	Patricia Farrell	01.03.25	Dublin	F	Dr Browne	80233	FT1	01.12.90	Dr Mayhew

Table 2.6 (a) The SELECT operator. (b) The PROJECT operator. (c) The JOIN operator. (d) The SEMI-JOIN operator.

SELECT FROM INPATIENT WHERE sex = 'F'

patient#	name	date_of_birth	address	sex	gp
41268	Mary Geraghty	12.09.35	Cork	F	Dr Corrigan
19743	Ann Mahon	08.12.89	Belfast	F	Dr White
80233	Patricia Farrell	01.03.25	Dublin	F	Dr Browne

(a)

PROJECT OUTPATIENT OVER address

address
Dublin
Belfast
Limerick
Sligo
Donegal

(b)

JOIN LABREQ AND PATIENT OVER patient#

patient#	test_type	date	reqdr	name	date_of_birth	address	sex	gp
41268	FT4	30.11.90	Dr Keogh	Mary Geraghty	12.09.35	Cork	F	Dr Corrigan
41268	TT3	30.11.90	Dr Keogh	Mary Geraghty	12.09.35	Cork	F	Dr Corrigan
97231	TSH-RIA	28.11.90	Dr Smith	Joseph McArdle	05.12.49	Donegal	M	Dr Jones
80233	FT1	01.12.90	Dr Mayhew	Patricia Farrell	01.03.25	Dublin	F	Dr Browne

(c)

INPATIENT SEMI-JOIN LABREQ OVER patient#

patient#	name	date_of_birth	address	sex	gp
41268	Mary Geraghty	12.09.35	Cork	F	Dr Corrigan
97231	Joseph McArdle	05.12.49	Donegal	M	Dr Jones
80233	Patricia Farrell	01.03.25	Dublin	F	Dr Browne

(d)

to describe them all, with the exception of the semi-join which plays a particularly important role in query optimization in distributed DBMSs (DDBMSs) as described in Chapter 5. The SEMI-JOIN of two relations, A and B, is the join of A and B, projected back on the attributes of A. Thus

INPATIENT SEMI-JOIN LABREQ OVER patient#

would return the relation shown in Table 2.6(d). The semi-join operator is denoted

$$\lhd_{a=b}$$

so the above semi-join would be written

$$\lhd_{\text{INPATIENT.patient\#=LABREQ.patient\#}}$$

The importance of the semi-join is due mainly to the fact that it reduces the size of the relation produced by the full join, which can be significant in distributed databases, as it means that less data has to be transmitted across the network.

2.2.5 Hierarchical and network DBMSs

Hierarchical and network systems were developed and commercialized almost a decade before relational systems, and so their origins in traditional file processing systems are naturally more evident. Unlike relational DBMSs which support set-oriented processing, both hierarchical and network DBMSs are record-oriented, that is they process one record at a time. Furthermore, while relationships in relational DBMSs are represented solely by attributes drawn from a common domain, relationships in hierarchical and network systems are explicitly and visibly (to the user) implemented by pointers. Hence while relational systems adopt a declarative approach to database processing, hierarchical and network systems adopt a navigational approach. This not only makes the actual writing of programs more difficult but also requires the user to keep track of the current position in the database. Although relational systems are rapidly replacing all other DBMSs, it can be argued that hierarchical and network systems offer considerable advantages in performance. However, as relational DBMSs mature and disks and CPUs get faster, these disadvantages are being overcome, even for large databases.

We will use a banking database to illustrate hierarchical and network DBMSs. This DB stores information about customers and their accounts and the transactions against those accounts.

The best known **hierarchical DBMS** is IBMs information management system, IMS, one of the most widely used DBMSs in the 1970s. Data in a hierarchical DB is stored as a series of trees consisting of a root and zero or more sub-trees. Trees are a natural way of representing hierarchical or 1 : n relationships, such as a person has many children, a patient has many tests.

The general structure of the bank DB as it would be represented in a hierarchical system is shown in Figure 2.3(a) and a sample DB in Figure 2.3(b).

The major problem with hierarchical DBMSs is their inability to model satisfactorily m : n (many-to-many) relationships. For example, the

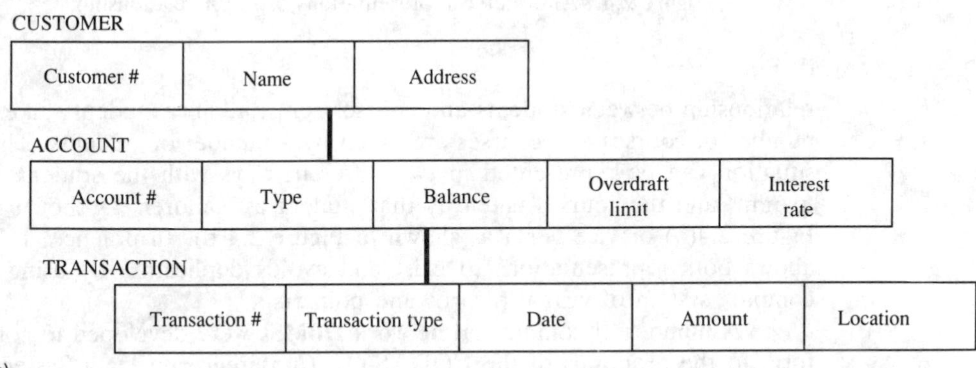

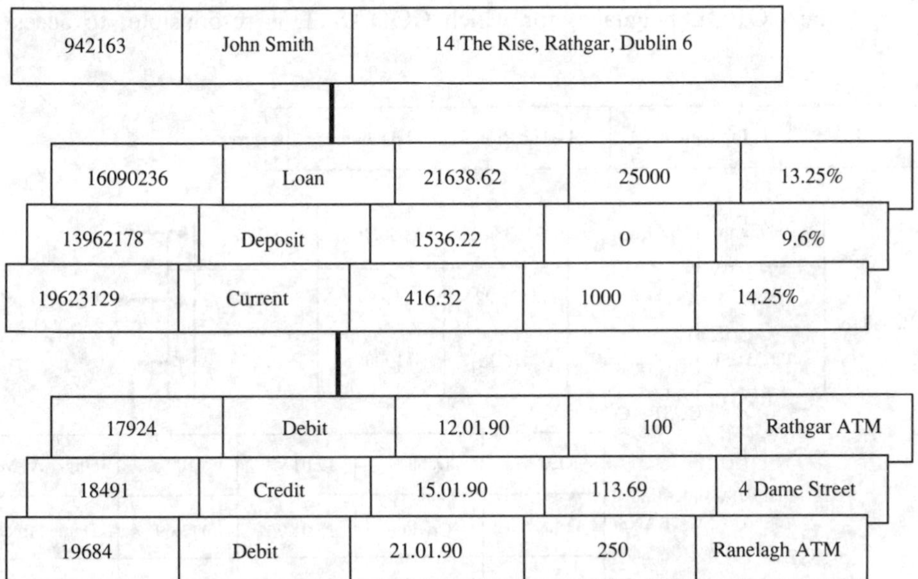

Figure 2.3 (a) Hierarchical database structure. (b) Example hierarchical database.

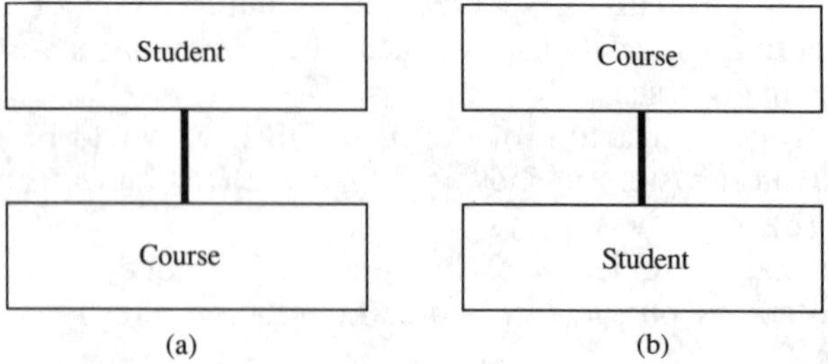

Figure 2.4 Alternative representations of $m : n$ relationship.

relationship between students and courses is $m : n$, since students take a number of courses and courses are taken by a number of students. This situation can be represented in two different ways with the student as 'parent' and the courses taken by that student as 'children' as shown in Figure 2.4(a) or vice versa as shown in Figure 2.4(b). In practice, IMS allows both representations to exist and avoids duplication by using a complex system of virtual records and pointers.

A number of commercial **network DBMSs** were developed to conform to the proposals of the CODASYL (Conference on Data Systems Languages) Data Base Task Group (DBTG) which were finalized in 1971. The original objective of the DBTG was to define standard extensions to the COBOL language, for which CODASYL is responsible, to access

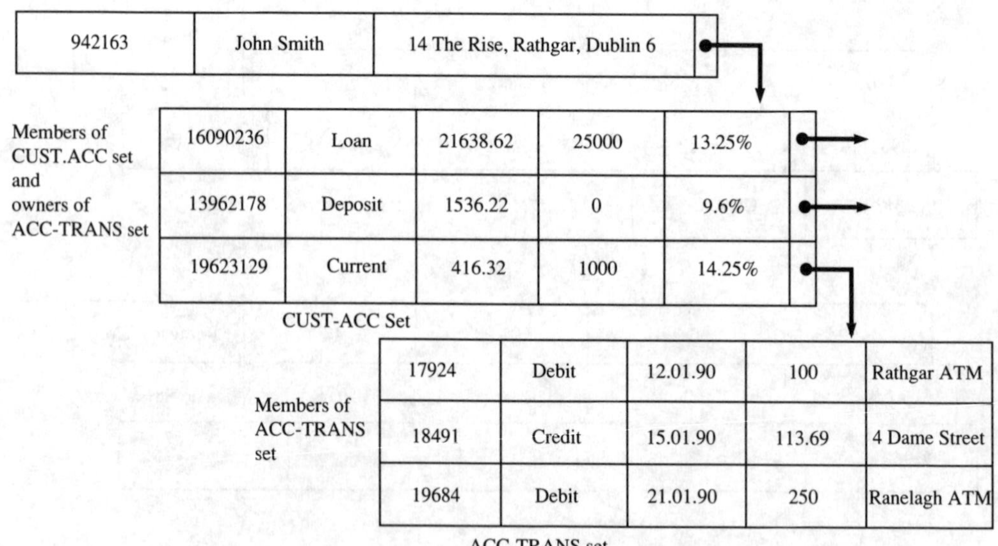

Figure 2.5 Example network database.

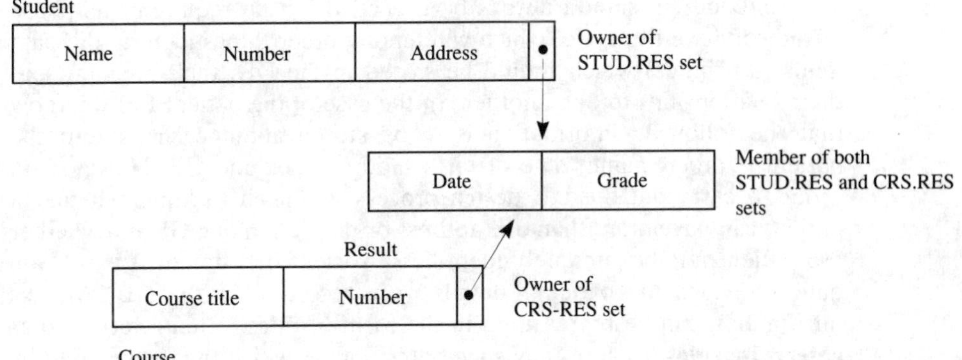

Figure 2.6 Representing an $m : n$ relationship in a network database.

DBs. However, the work evolved into the specifications of a DBMS architecture. Network DBMSs are often referred to as CODASYL DBMSs. Although network DBMSs have effectively been overtaken by relational systems, the original CODASYL DBTG report contained one of the first specifications of a layered architecture for a DBMS, which has since been formalized in the ANSI/SPARC three-level architecture discussed in Section 2.2.2.

Network DBMSs support two different data constructs, namely records and sets. Related records are grouped together into sets; each set having an owner record and a number of members, thereby modelling hierarchical or $1 : n$ relationships. Figure 2.5 shows how the bank DB would be represented in a network DB. It is also possible to represent $m : n$ relationships relatively easily by incorporating a **connector** record. For example, to represent the student and course DB, we would introduce a connector record, RESULT, containing the date on which the student took the course and the grade obtained as shown in Figure 2.6.

Network DBMSs offer some advantages over hierarchical systems, especially in relation to modelling $m : n$ relationships. However, they suffer from similar disadvantages due to their complexity in comparison to relational systems.

2.2.6 Database design and normalization

The development of relational DB technology has resulted in the parallel development of techniques for good logical DB design, that is the design of the conceptual schema. Logical DB design involves taking all the attributes that are to be stored in the DB, examining the relationships between them with a view to grouping them into relations in such a way as to eliminate unnecessary data redundancy and avoid other undesirable features. This process is known as **normalization**.

DB design should always be preceded by the requirements phase of the software life cycle, which will among other things identify the data items (attributes) which should be stored in the DB, their meaning and their relationships to one another. In the case of the patient DB we know that the following information is to be stored about each patient: the patient number, name, date of birth, address, sex and GP. However, in order to carry out the DB design process, we need to know whether a patient can have more than one address or more than one GP and whether the patient number uniquely identifies a patient or whether it is just the date on which the patient's details were recorded on the DB. All this information can be represented in the form of rules, often referred to as **enterprise rules** because they specify the way in which the data is used by the enterprise being modelled in the DB. The rules for the patient DB are:

(1) Each patient is identified by a single, unique patient number,

(2) Each patient has only one name, one date of birth, one address, one sex and one GP.

Thus by the first rule, if we are given a patient number, then associated with that patient number is a single unique name, date of birth, address, sex and GP. In this case, we say that patient# **determines** or is a **determinant** of name, address, date of birth, sex and GP; or alteratively name, address, date of birth, sex and GP are **dependent** on patient#. The standard notation is

patient# → name
patient# → address
patient# → date of birth
patient# → sex
patient# → GP

The identification of these **functional dependencies**, as they are known, is a vital part of the DB design process. Note that name does not determine patient#, unless of course no two patients could have the same name. In fact there are no other dependencies in the patient DB.

Functional dependencies are examples of integrity constraints (see Section 2.2.4) on the values that attributes can take. When a new tuple is being added to a DB, each attribute's values would be checked against any of these constraints which include that attribute. A DBMS module called a **constraint checker** is responsible for this validation. For example, if someone tried to add a second address for a patient in DB with the functional dependency

patient# → address

the integrity checker would signal an error.

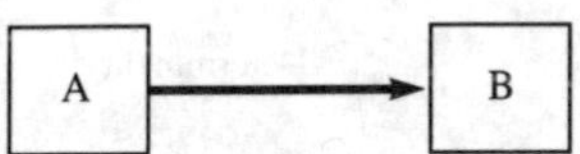

Figure 2.7 Sample determinancy diagram.

The process of normalization involves identifying the functional dependencies from the enterprise rules and producing a set of fully normalized relations. There are various ways to carry out this normalization process and the technique which will be used here is that of determinancy or dependency diagrams. If A determines B, that is A → B, then this is represented as shown in Figure 2.7. The determinancy diagram for our patient DB is shown in Figure 2.8. If we add the laboratory test information, then we would need to specify the following additional rule (rules 1 and 2 are as before):

(3) Patients can have any number of tests on any date but (for simplicity) only one test of any given type on any one day ordered by one doctor.

The laboratory test data is included in the determinancy diagram shown in Figure 2.9. Note that {patient#, test-type, date} are all needed together to determine reqdr because a patient could have the same test on a different day or a different test on the same day. Hence both patient# and the composite set of attributes {patient#, test-type, date} are determinants.

In Section 2.2.4, we introduced the notion of primary keys: an attribute, or set of attributes, which uniquely identifies the tuples in a relation. It is sometimes possible to have more than one attribute which could fulfil the role of primary key, so we refer to potential primary key attributes as **candidate keys**. In Figure 2.8, the candidate key is patient#.

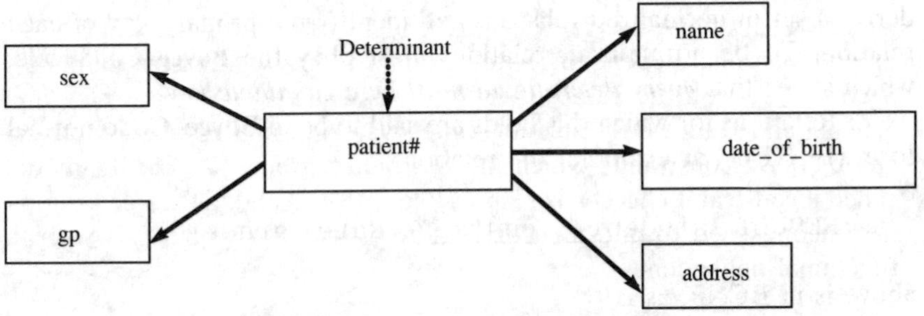

Figure 2.8 Determinancy diagram for simple patient database.

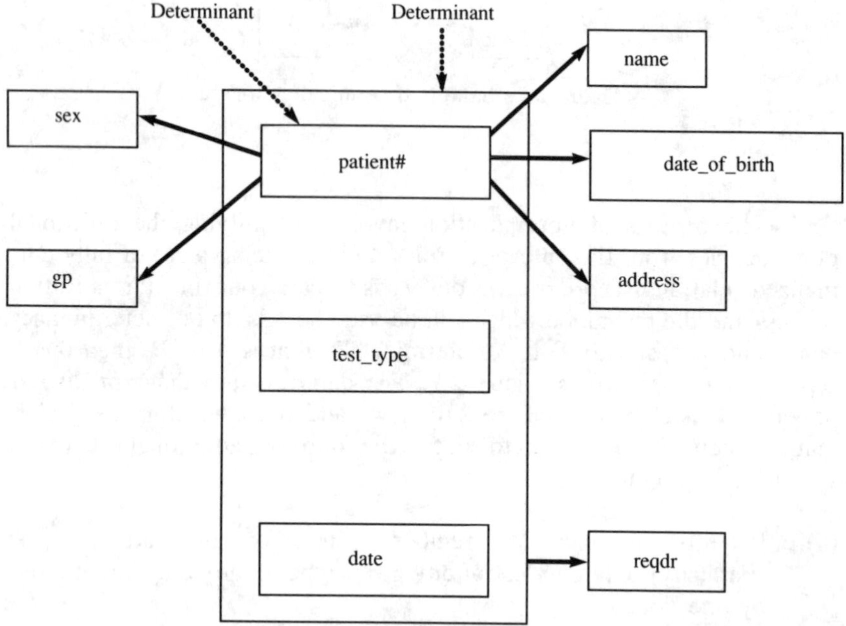

Figure 2.9 Determinancy diagram for simple patient and laboratory test database.

Consider the relation

RESULT (<u>student#</u>, <u>course#</u>, date, grade)

which records the results of students in various courses. Since students can take many courses and courses can be taken by many students, the candidate key is the composite attribute {student#, course#} and the dependency diagram is shown in Figure 2.10. Note that if students were allowed to repeat courses, then date would have to be included as part of the primary key.

Having drawn the determinancy diagram, it is a simple matter to derive a set of normalized relations and identify the primary key of each relation. To be normalized, relations must obey the **Boyce–Codd rule**, which states that *every determinant must be a candidate key*.

Relations for which this holds are said to be in Boyce–Codd normal form (BCNF). For example, the relation

RESULT (<u>student#</u>, <u>course#</u>, date, grade)

above is in BCNF, as is

PATIENT (<u>patient#</u>, name, date_of_birth, address,
sex, gp).

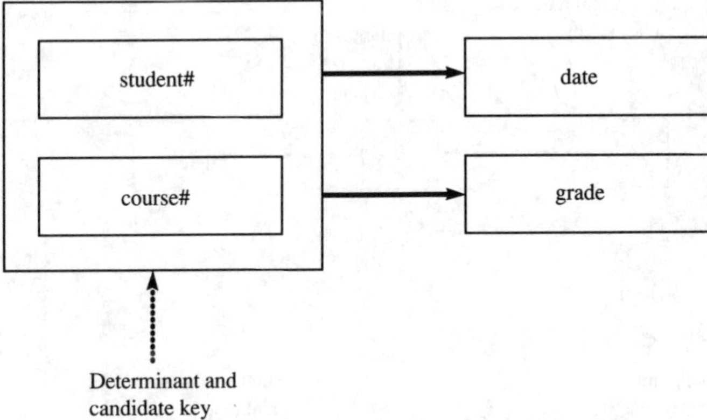

Figure 2.10 Determinancy diagram for RESULT.

However, examination of Figure 2.9 shows that there are two identifiers, both of which are determinants, but not of the same attributes. Patient# is a determinant of and a candidate identifier for name, date_of_birth, address, sex and gp, whereas the composite attribute {patient, test_type, date} is a determinant of and candidate identifier for reqdr. Hence to normalize this relation we must split the relation into two, such that each relation is in BCNF:

```
PATIENT (patient#, name, date of birth, address,
         sex, GP)
```

and

```
LABREQ (patient#, test-type, date, reqdr).
```

Relations in BCNF overcome most of the problems regarding redundancy and insertion and deletion anomalies present in un-normalized relations. In particular, they eliminate the presence of transitive dependencies. If

$A \rightarrow B$ and $B \rightarrow C$, then $A \rightarrow C$

or A is **transitively dependent** on C. If transitive dependencies occur in a determinancy diagram (Figure 2.11(a)) then these are eliminated by splitting the relation into two as shown in Figure 2.11(b). It is generally agreed that good DB design requires that relations be in BCNF. However, it is possible for non-functional dependencies such as multivalued and join dependencies to be present in BCNF relations and these dependencies can give rise to problems. Such non-functional dependencies are beyond the scope of this book. Details are given by Howe (1989), Date (1990) and Elmasri and Navathe (1989). There is an extensive literature on the

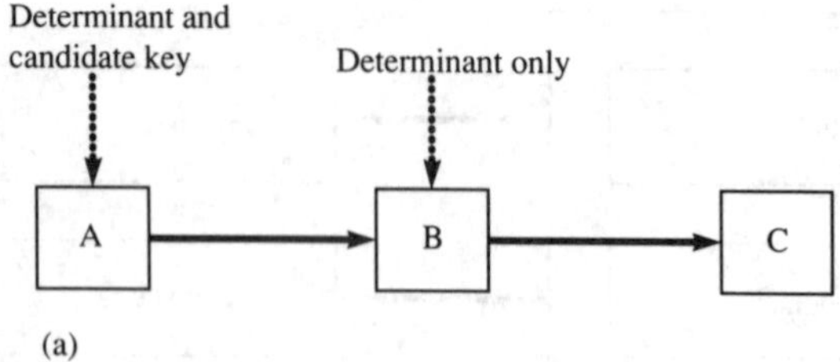

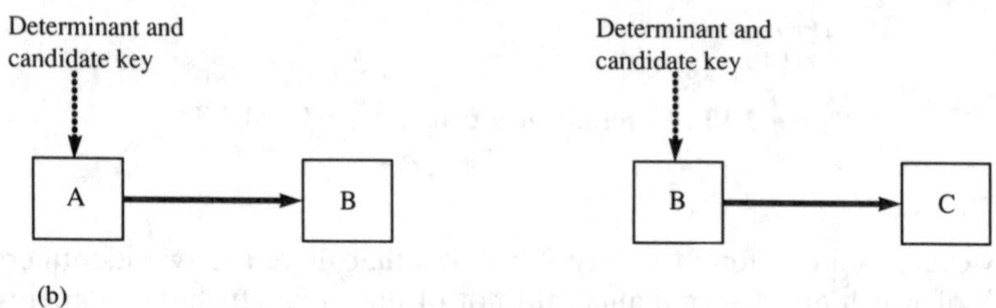

Figure 2.11 (a) Transitive dependency. (b) Elimination of transitive dependency by splitting.

theory of dependencies. A good introduction can be found in an early paper by Beeri *et al.* (1978).

2.2.7 Query languages

Most DBMSs offer users a variety of interfaces through which they can store, retrieve and update data in the DB. In addition, they provide a facility through a data definition language (DDL) to describe the data that is to be stored in the DB. From the point of view of this book, it is the former class of languages, namely the query languages, which are of most importance. Although the term query would seem to imply retrieval only, in practice it covers both storage and update.

These languages come in many forms, from calls to special DB procedures embedded in procedural 3GLs, powerful 4GLs, general-purpose DB languages such as SQL and special purpose, high-level languages which are designed for a particular application (e.g. the language used by travel agents to communicate with airline passenger seat reservation systems). The language which will be used to illustrate concepts throughout this book is SQL, since virtually all relational DBMSs today offer an SQL interface to the DB.

The basic retrieval command of SQL is the SELECT statement which extracts data from one or more relations. It subsumes all three relational operators, that is it includes not only the select operator but also projection and join. The basic syntax of the SQL SELECT is

```
SELECT ⟨attribute list⟩
FROM   ⟨relation name(s)⟩
WHERE  ⟨predicate(s)⟩;
```

For example, to retrieve all the female patients from Dublin from the INPATIENT relation of Table 2.1, the command would be

```
SELECT *
FROM   INPATIENT
WHERE  sex = 'F' AND address = 'Dublin';
```

The result is shown in Table 2.7(a). The * simply indicates that we want *all* attributes of the relation. If we only wanted the patient numbers and names, then the query would be in the form

```
SELECT patient#, name
FROM   INPATIENT
WHERE  sex = 'F' AND address = 'Dublin';
```

and the resulting relation is shown in Table 2.7(b). This example combines both the relational select and project operators. Similarly, we can use the SQL SELECT command to implement the relational join operator. The example given in Table 2.6(c) would be specified in SQL by

```
SELECT *
FROM   INPATIENT, LABREQ
WHERE  INPATIENT.patient# = LABREQ.patient#;
```

It is possible to combine all three relational operators in a single command. For example, if we wanted to find out the names of all Dr Corrigan's patients for whom laboratory tests had been ordered, we could issue the following query:

```
SELECT name
FROM   INPATIENT, LABREQ
WHERE  INPATIENT.patient# = LABREQ.patient#
       AND INPATIENT.gp = 'Dr Corrigan';
```

The result is shown in Table 2.7(c). Note that while two tests, FT4 and TT3, had been ordered for patients of Dr Corrigan, they are both for the same patient, Mary Geraghty and since duplicates are eliminated, only one tuple appears in the final relation.

Table 2.7 (a) Example of simple SQL SELECT. (b) Example including relational project. (c) Example incorporating relational select, project and join operators.

patient#	name	date_of_birth	address	sex	gp
80233	Patricia Farrell	01.03.25	Dublin	F	Dr Browne

```
SELECT
FROM INPATIENT
WHERE sex = 'F' AND address = 'DUBLIN'
```

(a)

patient#	name
80233	Patricia Farrell

```
SELECT patient#, name
FROM   INPATIENT
WHERE sex = 'F' and address = 'Dublin'
```

(b)

name
Mary Geraghty

```
SELECT Name
FROM   INPATIENT, LABREQ
WHERE INPATIENT. patient# = LABREQ.patient#
       AND INPATIENT.gp = 'Dr Corrigan'
```

(c)

SQL also supports the relational set operators of union, intersection, difference and Cartesian product and the examples given in Table 2.3 would be specified in SQL as

```
INPATIENT UNION OUTPATIENT;
INPATIENT INTERSECT OUTPATIENT;
INPATIENT MINUS OUTPATIENT;
INPATIENT PRODUCT LABREQ;
```

Note that most versions of SQL allow **nesting** of statements up to many levels, where one query (SELECT, FROM, WHERE) is embedded within another query.

SQL is a powerful language offering many features which allow users not only to store, retrieve and update their data, but also to create views, set access permissions and so on. In addition to being used in interactive mode for *ad hoc* queries (**interactive SQL**), SQL commands can also be embedded in procedural languages (**embedded SQL**) thereby providing a powerful database programming language for the development of complex applications. There is an international standard for SQL specified by ANSI. As with many standards, the 1986 SQL standard has been subjected to many criticisms and many RDBMSs offer additional features which are not part of the standard. Some of the commonly voiced criticisms of standard SQL include:

- No support for referential integrity (most RDBMSs now support this as an extension);
- No method for consistent handling of updates through views;
- No easy way of storing interim results of queries for subsequent processing – the only way to pass query results is through nesting of queries.

2.3 Computer networks

Database management systems were originally promoted as providing the total solution to information processing problems within large organizations. However, it was not long before users discovered that they provided no such universal panacea. As was indicated in Chapter 1, a growing movement developed away from centralized to distributed systems. This was brought about in the main by the microcomputer revolution at the end of the 1970s and the availability of increasingly reliable telecommunications systems to support networking. It was the availability of telecommunications software that made distributed database management systems (DDBMS) technically feasible. Most DDBMS researchers take for granted the existence of a reliable data communications facility in much the same way as most software assumes the existence of an operating system which provides certain standard services. Thus while DDBMSs do have to take into account the reliability of the data communication facilities provided and in particular develop methods to maintain the consistency of the DDB in the event of failure, the actual details of the communications protocols are not normally of great concern. However, some basic understanding of the issues involved in computer networks is essential for a full understanding of distributed database technology.

Computer networks are now very widely used; they range from simple systems connecting a few personal computers (PCs) together to worldwide networks with over 10 000 machines and over a million users. A network can be defined as an interconnected collection of autonomous computers. A distributed system, such as a distributed database management system (DDBMS), is built on top of a network in such a way as to hide the network from the user.

Computer networks are generally classified according to whether the computers they connect are separated by long (wide area network) or short (local area network) distances.

Wide area networks (WANs) are used where the computers are separated by distances greater than, say, 10 km. Typical transmission rates for WANs are from 2 to 2000 kilobits per second.

The computers, which are referred to as **hosts**, **nodes** or **sites**, are connected to a **subnet**. A subnet consists of two parts:

(1) Transmission lines along which the data travels;

(2) Packet-switch exchanges (PSEs), open relay systems or interface message processors.

PSEs are responsible for receiving messages from hosts on the network or from other PSEs and deciding how to route them onward through the network as shown in Figure 2.12. The PSEs themselves are connected in various ways discussed below. Conceptually PSEs are separate, dedicated processors, but often the host computer provides the function of the PSE directly. When a host on a network wants to send a message to another host on the network, that message must be assembled in groups of bytes known as **packets** before being transmitted across the network. WANs are generally based on a **point-to-point** (also known as **packet-switched**) network, in which message packets are stored at PSEs until the line for onward transmission is free. This is often referred to as **store and forward** communication, since packets are temporarily stored at one node before being forwarded to the next node. Examples of this approach are the UNIX† uucp network and internet. An important aspect of point-to-point systems is the way in which the PSEs are connected, that is, the **topology** of the network. There are a number of possibilities as shown in Figure 2.13.

Local area networks (LANs) are intended for connecting computers located on the same site, separated by distances of under 1 km. Transmission rates for LANs are much higher than for WANs, being between

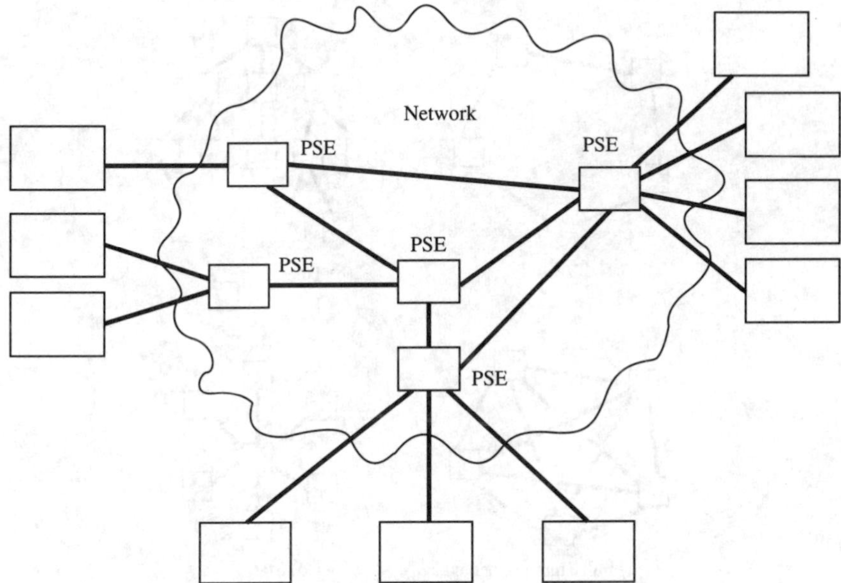

Figure 2.12 Conceptual representation of a network.

1 to 100 Megabits per second. It is thus clear that a DDBMS using a LAN for communication is going to give a much faster response time to users than one using a WAN.

LANs generally use broadcasting instead of point-to-point communication. In a **broadcast** network, packets are transmitted onto the network – all nodes can listen, but a message is only picked up by the node to which it is actually addressed. Other nodes simply ignore the message. Messages can also be sent to *all* nodes or to a subset of the nodes (**multicasting**), depending on the facilities offered by the network. Broadcast networks are generally configured into one of three common topologies as shown in Figure 2.14.

2.3.1 Network architecture

Networks are concerned with connecting (often heterogeneous) components and it is therefore essential to agree a set of rules governing the manner in which they can communicate. This set of rules is called a **protocol**. Furthermore, this language must be very structured so that messages do not get muddled, like two people talking at the same time on a half-duplex radio or normal telephone. The standard approach is to divide the network into a series of layers, each layer offering a particular service to the layer above, while at the same time hiding the implemen-

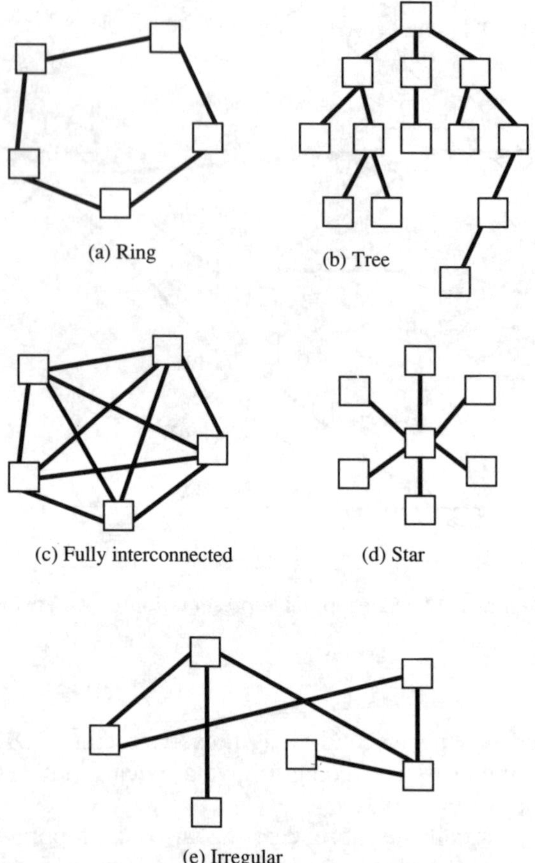

Figure 2.13 Alternative point-to-point network topologies.

tation details from the upper layer. The International Standards Organization (ISO) has defined a seven-layer manufacturer-independent protocol, known as the **ISO OSI Open Systems Interconnection Reference Model** and most existing systems are migrating towards this standard.

2.3.2 ISO/OSI reference model

The aim in defining the layers of the ISO/OSI model was to group functions together in a single layer in a logical fashion such that the interface between adjacent layers is clean and well defined. The basic ISO/OSI architecture is shown in Figure 2.15. Conceptually, layer n on host A communicates directly with its counterpart layer n on host B. In practice, however, communication is between layer n on host A, down to layer $n-1$, $n-2$ and so on, on host A, across the communication subnet

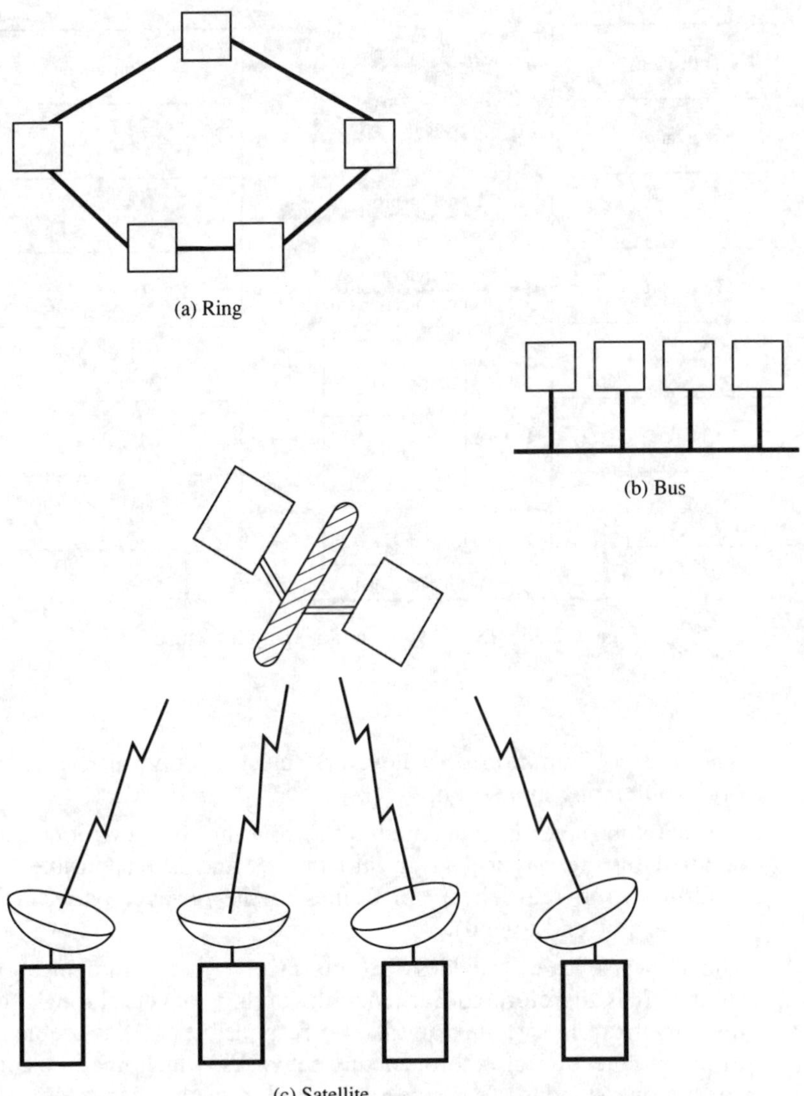

Figure 2.14 Alternative broadcast network topologies.

via open relay systems (OSI terminology for PSEs) to the corresponding physical layer on host B and then up through the 'stack' on host B to layer *n*. The functions of the various layers can be summarized as follows:

(1) The **physical layer** is concerned with the actual physical transmission of bits across the communications media. It therefore addresses issues such as whether the link is simplex, duplex or half-duplex,

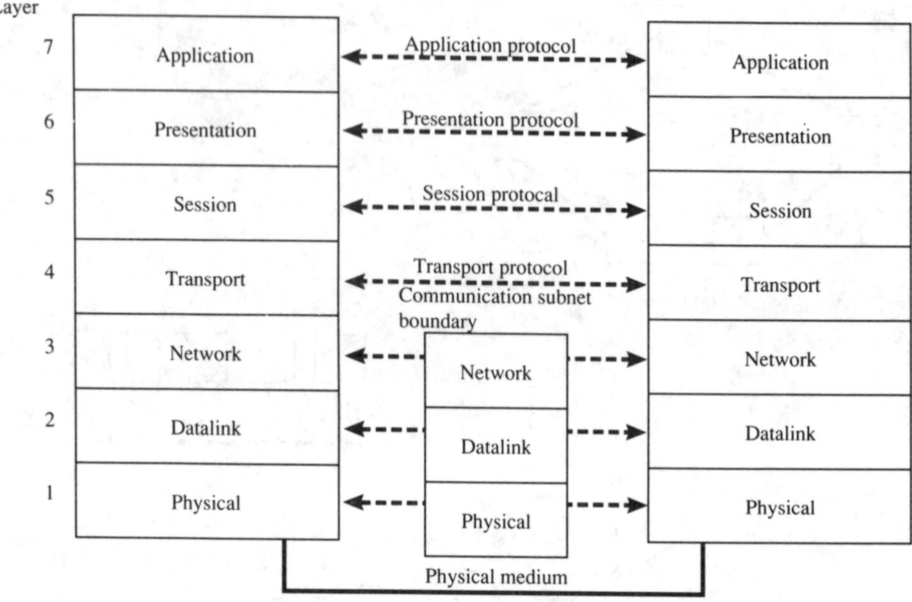

Figure 2.15 ISO/OSI seven-layer architecture.

type and configuration of connectors, electrical/optical characteristics, bit timing and so on.

(2) The **datalink layer** is concerned with grouping the raw bit stream handled by the physical layer into frames and is responsible for ensuring error-free delivery of frames to the receiver on a single link (i.e. not end-to-end).

(3) The **network layer** provides the interface to the communication subnet. It is therefore concerned with routing packets through the network from link to link and is also responsible for the problems of interconnection of heterogeneous networks, which involves converting one standard (e.g. packet size, addressing scheme, etc.) to another. The network layer also ensures that the network does not get swamped with packets leading to bottlenecks.

(4) The **transport layer** forms the division between the upper layers, which are concerned with the nature of the dialogue between end-systems (i.e. from originator to recipient), and the lower layers, which are concerned with point-to-point transport of data. It decides what type of end-to-end connection is needed depending on the requirements. An error-free end-to-end connection, which delivers messages in the same order in which they were transmitted, is an example of a common transport connection.

(5) The **session layer** manages sessions between different machines. It controls the dialogue between the two sides so that if, for example, both sides are not allowed to transmit simultaneously. The session layer ensures this by using a system of tokens. Only the side with the token is allowed to transmit. This layer breaks the dialogue up into sessions/activities, which can be further structured using major/minor synchronization points. Synchronization points are very important for DB systems because they facilitate recovery in the event of failure. They are used in a similar way to checkpoints in DB recovery subsystems (see Chapter 7).

(6) The **presentation layer** deals with the syntax and semantics of the data, whereas layers 1 to 5 are mainly concerned with simply moving the data about the network. Different computers have different ways of storing data (e.g. ASCII versus EBCIDIC) and it is the responsibility of the presentation layer to perform any format conversion. It also is responsible for data compression and encryption.

(7) The **application layer** at the top of the OSI stack provides the interface between the application and the network. It is concerned with problems associated with incompatible terminal types, different file naming conventions, electronic mail, remote job entry and so on.

As far as the network is concerned, a distributed database management system (DDBMS) is just another application, which is effectively half in and half out of the application layer of the ISO/OSI model. It is the responsibility of the DDBMS to define the elements in a dialogue, to enable one node in the DDBMS to communicate with another.

The layers of the ISO/OSI model are designed to facilitate specification of standards for each layer. Virtually all public networks worldwide adhere to the lower layers of the ISO/OSI architecture. CCITT (Comitié Consultatif International de Télégraphique et Téléphonique) – the international committee of national Post, Telegraph and Telephone companies (PTTs) – have issued a standard known as X.25 which covers layers 1 to 3 of the ISO/OSI model. Many of the existing DDBMSs have been developed on top of X.25 since standards for the upper layers have only been agreed relatively recently and implementations are not yet available for all the layers. However, there are a number of services provided by the upper layers, which could be very useful to a DDBMS. The remote database access protocol (RDAP) of the application layer specifies a standard which facilitates interworking of DB systems. DDBMSs of the future could make good use of RDAP. For example, the commitment, concurrency and recovery (CCR) service element provides basic support for a two-phase commit protocol. These issues are discussed in detail in Chapters 6 and 7.

2.4 Distributed databases

In Chapter 1, the reasons for the development of distributed database (DDB) technology were outlined. It was the availability of reliable data communications facilities, however, that has enabled the technology to develop. Moreover, as was indicated in Section 2.1, DDB technology combines both distribution and integration. The distribution aspect is provided by distributing the data across the sites in the network, while the integration aspect is provided by logically integrating the distributed data so that it appears to the users as a single, homogeneous DB. Centralized DBMSs, by contrast, require both logical and physical integration.

A distributed database (DDB) can be defined as a *logically integrated collection of shared data which is physically distributed across the nodes of a computer network.*

A distributed database management system (DDBMS) therefore is the software to manage a distributed database in such a way that the distribution aspects are transparent to the user.

A centralized DBMS is a system which manages a single DB, whereas a DDBMS is a single DBMS which manages multiple DBs. The terms global and local are often used when discussing DDBMSs (and indeed distributed systems in general) in order to distinguish between aspects which refer to a single site (local) and those which refer to the system as a whole (global). For example, the local DB refers to the DB stored at one site in the network, whereas the global DB refers to the logical integration of all the local DBs. Note that the global DB is a virtual concept since it does not exist physically anywhere.

2.4.1 Classification of DDBMSs by architecture

The ANSI–SPARC three-level architecture for centralized DBMSs presented in Section 2.2 has now gained widespread acceptance and most commercial DBMSs in the main adhere to this architecture. There is no such equivalent for DDBMSs. The technology and prototypes of DDBMSs have developed more or less independently of each other and each system adopts its own particular architecture.

Distributed data systems are divided into two separate types, based on totally different philosophies, and are designed to meet quite separate needs:

(1) Homogeneous distributed database management systems
(2) Heterogeneous distributed database management systems.

The full taxonomy of distributed data systems is shown in Figure 2.16. In keeping with practice elsewhere and reflected in the title of this book, we

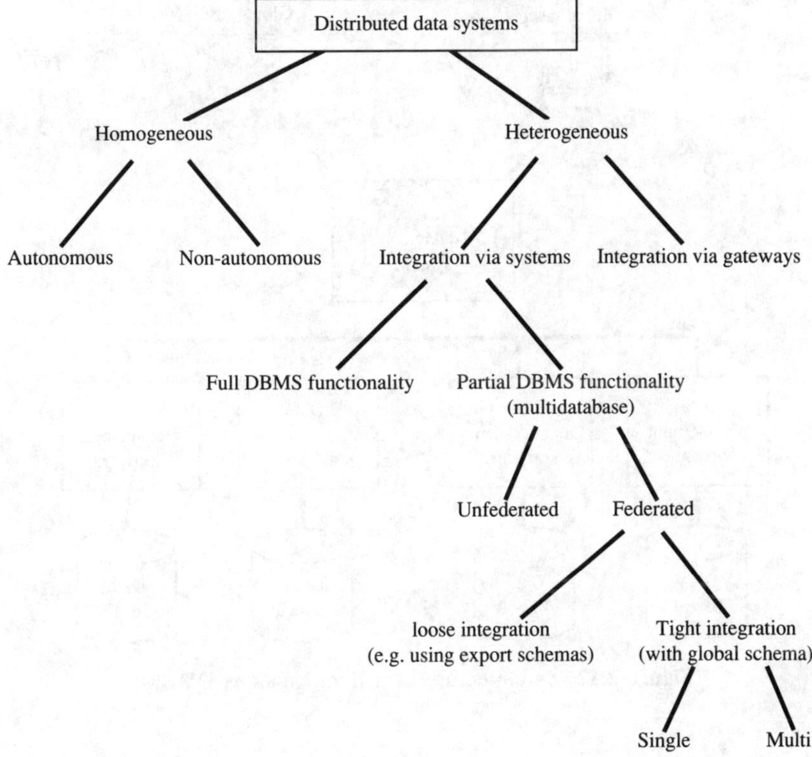

Figure 2.16 Taxonomy of distributed data systems.

use the term **distributed database management system** to cover both types and only differentiate when necessary. Most of the concepts described in this book are applicable to both types of DDBMS. We give examples of each sub-class in Chapter 3.

A **homogeneous DDBMS** has multiple data collections; it integrates multiple data resources. Some of the most venerable systems fall into this class. They can be further divided into classes depending on whether or not they are autonomous. We look at autonomy in more detail later on, but in the meantime we will use this term to indicate a declared aim of the systems designers to give the local systems control of their own destinies.

A homogeneous DDB resembles a centralized DB, but instead of storing all the data at one site, the data is distributed across a number of sites in a network. Figure 2.17 shows the overall architecture of a pure DDBMS. Note that there are no local users; all users access the underlying DBs through the global interface. The global schema is the union of all underlying local data descriptions (not specified in a schema) and user views are defined against this global schema.

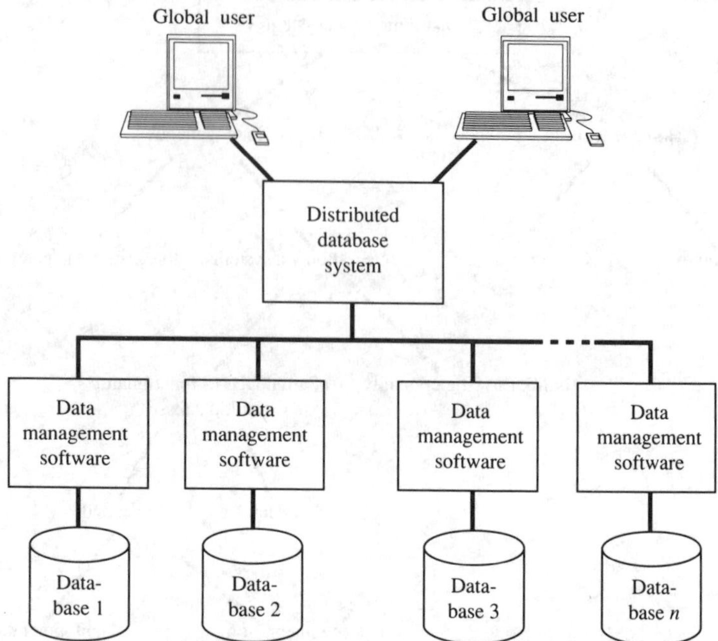

Figure 2.17 Architecture of a homogeneous DDBMS.

In Figure 2.17, we have not considered the case where there are local schemas for the local databases. If we want to come up with a standard conceptual architecture for a DDBMS evolved from the ANSI–SPARC architecture, we could include local DBMSs and local schemas, remembering that these do not have to be explicitly present in any particular implementation. Indeed, in practice, most of the homogeneous systems do not have local schemas and have limited data management software at the local level.

To handle the distribution aspects, we must add two additional levels, as shown in Figure 2.18, to the standard three-level ANSI–SPARC architecture shown in Figure 2.2, namely the **fragmentation** and **allocation schemas**. The fragmentation schema describes how the global relations are divided amongst the local DBs. Figure 2.19 gives an example of a relation, R, which is divided into five separate fragments, each of which could be stored at a different site. To **materialize** R (i.e. to reconstruct it from its fragments), the following operations are required:

```
R = (A JOIN B) UNION (C JOIN D) UNION E
```

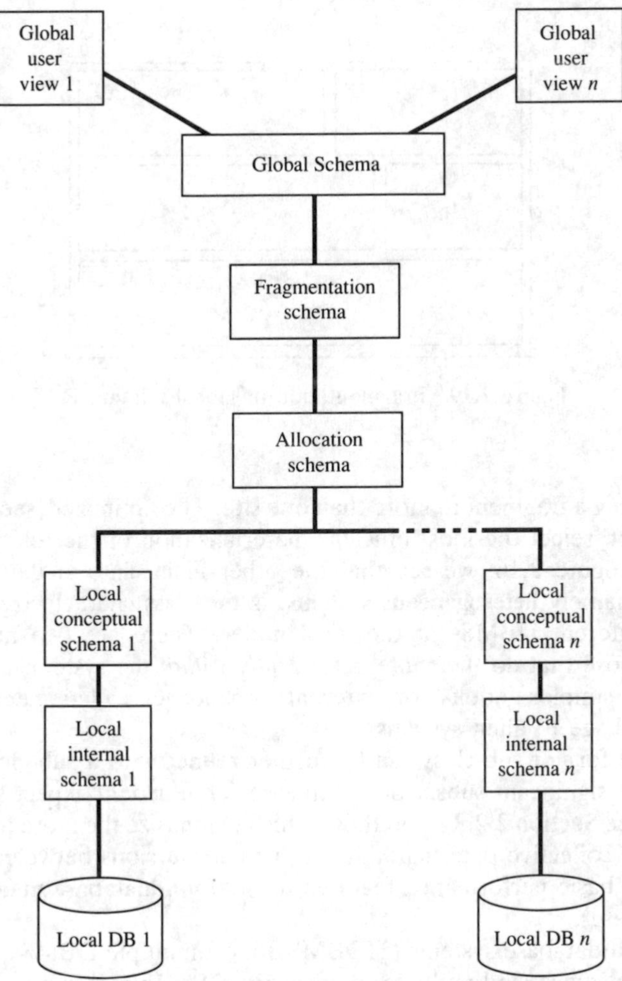

Figure 2.18 Schema architecture of a homogeneous DDBMS.

where JOIN and UNION have the normal relational meaning. It must of course be *possible* to reconstitute a global relation from its fragments by the application of standard relational operators. In practice this means that the primary key of the relation R must be included in all vertical fragments. Thus both A and B, and C and D, must be joinable and (A JOIN B), (C JOIN D) and E all union compatible. A collection of materialized relations at some particular time is called a **snapshot**.

The **allocation schema** then specifies, at which site each fragment is stored. Hence fragments can migrate from site to site in response to changing access patterns. Also, replication of fragments is easily supported

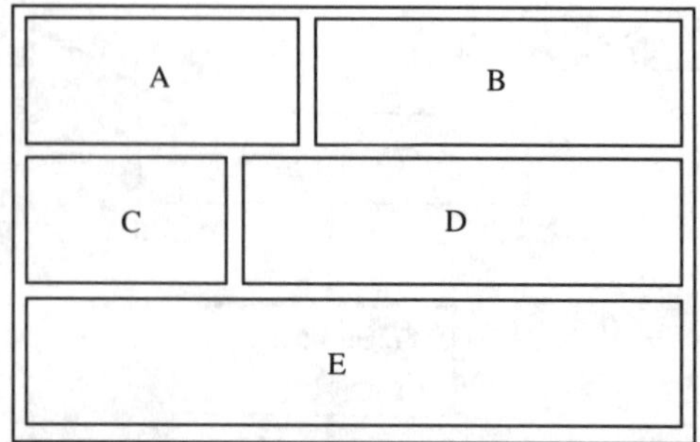

Figure 2.19 Fragmentation of global relation R.

by allocating a fragment to more than one site. The optimizer (see Chapter 5) can then select the most efficient materialization of the relation.

In Figure 2.16, we see that the other main class of data sharing systems, namely **heterogeneous systems**, is the class characterized by the use of different DBMSs at the local nodes. There are two main sub-classes: those that do their integration *fully within* the system, and those providing simpler 'hooks' or external appendages called **gateways**, to permit linkage to alien systems.

The former sub-class can be further refined into a sub-class which provides a significant subset of the functions one would expect from any DBMS (see Section 2.2.3), and those which emphasize the more pragmatic aspects of collective data handling, such as conversions between systems and some basic performance features (called **multidatabase management systems** here).

Multidatabase systems (MDBMSs) have multiple DBMSs, possibly of different types, and multiple, *pre-existing* DBs. Integration is therefore performed by multiple software sub-systems. The overall architecture of an MDBMS is shown in Figure 2.20. Note that in contrast to the homogeneous DDBMS, there are both local and global users. MDBMSs integrate pre-existing, heterogeneous data resources, although homogeneous systems can also be accommodated. It is an important feature of these systems that local users continue to access their local DBs in the normal way unaffected by the existence of the MDB. We follow the taxonomy of Sheth and Larson (1990) in Figure 2.16 closely for MDBMSs.

There are federated and unfederated MDBMSs. In unfederated systems, there are no local users and this is a relatively obscure sub-class. The federated systems are split into those that have a global schema (**tightly coupled**) and those which do not (**loosely coupled**).

The schema architecture for a typical tightly coupled MDBMS is shown in Figure 2.21. The global conceptual schema is a logical view of

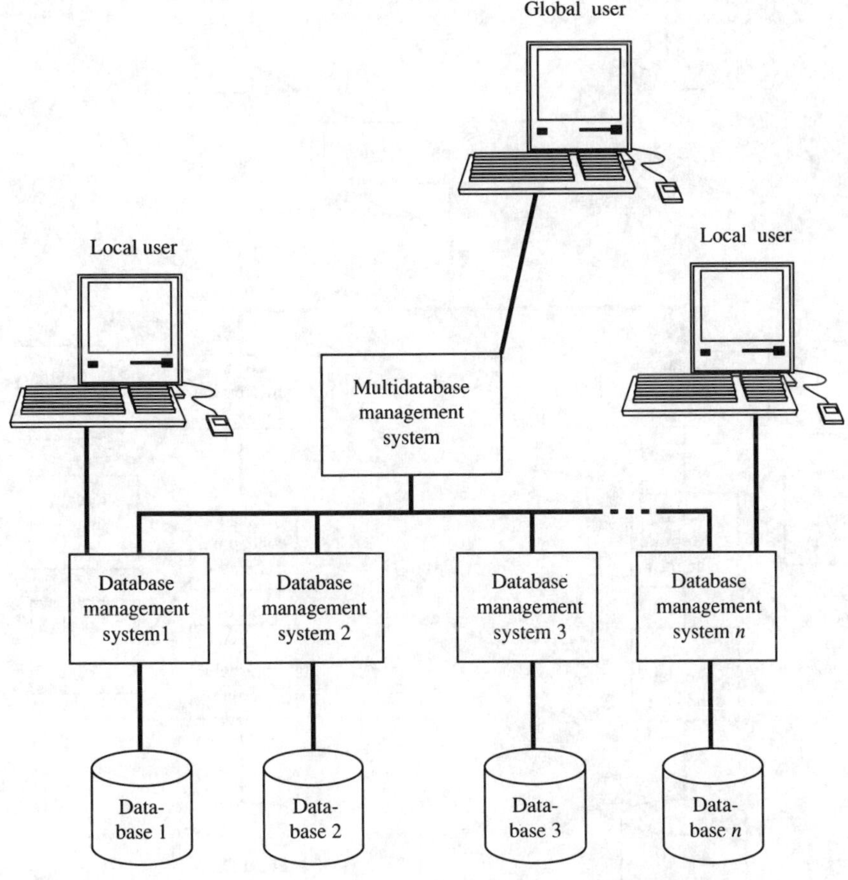

Figure 2.20 Overall architecture of a multidatabase system.

all the data in the MDB. It is only a subset of the union of all the local conceptual schemas, since local DBMSs are free to decide what parts of their local DBs they wish to contribute to the global schema. This freedom is known as local autonomy (see Section 2.4.2). An individual node's participation in the MDB is defined by means of a participation schema, and represents a view defined over the underlying local conceptual schema. Three additional levels – the participation schemas, the global conceptual schema and the global external views – have been added to the ANSI–SPARC architecture. Support for user views is possibly even more important in DDBMS environments, where the global schema is likely to be extremely large and complex, representing as it does the integration of the entire organization's data resource. The **auxiliary schema**, which is shown in Figure 2.21, when it is used, describes the rules which govern the mappings between the local and global levels. For

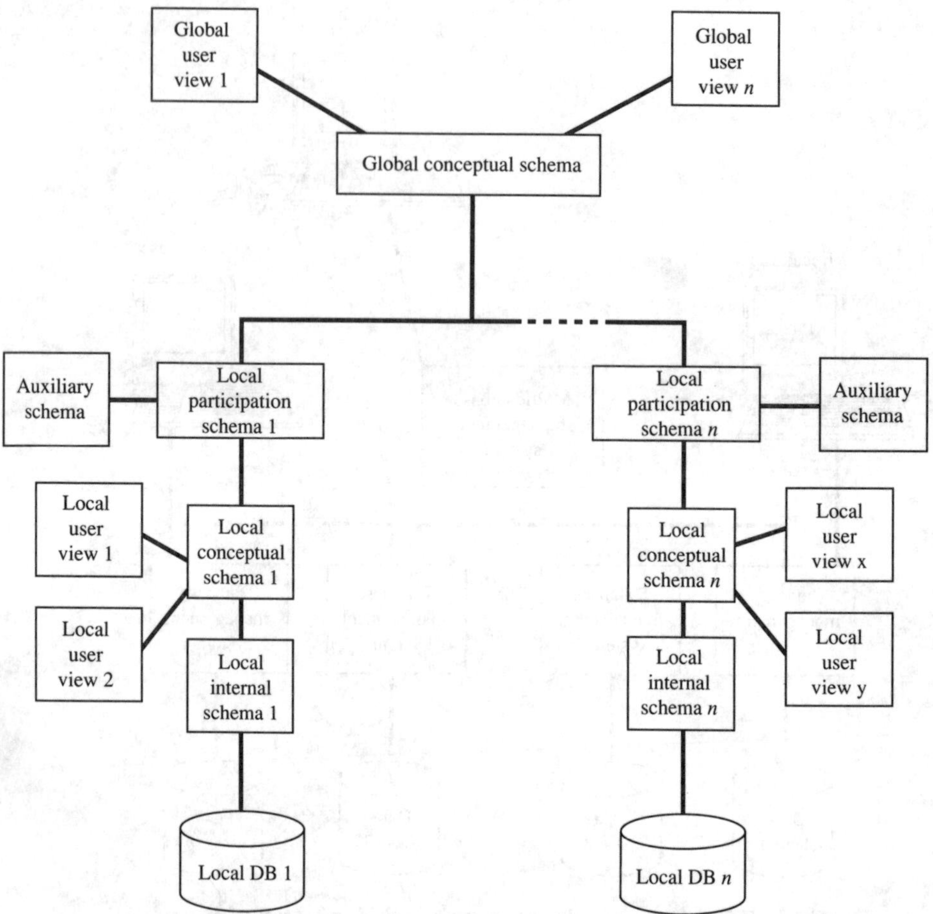

Figure 2.21 Schema architecture of a tightly-coupled multidatabase system.

example, rules for unit conversion may be required when one site expresses distance in kilometres and another in miles. Rules for handling null values may be necessary where one site stores additional information which is not stored at another site, for example one site stores the name, home address and telephone number of its employees, whereas another just stores names and addresses. Some MDBMSs also have a fragmentation schema, although not an allocation schema, since the allocation of fragments to sites is already fixed as MDBMSs integrate *pre-existing* DBs.

The loosely coupled MDBMS, in which there has been growing interest recently, is sometimes called an **interoperable database system**. The important characteristic of these systems is that they have no global conceptual schema. The construction of a global conceptual schema is a difficult and complex task and involves resolving both semantic and syntactic differences between sites. Sometimes these differences are so extensive that it does not warrant the huge investment involved in developing the global schema, especially when the number of multisite global queries is relatively low.

There are two main approaches to building loosely coupled MDBMSs. In one the onus is on the users to build their own views over the local conceptual schemas, as shown in Figure 2.22, using powerful query languages such as Litwin and Abdellatif's MSQL. Alternatively, local DBs can define their contribution to the federated DB by means of an export schema (analogous to the participation schema of MDBMS), as shown in Figure 2.23.

The reader should be aware that there is, as yet, no standard agreement as to terminology in this field.

2.4.2 Classification of DDBMSs by non-architectural issues

One of the main reasons for confusion in the classification of DDBMS is they can be grouped according to many different issues. In Section 2.4.1, we grouped the systems according to their architecture. However, orthogonal to the three broad classifications given, we can also categorize systems

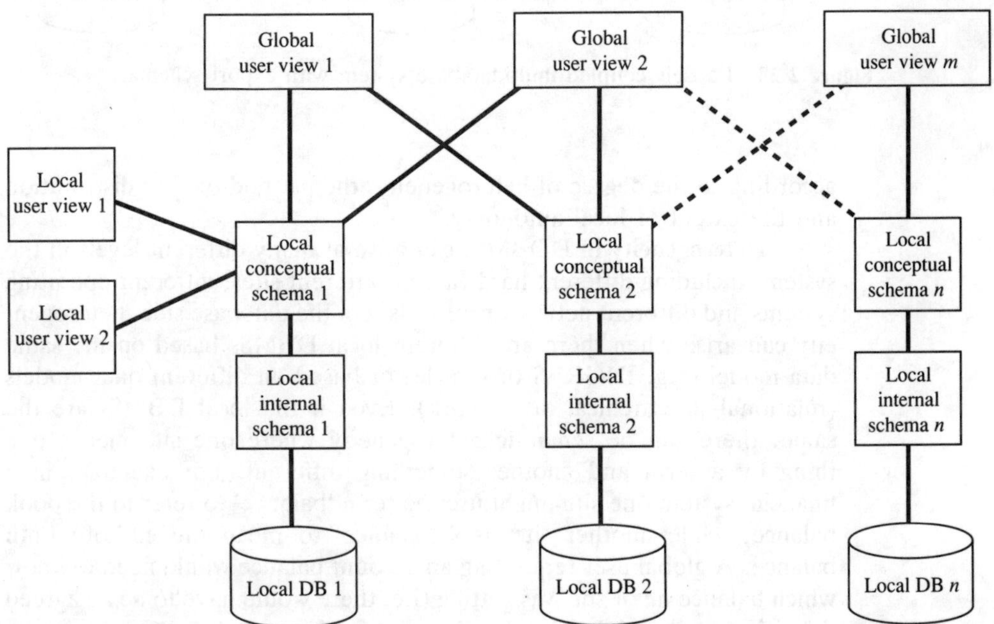

Figure 2.22 Loosely-coupled multidatabase system with no export schema.

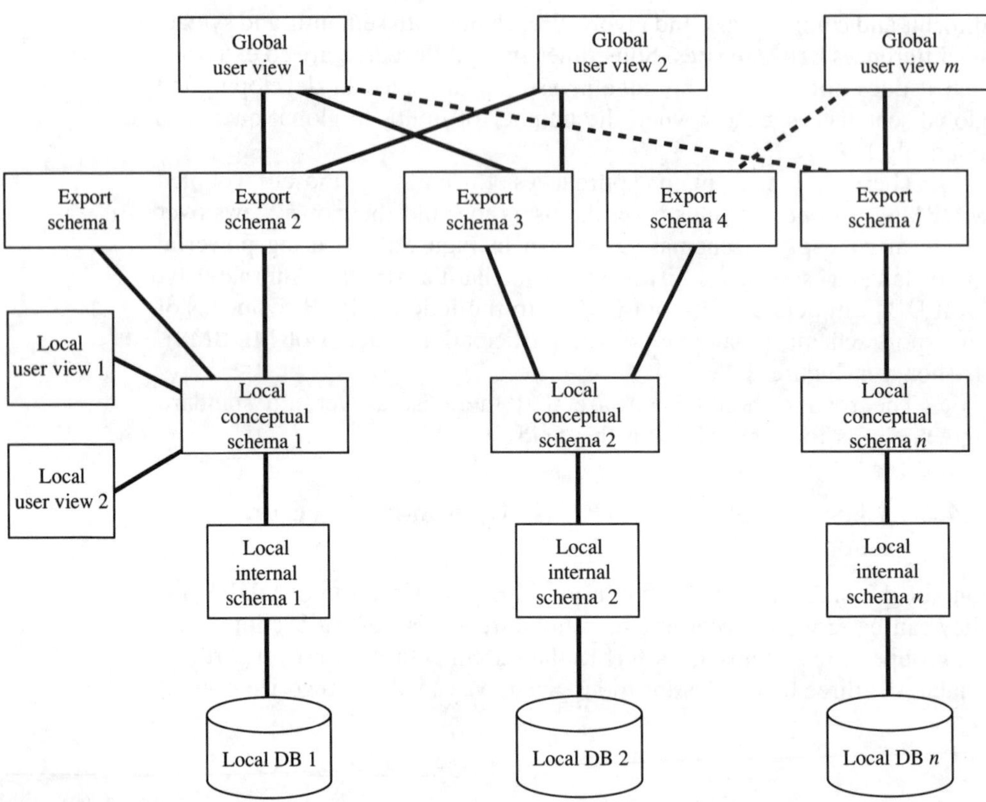

Figure 2.23 Loosely-coupled multidatabase system with export schema.

according to the degree of heterogeneity, the method of data distribution and the extent of local autonomy.

Heterogeneity in DDBMSs can arise at many different levels in the system, including different hardware at different sites, different operating systems and different network protocols. On the database side, heterogeneity can arise when there are different local DBMSs based on the same data model (e.g. INGRES or Oracle) or based on different data models (relational, hierarchical or network). Even if the local DBMSs are the same, there can be semantic heterogeneity where one site means one thing by a term and another something different. For example, in a financial system one site might use the term 'balance' to refer to the book balance, while another site uses 'balance' to mean the end-of-month balance. A global user requesting an account balance would need to know which balance he or she was getting (i.e. there would have to be an agreed definition at the global level). One site might record distances in miles and another in kilometres. A date might be stored as DD-MM-YY at one site and as MM-DD-YY at another. More subtle differences can also arise in relation to the interpretation of local integrity constraints at the global level. For example, all sites might have a constraint which states that an employee can only have one basic salary. Imagine the case of an employee who is working part-time and is recorded on two different local DBs. The DDBMS would have to have a way of resolving such difficulties and presenting the global user with a uniform, integrated view.

Much of the early work on distributed databases focused on the problems associated with integrating heterogeneous data models. The basic decision which had to be made was whether to adopt a single model at the global level and map all the local models onto this model or whether to simply provide bidirectional translators between all pairs of models. This latter approach has the advantage that a user of the IDMS network DBMS can view the entire DDB as a network DB, thereby avoiding the necessity of learning another model and language. However, this approach requires $n(n-1)$ translators, where n is the number of different models. The alternative and much more widely used approach is to adopt a single model, the so-called **canonical model**, at the global level and map all the local models onto it. This only requires $2n$ translators. Moreover, most systems adopt the relational model as the canonical model, and since many of the local models are already relational, the mapping can concentrate on semantic rather than syntactic issues.

The data can be distributed across the sites in different ways. The data may be **fully replicated**, in which case the entire global DB is stored at each node. Full replication is used when fault tolerance and performance are important; the data is still available even in the event of site and network failure and there are no communication delays (for retrieval). Fully replicated DBs are designed top-down since they really do consist of a single DB duplicated in its entirety across the network. The problem of supporting updates and recovering from failure in replicated databases is discussed in Chapters 6 and 7.

At the other extreme, the global DB can be **fully partitioned**, that is there is no replication whatsoever. Such a situation is common with multidatabases where local pre-existing DBs are integrated in a bottom-up fashion. In between these two extremes is **partial replication** of data. Partial replication is generally required when certain parts of the global DB are accessed frequently from a number of different sites in the network.

The degree of **local autonomy** or local control supported in a DDB environment is another important factor. Where a system allows full nodal autonomy, integration is more difficult, as will become apparent in later chapters of this book. Autonomy is concerned with the distribution of control as opposed to the distribution of data. Thus, at one extreme, if there is no local autonomy this implies that there is full global control. Such a situation could be found in a homogeneous distributed database environment which was designed top-down. Effectively such a system has no local users and while the local DBs are managed by local DBMSs, the local DBMSs do not operate independently (see Figure 2.17).

By contrast, in a multidatabase there are both local and global users and local autonomy guarantees that these local users access their own local DB independently of, and unaffected by, the existence of the multidatabase and its global users. Even with the degree of local freedom involved in a multidatabase, it could still be argued that the local node has, by participating in a multidatabase in the first place, relinquished a degree of autonomy!

Researchers often distinguish between different types of autonomy – design autonomy, communication autonomy, execution autonomy and participation autonomy.

Design autonomy is in many ways the most fundamental since it gives the local sites complete design and implementation freedom including deciding on the information content of the DB, selection of the data model and choice of storage structures. In multidatabases where the aim is to integrate *pre-existing* DBs, local design autonomy is taken for granted.

Participation autonomy gives local sites the right to decide how to participate in the distributed system, namely what data to contribute and when. Local sites should ideally be free to come and go as they please.

Communication autonomy gives sites the right to decide how, and under what terms, to communicate with other sites in the network. In practice most of this function is taken over by the computer network itself.

Execution autonomy affords to local sites the right to decide whether and how to process local operations to store, retrieve and update local data. For example, the local transaction manager should have the freedom to abort a global transaction if it is in conflict with a local transaction.

SUMMARY

In this chapter, we have presented a brief overview of the two technologies of database management and computer networks, which are combined together to produce distributed database systems. This overview is intended to remind the reader of concepts with which the reader is assumed to be familiar.

In Section 2.4 we present a comprehensive and consistent taxonomy of distributed data sharing systems which will be used throughout the book. Systems are classified at the top level as being either homogeneous or heterogeneous. Although much of the research to date, especially in areas such as concurrency control and recovery, has been carried out on homogeneous systems, it seems likely that the systems of the future will be heterogeneous. Of particular interest is the sub-class of these systems known as multidatabase systems (MDBMSs), which in turn can be tightly coupled through a global schema or loosely coupled without a global schema. Terms such as federated and interoperable database system are explained and fitted in to the taxonomy.

EXERCISES

2.1 (a) Is the natural join operator commutative?
i.e. is

$$A \bowtie B = B \bowtie A$$

(b) Is the semi-join operator commutative?
i.e. is

$$A \lhd B = B \lhd A$$

2.2 A relational DBMS contains the following relations:

STUDENTS(student#,student_name,student_address)
GRADES(course#,student#,result)
COURSES(course#,course_title,lecturer)

write a series of SQL statements to

(a) List the student_name and student_number for all students who obtained a result = 'A' in the course identified by course# = '3BA3';
(b) List the student_name, student_address and course_title for all courses taught by lecturer = 'Prof Brown' in which the students have obtained a result = 'F'.

2.3 For each of the determinancy diagrams shown in Figure 2.24:
(a) specify the candidate identifier(s)
(b) derive a set of normalised relations (BCNF).

2.4 A computer science department has decided to establish a relational database for its degree course. This database is to contain information about students, lecturing staff, tutors, courses and examination results. Note that at any time the database will store data about the current academic year only. Data from

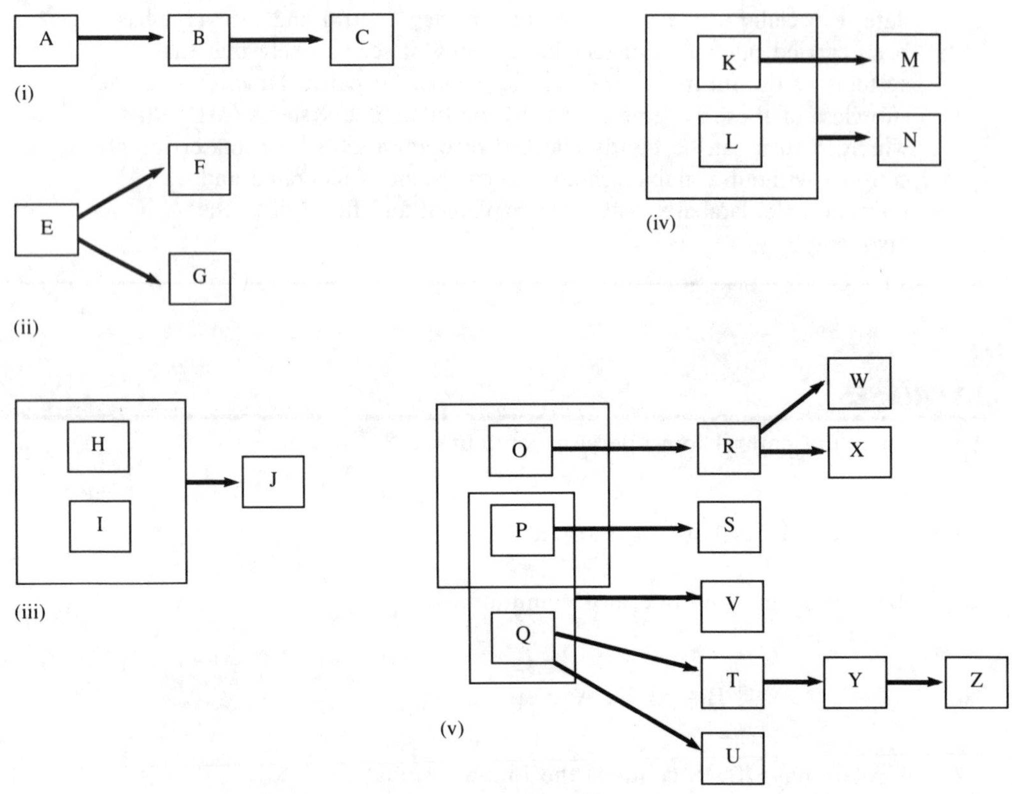

Figure 2.24 Examples of determinancy diagrams (Exercise 2.3).

previous years is stored in a separate database, which is not your concern. The following information is to be recorded:

For each STUDENT:

Number (unique)
Name
Address
Tutor
Year of course
Overall result (i.e. I, II.1, II.2, III, Pass, Fail, Repeat, Proceed carrying a subject),

together with the list of courses the student is taking and the result obtained in each course.

For each LECTURER:

Staff number (unique)
Name
Position (i.e. lecturer, senior lecturer, etc.)

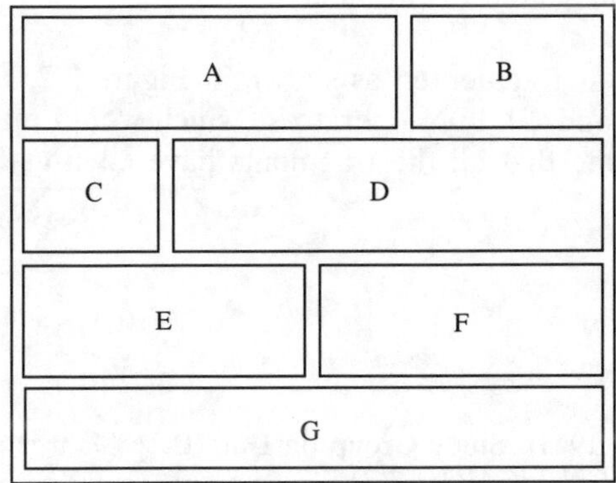

Figure 2.25 Fragmented global relation R (Exercise 2.9).

together with a list of courses which they teach.

For each TUTOR (who must be a lecturer):
  Tutor number (unique)
  Name

For each COURSE:
  Number (unique)
  Title
  Year taught (i.e. 1st, 2nd, 3rd or 4th year course)
  Compulsory or optional,

together with a list of lecturers who teach the course

(a) Assume plausible enterprise rules and state these clearly

(b) Draw a determinancy diagram for the database

(c) Derive a set of fully normalized relations for the database and identify the primary key of each.

2.5 What is the difference between point-to-point and broadcast networks? For each type, describe a number of alternative topologies.

2.6 Explain the seven layers of the ISO OSI Reference Model.

2.7 Explain in detail the difference between homogeneous and heterogeneous data sharing systems.

2.8 Why do you think homogeneous distributed database systems have been described as 'solutions in search of problems'?

2.9 If a global relation R was fragmented as shown in Figure 2.25, write a command (using JOIN and UNION operators) which would materialize this relation. You may assume that all the fragments have been gathered together at one site.

Bibliography

ANSI/X3/SPARC (1975). Study Group on Data Base Management Systems. Interim Report, *ACM SIGMOD* **7**(2)

This report presents the standard reference architecture for DBMSs consisting of three levels: conceptual, external and internal schemas (see Section 2.2.2)

ANSI (1986). *American National Standard for Information Systems, Database Language-SQL.* ANSI X3.135-1986

The ANSI SQL standard, see also Date (1990).

ANSI/ISO (1988). *Information Processing Systems – Remote Database Access*, Draft proposal ISO/IEC DP 9579

This proposed standard for remote database access could provide a lot of useful functions (e.g. atomic commit) to distributed data sharing systems which are built using the RDAP protocol (see Section 2.3.2).

Beeri C, Bernstein P.A. and Goodman N. (1978). A sophisticate's introduction to database normalization theory. In *Proc. VLDB*, West Berlin.

Breitbart Y. (1990). Multidatabase interoperability, *ACM SIGMOD* **19**(3), 53–60

This short paper gives a brief introduction to multidatabases, focusing in particular on the problems of schema integration (producing a single, unified global conceptual schema) and transaction management.

CODASYL Programming Language Committee (1971). *Data Base Task Group Report of CODASYL Programming Language Committee*

This report contains the specification of network DBMSs; the so-called CODASYL systems (see Section 2.2.5.2).

Codd E.F. (1970). A relational model of data for large shared data banks, *CACM,* **13**(6)

The seminal paper on the relational approach to DBM.

Coulouris G.F. and Dollimore J.B. (1988). *Distributed Systems, Concepts and Design.*. Wokingham: Addison-Wesley

An excellent introduction to distributed systems, concentrating on distributed file as opposed to database systems. Many of the issues discussed (e.g. concurrency control, recovery) are equally relevant to DDBMSs.

Date C.J. (1982). *An Introduction to Database Systems*, vol. II. Wokingham: Addison-Wesley

Date C.J. (1990). *A Guide to the SQL Standard* 2nd edn. Wokingham: Addison-Wesley

Date C.J. (1990). *An Introduction to Database Systems* vol. I 5th edn. Wokingham: Addison-Wesley

Day J.D. and Zimmermann H. (1983) The OSI reference model. *Proc. IEEE,* **71**, 1334–1340

A comprehensive description of the ISO OSI reference model for open systems interconnection (see Section 2.3.1).

De Marco T. (1979). *Structured Analysis and System Specification*. New York: Yourdon Inc

A classic reference on the software life cycle (see Section 2.2.6).

Elmasri R. and Navathe S.B. (1989). *Fundamentals of Database Systems*. New York: Benjamin/Cummings

Gray J.N., McJones P., Blasgen M., Lindsay B., Lorie R., Price T., Putzolu F. and Traiger I. (1981). The recovery manager of the System R data manager. *ACM Computing Surveys* **13**(2), 223–242

Grimson J.B. (1986). Guidelines for data administration. In *Proc. IFIP 10th World Computer Congress*. Amsterdam: North Holland, 15–22

This paper includes a discussion on the role of DDB technology as a useful tool for data administration.

Halsall F. (1988). *Data Communications, Computer Networks and OSI* 2nd edn. Wokingham: Addison-Wesley.

A good introduction to networks, demystifying a lot of the rather confusing terminology.

Howe D.R. (1989). *Data Analysis for Data Base Design* 2nd edn. London: Edward Arnold

This book provides an excellent introduction to logical DB design with lots of worked examples. The treatment of normalization (see Section 2.2.6) is particularly well done.

Litwin W. (1988). From database systems to multidatabase systems: why and how. In *Proc. BNCOD 6,* (Gray W.A., ed.), 161–88. Cambridge University Press

Litwin W. and Abdellatif A. (1986). Multidatabase interoperability. *IEEE Computer,* **19**(12), 10–18

Litwin W., Mark L. and Roussopoulos N. (1990). Interoperability of multiple autonomous databases. *ACM Computing Surveys,* **22**(3), 267–93

This paper gives a good overview of the need for and features of loosely coupled multidatabase systems (i.e. those with no global schema).

Merrett T.H. (1978). The extended relational algebra, a basis for query languages. In *Databases: Improving Usability and Responsiveness* (Shneiderman B., ed.) London: Academic Press

This paper presents a number of additional relational operators beyond the standard selection, projection, join and semi-join.

Öszu M.T. and Valduriez P. (1991). *Principles of Distributed Database Systems*. New York: Prentice Hall

Sheth A.P. and Larson J.A. (1990). Federated database systems for managing distributed, heterogeneous, and autonomous database systems. *ACM Computing Surveys,* **22**(3), 183–236

A good survey paper in which the comprehensive taxonomy of distributed data sharing systems is given with particular emphasis on what we have referred to throughout this book as loosely coupled multidatabase systems (see Section 2.4.1). The main research areas for these systems are discussed briefly and there is an extensive bibliography.

Tanenbaum A.S. (1988). *Computer Networks* 2nd edn. New York: Prentice Hall

The classic reference text on computer networks.

Ullman J.D. (1980). *Principles of database systems*. Rockville, Maryland: Computer Science Press.

SOLUTIONS TO EXERCISES

2.1

(a) Yes (see Ullman (1980) for proof)
(b) No

$$A \lhd B = \pi_A (A \bowtie B)$$

$$B \lhd A = \pi_B (A \bowtie B)$$

2.2

```
(a) SELECT  student#,student_name
    FROM    STUDENTS, GRADES
    WHERE   course# = '3BA3' AND grade = 'A'
            AND GRADES.student# = STUDENTS.student#;
(b) SELECT  student_name, student_address, course_title
    FROM    STUDENTS, COURSES, GRADES
    WHERE   STUDENTS.student# = GRADES.student#
            AND GRADES.course# = COURSES.course#
            AND COURSES.lecturer = 'Prof Brown'
            AND GRADES.result = 'F';
```

2.3

(i) (a) A
(b) R1 ($\underline{A}$, B) R2 ($\underline{B}$, C)

(ii) (a) E
(b) R3 ($\underline{E}$, F, G)

(iii) (a) {H, I}
(b) R4 ($\underline{H}$, $\underline{I}$, J)

(iv) (a) {K, L}
(b) R5 ($\underline{K}$, $\underline{L}$, N) R6 ($\underline{K}$, M)

(v) (a) {O, P, Q}
(b) R7 ($\underline{O}$, R) R8 ($\underline{R}$, W, X) R9 ($\underline{P}$, S) R10 ($\underline{P}$, $\underline{Q}$, V) R11 ($\underline{Q}$, T, U) R12 ($\underline{T}$, Y, Z) R13 ($\underline{O}$, $\underline{P}$)

2.4

(a) The following assumptions are made.

- Students can take several courses and each course can be taken by several students;
- Lecturing staff can teach on more than one course and a course can be taught by more than one lecturer;
- A student has only one tutor, but a tutor can have many students;
- A given course is taught to one year only;
- Names are not necessarily unique;
- Addresses are not necessarily unique;
- Not all lecturers are tutors, but all tutors are lecturers.

(b) See Figure 2.26.

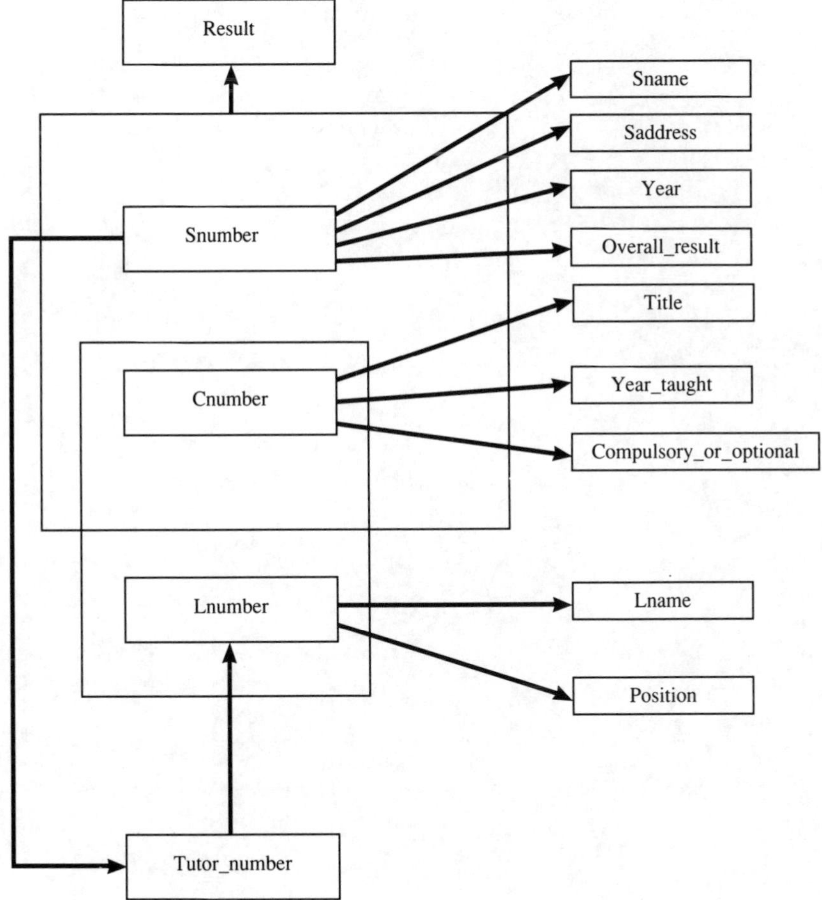

Figure 2.26 Determinancy diagram for Exercise 2.4.

(c) STUDENT (Snumber, Sname, Saddress, Year, Overall_result, Tutor_number)
COURSE (Cnumber, Title, Year_taught, Compulsory_or_optional)
CSRESULT (Snumber, Cnumber, Result)
STAFF (Lnumber, Lname, Position)
TUTOR (Tutor number, Lnumber)
TEACH (Cnumber, Lnumber)

2.9

R = (A JOIN B) UNION (C JOIN D) UNION (E JOIN F) UNION G

3 The State of the Art

3.1 Introduction

The purpose of a database is to integrate and manage the data relevant to a given enterprise, such as a health provision network, an industrial corporation or a bank. The motivation for establishing a database is to get all of the data relevant to the operations of the enterprise gathered together in a single reservoir, so that all of the problems associated with applications in the enterprise can be serviced in a uniform manner. This is to be done through a consistent set of languages, physical data structures, constraint checkers, consistency checkers, development tools and other data management functions.

However, we have already seen that centralized databases are beset with problems that cannot be solved without a radical revision of the basic concepts of data sharing, and this has led to the DDB concept. An important factor to be considered if a change from centralization to distribution of data is contemplated is that the user will typically have to deal with more than one DBMS. It may be necessary to pull data derived from a system managed by a particular DBMS into an apparently incompatible one or to write a query that simultaneously invokes more than one 'brand' of DBMS. The user of course requires as much system support as he/she can get for this and preferably 'off-the-peg' software offering this support is desired.

DDBS were originally mooted on the grounds of providing precisely these features. Their advocates talk enthusiastically of their substantial advantages in the areas of reliability, reduction of communications costs for remote access, ease of expansion and contraction and enhanced performance. The question now arises: on the basis of experience so far and looking at the availability of products in this area, to what extent are such systems available, and can fully functional DDBs still realistically be expected to be available in the reasonably near future? Even if they can, do the overheads they incur still outweigh any advantages we could expect to gain from their adoption? In this chapter overviews of a number of DDB systems are presented with a view to providing insights into the availability of the functionality promised by DDB advocates. The issue of performance is still open since most of the experience so far gained by the end users of applications has been in areas where the objective of high performance is secondary to the main goal of providing openness of access and flexibility of use of data, and we can discuss only the efforts being made by researchers and developers to boost the attractiveness of DDBs for more performance-conscious applications. We do this in later chapters. It should be noted that we use some technical terms in this chapter which will be fully clarified in subsequent chapters.

3.2 Distributed database products, prototypes and proposals

The DDB approach is usually characterized by the principle that the user need not be bothered about architectural, language, schema or location details. Software systems claiming to supply this feature and yet provide even a good subset of the essential data management support expected from current centralized DBs are not so rare as they were five years ago. Comprehensive products are being phased in, albeit at a rate which is at odds with the predictions of pundits several years ago. The results of the phases completed so far would probably surprise someone who had read a well-known EC report in 1982 (Esculier, 1982) on the products current or imminent in the DDB area then. From that report it was evident that even among the seven 'products' identified there, some did not really merit the name of DDB, and some are still not available commercially many years later! However that report, and subsequent observation, has proved useful in highlighting the difficulty of attaining the goals set by developers of DDB systems.

Most, but not all, of the systems described in the report suffered from being restricted to a single manufacturer's hardware and some omit many features normally considered essential in a DDB. Moreover, many were not suitable for what is clearly a common scenario for DDB development, where considerable investment has already been made in developing a variety of local databases on a variety of types and sizes of machines. Most of them are homogeneous systems. These products were really only suitable for adoption in 'green fields' situations.

From now on we simplify our terminology considerably by using a common definition of the **multidatabase approach**. This is taken to be simply an approach which allows a collection of pre-existing databases to be treated as a single integrated unit. The software is superimposed on local, possibly heterogeneous, DBs to provide transparent access to data at multiple sites. Local accesses proceed as usual through the local DBMS. Products which use this approach are starting to appear.

For many applications the multidatabase approach is likely to be more feasible than the homogeneous, logically-integrated DDB approach since it allows DBs to contract in to or out of the global DB almost as desired and appropriate, thereby eliminating the need for design of a finished DDB before any implementation takes place. The interfaces needed for the addition of a new DB using a DBMS which is different from all those already in the system require 'mere hours of coding'. There are also several well known, non-multidatabase system prototypes which manage data spread over heterogeneous computers.

The products already available, despite their immaturity, and even the existence of impressive research prototypes, mean that the DDB approach is worthy of serious consideration by those planning distributed data handling systems in the 1990s. In the next sections we consider the features of two representatives of each of the three classes of system. The classes are: products (and we limit our attention here at least predominantly, to homogeneous systems), multidatabase systems and research systems.

3.3 Two products

With the current emphasis on harmonization and openness in computing, many vendors of DBMSs have realized that DDB support systems will be essential for future products. To illustrate the sorts of products already on the market we have chosen the *de facto* market leader, INGRES/STAR, and a system which has been around for some time, but which offered substantially less functionality until it more recently had some new life breathed into it, ADR/D-NET, and its successors. Other products will be briefly mentioned for completeness later in this section, and some multidatabase systems, soon to become products, will be introduced in the next section.

3.3.1 INGRES/STAR

The DDB manager developed and marketed by Relational Technology Incorporated (RTI), INGRES/STAR, was originally restricted to running on Unix computers which hosted their DBMS, INGRES. It has now been further developed to become a useful general purpose DDB system which can deal, albeit at a lower level of functionality and performance, with data distributed over a large number of different computers, and managed by a variety of DBMSs (see Figure 3.1). It provides a good subset of the data management functions one expects from a centralized DBMS, and future releases are promised to extend the size of that subset. It seems to be well suited to a distributed environment where about 10% of the data accesses are to remote sites. A user views the DDB as though it were a local DB, and existing INGRES DBs can be integrated or a

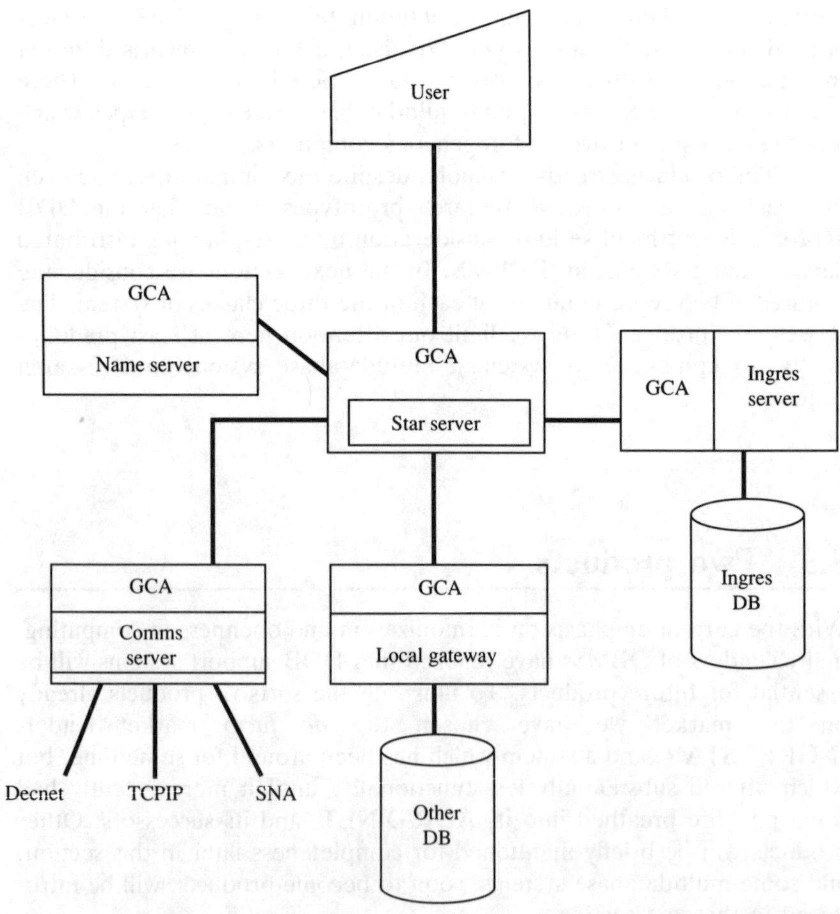

Figure 3.1 INGRES/STAR (INGRES* architecture).

completely new DDB can be set up in a 'green field'. An INGRES/STAR DB is accessible from all the nodes in the network without the user having to know where the data actually resides. Participating local DBs can still be accessed directly if the controlling node's location is known, and the existing applications are not disturbed by the definition of a DDB. An important fundamental component of the system is the global communications architecture (GCA). In each node a copy of the global part of the DDB system – the INGRES/STAR server – controls the decomposition of queries to, and the recomposition of responses from, the system components. INGRES/STAR is described by its developers as conforming to the server – client process paradigm. An independent server can accept a request for data in SQL encoded in GCA format from a remote or local client process. It decomposes the request into an efficient set of remote, local, and 'gateway' queries (i.e. queries to other systems to which the INGRES system is connected) on the basis of information from a 'name server' and subsequently receives and correctly combines the results of the queries and supplies the final result of the user's request at the originating site. This means that the user can have a perception of a single, local database, despite the fact that the data is dispersed over several contributing hardware platforms, such as DEC, IBM and other MSDOS and Unix kit. At the distributed sites, remote requests are received through the local communications servers and GCA is invoked again to link with the local database systems. In INGRES the physical data structures for accessing data are heap, hash, ISAM and B-tree.

In release 6 of INGRES by RTI, the developers have taken the first product step towards their cooperative system architecture (CSA). In this release of this well known and relatively mature system (it reflects nearly 20 years of research and development into basic relational structures and architecture) the architecture of the network protocol support component of the product, INGRES/NET, has been completely reworked. INGRES/NET was first delivered in 1983, and was aimed at the market slot where a relational DB was to be integrated with distributed computing. This is not the same as a DDB, of course, because no specific database functionality was on offer at the global level.

First a DEC VMS version was released, and then the following year this was integrated with DEC Unix machines. PC links were provided in 1985. The basic approach to the operation of this system was governed by a back-end–front-end principle. The back-end RDB engine with SQL runs on the node holding the data; the front-end, incorporating such tools as query-by-forms, terminal monitor and applications programs, resides on the enquirer's machine.

The GCA architecture, resulting from a comprehensive review of INGRES/NET, conforms to the OSI reference model, thereby offering the openness required to evolve INGRES/STAR into a system offering heterogeneous (but at present relational only) DDB support. This heterogeneity is provided by a database gateway feature. Gateways provide the transparency required to shield the user from the various dialects of SQL that the participating systems (e.g. INGRES, SQL/DS, DB2, RMS and Rdb) offer, and also from the nasty diversity of error messages submitted by the heterogeneous systems. Non-relational gateways are also being developed, and this requires the provision of relational interfaces to the alien systems (see Chapter 4). The gateway carries out the parsing and evaluating of a query over the INGRES 'view' of contributing databases. The local data managers retrieve the data. A key goal of the gateway feature is to keep the architecture fixed regardless of both the particular INGRES product using it and the local database systems. GCA makes INGRES/ NET topology-independent, makes it easier and more efficient to add new protocols and gives it the multiserver architecture needed to enhance system throughput and to allow an unlimited number of simultaneous users. This release also improves distributed query optimization (see Chapter 5) and simplifies information management through the introduction of the STAR*VIEW distributed database monitor.

The data is catalogued in the 'name server', and the user views the data as a set of local relations. These are referred to by 'synonyms' which translate to particular remote data objects (which form, for example, fragments of a global relation). The location transparency this gives allows existing database applications to be used without pain or extensive user retraining. The local DBs retain their autonomy. Many useful products, such as business support interfaces developed by RTI's 'corporate partners' for centralized INGRES DBs carry over to DDBs.

The history of this product typifies the phased approach mentioned earlier. The developments listed above mark the end of the second phase of a four-phase development project for INGRES/STAR. The first phase, completed in 1986, was to develop the homogeneous version of the system. Several local and remote INGRES databases running under UNIX or VMS operating systems on computing facilities linked by DECnet or TCP/IP could be integrated into a single DDB using this software. In phase 3 the functionality will be further improved by adding better distributed transaction processing support, replication management, efficiency, security and administration features. We will be examining features of the subsystems needed to deal with these facilities in distributed database systems in general in subsequent chapters.

The more futuristic object-oriented system features (see later) being designed and prototyped in POSTGRES will be merged with INGRES/STAR in phase 4, and the issues of nested configurations, fragments and better configuration strategies are also being addressed for that phase.

In summary, INGRES/STAR provides

- A global query optimizer
- Vertical and horizontal fragmentation/partitioning

- A global data dictionary
- Several relational DB interfaces
- Heterogeneity of operating systems and machines through the gateway feature.

It will provide non-relational gateways and two-phase commit (see Chapters 6 and 7) in the next phase, but it does not support dynamic replication (but only snapshots) or dictionary updates.

3.3.2 CA-DB:STAR and ADR/D-NET

In the early 1980s, Applied Data Research, Inc. (ADR) developed a homogeneous relational system called ADR/DATACOM/DB for linking ADR relational DBs on IBM mainframes. Its target was therefore systems somewhat larger than those targetted by INGRES/STAR. It was billed by its vendors as a DDB but it lacked the important feature of supplying a unified view of the 'global database' and a standardized query language to pose queries over the collection of DBs as if it were a single DB. There are some differences in opinion between experts as to whether this system as first introduced merited the title of DDB, which many would reserve for more comprehensive systems such as INGRES/STAR. However, though limited in terms of distributed query optimization and other high-level logical data independence features, it was a useful software product in that it provided the following capabilities:

- Support for multiple databases at various network nodes;
- Processing of shared databases by many machines;
- Replication and partitioning of data;
- Location transparency and independence for users and their programs;
- Excellent security and authorization features, and efficient scheduling of concurrent transactions.

It should also be noted that, as we shall see at the end of this product description, this early system has evolved significantly in recent years.

The ADR/D-NET software module (see Figure 3.2) manages the entire DDB environment, coordinating all activities within the system, including interaction with the user, filtering and routing data requests to the extent that the system supports this (remember it has no query decomposition, and it does not concatenate partial results from the invoked databases), handling telecommunications links between nodes using IBM's ACF/VTAM, and maintaining the status of the distributed directory.

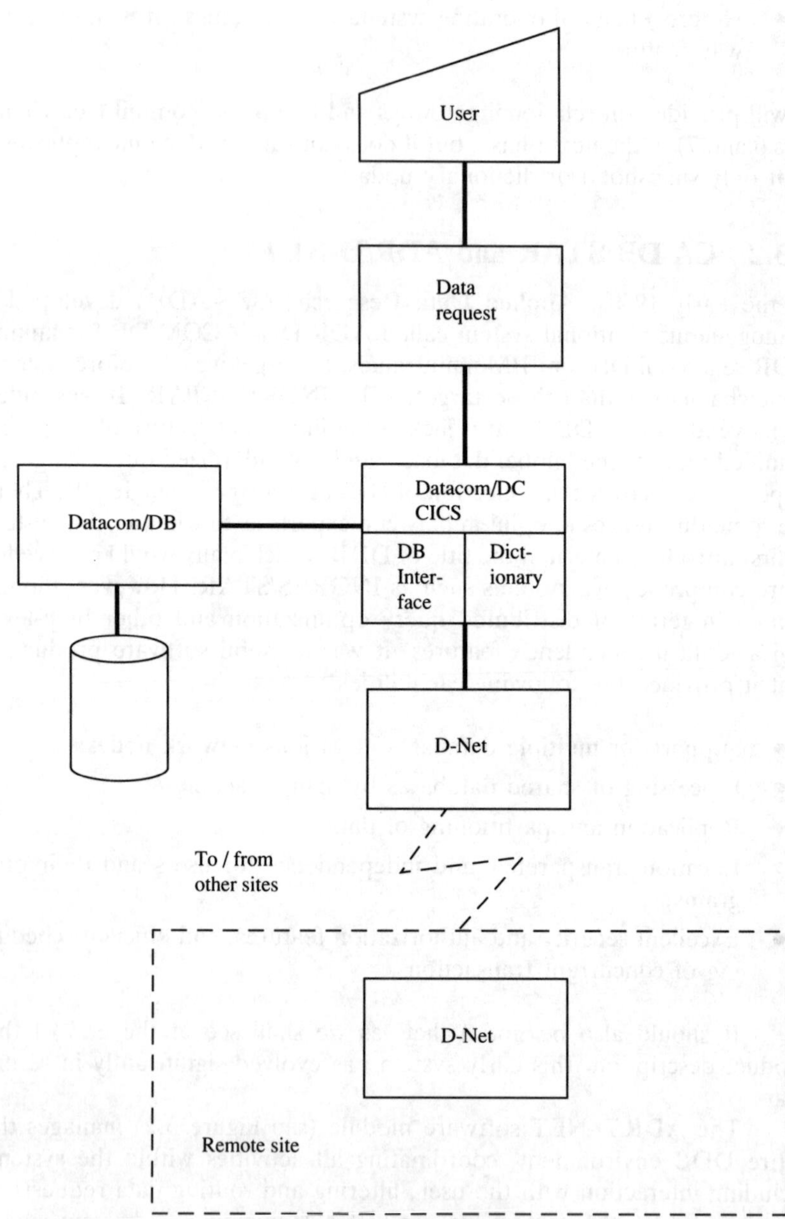

Figure 3.2 ADR/D-NET.

Transactions arriving at the system make references to files (ADR calls these 'databases') as the basic unit of distribution. The data dictionary, which can be replicated (perhaps partially) or centralized and holds the data definitions for the database, is consulted by D-NET to see where the file is located, thereby making access location-transparent.

A CALL DB command can be embedded in the user's host program code, written in RPG or COBOL. Alternatively the DATACOMM/DB query language, DQ, can be used for record-at-a-time access, which is very restrictive (see below). Physical accesses are made via a VSAM-like structure.

This product was designed to operate under a variety of IBM operating systems, maintaining compatibility through a feature called Virtual Program Environment. So it will function on IBM 370, 43-hundreds, 303s and 3081 under these operating systems.

The physical connection between computers can be through a communications network, a channel-to-channel connector, or a combination of these. All users at all nodes in the network have equal capability for all kinds of transactions, including update, subject to their authors' access privileges.

A major design feature for this system was the assurance of availability and reliability of the data in the network, and these features account for a very large percentage of the code in the system. Recovery, restart and transaction backout are available throughout the network.

A primary-copy system is used for concurrency control and locking is available to protect transactions from interference by others running at the same time. The deadlock detection and prevention schemes of DATACOM/DB are inappropriate for distributed environments because they would entail the inefficiency of consultation of active transactions tables at different sites to detect wait-for cycles. So a time-out mechanism is used for this. When the time quantum (specified by the DBA) elapses, D-NET builds the appropriate active transaction table dynamically, and decides upon a victim, usually the most recently started transaction, to be backed out and restarted.

A few years ago this system was acquired by Computer Associates, Inc., and it has undergone a number of name changes since then. The current name is CA-DB:STAR and it is being marketed energetically by Computer Associates.

A new version of the DBMS has been implemented to support set-at-a-time accesses. All of the application development products one would expect with a modern DBMS are provided. Moreover, heterogeneity is accommodated, so that a similar evolutionary path to that of INGRES is being taken (but aimed at mainframes here). Computer Associates have also now acquired the well-known IDMS network database manager system and this is obviously going to account for a priority porting exercise to accommodate it in the DDBS. Currently an IDMS system with SQL interface is going to final practical testing. Distributed optimization and updating features promise to make this a key contender for large installations.

Complementing this larger scale capability, a system to allow full portability between PCs and mainframes, called CA-DB/PC, is being developed. This system provides the attractive feature of allowing development work to be offloaded to PCs. A 'star' version will support the transportation of data between the large and small systems.

There are already several very large volume users of the CA-DB:STAR system. Unconventional uses of the functionality are sometimes encountered. For example, one large user selected the system purely for its ability to partition data. The complete volume of data is broken up into chunks which can be maintained autonomously in a reasonable time span, while retaining their integration. The communications facility supporting this product uses SNA protocols and high-speed channels. Network transparency is supported and all communications advances from IBM can be exploited.

3.3.3 Other products

Most suppliers and developers of centralized DBMSs have realized for some time that it is a marketing necessity to move into the DDB sector. For example, distributed versions of ORACLE, ADABAS and IDMS/R have been announced.

So far, however, many of them suffer grievous deficiencies such as there being no global query optimization offered, no two-phase commit, deadlock resolution, poor fragmentation and sometimes no location transparency. Often they operate on only a very limited set of hardware platforms, for example IDMS/R can apparently only be distributed at all over IBM 370 boxes.

Well-known systems such as IBM's DB2 are still dragging their feet. It will be very interesting to see just when IBM finally take a decisive plunge into this particular pool.

3.4 Two multidatabase systems

There are prototype software systems in existence which aim to permit any kind of pre-existing, heterogeneous, independent DB, whether on the same computing facility or not, to be interrogated via a uniform, integrated logical interface. Many of these have appeared as pre-development prototypes or industrial prototypes in very recent years. Some of these are on the verge of being offered by their producers as product systems. However, we choose to review first in this section what is widely regarded as one of the earliest and most definitive examples of a multidatabase architecture, namely Multibase. The developers of this system did not continue its development to the stage where it would have been within striking distance of being a product, although an extensive working prototype was developed in 1985. Nonetheless, it warrants a description in this section because it illustrates the concepts of this approach to DDBs so well. The second example presented here is that of DQS, which is about to be launched on the market at the time of writing. We attempt to highlight the major differences between the two systems.

3.4.1 Multibase

In the Multibase system, which was designed by Computer Corporation of America (CCA), a simple functional query language (DAPLEX) is used to reference and manipulate distributed data, which is viewed through a single global schema. DAPLEX is also used for defining the data. The users of the system are therefore enabled to access in a uniform manner, and with ease and efficiency, data which is of interest to them but is scattered over multiple, non-uniform local databases (Figure 3.3(a)). The users are each provided with a view of the data as belonging to just one non-distributed database. The pre-existing DBs, their DBMSs, and their local applications programs are unaffected (at least logically but probably not performance-wise), so that a global DB is easily extensible.

All of the underlying operations which are necessary to access data relevant to a query are provided automatically and transparently to the user, by Multibase. These operations include: locating the data needed to service the query; knowing the local formats and the query languages that have to be used to access the local data; breaking the global query down into subqueries which can each be evaluated at a local site; correctly resolving any inconsistencies that may occur between data from different sites; combining the partial results to obtain an answer to the global query; and presenting the result to the original user's site. By providing the functions transparently within the system, many sources of error and many tedious procedures can be eliminated.

The local host computers are all connected to a communications network to permit global access through Multibase. The network can be a local area network or a wide area network. The global user has to have an interface to this network, so Multibase is connected into the network in order to permit use to be made of its services at his/her node. Local sites retain autonomy for local operation and for updates – a local DB can be updated only locally in Multibase. Global concurrency control therefore requires control of specific locking and timestamping mechanisms, for example. For instance, global deadlock detection algorithms could well depend upon having local wait-for graphs available from the

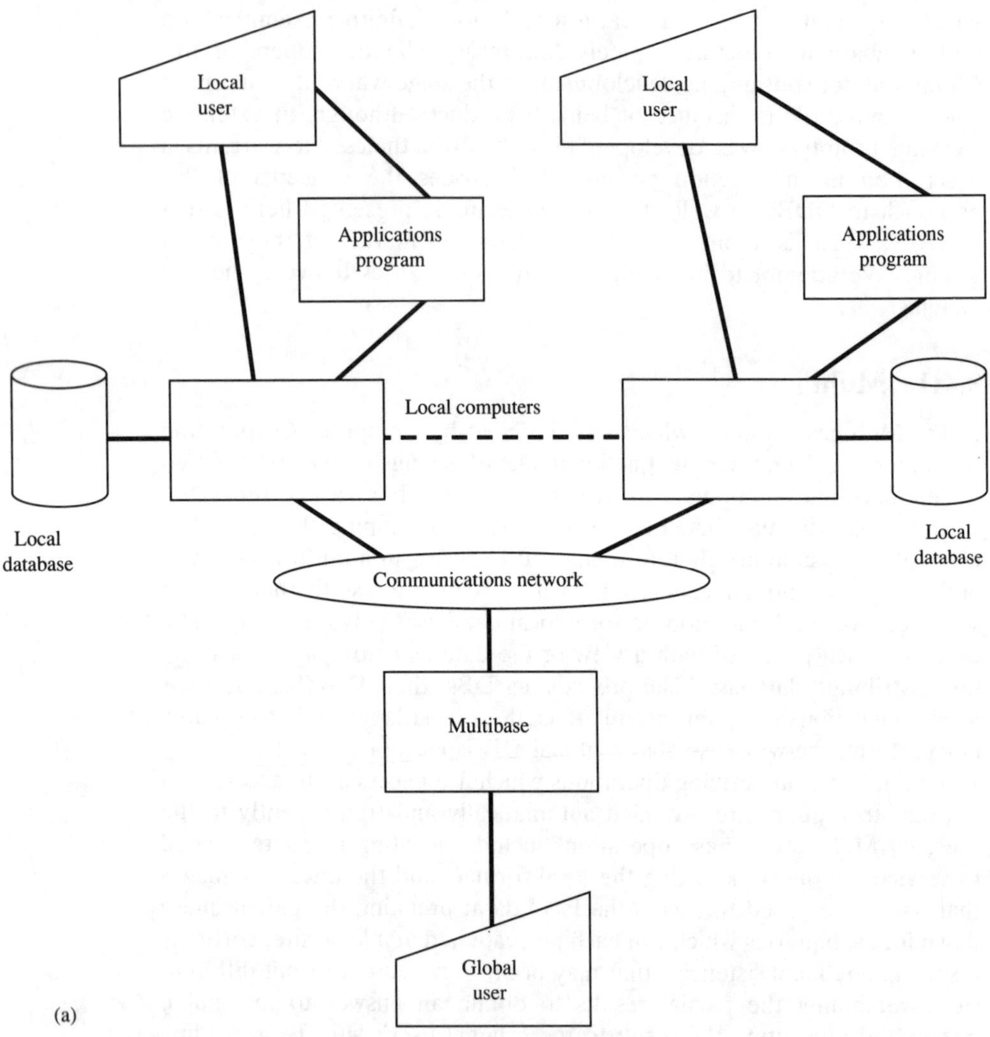

Figure 3.3 (a) Multibase architecture.

heterogeneous DBs. This information is often not available from the contributing DBMSs, and so Multibase guarantees no more global user data consistency than that which is supplied locally.

To provide the global user with a level of indirection from the locations and details of contributing data collections, Multibase handles the issues of data harmonization (i.e. removal of inconsistencies) and interrogation at global level, separately from the homogenization of the different models of data, which is carried out locally. DAPLEX local schemas are presented as views of the local data, homogenization being

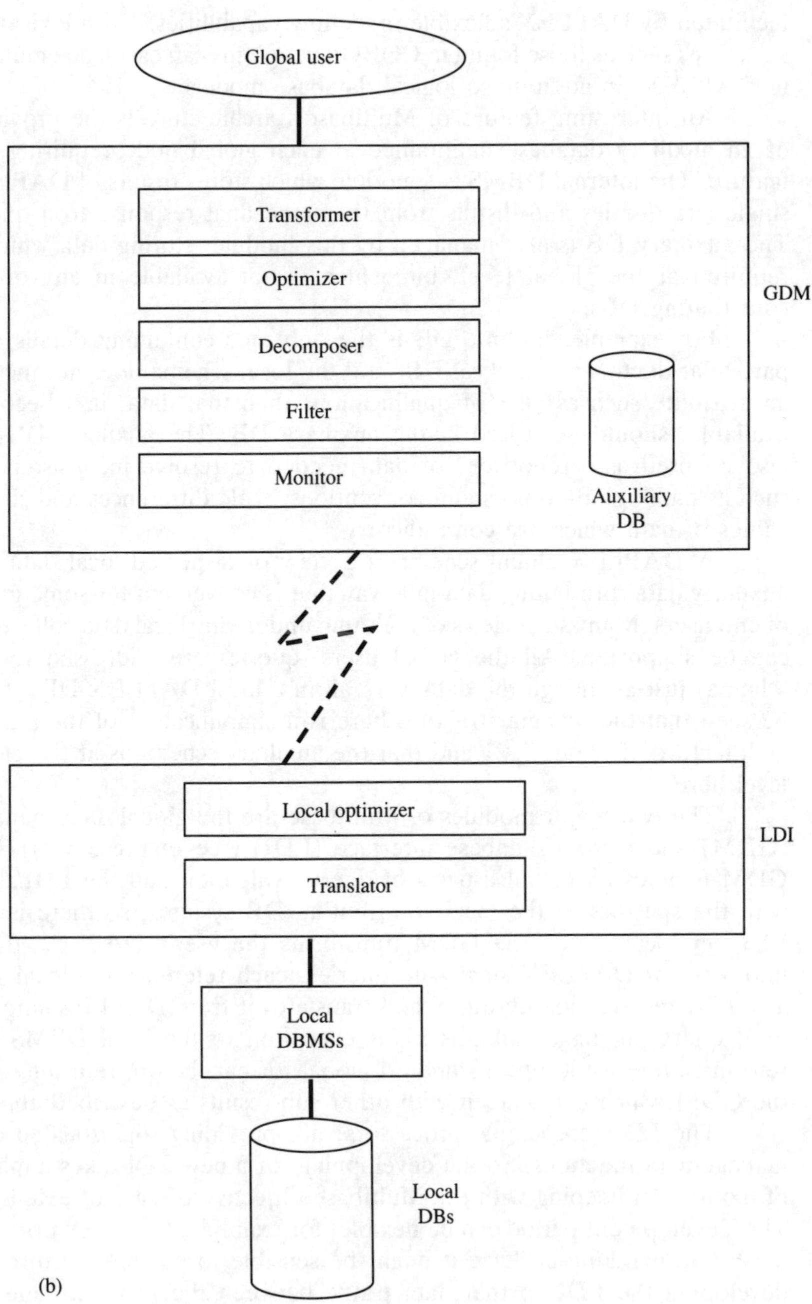

Figure 3.3 (b) The two major modules of Multibase.

facilitated by DAPLEX's flexible modelling capabilities. Even logical file structures such as those found in COBOL programs can easily be emulated in DAPLEX, in addition to logical database models.

An interesting feature of Multibase's architecture is the provision of an auxiliary database maintained at each global node requiring this feature. The internal DBMS is a module which stores results of DAPLEX single site queries and distills from them the final response to a query. The auxiliary DB is also managed by this module, storing data which is required at the global level, but which is not available in any of the contributing DBs.

For example, if some DB is the only one containing details of a particular doctor in a medical DB, and the local schema does not include an attribute such as year of qualification, then that data, if it becomes available, should be stored in the auxiliary DB. The auxiliary DB can also be used as a repository of data needed to resolve inconsistencies, such as naming differences and conventions, scale differences and simply values of data which are contradictory.

A DAPLEX global schema is a view of dispersed local data and auxiliary data, presenting data in a way that is convenient for some group of end users. Many such views of the same underlying local data collections can be supported. All the global users' queries are addressed to this schema, just as though the data were all in a local DAPLEX DB. It can be seen that the schema structure here is a simplification of the schema architecture of Figure 2.21 and that the auxiliary schema is at the global level here.

The two major modules of Multibase are the global data manager (GDM) and a local database interface (LDI) (see Figure 3.3(b)). The GDM handles all global aspects of query evaluation and the LDI deals with the specifics of the local contributing DB systems, so there is one LDI per local node. The GDM transforms the user's DAPLEX query into a set of DAPLEX single-site queries, each referencing a local DB. The LDI receives its sub-query and translates it from DAPLEX into the local query language, submits it for execution to the local DBMS and reformats the result into a standard global format, before returning it to the GDM which combines it with other sub-results as described above.

The LDIs are simple processors, not providing sophisticated data management functions. So the development of a new LDI takes a matter of months, in keeping with the Multibase objective of ease of extension. This development period can be flexible, for example, for a very primitive local data handling package it might be sensible to put more effort into developing the LDI so that data traffic between the local site and the global query site can be reduced.

Although Multibase was never developed into a product, the researchers on the project continued to study key areas in multidatabase research. In particular, contributions were made in the model transformation, view-handling and query processing areas.

3.4.2 Distributed query system (DQS)

A prototype for a system called NDMS (Network Data Management System) was implemented at a very early stage in the history of multidatabase systems. As early as 1983, it had been implemented to interface with a variety of DBMSs, namely IDMS DB/DC, ADABAS and RODAN, installed in the IBM OS environment and with INGRES in the DEC VAX VMS environment. Access to traditional data files is also facilitated by interfaces to the access methods of major operating systems.

Like Multibase, NDMS provides for integration of pre-existing databases managed by heterogeneous DBMSs at heterogeneous nodes of a computer network. However the DAPLEX views are replaced by relational views which are defined at three levels and are materialized (generated) during query evaluation (see Figure 3.4). The definition levels form a hierarchy of data abstractions using data aggregations and gen-

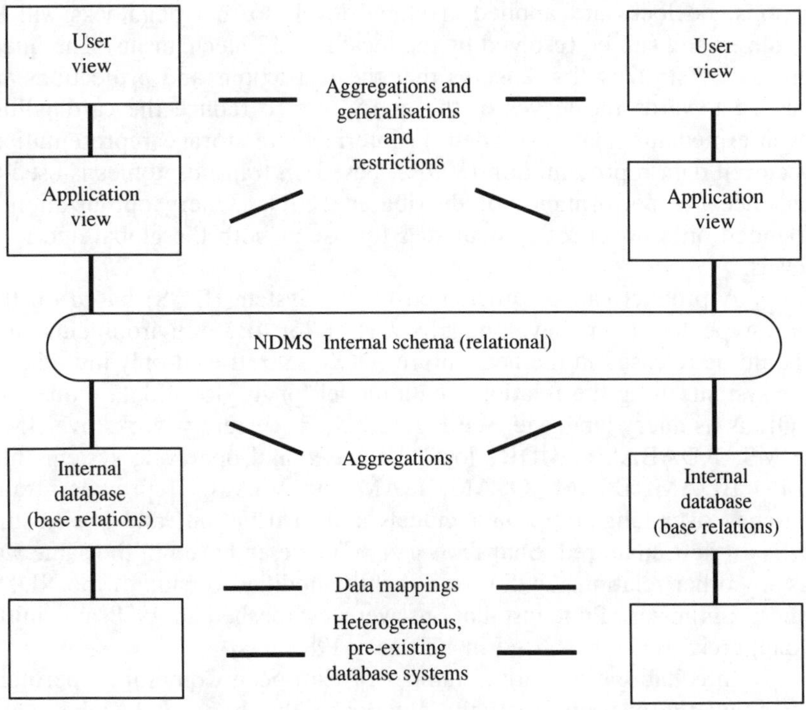

Figure 3.4 Data abstractions in NDMS.

eralizations. Again it can be seen that Figure 2.21 has been interpreted somewhat.

The view definition mechanisms of the local DBMSs are enhanced by mapping languages to arrive at the NDMS internal schema and use is made of semantic constraints to resolve conflicts due to semantic incompatibilities at the local level.

A system encyclopaedia containing all definitions pertaining to a node is stored at the node, together with the NDMS control software. This represents the local part of the global data dictionary. The local DBA defines the relational application views needed at the node over the internal schema. The end users may define, or have defined for them, their own data abstractions over these views. Both permanent views and periodically updated (by the system) snapshots are supported.

Local or distributed on-line and queued transactions, which can be initiated at any point of the NDMS controlled network and executed at any node, are controlled by the distributed transaction processing facility. These may exchange messages and are synchronized by a two-phased commit protocol. A transaction recovery mechanism, supported by a system journal, is also available. Thus, unlike Multibase, update transactions are supported. In ensuring the correctness of concurrent transactions, no locks are applied at global level, so that deadlocks will be localized and can be resolved by the local DBMS mechanisms. The query processing strategy first ensures that the restrictions and projections are pushed towards the leaves of the query tree to reduce the cardinalities of intermediate relations. Then an intermediate storage representation, vectorial data representation (VDR), based on transposed files is used to enhance the performance of distributed JOINs. Query optimization is founded on a novel set of heuristics for use at both the global and local levels.

A product called Distributed Query System (DQS) based on this prototype has been developed by CRAI for IBM environments, and should be released in the near future. DQS is a retrieval-only multidatabase system, using the relational data model for its global data model and SQL as its query language (see Figure 3.5). It currently works over IMS, IDMS, ADABAS and DB2 local databases and operating systems files using BDAM, BSAM, QSAM, ISAM and VSAM. It provides transparency over languages, data models and distribution, and pre-existing DBs are left unaltered. Snapshots can be made and used in the same way as any other relation. DQS uses a slightly modified version of the NDMS query optimizer. Pilot installations were established in 1988 and initial commercial releases started in February 1989.

In collaboration with a number of European Community partners, including the institutions of the authors of this book, CRAI have also developed a further product, called Multistar (M*), which complements DQS by providing similar functionality for Unix environments. It is also

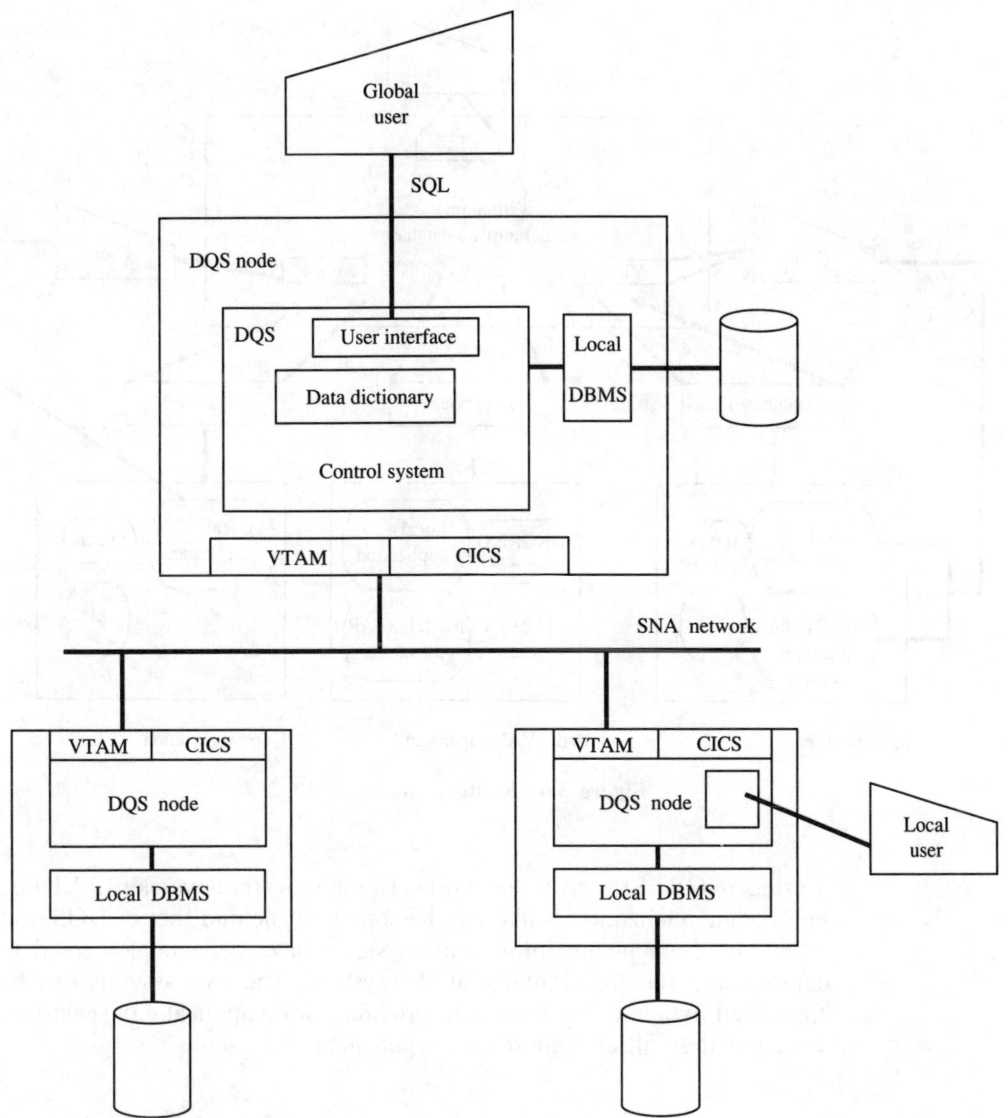

Figure 3.5 DQS architecture.

based on NDMS (see Figure 3.6). The global user accesses data via SQL, either in interactive mode or embedded in 'C' programs. Applications which generate SQL statements dynamically from a source other than a terminal will also be supported. A number of versions of the system have been implemented on DEC (VAX using INGRES), ICL (CLAN6 using INGRES and ORACLE and also Series 39 under OS VME), SUN (Series

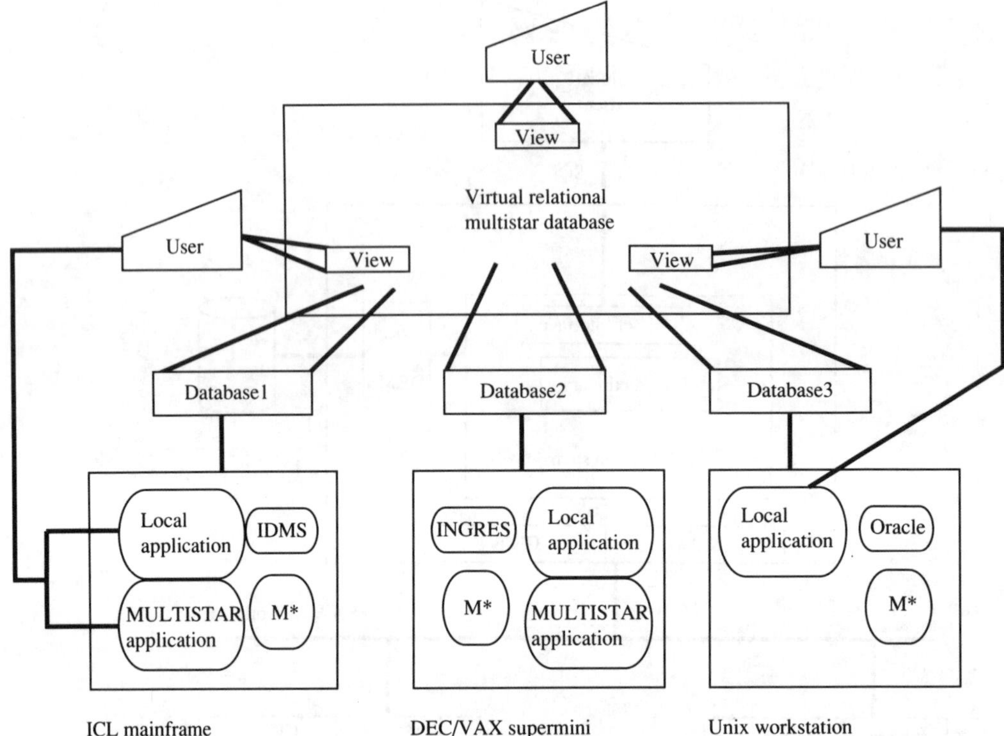

Figure 3.6 Multistar nodes.

3 using INGRES), and other hardware under various versions of Unix. Full commercialization is likely to be somewhat behind that of DQS, but exemplars from health information systems have been implemented to demonstrate the functionality of the system. The two systems can be connected by a gateway feature to provide a wide applicability spectrum. Together they fill an important market niche.

3.5 Two research systems

3.5.1 R*

A system called R* has been developed in the Almaden Research Centre of IBM (formerly the San José Research Laboratory) to extend their experimental centralized system, System R. This system permits the data collections comprising the database to be stored at geographically dispersed sites. The major objectives of this experimental homogeneous

DDB system include allowing each of the cooperating local databases to remain autonomous, giving good performance and, importantly, providing 'a single site image' of the data (i.e. data and location independence, and identical syntax for local and global invocation of an operation). There are four major components in R*.

A key component is RDS* (see Figure 3.7), a language processor which controls pre-compilation and execution of SQL statements. Being the distributed equivalent of System R's Relational Data System, RDS, it implements the conceptual schema matching the RSS* physical schema

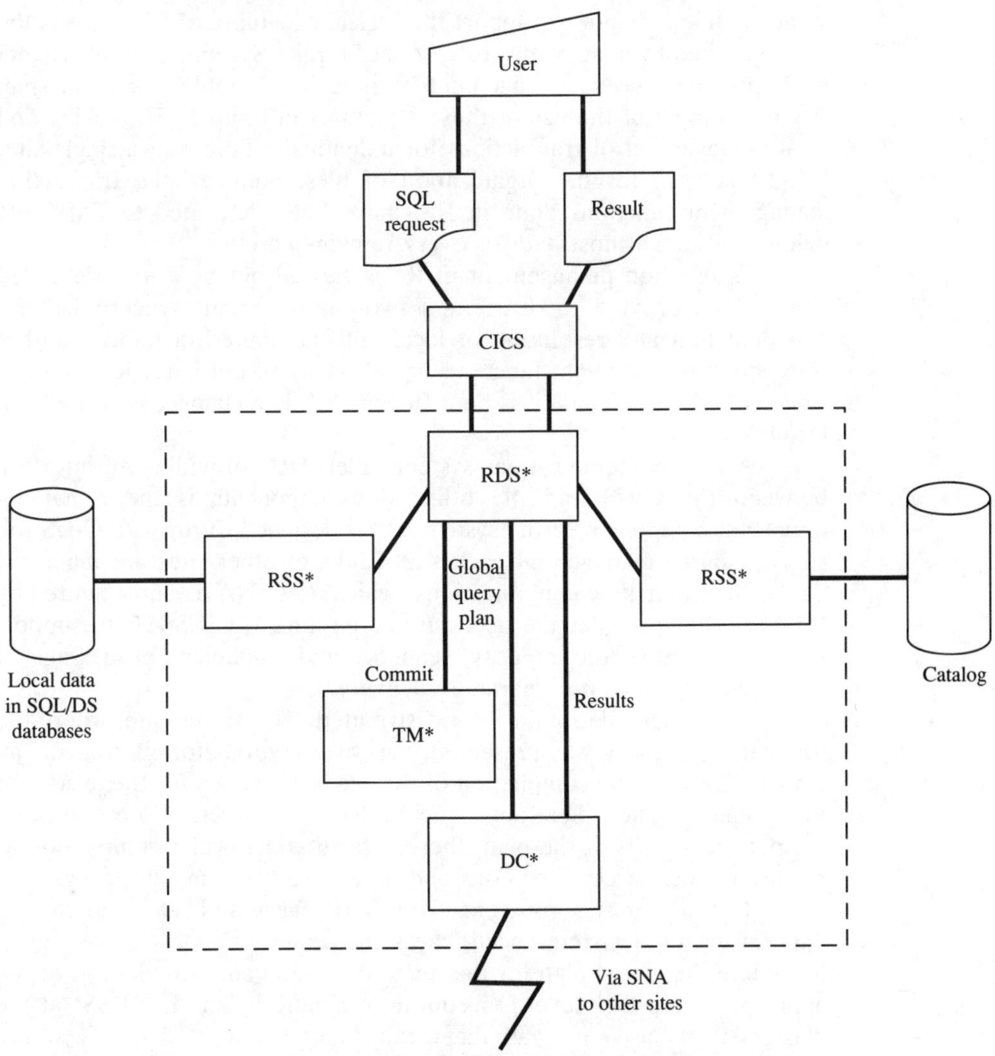

Figure 3.7 Components of R*.

(see below). It translates requests in conceptual terms into lower level RSS* calls. For this purpose it maintains a system catalog or data dictionary stored just like any other table at each site, for converting global names to local object names. Snapshots (materialized queries, refreshed periodically for subsequent use), views (unmaterialized sub-query results which are materialized dynamically as required) and local data tables can all be set up at various sites and global queries can be expressed over combinations of these. RDS* can also be used to create, delete or migrate tables. User authorization and query optimization are the responsibility of RDS*.

Underpinning RDS* is RSS*, which is a physical storage management module for data to support the logical capability of RDS*. It is the distributed equivalent of the Relational Storage System, RSS of System R. It provides access management by indexing or table scans (we shall see an example of the use of these structures in Chapter 5), locking and local management of transactions for individual relations at a single site. VSAM is used for the organization of files. Some of the transaction management functions done in RSS have been delegated to TM* (see below), although most data recovery remains here.

Transaction management in R* is carried out by a module called TM* which provides a distributed two-phase commit synchronization, and detection and resolution of local and distributed deadlocks. Other transaction management functions are also carried out here. Recovery to support two-phase commit is here (logging of data changes is carried out locally).

A data communications system called DC* providing an interface between the CICS and the other R* components is the remaining important component of the system. R* is designed to run as a CICS job step (resource manager) at each site. Links to other sites are made via CICS/ISC (intersite communications) which uses SNA as implemented by VTAM. DC* provides the necessary extensions to CICS/ISC to support this. It guarantees the integrity, sequence and uniqueness of messages if delivered, but does not guarantee delivery.

Query compilation in R* is distributed. The master site, where the original SQL query was presented, acts as a coordinator. It controls all global aspects of the compilation of the accesses needed for the execution of the query. The other (apprentice) sites to be accessed are delegated the pertinent parts of the plan, thereby facilitating local recompilation as required. Local access decisions and access plans are made locally.

The master site must parse the SQL query and fetch the catalog data for each object referenced, check the requestor's local access rights, formulate the global plan for the query execution and broadcast it to the apprentices in a high level procedural distribution plan. The RSS* at the master site is used to read the catalog and the local data. Each site participating in the execution of the query receives and stores the original

SQL query with the names having been changed using information from the system catalog and other transformations having been carried out. The work done at the master site is repeated, but here only the centralized versions of the modules are activated. Clearly no distribution plans or such like objects are required at this stage. The input to this process is not shown in Figure 3.7, but the outline of the execution is similar to that shown for the local access to data at the master site. A low-level access plan and program for the local part of the query is then produced and executed. Independent local recompilation is possible if required because all of the original SQL query is stored at the local site.

3.5.2 Experimental Distributed Database System (EDDS)

Experimental Distributed Database System, EDDS, is a research prototype, developed by the authors of this book, which is distinguished by having a number of features which make it more efficient and flexible than systems on which its architecture was modelled, such as Multibase, Preci* and some of the early Sirius Delta project systems. The system was designed as a testbed for solutions to a variety of open research questions in multidatabase technology. Architectural features, algorithms and detailed structures vary over time in such research prototype systems, and at any given time the EDDS 'standard' is the current best mix of components.

The basic architecture is very similar to that of Multibase, with the Global Transaction Manager, GTM, replacing the global data manager of Multibase, and the Local Data Manager, LDM, replacing the local database interface. In principle the operation of these two modules mirrors those of Multibase.

The schema architecture of EDDS is also similar to that of Multibase (see Figure 3.8). The global schema, based on the relational model, describes the logical view of pertinent data as a single database. Each DBMS has a participation schema which shows the data it offers to contribute to the global database; this sits notionally on top of the local conceptual schema. Replication of data is permitted. An auxiliary database schema may be maintained at some sites to support resolution of inconsistencies and handling of null values arising from distribution. Other difficulties can also be handled using this facility, and this is an interesting area for research.

Access to data is through SQL, perhaps embedded in applications programs. The system returns a single answer in a manner which leaves the configuration and other details invisible to the user. Tuples comprising global schema relations are materialized only when demanded. As with the other multidatabase systems, local DBMSs remain undisturbed.

The system architecture is built on the two major modules mentioned above, the GTM and the LDM (see Figure 3.9). A third module

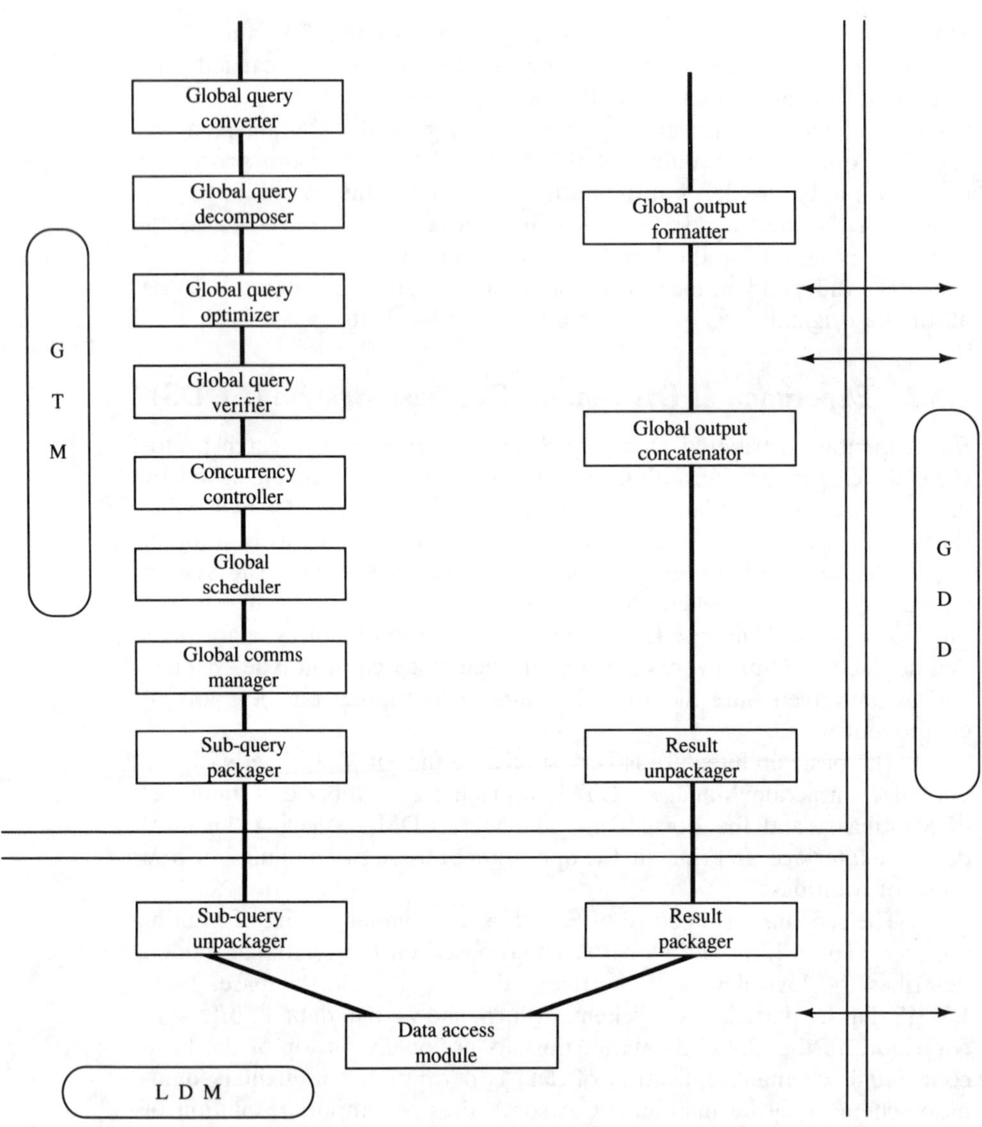

Figure 3.8 Components of EDDS.

is the global data dictionary, GDD, which has received special attention in EDDS. For small system nodes an additional system layer is required to generate global queries and return their results when the local system needs supplementation.

The GDD holds all the meta-data for the system. Participation schemas, view mappings, security and integrity constraints and information about sites and networks are all held here. In early implemen-

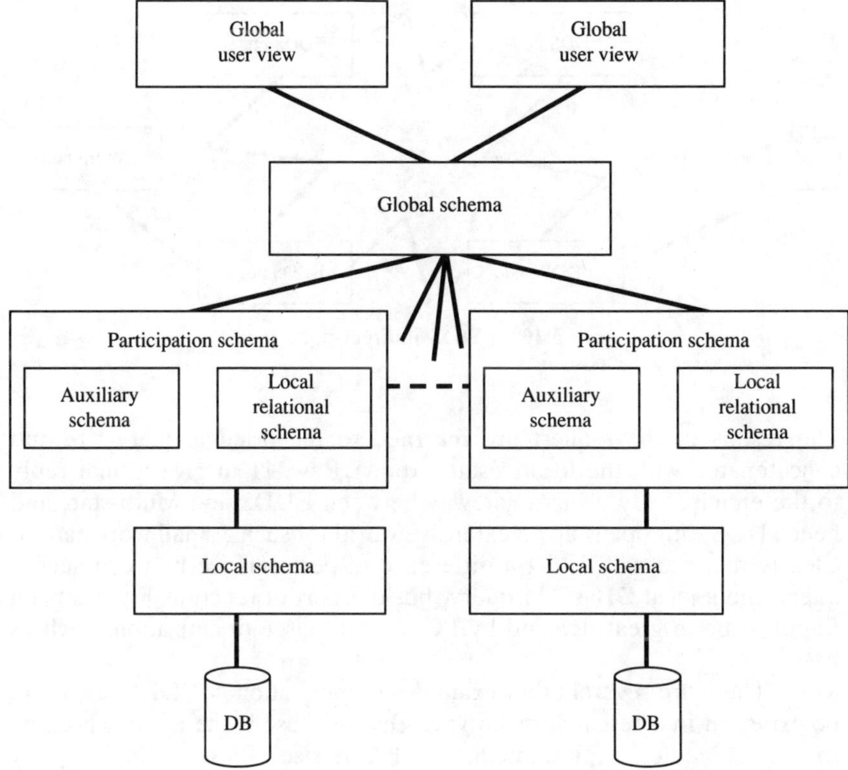

Figure 3.9 Schema architecture of EDDS.

tations the GDD was replicated at each site, and it performs its tasks in an active management manner, as well as a passive administrative one. A more sophisticated version where the GDD is distributed and managed by a database management system is also available.

Perhaps the most interesting feature of the system is its usefulness for linking local systems with very limited capability, such as small PCs, into the DDB system in a manner which permits them to act as workstations in tandem with computing facilities with much greater capability, albeit with somewhat reduced performance and functionality. The developers offer an 'indirect node' facility to support this feature. For example (see Figure 3.10), a microcomputer hosting a limited DBMS, such as DBase111, can be fitted with interfacing software which permits the user to access data to which access rights are held using only the query facilities of the local DBMS. In a manner transparent to the user, any data not held locally is requested by an EDDS SQL query, generated by the interfacing software, and posted off to a node of the pertinent EDDS DDB for evaluation as though it were a conventional EDDS global query.

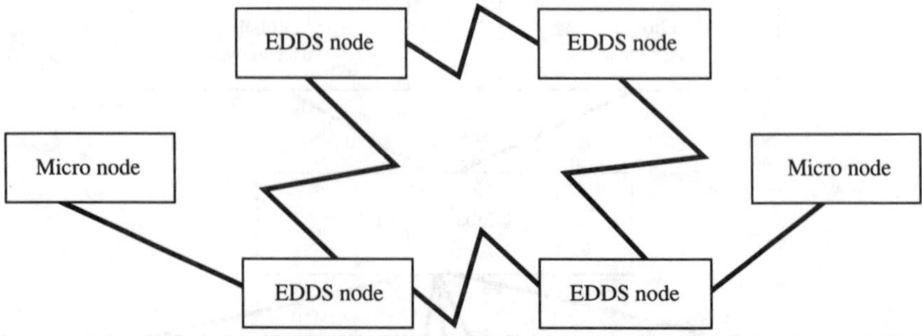

Figure 3.10 EDDS indirect-node facility.

The results of the request are returned to the original query site and concatenated with the local results from DBase111 to give a final reply to the enquirer. By using a gateway between EDDS and Multi-star, and hence DQS, this opens up an extensive world for such a small workstation. Clearly the user will detect a difference in performance between such a query and a local DBase111 query, but this sort of functionality has been found to be in great demand by PC users in large organizations such as hospitals.

There are several other examples of innovation in EDDS, as would be expected in a research prototype. One of these is the approach taken to the estimation of intermediate relation sizes for distributed query optimization (see Chapter 5).

SUMMARY

In this chapter we have endeavoured to present an overview of the state of the art both of the available commercial products in the DDB area and of the rising stars of research and development. We focused on two products, of which the first, INGRES*, marks what we consider to be the leading edge of commercial package development. Although only two out of four phases of its development have been completed, a good subset of database functions have been provided in INGRES* for systems where the data is distributed. The other product for larger IBM system configurations, CA-DB:STAR, gives a range of capabilities which is representative of a number of other systems at an earlier stage of evolution than INGRES*. However, in another sense this product is more mature than INGRES*, having been around for a longer period in product form. It is a worthwhile contender for some environments.

The two multidatabase systems reviewed were Multibase and DQS. The former, based on the DAPLEX data model, in many senses marked the goal for such systems in the early 1980s and inspired efforts at development of working prototypes, although it never itself became a product. This contrasts with DQS, which together with its 'stablemate' Multistar, is based on an early relational prototype, NDMS, which has a number of features making its design novel. In tandem, DQS and Multistar, which can be linked by a tailored gateway feature, cover IBM and Unix configurations, running a variety of DBMSs.

The examples we have chosen to illustrate current research frontiers are R* from IBM's research labs and EDDS, a system produced as a result of a number of European Community Programme projects in the DDB area. R* is a respected system and many research papers have resulted from work done on it. In particular contributions to query optimization, which will be dealt with in a subsequent chapter, have been very influential on research and development in this area. EDDS is a research vehicle which emphasizes global data dictionary structure and the accommodation of users of small systems in DDB systems, and is interesting for the research issues addressed within it.

Interest in producing DDB prototypes appeared to wane a little in the mid-1980s, but there is currently a new wave of enthusiasm for producing heterogeneous DDBs, which promises to bear fruit for the next few years.

Figure 3.11 adds some leaves to the tree in Figure 2.16 by indicating some of the systems falling in the various classes.

The performance issues remain a major focus for development and we shall have to wait for a few more years for a full answer to the questions posed at the beginning of this chapter.

EXERCISES

3.1 In a university many kinds of database are in use for three basic types of application function, dealing respectively with:

- Student records
- Salaries
- Resources (including rooms and equipment).

Write a report to the university finance officer explaining how an INGRES-STAR DDB can help in the integration of data in this environment. Assume that the present system is UNIX-based. Pay particular attention to explaining the roles of the system modules and schemas, and how they can save on development costs for a replacement application system which consultants have identified as essential.

3.2 Repeat Exercise 3.1 but assume that the present system is IBM-based and so you are advocating the adoption of CA-DB:STAR in your report.

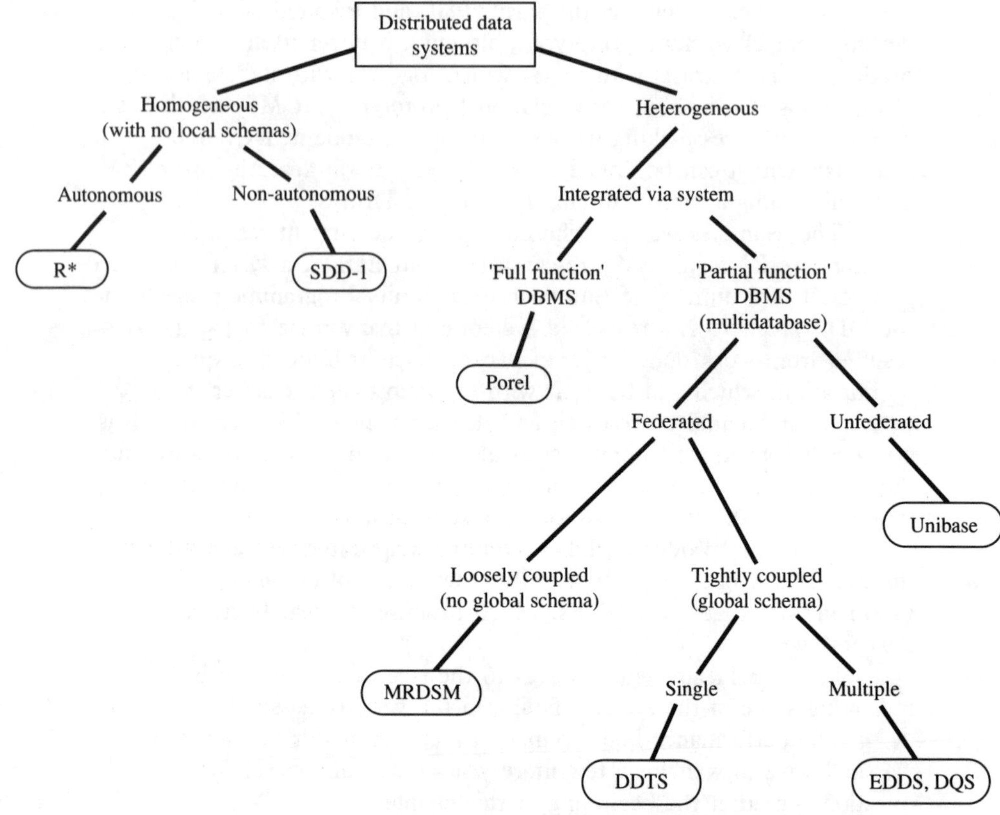

Figure 3.11 A taxonomy of distributed data systems.

3.3 What functions would you expect to have most impact on the decision as to whether or not DQS would be more appropriate than CA-DB:STAR for integrating data when three banks with IBM computer installations merge?

3.4 Distinguish between the suitability of the facilities offered by laboratory prototypes of multidatabase systems and homogeneous products for integrating research files which have been independently accumulated at great cost (in computing systems terms) in research centres worldwide. Ignore considerations of availability and support for the packages (i.e. assume that they are all at the released product stage).

3.5 Someone has calculated that all of the recorded information in the world (less than 10^{20} bytes) could be accommodated on the available computer storage devices which are currently in existence, or which could be made available within a reasonable period of time by obliging suppliers if ordered. Why do you think that this has not happened?

Bibliography

Bell D.A., Fernández Pérez de Talens A., Gianotti N. *et al.* (1987). Multi-star: a multidatabase system for health information systems, *Proc. 7th Int. Congress on Medical Informatics*, Rome, Italy

The Multistar prototype was developed by a group of collaborators in an EEC-funded project. It is largely based on NDMS and has been influenced by EDDS. Its functionality is illustrated by reference to medical examples which were studied in detail in this project.

Bell D.A., Grimson J.B. and Ling D.H.O. (1989). Implementation of an integrated multidatabase-Prolog system. *Information and Software Technology*, **31**(1), 29–38.

This paper gives some implementation and design information on the EDDS prototype.

Breitbart Y.J. and Tieman L.R. (1984). ADDS – heterogeneous distributed database system. *Proc. 3rd Int. Seminar on Distributed Data Sharing Systems*, Parma, Italy

Another DDBS, previously called Amoca Distributed Database System, was a multidatabase system developed for the oil industry. An interesting feature of the system was that its designers considered the problems associated with concurrent access to the DDB which many other similar systems ignore. Breitbart has continued his work in this area and, for example, presented a paper at the 1987 SIGMOD Conference on the multidatabase update problem.

Brzezinski Z., Getta J., Rybnik J. and Stepniewski W. (1984). UNIBASE – An integrated access to data, *Proc. 10th Int. Conf. on VLDB, Singapore*.

Deen S.M., Amin R.R., Ofori-Dwumfo G.O. and Taylor M.C. (1985). The architecture of a generalised distributed database system – PRECI*, *Computer J.* **28**(3), 282–290.

PRECI* is the distributed version of the centralized research vehicle, PRECI, developed at the University of Aberdeen. An interesting feature of its architecture is that, like PRECI itself, it attempts to be all things to all men to some extent. In the present context this means being a suitable architecture for both heterogeneous and homogeneous DDBs, each giving full DDB functionality, and also for multidatabases where the goal of distribution transparency was shed.

Esculier C. and Popescu-Zeletin R. (1982). *A Description of Distributed Database Systems.* EEC Report ITTF/2024/83.

This EC reports presents some details of each of the systems available in Europe which, in 1982, were either products or 'would be within two years'. The products were

- ADR's D-net
- Intertechnique's Reality D-DBMS
- ICL's DDB-50
- Siemen's Sesa***
- Nixdorf's VDN
- Tandem's Encompass
- Software AG's Datanet.

It is enlightening to note how few of these systems actually appeared on the market.

Holloway S. (1986). ADR/DATACOM/DB – the high-performance relational database management system. In *Pergamon Infotech State of the Art Report on Relational Database Systems* (Bell D.A., ed.), pp. 114–135. Oxford: Pergamon Infotech

This paper gives an excellent account of the system from which CA-DB:Star evolved.

Landers T. and Rosenberg R.L. (1982). An overview of Multibase. *Proc. 2nd Int. Symposium on Dist. Databases*, Berlin, Germany

This is an excellent, readable account of the Multibase system architecture.

Litwin W., Boudenant J., Esculier C. *et al.* Sirius systems for distributed database management. In *Distributed Databases* (Schneider, H.-J., ed.), pp. 311–66. Amsterdam: North-Holland

Like SDD-1, the Sirius series of designs and prototypes from INRIA in France had a significant influence on the design of full DDBs and multidatabases. This is a very comprehensive paper, and it contains a rich collection of well-considered solutions to DDB management and design problems. The latter part of the paper describes MRDSM (see also Wong and Bazex (1983)) which is a 'multidatabase system' by a slightly different definition than that used most frequently in this book (see also Wolski (1989) and Figure 2.16). In MRDSM, when data from different local databases is to be accessed, the query must refer to the data items by qualifying them by their respective database names (in a way analogous to the way attribute names are qualified by relation names if necessary). This somewhat waters down the aspirations of those seeking data transparency, but could be exceedingly effective in some practical application environments. Litwin has recently been continuing his work in interdatabase dependencies and other interoperability issues.

Lohmann G., Mohan C., Haas L.M. *et al.* (1985). Query processing in R*. In *Query Processing in Database Systems* (Kim, W., Batory D. and Reiner D., eds), pp. 31–47. Heidelberg: Springer.

Mallamaci C.L. and Kowalewski M. (1988). DQS: a system for heterogeneous distributed database integration. *Proc. Eurinformation Conf.*, Athens, Greece

DQS is a product based on the NDMS prototype.

Neuhold E.J. and Walter B. (1982). Architecture of the distributed database system POREL. In *Distributed Databases* (Schneider H.-J., ed.), pp. 247–310. Amsterdam: North-Holland

POREL is another of the DDB proposals which became trend-setters in the late 1970s and early 1980s. It is a heterogeneous system, although it appears to be aimed at 'green fields' situations mainly, which pays particular attention to communication issues which have arguably become somewhat irrelevant since 1982 with, for example, the advent of the ISO/OSI reference model.

Rothnie J.B., Bernstein P., Fox S. *et al.* (1980). Introduction to a system of distributed databases (SDD-1). *ACM TODS*, **5**(1), 1–17

SDD-1, one of the first comprehensive specifications for a DDBMS, was produced by Computer Corporation of America. Its general structure is built around three types of module or 'virtual machine'. Transaction modules plan and monitor the execution of the distributed transactions, data modules can read, move, manipulate or write sections of a DDB, and the reliable network connects the other two kinds of module, guarantees delivery of messages, all-or-nothing updates, site monitoring and synchronization.

The access language is Datalanguage which can be used in stand-alone mode or embedded in an application program. The term 'transaction' is used to describe a statement in Datalanguage; an atomic unit of interaction between the world and SDD-1.

This particular paper, one of a well-known series on SDD-1, marked an important milestone in the history of research on DDBs. It describes a prototype (first built in 1978) homogeneous DDB system which worked on the ARPA network, and gave a pragmatic and sentinel approach to a number of important DDB problems: concurrency control, distributed query execution and run-time organization and structure.

Staniszkis W., Kaminski W., Kowalewski M., Krajewski K., Mezyk S. and Turco G. (1984). Architecture of the Network Data Management System. *Proc. 3rd Int. Seminar on Dist. Data Sharing*, Parma, Italy

In its time this paper represented a milestone in the development of multidatabase systems: NDMS was one of the earliest prototypes with anything like the full multidatabase functionality.

Stonebraker M. and Rowe L. (1986). The design of Postgres. *Proc. ACM Conf. on Management of Data*, Washington DC

Postgres is based on an extension to the relational data model which is claimed to meet the needs of applications which traditionally would not consider the use of a relational DBMS because of its modelling constraints. It includes 'object-oriented' features, for example, it permits functions as well as data to be stored in the database. These can be invoked and executed using new commands inserted in SQL.

Wolski A. (1989). LINDA: a system for loosely integrated databases, *Proc. IEEE Conf. on Data Engineering*, Los Angeles CA

This system is somewhat similar to MRDSM and like it avoids the need for a global schema, this time by providing homogenizing views on pre-existing data accessed by a common data language. This data language is simpler than that required for the INRIA system.

Wong K.K. and Bazex P. (1985). MRDSM: a relational multi-databases management system. In *Distributed Data Sharing Systems* (Schreiber F.A. and Litwin W., eds), pp. 77–85. Amsterdam: North-Holland

This is in our view a key paper describing what is often called the loosely-coupled federated systems approach, but which is called here and by Litwin the multidatabase approach. It is distinguishable from the other federated multidatabase systems by the fact that it does not use a global schema. The user must know the schemas of the participating local schemas.

4 Data Handling – Distribution and Transformation

4.1 Introduction

An essential aspect of handling distributed data arises when we are deciding how to distribute the data around the sites in order to take advantage of the 'natural' parallelism of execution inherent in the distributed system or simply to get the best level of 'localization' of processing. We explain this term later. Another fundamental issue is that of providing automatic methods of transforming accesses to data which are written in an 'alien' access language (in this case the global query language), into access requests which can be dealt with by a given local DBMS.

In the first half of this chapter the data distribution issue is addressed and a simple solution is provided. In Section 4.2 we establish the case for careful allocation and placement of data over the storage devices of the available computing facilities, and this is followed by a section giving some examples which illustrate the advantages of careful data design. Section 4.4 (which can be omitted on a first reading) shows how a semantic approach to these problems can be used to supplement the usual quantitative approach, which itself is dealt with in Section 4.5.

The second part of the chapter is concerned with problems of integrating data models of various kinds. Section 4.6 highlights the issues and Section 4.7 examines some contenders for the global data model briefly. This is followed by two sections dealing with the particular case of mapping between the relational and network DDLs and DMLs respectively.

4.2 The data placement and allocation problem

This problem is concerned with ensuring that data objects are well placed with respect to other objects with which they are related. At this stage we introduce the concept of 'well-placedness' by means of an example. If the data objects O_1 and O_2 are required consecutively in a particular query, we might like them to be placed near one another, for example on a single page, or at a particular site, preferably that where the query or transaction accessing them arises. The rationale here would be that such localization of data is likely to be beneficial, because intersite transmissions are kept low. However, this situation is complicated by a number of factors, some of which are expressed here as questions.

What happens when the storage capacity available locally is too small to hold all the data for a particular query?

What happens when a given object, O_1, say, wants to be 'near' both O_2 *and* O_3, and they are at different sites?

What effect does the query optimizer have on this process?

Can we improve on this well-placedness in cases where it is possible to exploit the natural parallelism provided by a network of computers?

In a particular instance of the latter cases it might be better, for example, to have part of object O_1 and part of object O_2 at one site and the rest of both objects at a different site.

The problem of data placement and allocation is not an extensively studied one. Most of the work on it has been done in terms of 'the file allocation problem' or 'the efficient file segmentation problem'. The first is concerned with dispersing files efficiently around a network and the second addresses the problem of splitting records up so that the most 'busy' parts are allocated the best performing facilities. Solving either of these individually is by no means a complete solution to the problems of data placement on networks of computers. However, when the solutions are coupled with other approaches to this problem and to related problems, methods which are valuable in a number of reasonably general cases are obtained.

In the next section we demonstrate how careful placement of data and allocation of data to sites can make a great difference to query cost or performance. We restrict our attention to retrieval at this stage, but the overall objective is to maximize efficiency for both update and retrieval operations.

4.3 Some examples of data placement and allocation

We start this section by showing how judicious allocation of data objects to sites in distributed computer networks can have an important impact on both performance and costs.

4.3.1 Single-relation case

Suppose we have a single relation whose tuples are to be placed around the nodes of the network. To start with we assume that just one site is involved, but that there are many pages of data over which the tuples can be spread. As we said in the introduction to this chapter, a common goal is to maximize *data locality*. That is, we would like each tuple to be placed 'near' other tuples which should appear in the answer set of each pertinent query, so that when we fetch a page from secondary storage we have a good chance of being able to answer any given queries from it alone.

EXAMPLE 4.1 (see Fang *et al.* (1986))

Consider the following solution to a rather simple placement problem.

(1,p)	(1,q)	(1,r)	(1,s)	
(2,q)	(2,r)	(2,s)	(2,p)	
(3,r)	(3,s)	(3,p)	(3,q)	(1)
(4,s)	(4,p)	(4,q)	(4,r)	
page 1	page 2	page 3	page 4	

Suppose the following query is addressed to this 'database': get all tuples with a '1' in the first position (attribute).

We could imagine that here the numbers represent parts and the letters represent suppliers. So the inquirer would then be interested in an answer to the following query: get all suppliers supplying part 1.

Clearly *all four pages* have to be accessed to evaluate this query (call it (1,*)?). The same is true for each member of the query set,

Q: Q = {(1,*)?,(2,*)?,(3,*)?,(4,*)?,(*,p)?,(*,q)?,(*,r)?,(*,s)?}

So the placement in (1) above is really rather poor.
An alternative placement is as follows:

(1,p)	(1,r)	(3,p)	(3,r)	
(1,q)	(1,s)	(3,q)	(3,s)	
(2,p)	(2,r)	(4,p)	(4,r)	(2)
(2,q)	(2,s)	(4,q)	(4,s)	
page 1	page 2	page 3	page 4	

Here each query in Q requires access to *only two pages*. So it can be seen that good placement can affect the responsiveness *performance* index, even for one relation and one site.

Now assume that we can, or have to, spread tuples of the same single relation over many sites in a distributed network. Assume there are no application-related reasons for having particular data items stored at particular sites. We can have either of two objectives here: to maximize parallelism of query execution (i.e. process as many tuples as possible at a time); *or* to minimize intersite data traffic (i.e. process as many tuples as possible at one site).

Suppose we take the 'good' tuple-to-page *placement* of (2) above and *allocate* pages to sites as follows:

site 1	site 2
pages(1,4)	pages(2,3)

Consider the queries of Q again. It can be seen that the evaluation of each query in Q requires access to be made to both sites. In contrast, either of the following allocations to sites is better than that above because, while in each case four of the queries still need to access two sites each, the remaining four need access only one site each.

site 1	site 2
pages(1,2)	pages(3,4)

or

site 1	site 2
pages(1,3)	pages(2,4)

4.3.2 Multiple-relation case

The situation is more difficult when we have to distribute the tuples of more than one relation over the sites. We illustrate the benefit of good placement in this case by considering just two relations. To do this the query set is now expanded to include queries which span both relations. Consider a simple, and artificial, case where the query set is composed of queries requiring the system to get all of the tuples in relation 2 having an entry in a column (the JOIN column) which matches an entry in the JOIN column of relation 1. Without loss of generality, consider again R_1 and R_2 to be binary (two attributes) relations and assume that the JOIN columns are columns 2 and 1 respectively.

For instance we could consider R_2 to be the (parts,supplier) relation of the previous example with the atributes reversed in order. R_1 could be a (city,supplier) relation. Possible queries would involve linking parts with the cities in which their suppliers are sited (say for delivery purposes).

EXAMPLE 4.2

The case where there is a 1 : N (one to many) relationship between the tuples of the two relations is relatively simple and so we focus on the M : N case (many-to-many). Assume that the tuples of both relations have the same width, and consider the following placement on a single site. (Note that the pages in this example are twice as big as those in the preceding example).

(a,p)	(p,1)	(a,q)	(p,2)	(a,r)	(p,3)	(a,s)	(p,4)	
(b,q)	(q,2)	(b,r)	(q,3)	(b,s)	(q,4)	(b,p)	(q,1)	
(c,r)	(r,3)	(c,s)	(r,4)	(c,p)	(r,1)	(c,q)	(r,2)	
(d,s)	(s,4)	(d,p)	(s,1)	(d,q)	(s,2)	(d,r)	(s,3)	(3)
R_1	R_2	R_1	R_2	R_1	R_2	R_1	R_2	
page 1		page 2		page 3		page 4		

Consider the following query: get all R_2 tuples with a 1 in column 2 which match (via the JOIN column) R_1 tuples with an 'a' in column 1.

In our interpretation of the relations this would mean: get all the (parts,supplier) pairs for, say, 'nuts' with suppliers in, say, 'London'.

$$\underset{\text{col } 1 = \text{'a'}}{\sigma(R_1)} \quad \underset{\text{col } 2 = \text{col } 1}{\bowtie} \quad \underset{\text{col } 2 = 1}{\sigma(R_2)}$$

Here we have to access all four pages, even if we try to optimize by doing the SELECTs first and make use of an index on both selection columns to home in on the pertinent data. That is, this query optimization and (in this case) the access support mechanisms, do not solve the problems raised by having a bad allocation of tuples to sites. Four pages also have to be accessed for queries with the same basic template and the first selection condition constant changed to 'b'. If this condition is changed to be on 'c' or 'd' respectively, and the constant in the second condition is changed to '3', the same is true.

Notice that if the buffer of the computer carrying out the JOIN can hold only a few pages we will need to be careful when carrying out the JOINs, if we use some of the common algorithms. For simplicity, in the present discussion we ignore this complication, but still assume that there is a performance advantage in minimizing the number of pages accessed.

Consider now an alternative placement.

(a,p)	(p,1)	(c,p)	(p,3)	(a,r)	(r,1)	(c,r)	(r,3)	
(b,p)	(p,2)	(d,p)	(p,4)	(b,r)	(r,2)	(d,r)	(r,4)	
(a,q)	(q,1)	(c,q)	(q,3)	(a,s)	(s,1)	(c,s)	(s,3)	
(b,q)	(q,2)	(d,q)	(q,4)	(b,s)	(s,2)	(d,s)	(s,4)	(4)
R_1	R_2	R_1	R_2	R_1	R_2	R_1	R_2	
page 1		page 2		page 3		page 4		

Here (given appropriate access mechanisms) only pages 1 and 3 need to be accessed to answer our query (and only two pages have to be accessed for the other queries with the template given above).

Now suppose that communication times are much greater than local access and processing times. Also, suppose we allocate the pages to sites as follows:

site 1	site 2	
pages 1 and 2	pages 3 and 4	(A)

For both placements (3) and (4) above, we need to access both sites to answer our original query. For the allocation

site 1	site 2	
pages 1 and 3	pages 2 and 4	(B)

we still need two site references for placement (3) above but for placement (4) we need only one site reference. So allocation (B) of pages to sites is better than allocation (A) for placement (4) for the original query.

On the other hand, the converse could be true if local access times are dominant, as we will now show. We assume in the following that one unit of time is required to access a page locally with sequential, page-by-page, access, and that a much smaller time is needed for communication. In this case, for placement (4) the allocation (B) of pages to sites above costs 2 units of time to access the two pages because they are on the same site. In allocation (A), however, both accesses can proceed in parallel and so only 1 unit of time (and a small amount of communications time) elapses as the data is accessed.

From these rather contrived and idealized examples it is clear that both the placement of tuples on pages and the allocation of pages to sites in a network can have a significant impact upon the costs in terms of responsiveness. Both techniques are made more complex by permitting redundancy (i.e. letting more than one copy of a tuple reside in the network). However, this extension can bring compensating rewards as well.

It has been shown that these file placement and allocation problems are very hard in that it is unlikely that an algorithm with polynomial time complexity function can be found for solving them. Bell showed that a number of data placement problems are NP-complete, by identifying one-to-one correspondences between them and a number of very difficult graph and other problems. This indicates that it is unlikely that an algorithm will be found for any of these problems to give a full solution for realistically-sized instances within an acceptable time. Chang and Shielk have proved that the file allocation problem itself is NP-complete, by demonstrating a one-to-one correspondence with a classical problem called the colorability problem which is known to be NP-complete.

This does not mean that we should give up the search for the most efficient methods of solving these problems, but rather that we should use heuristic methods or perhaps consider sub-problems which have simpler solutions but have good practical applicability.

4.4 A semantic approach to the problem

In this section we explore the possibility of optimizing the placement and allocation of data without considering the requirements of any quantitative cost model directly. We transform the problem from the very general one discussed in the previous section into a more restricted, but currently more pragmatic one. The goal here is to split a global database up into fragments, not necessarily disjoint, to maximize the efficiency of query execution. The fragments will typically be somewhat larger than the single tuple fragments considered in previous sections.

In this brief section we address the issue of determining the extent to which we can extract *qualitative* aspects of data distribution. We show that it is possible to identify limited but interesting classes of distribution strategies with certain desirable properties from purely semantic and qualitative considerations. Later we will consider methods where the major role is played by specific quantitative cost models.

Given a collection of queries, Q, as before, we say that a given partition and allocation of the global database is **locally sufficient relative to Q** if any given query, $q \in Q$ can be split up into **local queries** $\{q_i\}$ (each expressed over a single local fragment of the global database) in such a way that the evaluation of q is the UNION over i (i here is the site index) of the local evaluations of the q_i.

That is, if G is the global database $= \cup_i L_i$ where the L_i are the local fragments then

$$\text{evaluation}\ (q,G) = \cup_i\ \text{evaluation}\ (q_i,L_i)$$

Having this property means that to process any query in Q, no data transfers between sites are required apart from a final transmission of a partial result from each L_i to the querying site, where the UNION is formed. Usually redundancy among the fragments is required for this property to be attainable. This is acceptable for retrieval queries, provided the storage costs do not rule it out. However, for update queries, which have costs which are a non-decreasing function of the 'extent' of the redundancy, we would certainly like to minimize redundancy. That is, we would like to find a distribution strategy with minimal redundancy.

Putting this together with the local sufficiency goal above we can express our goal here as being to find a locally sufficient set of local fragments $\{L_i\}$, such that $\{J_i\} = \{L_i\}$ for any other locally sufficient set of fragments $\{J_i\}$ for which J_i is as small as L_i for every i. That is, there is no different locally sufficient distribution less redundant than $\{L_i\}$.

To demonstrate this qualitative approach to data distribution, we assume in the rest of this section that we have only one relation for each primitive object in our database and we restrict our queries to have either only one variable (a unary operation), or to have an equi-JOIN on a primary key or a foreign key, or to have finite combinations of both of these. Although apparently very restrictive, this characterizes a large natural class of queries and is therefore likely to be of practical value and, perhaps more importantly in the present context, the queries so defined reflect the semantic structure of the real world. So we use them as the basis of the qualitative distribution approach outlined here.

An example of such a query in SQL is

```
Select doctor-name, patient-name
 From doctor, patient
  Where doctor.age =patient.age
```

If we consider only horizontal subdivisions of the relations, which is reasonable since we are considering only simple queries, we can define 'forests' of 'trees' which we can use as the basis of our data distribution.

A **partition tree** is a directed graph with an underlying tree structure. Its nodes are in one-to-one correspondence with the relations of our database schema and its edges are in one-to-one correspondence with foreign keys, directed from the foreign key of a relation to the corresponding primary key (in another relation), and the direction is from son to father relations of the tree structure. It can be shown that a partition of the root relation in such a partition tree indicates a unique partition of every relation in the tree.

A **partition forest** is a group of partition trees having the property that each relation of the schema corresponds to a node in precisely one tree.

By partitioning the root of each tree in a forest we induce a unique partition of the other nodes. If the root partitions are allocated to sites then the fragments at the lower levels of the trees follow perfectly the corresponding fragments of the roots. We call the resulting partition $\{L_i\}$.

A class of queries for which $\{L_i\}$ is locally sufficient can now be determined from this forest. It is the smallest class of queries that includes all one-variable queries on the schema relations, and which is closed under PROJECT, SELECT and JOIN on relation attributes corresponding to edges in the trees of the forest.

Notice that, in addition to limiting the class of queries for which this optimization works, we have ignored differences in communication costs between the sites, we have assumed that there are as many sites as we require and that they have no restrictions on their local storage capacity, we have taken no account of query optimization strategies (not too essential here) and we have not considered queueing delays. Moreover, the distribution obtained while achieving, minimally, local sufficiency, results in more complex updates even for non-redundant distribution, because an interrelational integrity constraint must be checked.

However, one class of updates, namely the class of all one-variable updates except changes to primary and foreign keys, can be completed without synchronization delay.

This approach can be extended to permit redundancy in the distribution in order to extend the cardinality of the locally sufficient query set.

This discussion has demonstrated the value and promise, despite the restrictions, of using a semantic approach to the problem of finding an efficient allocation strategy. It also serves to illustrate the complexity of this approach. Ideally this method should be used to supplement a quantitative method such as that discussed below. We find that there is a parallel between this and the situation in (semantic) query optimization as we shall see in Chapter 5.

4.5 A practical combinatorial optimization approach to the file allocation problem

In the present context (that of distributed databases) we are more concerned with the file allocation problem than with the placement problem. For practical purposes, we restrict our attention to cases where complete files rather than records are the objects to be placed.

This is realistic when we consider that most files are not fragmented because many important accesses need to fetch *all* records in the files and it is relatively hard, in general, to determine 'hit-groups', or active parts of files or records, which are to be treated separately from the rest. Anyway, sub-files can be treated just as complete files are, in cases where they can be identified.

Furthermore, in real design situations it is unlikely that we will try to exploit parallelism in our file allocation. The current conventional wisdom is that this task should be delegated to the query optimization sub-module of the distributed database management system.

The problem of optimizing the allocation of files to sites in distributed databases has a fairly long and varied history. Many of the solutions are too general (and hence too complex) to be used on practical problems because the number of parameters to be considered tends to be prohibitive.

In this section we present a solution which is applicable only for a particular manifestation of the problem, but which is pragmatic and useful and also has the virtue of being illustrative of the solutions one can find to this problem.

The particular solution given here was developed for distributing data in a dedicated network of computing facilities which have tight limits on their local mass storage capacity. It is obtained by transforming the original problem (that of minimizing access costs) into the isomorphic problem of maximizing local accesses.

Storage is considered to be a constraint on the optimization, rather than as a cost: adding a file to a site does not incur any additional cost, so long as the site capacity is not exceeded. The cost of accommodating and exceeding the capacity at a site is considered to be so great, involving as it does reconfiguring and reorganizing local mass storage, that it is out of the question.

Another characteristic of the method considered here is that it is assumed that the transaction traffic is known in advance – any *ad hoc* queries are therefore optimized purely by the run-time query optimization module in the DBMS. A given transaction can arise at any of the network's nodes, and the frequency of occurrence at each site is input to the algorithm as a table (see Example 4.3 for an illustration). Each transaction is specified to the allocator simply as a set of entries in a table. These show the number of update or retrieval accesses from the transaction to each of the files (see Example 4.3 for an illustration). Reads and updates are assumed to have equal costs. Local accesses are assumed to be much cheaper than remote accesses. Remote accesses all have the same unit cost, which is a reasonable assumption if we assume that the communication network underpinning the DDB is the same throughout. In the version of the algorithm given here, no redundancy is permitted and fragmentation of files is forbidden. So each file is assigned to one and only one site in the network.

We use the following notation for the problem

- There are N nodes, indexed by j, capacity = c_j
- There are M files, indexed by i, size = s_i
- There are T transactions, indexed by k, frequency from node $j = f_{kj}$
- There are n_{ki} accesses (for retrieval or update) from transaction k to file i
- x_{ij} is a decision variable which is 1 if file i is allocated to node j, 0 otherwise.

We know therefore that

$$\Sigma_j x_{ij} = 1 \; \forall \, i \,|\, 1 \leqslant i \leqslant M \tag{4.1}$$

The constraints on the storage space can be written

$$\Sigma_i x_{ij} s_i \leqslant c_j \; \forall \, j \,|\, 1 \leqslant j \leqslant N \tag{4.2}$$

It can easily be shown that the problem of allocating files to minimize the total remote and local access costs for the given set of transactions is equivalent to a maximization problem

$$\text{maximize } (\Sigma_{i,j} X_{ij} V_{ij}) \tag{4.3}$$

where $V_{ij} = \Sigma_k f_{kj} (n_{ki}) \times$ cost of local retrievals

The reason for this is that the total number of accesses, local and remote, is independent of the allocation, and so, because the remote accesses are much more costly than the local accesses, their minimization (or alternatively, the maximization of the local accesses) characterizes the optimal solution.

The non-redundant File Allocation Problem (FAP) considered here can therefore be formulated as Equations 4.1, 4.2 and 4.3 above. To solve it we disregard, temporarily, the size constraint.

Step 1

Calculate $J(i) = \{j' | V_{ij'} = \max V_{ij}\}, \quad 1 \leqslant j \leqslant N$

Step 2

An optimal set of x_{kj} is given by $x_{ij} = 1$ for some $j \in J(i)$ and $x_{ij}=0$ otherwise.

Step 3

Inspect

If this solution is feasible (i.e. meets the constraints of Equation 4.2) it is our answer; go to Step 7.

Step 4

Otherwise, identify all nodes which cause the constraints in Equation 4.2 to be broken.

Step 5

For every such over-subscribed node, solve the corresponding knapsack problem (see below), thereby eliminating a node and the files allocated to that node from further consideration. (If there is more than one such node this step treats them in order of 'allocated value' and eliminates them all.)

Step 6

Consider $J(i)$ for any nodes j which remain. If there are some such nodes go to Step 2.

Step 7

Otherwise, we have finished.

The knapsack problem is a classical problem in operations research where a scarce resource (here a node's storage capacity) is to be allocated to a number of competing users. In this case we want to 'pack' the node's storage in a way which maximizes the 'value' of the contained goods, V_{ij}. For an introduction to solution methods see Daellenbach *et al. (1983)*. The knapsack problem instances to be solved in the exercises in this chapter, and in many real design problems, are sufficiently small-scale to permit exhaustive search for the answer.

EXAMPLE 4.3 (see also Ceri *et al.* (1980))

Suppose we are to allocate eight files among five sites, each with 20 Mbytes disk storage and given the following access rates of transactions to files (n_{ki})

	Files (size/Mbytes)							
Transactions	1 (10)	2 (5)	3 (18)	4 (9)	5 (9)	6 (7)	7 (4)	8 (4)
1	10	10			10			20
2					20			10
3			75	75	150	15		
4			5	5	10	10		10
5			5	5			10	10
6	10	2	5	1				
7	2	10	1	5				
8	6	6	3	3				
9	1	1						
10								5

Also suppose that the frequency of transactions in sites (f_{kj}) is as follows:

	Sites				
Transactions	1	2	3	4	5
1	30				
2	20	10			
3	3		5	4	4
4			12	9	9
5			10	7	3
6	180	20	100	1	1
7	100	1		30	35
8	30	20	10	10	10
9	3	3			
10	4				

From these two we can calculate the following V_{ij} table

	File i (size)							
	1	2	3	4	5	6	7	8
Site j	(10)	(5)	(18)	(9)	(9)	(7)	(4)	(4)
1	**2483**	**1843**	**1315**	**995**	**1150**	45	0	**820**
2	325	173	161	85	200	0	0	100
3	1060	260	1015	615	870	**195**	**100**	220
4	130	362	445	561	690	150	70	160
5	140	412	430	566	690	150	30	120

Step 1

At Step 1 of the algorithm the $J(i)$ are the bold elements for each i.

Step 2

If we assign $x_{ij} = 1$ for these and 0 for the other entries we have our first 'solution'.

Step 3

Site 1 has been allocated 55 Mbytes of files. Its capacity is only 20 MBytes, and so this is not a feasible solution.

Step 4

Site 1 (has been allocated too much)

Step 5

The maximum value (V_{ij}) we can get from storing any files on site 1 is obtained by storing files 1, 2 and 8 there.

Step 6

Our new V_{ij} table is obtained by eliminating row 1 above and columns 1, 2 and 8.
The new $J(i)$ are the underlined entries (all allocated to site 3)

Step2'

Assign $x_{ij} = 1$ to these, $x_{ij} = 0$ to the remainder of the entries.

Step3'

Site 3 has been allocated 47 MBytes of files, but it can only store 20 MBytes.

Step4'

Site 3 (has been overloaded)

Step5'

The maximum value we can get from storing files on site 3 is obtained by storing files 4 and 5 there.

Step6'

Our new V_{ij} table is obtained by eliminating row 3 and columns 4 and 5 from the reduced table.

	File		
Site	3	6	7
2	161	0	0
4	<u>445</u>	<u>150</u>	<u>70</u>
5	430	150	30

The new $J(i)$ are underlined (all allocated to site 4)

Step2″

Assign 1 to x_{ij} for these entries, 0 for the rest.

Step3″

Site 4 has been allocated 29 MBytes, but it can take only 20 MBytes.

Step4″

Site 4 (has been overloaded)

Step5″

Store file 3 at site 4.

Step6″

Our new V_{ij} table is obtained by eliminating row 2, column 1 from the table above.

Without spelling out the details it is clear that the remaining 2 files, 6 and 7, are allocated to site 5.

So our solution is

Site	File	Total space used (MBytes)
1	1,2,8	19
2		0
3	4,5	18
4	3	18
5	6,7	11

4.6 Integration of heterogeneous database systems

A fundamental concept in the integration of heterogeneous databases is that of providing a DBMS-independent global conceptual schema. The global data model provides a 'virtual' level of representation to support manipulation of the local data collections.

The steps to be taken when defining this global view form a hierarchy. The global schema cannot contain more information than the sum of the information contained in the contributing local schemas and any auxiliary schemas. So these steps take the form of a series of data abstractions. For each of these some details are deliberately omitted from the representation.

One of these abstractions is **aggregation**, where a relationship between entities is represented as a higher level object. For example an 'appointment' entity could be used to represent a relationship between a patient, a doctor and a clinic. Another abstraction is **generalization**, where a set of similar entities is considered to be a single generic entity. For example a 'person' object could be a generalization of doctor, patient and nurse entities. **Restrictions** on the particular class of objects in order to obtain a subset of interest give another abstracting mechanism. For example, the set of patients in the orthopaedic department could form an object called 'orthopaedic patients'.

There are various other conversions and transformations that can take place between schemas. Some are needed for syntactic reasons, for example, if different units such as millilitres and fluid ounces are used to measure volume in two different laboratories. Another syntactic transformation would be needed if the structure of the records (or relations, for example) in the local databases were different.

Another set of transformations may be needed for semantic reasons. For example where some hospitals in a region refer to themselves as a default in a file used for transporting patients between hospitals by ambulance. The other hospital for a particular transfer might be represented explicitly, and the way this is done could vary between local systems. A particular trip could then be represented twice within the distributed system, but it might not be obvious that this is the case from any syntactic considerations. The DDB system would have to 'figure out' the meanings of the different structures from semantic information provided by the system designer.

Each local data model is defined by the corresponding DDL and DML semantics. In order to integrate pre-existing heterogeneous databases, special methods of mapping between different data models are needed. An important goal for such mapping is that both the information stored under the local data models and the operators which can be addressed to them should be 'preserved'. That is, we should ideally be able to access precisely all of the local data via the global model, in all of the ways supported by the local DBMS. The use of this capability is, of course, subject to logical and physical access constraints which exist in a particular environment.

The pattern used here for transforming data models is that of mapping a **source** data description, according to a source data model, into a **target** description, according to a target data model. These descriptions, or schemas, are said to be **equivalent** if they produce sets of database **states** (actual databases) which are one-to-one and onto (i.e. nothing is left out), the one-to-one states being equivalent. Database states under the source and target data models are, in turn, said to be equivalent if they can be mapped to the same state in some **abstract meta-model**. Essentially this means that they both represent the same state of the real world. Formal methods of establishing this equivalence depend on the identification of, and agreement on, such an abstract meta-model. As no such meta-model has been universally accepted, rather informal methods are used to establish the equivalence of states.

Ideally we would like the set of operators available in the DML for each data model to be complete, in the sense used by Kalinichenko, namely that for every object in the DDL, retrieval, update and deletion can be expressed in the DML; and for every pair of states of a database, a sequence of operators can be defined to transform one into the other.

If each data model had this property then we could guarantee that, for any pair of databases with equivalent schemas, queries on one could be run on the other.

To put our goal for data model transformation into more pragmatic terms: we aim to ensure that database transactions which run on a database described by one data model, and are required to run on a database described by the other data model, can be rewritten to do so. We require this rewriting to be done automatically by the system.

The problem of determining the extent to which this can be done has been summarized for practical purposes as follows: given a database program (or transaction) and a description of the database schema with which it interacts; given also a description of a second schema of the same database and a definition of the logical restructuring to this second form; then, to what extent is it possible to mechanically produce an equivalent (with respect to file and terminal I/O) program or transaction, interacting with the database via the second schema.

4.7 The global data model

It is possible to identify contenders for a global data model which are general enough to cope with all idiosyncrasies of any of the data models likely to be encountered in pre-existing databases. To form such a basis of homogenizing *all* data models in a totally complete way we need to ensure the following:

(1) that the global data model at any stage of its evolution is capable of absorbing new data models (by extending the DDL and DML using a system of axioms expressed in global data model terms);

(2) that the information and operators are preserved in the sense above (i.e. there are commutative, or order-independent, mappings between the schemas and operators, and a one-to-one, onto mapping between the database states);

(3) that the local data models can be synthesized into a unified global data model (by constructing global data model kernel extensions equivalent to the local data models, and unifying these extensions).

One such global data model, called the unifying conceptual data model (UCDM), has been developed by starting from the relational data model and extending it incrementally as in (1) above by adding axiomatic extensions equivalent to various well-known (local) data models. The principles in (2) and (3) above were systematically applied in order to obtain these results.

Examples of simple axioms added to the RDM in order to make it equivalent to the network model are the axioms of uniqueness, conditional uniqueness and obligation for unique, unique non-null and mandatory attributes (data items) respectively. More complex interrelational axioms include the axiom of total functional dependency (between attributes in different relations).

Another, perhaps more pragmatic, contender is DAPLEX. This is a special purpose system for use as a pivot language and common data model to which each local data model maps in order to integrate the pre-existing databases. This system uses the **functional model** as a pivot representation onto which the heterogeneous contributors map on a one-to-one basis. Real-world entities and their properties are represented as DAPLEX entities and functions respectively. Separate views of the integrated 'database' are provided to meet local requirements.

Mapping between most well-known data models, and even operating system files, is simple using DAPLEX. For example, a relational database can be accommodated by representing each relation as a DAPLEX entity and each domain as a DAPLEX single-valued function. The network data model can be described in a similar way. Sets are represented as multivalued functions which return member entities.

EXAMPLE 4.4

Consider the network schema at the 'remote' site as given below in Figure 4.1. The DAPLEX representation for this is given in Schema 4.1. The two figures in the above example can also be used to outline how DAPLEX can be used to integrate heterogeneous (here relational and network) databases. DAPLEX views of the distributed data are defined using **view derivation** over the DAPLEX versions of the local schemas.

Imagine a second DAPLEX schema equivalent to the relational local schema at a site, which is very straightforwardly mapped from the 'local' schema, containing, in particular, an entity called LOCAL-CUST. The view derivation for a global entity called GLOBAL-CUSTOMER is given in Algorithm 4.1. This shows how to get the data from a local database into the format required for global usage. It shows when cus-

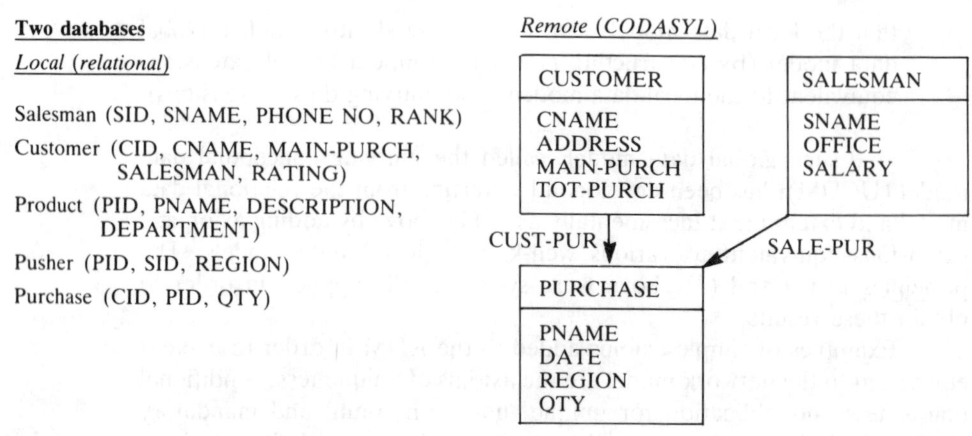

Figure 4.1 Network schema at 'remote' site.

tomers of both sites are equivalent. A query such as that in Algorithm 4.2 can be addressed against the global entity. The view derivation is used to translate it to queries over the local DAPLEX queries. The view derivation statements are inserted into the global query and the given query is split into a set of single-site queries. The local DAPLEX queries proceed next to the local database interfaces at the local sites. There they are translated into queries over the schemas expressed using the local data models. These transactions are fairly straightforward, and are not too dissimilar to the equivalent process for the relational–network translation discussed below.

4.8 Getting a relational schema equivalent to a network schema

Many implementors of co-existence architectures for the integration of collections of data models agree that the relational data model, without axiomatic or other extensions, is adequate for the harmonization of different database systems. Examples of systems which use the relational model as global data model are the multidatabase systems NDMS, ADDS, MULTISTAR and EDDS.

Schema 4.1 DAPLEX schema at remote site.

```
REMOTE (Daplex Schema)
Type    PURCHASE is entity;
          Pname:  string;
           Date:  integer;
         Region:  string;
            Qty:  integer;
End entity
Type    REMOTE-CUST is entity;
                Cname:  string;
              Address:  string;
           Main-purch:  string;
              Tot-pur:  integer;
             Cust-pur:  set of PURCHASE;
End entity
Type    SALESMAN is entity;
            Sname:  string;
           Office:  string;
           Salary:  integer;
         Sale-pur:  set of PURCHASE;
End entity.
```

To use the relational model in this way, we usually need to provide relational views of the local, (in general) non-relational, data models. In this section we illustrate how this is done by considering a method based on one suggested originally by Zaniolo for getting a relational schema equivalent to a CODASYL (network) schema.

There are four sources of data in a network scheme which have to be used when getting a relational equivalent:

(1) The record and data item descriptions,
(2) The associations between the owners and members of set types,
(3) The 'duplicates not allowed' **location mode** for record types,
(4) The 'duplicates not allowed' declaration for set types.

Algorithm 4.1 Derivation of GLOBAL-CUSTOMER entity.

```
Derive GLOBAL-CUSTOMER from
  For each I in LOCAL-CUST + REMOTE-CUST
    case I is
      when LOCAL-CUST – REMOTE-CUST
        define GLOBAL-CUSTOMER to be
          CNAME -> CNAME(I);
          MAIN-PURCH -> MAIN-PURCH(I);
          RATING -> RATING(I);
      when REMOTE-CUST – LOCAL-CUST
        define GLOBAL-CUSTOMER to be
          CNAME -> CNAME(I);
          MAIN-PURCH -> MAIN-PURCH(I);
          RATING-> int(TOT-PURCH(I)/4);
      when REMOTE-CUST and LOCAL-CUST
        define GLOBAL-CUSTOMER to be
          CNAME -> CNAME(I);
          MAIN-PURCH -> MAIN-PURCH(I);
          RATING ->
            max(int(TOT-PURCH(I)/4),
              RATING(I));
    end case
  end loop
end DERIVE
```

The first two sources give the relations and attribute names, the third and fourth sources supply integrity constraints for the relational schema.

Making some simplifying assumptions which we will identify (for subsequent removal) later, the method derives a collection of relational

Algorithm 4.2 DAPLEX query over the global view.

```
'For each I in GLOBAL-CUSTOMER
  where I is in LOCAL-CUST
    and I is in REMOTE-CUST
      and RATING(I) <=3
Print(details.........)'
```

schemas which capture the network database's structure by making use of the 'database key' feature of CODASYL. The database keys are subsequently removed, along with the physical access path information which is present in a network schema, so that only the desired relational description is left.

STEP 1

Construct the 'first-fix' relations

Each record type generates one relation. Its database key, and a combined database key and set name for each set owning the record are appended. There is a tuple in the extension of a relation for every record of that type in the network database. **Candidate keys** (C-keys) are derived mainly from the 'duplicates not allowed' clauses and indicated in the relational schemas. **Foreign keys** are also derived from the logical linkage between an owner record and its member, so there is a one-to-one mapping between foreign key constraints and set types. The result of this step is a 'relational analog' of the network database, and it is now subjected to two refining steps.

STEP 2

Top-down Synonym Substitution

Data items are conducted from the owner to the member record occurrences of the sets. A **synonym** of a database key for record R is a combination of data items from its 'predecessors' which uniquely identify the occurrences of R. This step replaces an owner database key in any relation by a synonym (for example a key) of the owner relation. The synonym is added to the key of the relation under consideration. This process is repeated until no further substitution is possible.

STEP 3

Project out unwanted items

The database keys are eliminated from the schema. If there is a synonym for every owner in the database, projecting out the database key of each relation removes all database keys.

Hence we end up with a set of relations which have attributes corresponding to the original network database's data items, concatenated with some inherited attributes.

EXAMPLE 4.5

Consider the network database in Figure 4.2

STEP 1

First-Fix Relations

CUSTOMER

c-db-key, CNAME, ADDRESS, MAIN-PURCHASE, TOT-PURCH

C-Key CNAME

SALESMAN

s-db-key, SNAME, OFFICE, SALARY

C-key SNAME

PURCHASE

p-db-key, c-db-key, s-db-key, DATE, PRICE, QTY

C-key (– none)

Foreign Keys c-db-key
s-db-key

STEP 2

Replace owner record keys in member record by synonym

PURCHASE

p-db-key, CNAME, SNAME, DATE, PRICE, QTY

Key CNAME, SNAME
Foreign Key CNAME of CUSTOMER
SNAME of SALESMAN

STEP 3

Simplify

CUSTOMER

CNAME, ADDRESS, MAIN-PURCHASE, TOT-PURCH
KEY : CNAME

SALESMAN

SNAME, OFFICE, SALARY
KEY : SNAME

PURCHASE

```
CNAME,    SNAME,    DATE,    PRICE,    QTY
          KEY : CNAME, SNAME

          FOREIGN KEY : CNAME of CUSTOMER
                        SNAME of SALESMAN
```

Schema name is SALES

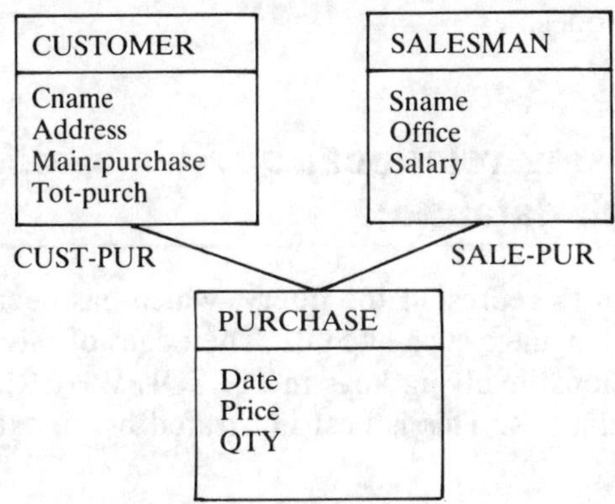


```
Record Name is CUSTOMER
  Location-mode is CALC using CNAME
  Duplicates not allowed
    CNAME is char 25
      ADDRESS is char 30
      MAIN-PURCHASE is integer 6
      TOT-PURCH is real 6.2
Record Name is SALESMAN
  Location-mode is CALC using SNAME
  Duplicates not allowed
    SNAME is char 25
      OFFICE is integer 5
      SALARY is integer 6
Record Name is PURCHASE
  Location-mode is via CUST-PUR
    DATE is integer 6
      PRICE is real 6.2
      QTY is integer 6
```

```
Set Name is CUST-PUR
Mode is Chain
  Order is First
  Owner is CUSTOMER
  Member is PURCHASE
  Set Sel is thru current of set
```

```
Set Name is SALE-PUR
Mode is Chain
  Order is First
  Owner is SALESMAN
  Member is PURCHASE
  Set Sel is thru
    Loc-Mode of owner
```

Figure 4.2 A CODASYL database.

As mentioned earlier, some simplifying assumptions have been made in this method. These can be removed by a series of simple devices in order to make the technique fully general. Examples of the assumptions are:

- No multimember sets are allowed,
- Repeating groups are prohibited,
- Data items are not allowed to have 'direct' and 'database-key' as location modes.

4.9 Processing relational queries against the network database

A graph is drawn to represent the query, which has been expressed in a relational query language such as SQL. The edges of this graph represent the JOIN conditions involving keys in the SQL WHERE clause and the nodes are the relations. This is best illustrated by an example.

EXAMPLE 4.6

Suppose we have the relational schema obtained in Example 4.5 and we have the following query addressed to it: Find the names of all those salesmen who sold bolts as main-purchase items to customers in Belfast in August. An SQL version of this query is

```
SELECT  SNAME, OFFICE
FROM    CUSTOMER, SALESMAN, PURCHASE
WHERE   (ADDRESS = "BELFAST") and
        (MAIN-PURCHASE = "BOLTS") and
        (CUSTOMER.CNAME = PURCHASE.CNAME) and
        (DATE = "AUG") and
        (PURCHASE.SNAME = SALESMAN.SNAME)
```

We now give a very much simplified method of translating this to a DML program for a network database. To illustrate the approach to translation we take a naïve approach to evaluating JOIN queries. A very basic nested loop method of evaluation is assumed.

This is an exceedingly crude approach, generating the Cartesian product of all the relations and testing, tuple by tuple, to see if the selection criteria hold for them. There are very simple ways of enhancing its performance using query optimization techniques (see Chapter 5). For example, a very obvious one is to move all the selections out to the outer loops and perform them as early as possible.

It is an easy task to map this algorithm, or a more efficient version of it, to a program in a network database's DML. Relations are simply mapped to record types, attributes to data items and key-JOINs are mapped to sets taking account of which record-type is owner and which is member. This information is available from the local network schema.

If a given relation is at the owner end of a key-JOIN, fetching a tuple from it is translated to FIND OWNER of the corresponding set. Otherwise a FIND FIRST, FIND NEXT pairing is generated.

EXAMPLE 4.7

Consider the query given in the previous example. Using the 'brute-force' nested loop method and ignoring complications such as duplicates, we get a simplified network DML program as follows.

```
    FIND FIRST CUSTOMER VIA SYSTEM.
      PERFORM FIRST-LOOP UNTIL finished.
FIRST-LOOP
    GET CUSTOMER.
        FIND FIRST PURCHASE RECORD OF CUST-PUR SET
    PERFORM SECOND-LOOP UNTIL finished.
    FIND NEXT CUSTOMER RECORD OF SYSTEM.
SECOND-LOOP
    GET PURCHASE
    FIND OWNER IN SALE-PUR OF CURRENT PURCHASE RECORD
    GET SALESMAN.
    IF ADDRESS OF CUSTOMER = "BELFAST" AND MAIN-PURCHASE
    OF CUSTOMER = "BOLTS" AND DATE OF PURCHASE = "AUG"
    THEN WRITE SNAME, OFFICE
      FIND NEXT PURCHASE RECORD OF CUST-PUR SET
```

It is very clear from this example how 'pushing' the selections (see Chapter 5), that is, doing them as the corresponding relations are encountered in the algorithm, would enhance the efficiency of this method.

SUMMARY

This chapter is in two parts. In the first part we have studied the question of how to allocate data to the nodes of a computer network in a manner which makes subsequent retrievals for the expected transactions as efficient as possible. The case for careful consideration of the basis of distribution of the data is made, and both qualitative and quantitative approaches to this procedure are presented.

The second part treats the problems associated with harmonizing heterogeneous systems which have to be integrated. The issues are discussed in detail and then we consider briefly some of the data models suggested for use for the global database description. The particular problem of translating between relational and network data models is treated in some detail.

EXERCISES

4.1 Find an arrangement of the tuples of relation R_1 and R_2 of the example in Section 4.3.2 for which just one page access is required to answer the original query. Discuss the effect of page to site allocations for this placement.

4.2 Work through Example 4.3 for the case where each site can hold 30 Mbytes, and file 7 has size 3 Mbytes instead of 4 Mbytes.

4.3 Determine an efficient allocation of six files to four sites, each of which is capable of holding 50 Mbytes. The access profiles of six transactions are as follows:

	File (size)					
Transactions	1 (30)	2 (20)	3 (35)	4 (10)	5 (30)	6 (25)
1	30		30			
2	15		15	100		
3				40	20	20
4		50	20			
5	10	10				10
6	10			10	30	

The frequency of transactions on sites is as follows:

	Sites			
Transactions	1	2	3	4
1			50	100
2	20	10		
3	20	10		
4	20	20		20
5		20	50	10
6			50	10

4.4 Explain why 'de-clustering' of data might be needed as well as clustering in distributed data systems (see references for material on de-clustering).

4.5 Discuss informally the interrelationship between query optimization (see Chapter 5) and file allocation. Illustrate your answer by reference to the design of roads in an urban development, and their subsequent use.

4.6 Explain the desirable features of a global schema for a heterogeneous database system.

4.7 Name some distributed database systems which use the relational data model for their global schemas. Suggest reasons for this choice, and discuss the difficulties it could raise.

4.8 Discuss the pros and cons of converting local databases to make them homogeneous, as an alternative to using the integrating methods presented in this chapter.

4.9 What is the difference between homogenization and integration of heterogeneous databases?

4.10 Integration can require conversions of units and various other changes between local schemas and a global schema in addition to data model homogenization. Give examples of three such conversions, and describe the 'integration rules' which would be required in the system for this purpose. Where in the system architecture would you suggest that this particular conversion functionality should be provided?

Bibliography

Bell D.A. (1984). Difficult data placement problems. *Computer J.*, **27**(4), 315–320

This paper establishes the fact that several interesting and practical data allocation problems are NP-complete.

Ceri S., Martella G. and Pelagatti G. (1980). Optimal file allocation for a distributed database on a network of minicomputers. In *Proc. ICOD 1 Conf.* Aberdeen, Scotland

A different version of the method described in Section 4.5, extended to the case where redundancy is permitted in the allocation, can be found here. Example 4.3 is based on figures given in an example in this paper.

Chang C.C. and Shielke. (1985). On the complexity of the file allocation problem. *Conf. on Foundations of Data Organisation*, Kyoto, Japan

The file allocation problem (see Section 4.5) is established to be NP-hard by reducing it to a well-known graph colouring problem.

Chen H. and Kuck S.M. (1984). Combining relational and network retrieval methods. *Proc. SIGMOD Conf.*, Boston, USA

These authors have made a number of contributions to different aspects of the conversion of data models, of which this paper is an example. It shows how to get efficient DML programs from relational queries.

Daellenbach H.G., Genge J.A. and McNickle D.C. (1983). *Introduction to Operational Research Techniques*. Massachusetts: Allyn and Bacon, Inc.

A treatment of the knapsack problem.

Dayal U. and Goodman N. (1982). Optimisation methods for CODASYL database systems. *Proc. ACM SIGMOD Conf.*, Orlando, USA

Fang M.T., Lee R.C.T. and Chang C.C. (1986). The idea of declustering and its applications. *Proc. 12th Int. Conf. on VLDB*, Kyoto, Japan

Declustering is the inverse procedure to clustering. It can be appreciated by thinking of the task of selecting two basketball teams for a match from a group of players, half of whom are over 7 feet tall and the rest are under 5 feet tall. If we want the match to be evenly balanced we choose dissimilar players, heightwise, to be on the same team. Similar requirements are met in some computing environments, for example when parallelism is to be exploited.

Kalinichenko L.A. (1987). Reusable database programming independent on DBMS. *Proc. 10th ISDMS Conf.*, Cedzyna, Poland

The UCDM, described briefly in Section 4.7, is developed in this paper. Various principles for conversion between data models are given, and a series of axiomatic extensions to allow well-known data models to be covered are given.

Katz R.H. and Wong E. (1982). Decompiling CODASYL DML into relational queries. *ACM Trans. on Database Systems*, **7**(1), 1–23

Rosenthal A. and Reiner D. (1982). An architecture for query optimisation. *Proc. ACM SIGMOD Conf. on Management of Data*, Orlando, USA

Shipman D. (1981). The functional data model and the data language DAPLEX. *ACM Trans. on Database Systems* **6**(1), 140–173

The DAPLEX language, which underlies the Multibase system, is presented here.

Smith J.M. and Smith D.C.P. (1977). Database abstractions: aggregations and generalisations. *ACM Trans. on Database Systems,* **2**(2), 106–133

This is something of a classic as a treatment of the issues of data abstractions (see Section 4.6).

Taylor R.W., Fry J.P. and Shneiderman B. (1979). Database program conversion – a framework for research, *Proc. 5th Int. Conf. on VLDB*, Rio de Janeiro, Brazil

The problem of finding out how well we can mechanically produce, from a given program and database, an equivalent program to interact with a converted database, is formulated and addressed in this paper. The precise definition given in this chapter is taken from this paper.

Wong E. and Katz R.H. (1983). Distributing a database for parallelism. *Proc. ACM SIGMOD Conf.*, San Jose, California

This paper describes the semantic approach to optimizing the placement and allocation of data. There is no need for the development of a quantitative cost model in this case. The approach described in Section 4.4 of this chapter is developed here.

Zaniolo C. (1979). Design of relational views over network schemas. *Proc. ACM SIGMOD Conf.*, Boston, Massachusetts

If the RDM is to be safely employed as a global data model for DDBs, as it frequently is (in contrast to systems using functional data models, such as

DAPLEX, or the more complete UCDM), we must have ways of mapping the various other data models to it. That is, we must provide relational views of databases conforming to other models. This paper explains in detail how this can be approached in the case of the CODASYL data model (see Section 4.8).

SOLUTIONS TO EXERCISES

4.2

Files 1, 2, 5 and 8 are allocated to site 1 in the first iteration

Files 3, 4 and 7 are allocated to site 3 in the second iteration

File 6 is allocated to site 4 in the third iteration.

4.3

The V_{ij} table is as follows:

	File (size)					
Sites	1 (30)	2 (20)	3 (35)	4 (10)	5 (30)	6 (25)
1	300	1000	700	<u>2800</u>	400	400
2	350	<u>1200</u>	550	1400	200	400
3	2500	500	1500	500	<u>1500</u>	<u>500</u>
4	<u>3200</u>	1100	<u>3400</u>	100	300	100

In this case the $J(i)$ entries are underlined. This would give two overloaded sites on the first iteration of the algorithm, namely sites 3 and 4.

Solving the knapsack problem for 4 first (because it has the greater 'allocated value') we store files 1 and 2 at site 4. Similarly we store files 4 and 5 at site 3. On the second iteration we still have two files to assign to either node 1 or node 2. Can you think of a better approach?

5 Distributed Query Optimization

5.1 Introduction

In databases in general, a major aim is to hide the structural details of the data from the user as much as possible. In distributed databases one of the main goals is that the distribution details should also be hidden, so that invoking the capabilities and functionality of the system are as easy and effective as possible.

The relational data model, which we focus upon here, can be used to provide a data-independent interface to a centralized database. The high level of this interface is due to its non-procedurality. An early example of a relational data language was the Relational Calculus which is considered by database experts to be a **non-procedural language**. Using it the data requested in the query is simply described and no procedure has to be specified for its extraction. On the other hand most people would say that Relational Algebra is a procedural language because when using it a method is specified for the retrieval of the requested data.

The Relational Calculus is a somewhat mathematically-oriented language. So, in order not to restrict the usability and applicability of the concept of non-procedurality, languages of equivalent power to that of the Relational Calculus, but avoiding its technical complexity and 'unfriendliness', have been developed for commercial database management packages.

SQL is the result of one such development, and it has been widely accepted in the computing industry. However, it is not universally regarded as being non-procedural, because judgements differ as to what is procedural and what is not. One way of removing some of the subjectivity associated with this is to use the following informal criterion as a basis of judgement.

Given two representative sets of specifications of a particular set of computations, the set which is characterized by having fewer operations, variable bindings and ordering constraints is the less procedural specification. This is an intuitive criterion but it has been elucidated by its proposers Welty and Stemple.

Even if a non-procedural language is used, getting an answer to a query still requires the specification of a procedure to search, access, manipulate and transfer data. The power of many query languages has been extended to include aggregate functions and transitive closure and corresponding new optimization techniques have had to be developed. These are beyond the scope of this book, but we consider them a little further in Chapter 11. We restrict our attention here to the basic relational operators, PROJECT, SELECT and JOIN. In the case of DDBs, sites at which intermediate and final processing are to be performed must also be indicated.

Non-procedurality of the data language implies that the onus of choosing these methods and sites must be on the system. **Query optimization** is the process of ensuring that either the total cost or the total response time for a query are minimized.

The choices to be made by a query optimizer sub-module of the query processor are fairly self-evident:

(1) The order of executing (relational) operations;
(2) The access methods for the pertinent relations;
(3) The algorithms for carrying out the operations (in particular, relational JOINs);
(4) The order of data movements between sites.

A query optimizer takes as inputs the requirements for data expressed in a query. This input, which is the output from the query parser submodule of the query processor of the system, is represented in an internal form which makes it amenable to manipulation by the optimizer. The optimizer then selects an appropriate strategy for accessing the data. Optimization of query execution is an intractable problem and perfect data on the system's behaviour is unlikely to be available, but satisfactory sub-optimal results, based on the heuristic methods described later in this chapter, can be obtained.

We can see from the above list of choices that in a distributed environment two essential aspects of query processing have to be considered alongside those for centralized databases:

- Data and messages have to be transmitted across communications lines, which has a tendency to slow down the whole process;
- The existence of multiple processors in the network means that there are opportunities for parallel processing and data transmission, which raises the possibility of speeding up responses.

The task of the query optimizer is to govern and expedite the processing and data transmission required for responding to queries. We discuss the issues of distributed query processing using a rather traditional and well-tried pedagogical approach.

We clarify these concepts in Section 5.2, and in Section 5.3 we look at methods of ordering relational operations that can be tried for giving the correct result more efficiently than an initial specification. Section 5.4 deals briefly with the issue of selecting query plans in centralized systems and in Section 5.5 we study the important issues of choosing a method for a JOIN execution, looking in detail at SDD-1's SEMI-JOIN method and also at the non-SEMI-JOIN method used in R*. The chapter ends with a summary of some issues currently engaging the minds of database researchers in this area.

5.2 The importance of query optimization

The most convincing argument for the provision of a query optimizer in a database system is that there can be very substantial savings in the cost of evaluating a query or in the length of time the user has to wait for a response. In this section we distinguish between these two types of optimizers, and then illustrate how response time and cost can be reduced.

5.2.1 Basic types of optimization

When distributed query processing techniques are compared, it is usually on the basis of cost of query execution (execution cost) or on the basis of time taken between the submission of the query and the receipt of the reply (response time). At the most general level, response time can be taken to represent a cost to an organization. For example, missed sales or other similar opportunities due to poor responsiveness are clearly undesirable from a financial point of view. However, here we distinguish, for pedagogical reasons and also for some pragmatic reasons, between the marginal costs of a given query as it is executed and the responsiveness of the system to the query.

Execution cost optimizers aim to minimize the use of the (total) system resources for a query and hence reduce its cost. The value of the objective function for the optimization process is therefore obtained from the sum of expressions representing the consumption of the individual system resources.

The most critical resources utilized in query evaluation in a centralized database are

- CPU
- I/O channels
- Telecommunications lines.

I/O channel usage contributes to the cost of loading data pages from secondary to primary storage and it is compounded by the cost of occupying secondary storage for temporary relations and buffer storage. Channels, intermediate storage and buffers may each be bottleneck resources of the system. Bottlenecks occur where there is more demand for resources than can be met at a particular time. Telecommunications lines can be bottleneck resources for similar reasons, being very similar in function to channels. CPU costs are often assumed to be low or even negligible in database systems, but they can be relatively high for complex queries or when cheaper communications lines are used.

Response time optimizers aim to minimize the response time for a query by exploiting parallelism, in particular that natural parallelism provided by having multiple processors in the network. Clearly sub-queries on the 'critical path', namely those determining the minimum response time for the complete query, merit most attention.

The value of the objective function for optimization in this case is obtained from the totality of expressions representing sub-queries on the critical path. It is easy to see that there could well be a difference between the 'fastest' and the 'cheapest' execution strategies in particular cases.

5.2.2 Variations in ways of executing queries

Even for the case of centralized databases, there are many ways to evaluate a given query. In general, as already indicated, query optimizers intend to minimize redundant and unnecessary operations, choose the cheapest or fastest way to perform basic database operations, schedule their execution well, and use standard and shared sub-methods where possible. There are, however, two basic tools for use in optimization. An example of the first, called *query transformation* is that the relational operators, such as JOIN and PROJECT, can be carried out in different orders. Other kinds of transformation can be identified, and examples can be found in the references at the end of this chapter. The operators can then be implemented using a variety of low-level algorithms and access devices, such as indices, pointers and methods of executing relational operators. This is called *query mapping*. Query mapping therefore corresponds to choices 2 and 3 in Section 5.1 above; query transformation corresponds to choice 1 (but it has an impact on choice 4 also, in distributed systems).

In distributed systems *message transmission* on data communications lines is required to control the query evaluation operations and the order in which they are executed; *data transmission* is needed to pass results and partial results between sites. An optimizer must choose these and this corresponds to choice 4 in section 5.1. Communications line transmission rates are usually assumed to be some factors of ten (orders of magnitude) slower in speed than I/O channels and so figure prominently for heavy traffic, but the orders of magnitude vary somewhat. For example, we may use a high-speed network (nominal speed 24 Mbits s^{-1}, actual speed 4 Mbits s^{-1}) for some communications and a medium-speed network (nominally 56 kbits s^{-1}, actual 40 kbits s^{-1}) for others. These speeds can be compared with corresponding disk costs of 23.48 ms for 4 kbytes (i.e. 1.3 Mbits s^{-1}). These figures come from a study carried out in 1985 by Mackert and Lohmann, so the factors should be considered with care in current environment.

We now illustrate the influence of the choices of ordering of operations with reference to a simple distributed database over 3 nodes. This shows how the CPU, I/O and data transmission costs are affected by the strategy chosen.

EXAMPLE 5.1

We use a simple JOIN and SELECT query over three relations at three different sites to illustrate the effect of changing the order of execution of the relational operations.

Site	Relation
Hospital	HOSPITALIZATION (pat-name, DOB, admit, discharge, dept) Cardinality 200 000
Health centre	PATIENT (pat-name, DOB, GP) Cardinality 10 000
Community care	SURVEY (pat-name, DOB, weight, type-of-work) Cardinality 100 000

Query: Find the names and the GPs of all patients who weigh over 100 kg and have been treated in the orthopaedic department since 1 January.

Assume that all the communications links have the same cost/tuple and that size=cardinality. Assume also that 0.1% of the patients in HOSPITALIZATION satisfy the criterion 'orthopaedic department since 1 January' and that this figure is reduced by 50% by the effects of the other operations, and that 1% of the patients weigh over 100 kg.

Option 1
Move PATIENT relation to community care site, JOIN it with the SURVEY relation there, and move the result to the query site for JOINing with the other relation, shipped from the hospital. See Figure 5.1 (a).

Costs (let the cost of transmitting a tuple be t and the overall cost of comparing and possibly concatenating two tuples be c):
JOINs . . . $10\,000 \times 1000c$ for PATIENT and restricted SURVEY (we assume here that this gives a 1000 tuple result)

$+ 200 \times 1000c$ for JOINing this result and restricted HOSPITALIZATION

Transmit . . . $200t + 10\,000t + 1000t$

Option 2
Send the restricted HOSPITALIZATION relation to the community care site. Join it with restricted SURVEY there. Join the result with PATIENT at the health centre, and ship the result to the query site. See Figure 5.1 (b).

Costs: JOINs . . . $1000 \times 200c$ at community care
$+100 \times 10\,000c$ at health centre.
Transmit . . . $200t + 100t + 100t$.

The latter strategy incurs less associated CPU cost and less traffic is involved, but there is less parallelism of execution than using the other strategy. So the ordering of operations can make a significant impact on both costs and responsiveness even for this simple example. This example is based on one developed by Hevner. A more dramatic illustration of the effect of the choice of strategy is given in the references. Using six different strategies, response times varying from seconds to days were obtained by Rothnie and Goodman!

The complexity of a query optimizer to handle even a simple query such as this can be appreciated as the example is studied. In practice the situation is often very much more complex than this. Consider, for example, the case where the patients are spread over several sites, and so the SURVEY relation is horizontally partitioned over the network. There are

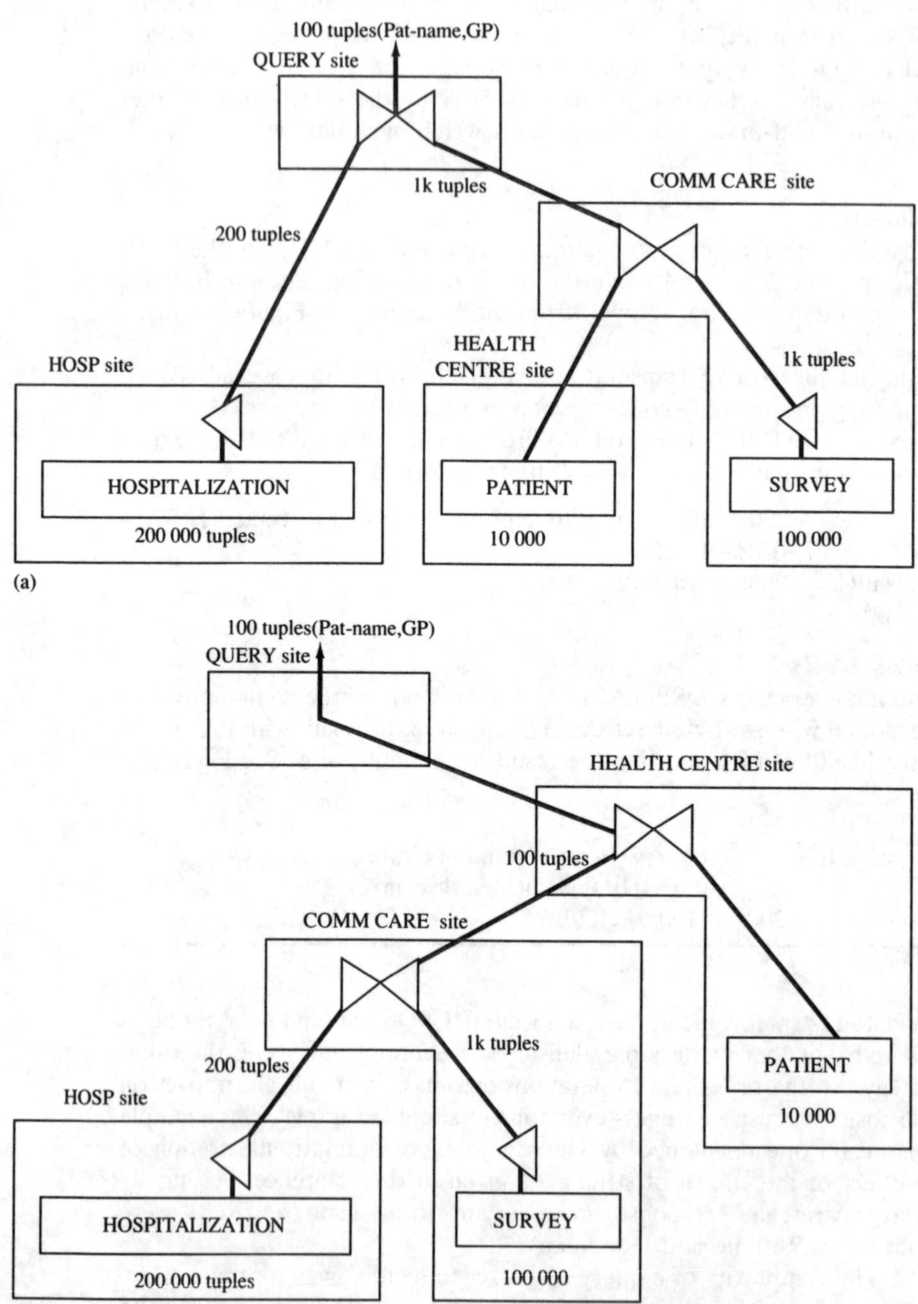

Figure 5.1 (a) A JOIN order for Example 5.1. (b) An alternative JOIN order for Example 5.1.

now a greatly increased number of possible routes and orders of intersite transmission and the parallelism of execution of partial JOINs and other operations adds to the problem of optimization. Some idea of the increase in complexity this causes is given by Example 5.6.

Examples of valid query transformations are distributivity of SELECT and PROJECT over JOIN, and commutativity and associativity of JOIN and PRODUCT (see Section 5.3). These transformations can be examined without knowledge of the physical characteristics of the database system, and there are several basic transformations which always result in benefits.

There are also a variety of ways of mapping queries to low-level structures and operations (using physical access methods, etc.) of the database system. We will see how IBM's System R does this in Section 5.5. Also there is a considerable choice of methods of executing JOINs locally and globally, as we will also see later. Transformations and mappings can be evaluated quantitatively. The cheapest or quickest overall result is then chosen from the alternatives.

At the query transformation level, conventional query optimization as described above searches for efficient sequences, possibly interleaved, of operations to be performed on the database for each query. Semantic query optimization, which we consider briefly in Section 5.6, uses a different approach which can be regarded as a generalization of these simple transformations. The original query is transformed into a semantically equivalent query (one still giving the required answer) which performs better. Examples are where transformations based on the conventional integrity constraints (such as functional dependencies) are used to check the semantic validity of updates. The techniques can be used in conjunction with the methods described earlier and thus offer the possibility of greater enhancement of performance.

In distributed query processing, a query is decomposed into subqueries pertinent to sites storing the required data and these are then decomposed locally much as they would be for centralized database systems. Query execution consists of a series of local executions, perhaps carried out in parallel, and a global execution which governs the movement of data between sites. The local executions do not all have to chronologically precede the global execution. For example, it is quite possible that some local sub-queries must be carried out at sites S_1 and S_2, the result assembled under control of a global process and the partial results used in another sub-query evaluation at a third site S_3 as in Figure 5.2. Furthermore, it is quite possible that another three sites S_4, S_5 and S_6 contribute to similar global and local processing and that the two partial results are combined with the result of local processing at a new site S_7.

So considerable interleaving of global and local executions is possible. It is clear from this example how parallelism of execution is possible. We will see detailed examples of this later (in Section 5.5).

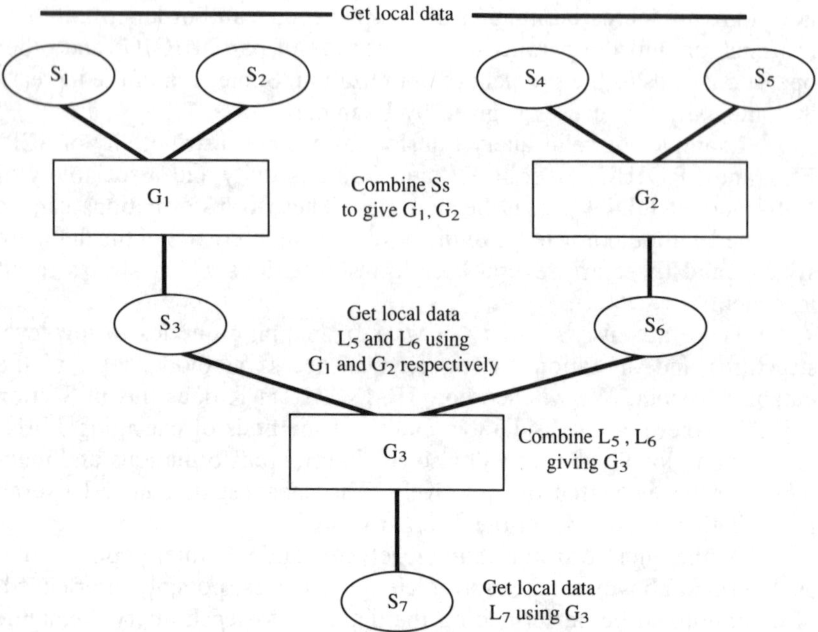

Figure 5.2 The potential for parallelism in distributed query evaluation.

5.3 Equivalence transforms

A general SQL query can be converted into an equivalent set of relational algebra expressions. The reciprocal conversion is also possible. This is true whether the query is addressed to a distributed database system or a centralized database system. This section is primarily concerned with the order of execution of operations against a DDB and so it is convenient to work with Relational Algebra expressions.

Two relational algebra expressions are said to be **equivalent** if we get identical results when the relations named are substituted by the same extensions (i.e. the same sets of data values for the types). As mentioned earlier there are a number of transformations which always result in an equivalent query. For queries with only two or three relations (called query variables) the following transformations are examples of those that *always* give identical results. Examples using operator graphs appear in the next section (Figure 5.3).

(a) For SELECT and PROJECT

(i) Commutativity

$$\sigma_F (\pi_A (R)) = \pi_A (\sigma_F(R))$$

provided that condition F involves only attributes in A.

(ii) Cascade

$$\pi_A (\pi_B (R)) = \pi_A (R)$$

where the set of attributes B includes A.

$$\sigma_F (\sigma_G (R)) = \sigma_{F \cdot G} (R) = \sigma_G (\sigma_F (R))$$

(b) For JOIN

(i) Commutativity

$$R \underset{F}{\bowtie} S = S \underset{F}{\bowtie} R$$

similarly for natural JOIN and PRODUCT.

(ii) Associativity

$$(R \underset{F}{\bowtie} S) \underset{G}{\bowtie} T = R \underset{F}{\bowtie} (S \underset{G}{\bowtie} T)$$

similarly for natural JOIN and PRODUCT.

(c) Some combinations of binary and unary operations

(i) SELECT over UNION and SET DIFFERENCE (the latter are denoted by * here)
distributivity $\sigma_F (R*S) = \sigma_F(R) * \sigma_F (S)$

(ii) SELECT over PRODUCT

commutativity $\sigma_F (R \times S) = \sigma_F (R) \times S$

(iii) PROJECT, over CARTESIAN PRODUCT and UNION

distributivity $\pi_A (R * S) = \pi_B (R) * \pi_C (S)$

where B, C are the subsets of A appropriate to R and S respectively. They must be identical for UNION.

(iv) SELECTION and PROJECTION are distributive under certain conditions over JOIN and SEMI-JOIN (SEMI-JOINs will be defined later). This is important for existing relational systems.

A few examples are given later in Figure 5.4. Ceri and Pelagatti present a comprehensive list of equivalence transforms in their book which is referenced below.

The rule of thumb used in centralized optimization that 'PROJECTIONS and SELECTIONS should be performed early, and JOINS (and other binary operations) late' applies to an even greater degree to distributed systems because large join sizes are undesirable for transfers between distributed sites.

In the case of distributed databases a global query is expressed over the relations described in the global schema. We assume here that the query is expressed in Relational Algebra. As mentioned in Chapter 2, each of these relations is constructed from local participation schema relations. If we substitute the construction of each global relation each time it is referenced in the global query we obtain an algebraic expression over the participation schema relations. This intermediate expression of the query is sometimes called its **canonical form**.

Since this is an algebraic expression it can be subjected to the normal equivalence transformations. A particularly useful transformation for this distributed case is the distributivity of the unary SELECTION and PROJECTION operations over the binary UNION and JOIN operations (see (c) above).

5.4 Generating and selecting access plans in centralized systems

Access plans for a query are descriptions of data and operations which lead from the database to the response to the query. Examples of ways of representing access plans are **operator graphs** and **object graphs**. The use of such query graphs to provide a visual representation of queries offers the additional advantages of the applicability of graph theoretic results to discover tree sub-graphs which are relatively easy to deal with, or to spot cycles in the graph which merit special attention.

Operator graphs incorporate the symbols:

Selection	Projection	Join
◁	▽	⋈

EXAMPLE 5.2

The second version of the query of Example 5.1 can be represented as an operator graph as in Figure 5.3.

Figure 5.4 shows some valid transforms of some queries based on Example 5.1 in operator graph form.

Object graphs are the other type of query graph. For illustration, Figure 5.5 shows the object graph for part of Example 5.1.

Clearly the optimizer should aim to provide sufficient access plans to stand a good chance of netting the optimal plan, but at the same time try to avoid the penalties associated with getting larger numbers of these than the system can cope with. An exhaustive search approach might be

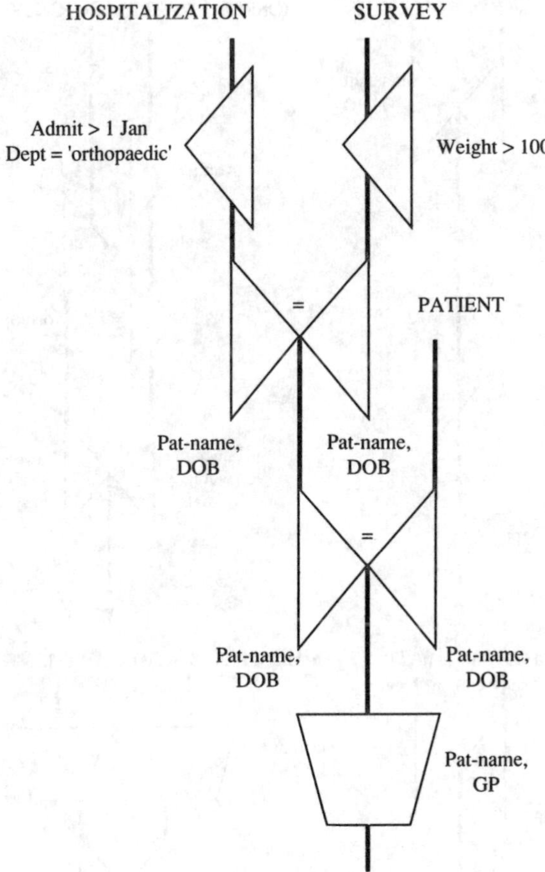

Figure 5.3 Operator graph for Example 5.1.

prohibitively expensive in many realistic situations. We return to the issue of exhaustive search as opposed to heuristic search later (Section 5.6). The method of obtaining the contender access paths varies a lot from system to system, and again these methods will be illustrated later (Section 5.6).

To give further insights into the complexity of query optimization we now consider briefly two problems which are dealt with at access path generation and selection time. These are nested SQL query handling and the management of common expressions.

In IBM's System R prototype, the basic access path selection techniques involve the use of a two-level hierarchical procedure based on SQL's unlimited nesting structure. Nested queries in SQL are associated

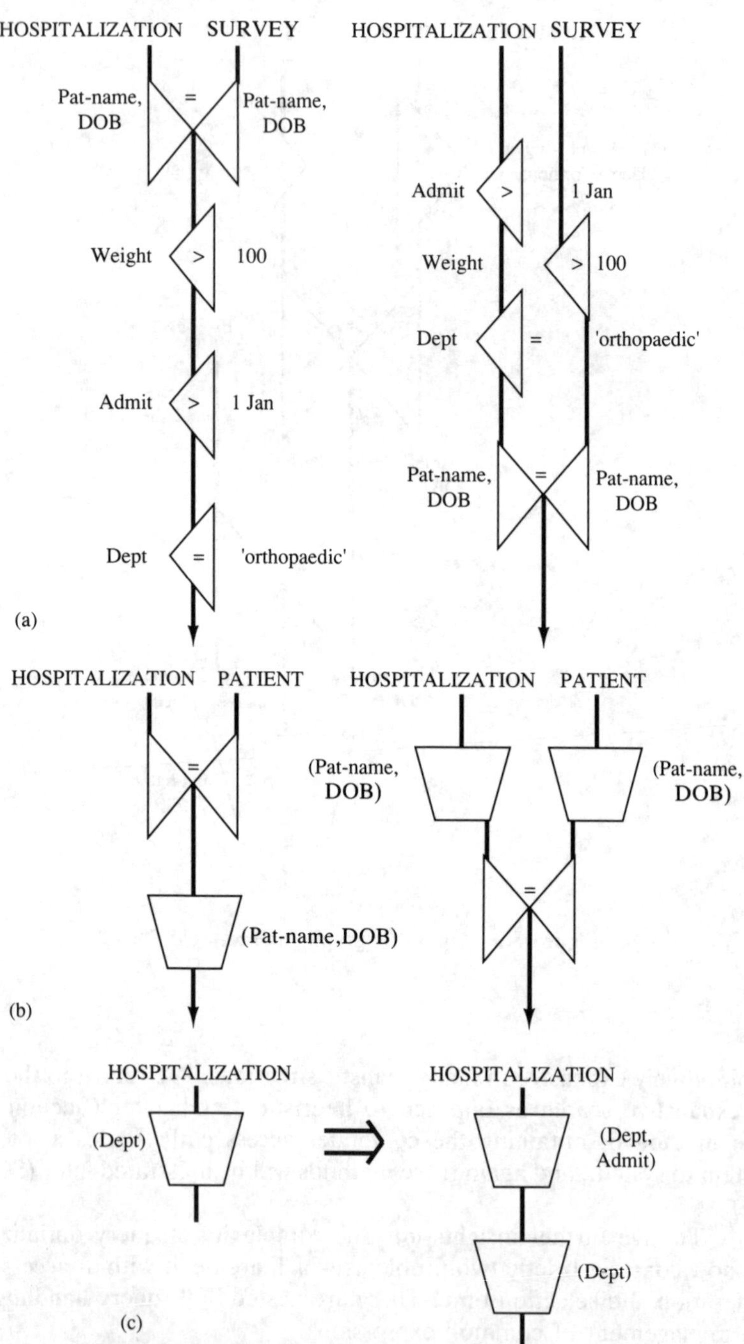

Figure 5.4 Some equivalence rules. (a) SELECT after and before JOIN—same result. (b) PROJECT after and before JOIN—same result. (c) Cascade of SELECT.

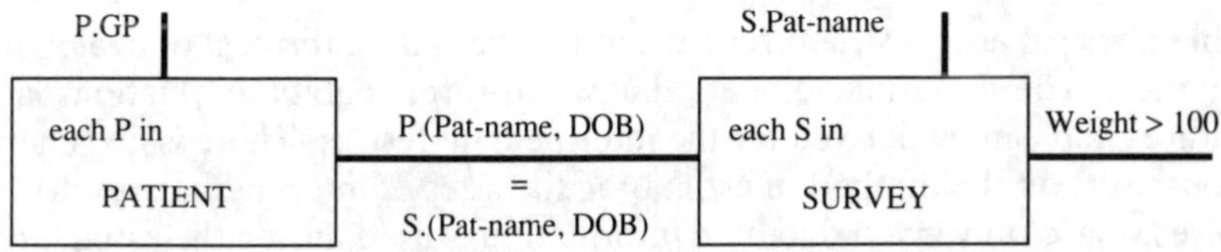

Figure 5.5 Object graph for Example 5.1.

with poor execution times and so have attracted the attention of query subsystem designers.

'Naïve' query evaluation involves exhaustive evaluation and comparison of the query blocks, and the top level determines the sequence of evaluation of the blocks. Evaluation is therefore clearly dependent on the user's block structure.

A number of efforts have been made to avoid this exhaustive enumeration approach. If we assume just two levels of nesting and call the nested SELECT . . . FROM . . . WHERE blocks outer and inner respectively with the obvious meaning, five basic types of nesting can be identified.

Four of these types are distinguished by whether or not the inner block has a JOIN predicate in its WHERE clause; and whether or not its SELECT clause contains an aggregate function such as a MAX, AVG or SUM operation. The remaining type has a JOIN predicate and a DIVIDE predicate.

Some of the types can still be treated by a conceptually simple nested iteration method, where the inner block is processed for each outer block tuple, but this is costly and algorithms are available to transform nested queries of four of the above types into standardized non-nested JOIN predicates and the fifth into a simple query that can be handled easily by System R. These cases and their treatments were identified and discussed by Kim. However, care is needed when applying these results, as has been pointed out by Kiessling.

A further, intuitive, approach to reducing the number of plans generated is common expression analysis. *Ad hoc* query evaluation can be greatly speeded up by making use of stored final or partial results from previous queries which have query sub-graph paths or individual nodes in common with the current query. Analysis shows that the processing costs are not significantly increased if none of these common expressions can be found. This sharing of processing is even more important if transaction 'scenarios' (sets of transactions which hit the system simultaneously) are identified, in which case multiple queries are optimized. We return to this subject in Section 5.6.

Cost models for selection of plans are usually based on the number of secondary storage accesses, buffer sizes and operand sizes. The available physical access structures such as indexes affect the cost of evaluating queries. These parameters are known for the database relations and indices and can be derived for the intermediate results. There is no general consensus on the method of estimating the sizes of intermediate results. In cases where only given database information is used during the estimation, rather a lot of assumptions are made. Typical assumptions made are:

- All records are equally likely to be selected
- Any record can be hit only once
- Any page can be hit only once.

These make the calculation of estimates of result sizes very simple, but suffer from a lack of fidelity to the real world (see Exercise 5.1 at the end of this chapter). Increasing the level of accuracy of estimates is not easy. How to use query selectivity in an accurate way is a complex and understudied aspect of this estimation. What proportion of the tuples of a relation contribute to the query evaluation? The result of this dearth of study is a lack of practically useful formulae striking the required balance between generality of the assumptions made and the bulk of data required. There have been some attempts to correct this situation (see Section 5.6).

Armed with the cost estimates, the selection procedure can advance in one of two ways: by exhaustive searching, where all possible paths are examined, or using heuristic searching, where the choices considered are reduced by applying 'compiled hindsight'. An example of such a heuristic is to discard non-minimal sub-plans for obtaining intermediate results (see Section 5.5 for how SDD-1 uses search reduction heuristics, and also Section 5.6).

5.5 Methods of performing JOINs

Of the basic relational operations (SELECT, JOIN, PROJECT) the most expensive in terms of both time and money is JOIN. It causes more page swaps than the other relational operations. The number of page swaps is an important contribution to response time and cost. In a paging environment the storage devices form a hierarchy based on speed (such as primary storage, fast disk, slow disk and archiving storage), so swapping between levels is required. The frequency of page swaps is often used as the cost measure when modelling these systems.

Procedures can be devised for reducing the cost of JOINs when all possible combinations of pages of two or more relations are matched. However, in many cases the number of page pairs to be considered can be quite dramatically reduced. Some of these cases occur when at least one of the relations being joined is affected by either a preceding JOIN or a preceding SELECT. Alternatively a directory holding information on the values stored on each page can be used in order to ignore page pairs with no matching values.

Graph methods are often used in the study of JOIN. Object graphs and operator graphs have already been met. In **query graphs**, in the present context, for a given query the nodes represent relations (the query variables). An edge exists between two nodes if there is a JOIN predicate (usually equality in which case we have an EQUI-JOIN) in the query linking attributes in the corresponding relations.

A **tree query** is defined as one with no cycles in the graph. Otherwise it is a **cyclic query**. Efficient procedures to test whether or not a given query is a tree query are available. Tree queries can be processed efficiently but cyclic query processing is difficult and any procedure for processing cyclic queries must convert them into tree queries. There are procedures to carry out the conversion of a cyclic query to a tree query but their details are beyond the scope of this book.

In the rest of this section we look at the two major approaches to the handling of JOINs in distributed databases, namely using SEMI-JOINs or not.

5.5.1 SEMI-JOIN methods

A SEMI-JOIN involves an increase in local processing of data in comparison to a JOIN, but saves on the cost of data movement between sites.

Informally, it is the projection of the tuples of the relation resulting from the JOIN on to one (named) relation, say, R_1, of the pair (R_1, R_2) of relations being joined.

In what follows we use the notation $\lhd$ for the SEMI-JOIN operation with an appended condition as in the JOIN operation.

Suppose π_i is the PROJECTION over the attributes of R_i and $\bowtie$ is the natural JOIN with the same appended JOIN conditions as $\lhd$. Then the SEMI-JOIN can be defined as follows

$$R_2 \lhd R_1 = \pi_1 (R_1 \bowtie R_2)$$

This formula can clearly be replaced (see Figure 5.4 (b)) by the equivalent form

$$R_2 \lhd R_1 = R_1 \bowtie (\pi R_2) \tag{5.1}$$

where π is over the JOIN attributes only.

This second representation has potential advantages over the first if R_1 and R_2 are at different sites A and B and the execution of a full

JOIN between R_1 and R_2 is to be done at a third site C. In the SDD-1 system the execution of the $\{\pi R_2\}$, transmission and local JOIN at A (giving the result of the SEMI-JOIN) is referred to as the **reduction phase** of a distributed JOIN. It is followed by a simpler **processing phase**, where the two reduced relations at A and B are shipped to a strategic site such as C and finally JOINed. This method can be used to reduce communication costs when a full JOIN is to be executed at C. First R_1 and R_2 are both 'SEMI-JOIN reduced' as above, and then both sub-results are sent to C for execution of the JOIN.

Suppose R_1 is the SEMI-JOIN relation (i.e. as in Equation 5.1 above) and that the result of the SEMI-JOIN is required at a third site C. The procedure is as follows:

Procedure SEMI-JOIN

Begin
Step 1. Project the JOIN attributes from R_2 at B ($= \pi R_2$), after applying any required SELECTIONs.
Step 2. Transmit πR_2 to A.
Step 3. Compute the SEMI-JOIN of R_1 at A.
Step 4. Move the result to C.
end

The advantages of the SEMI-JOIN algorithm are clearly greatest when πR_2 is relatively small (and so step 3 reduces the number of tuples from both local sites to be transmitted to the result site), and local processing costs are much smaller than transmission costs. The selectivities of SEMI-JOINS are what makes it worthwhile to use them (see Section 5.5.1). JOINs can increase the size of the database; SEMI-JOINS never do.

When the JOIN is done at A or B, let R_i^1 be the projection of R_i onto the JOIN columns, and let $|R_i \lhd R_j|$ be the size of the SEMI-JOIN result. A SEMI-JOIN will have a lower transmission cost than a conventional JOIN if the cost of initiating a message (remember that extra incurrence of this cost has to be included for SEMI-JOINs) added to min $(|R_2^1| + |R_2 \lhd R_1|, |R_1^1| + |R_1 \lhd R_2|)$ is less than min $(|R_1|, |R_2|)$.

We can generalize this discussion by considering cases where there are more than two relations. Here the reduction phase of query evaluation has the objective of translating a query into a cost effective series of SEMI-JOINs.

EXAMPLE 5.3

Suppose that a researcher in the orthopaedics department of a hospital suspects that the combination of the job a patient does and his/her weight is in some way related to the patient's likelihood of having a particular bone ailment. To investigate this the researcher wants to examine the type of work of all the people treated in orthopaedic wards since 1 January who are overweight. Accesses are made therefore to the two relations HOSPITALIZATION and SURVEY of Example 5.1. We ignore SELECT and PROJECT CPU costs.

A query is submitted to the DDB as follows:

```
Select pat-name, type-of-work, weight, admit
  From HOSPITALIZATION, SURVEY
   Where (HOSPITALIZATION.pat-name =
   SURVEY.pat-name)
   and (dept = orthopaedics) and (admit>1Jan)
   and (weight>100)
```

The result is required at the hospital site (where the researcher works).

To evaluate this query using SEMI-JOINs, the following steps are taken.

Step 1 (a) Restrict HOSPITALIZATION (dept = orthopaedics, admit > 1 Jan)

(b) PROJECT pat-name from restricted HOSPITALIZATION This gives a relation R of 200 tuples (each being of 'breadth' 1 attribute)

i.e. Card(R) = 200

Step 2 Transmit R to community care site

Transmission cost = 200 transmission cost/attribute (t_a)

Step 3 (a) Restrict SURVEY (weight > 100) – 1000 tuples

(b) JOIN R and restricted SURVEY – 100 tuples

(c) PROJECT these tuples over the required attributes.

Processing cost = 200 × 1000 cost per tuple comparison (c_t) + 100 cost/tuple concatenation (c_c)

(For increased precision we split variable c as used in Example 5.1 into two components, namely c_c and c_t and use a new unit for transmission costs, t_a.)

Step 4 Move result to hospital site

Transmission cost = $100 \times 3\ t_a$ (there are three attributes)

Step 5 JOIN result with restricted HOSPITALIZATION at hospital.

Processing cost = $200 \times 100\ c_t + 100\ c_c$

So total cost is

$$500\ t_a + 220\,000\ c_t + 200\ c_t \qquad \textbf{(5.2)}$$

Alternatively, suppose we used a crude JOIN instead of SEMI-JOINs here.

Step 1 Send qualified tuples in HOSPITALIZATION (projected over the three required attributes) to community care site.
Transmission cost = $200 \times 3\ t_a$

Step 2 JOIN with restricted SURVEY at community care.
Processing cost = $200 \times 1000\ c_t + 100\ c_c$

Step 3 Move result to Hospital site.
Transmission cost = $100 \times 5\ t_a$

Therefore total cost is

$$1100\ t_a + 200\ 000\ c_t + 100\ c_c \qquad \textbf{(5.3)}$$

So, under the assumption that t_a contributes much more significantly to the cost than c_t or c_c, (5.2) shows that we have probably about halved the cost of the JOIN by using SEMI-JOIN, despite having to JOIN at both sites. PROJECTing at Step 2 would reduce (5.3).

A more general case would be where the results are required at a third site. In this case the sending of the projected HOSPITALIZATION relation to the community care site is carried out in the hope that it reduces the size of SURVEY before SURVEY is transmitted to the JOIN site (say the health centre site). If size reduction does result from this, we say that the SEMI-JOIN is **beneficial**. In the above example this fact was not important because the *conventional* JOIN was carried out at community care. If the JOIN were not carried out until the requested data from community care was received at hospital, then the t_a figure would become 3000, because 1000 PROJECTed SURVEY tuples would have to be transmitted.

The main difficulty with this method is that of finding a minimum cost–response time sequence of SEMI-JOINs for a given query. The method for approximating this solution is exemplified by the algorithms used in SDD-1. We say that a SEMI-JOIN is beneficial if it reduces the size of the database. Having found a beneficial SEMI-JOIN we see if it is 'cost-effective' (i.e. its benefit is greater than its cost).

A heuristic is used in SDD-1 to accomplish the reduction phase of query execution for a class of JOIN queries.

It is presented in the form of an algorithm below. This algorithm results in a good sequence of SEMI-JOINS (referred to hereafter as S-Js).

Algorithm 5.1 (REDUCE)

---

begin
Phase 1
Step 1. Start with the null-reducer (no S-Js) as the best-so-far solution.
Step 2. Append cost-effective S-Js to the best-so-far solution.
Step 3. Repeat step 2 until there are no further such S-Js.

Phase 2

Step 4. Choose a final site for execution of the processing procedure and eliminate S-Js made unnecessary by this choice.

end

This algorithm is 'greedy' and is not claimed to be optimal, because it relentlessly proceeds forward; there is no backtracking to estimate the effect of local sub-optimization on the global execution. More sophisticated versions have been suggested in the literature.

The benefit of a S-J is the reduction it gives. Rules are defined for conducting the cost–benefit analysis decision making required for the REDUCE algorithm by formulae based on a statistical **profile** maintained by SDD-1, as follows:

Benefit estimation:

Notation: B (R) = Number of bytes/tuple in R
C (R) = Cardinality of R
C (RA) = The inverse selectivity (i.e. the number of distinct values) of attribute A in R. This is sometimes called 'term degeneracy'.
B (X) = Number of bytes in attribute collection X.

Estimation formulae:

(1) Benefit of PROJECTing R over attribute collection X in R = $[B(\mathrm{R})-B(\mathrm{X})] \times C(\mathrm{R})$

(a) It should be noted that we have taken some liberties with the estimation formulae given here. There are some variations from the SDD-1 formulae, but we feel that the derivations of our formulae are easier to understand.

(b) This first formula ignores the possibility of having duplicated tuples after removing unwanted attributes;

(2) Benefit of restricting R to tuples with R.A=c (a constant) $= B(\mathrm{R}) \times C(\mathrm{R}) \times (1-1/C(\mathrm{RA}))$

(3) Benefit of SEMI-JOINing R and S over attribute A

$$= \text{MAX} \begin{cases} 0 \\ B\ (\text{R}) \times C\ (\text{R}) \times (1 - C(\text{RA})/C(\text{SA})) \end{cases}$$

(Assume R is the relation contributing attributes to the S−J.)

Clearly Formula 3 is a rather rudimentary measure of benefit, as can be seen by applying it to Example 5.3. Moreover, there is an assumption of uniformity of the distribution of the A values.

Cost estimation:

The SDD-1 formula for the cost of S-J R and S over attribute A is

Cost = number of bytes transmitted to get the A values from S to R site.

$$= \begin{cases} C\ (\text{SA}) \times B\ (\text{A}) \text{ for non-local SJs} \\ 0 \text{ for local SJs} \end{cases}$$

The heuristic used in algorithm REDUCE is 'A S-J is cost effective if cost < benefit'.
(Notice that JOIN costs are not considered here; see exercises.)

EXAMPLE 5.4

Suppose a relation DOC has three attributes:

- Dr-no (6 bytes)
- Clin-no (6 bytes)
- Salary (5 bytes)

and it has 10^6 tuples.

What is the benefit of each SEMI-JOIN?

1) Calculate the benefit of PROJECTing over Dr-no.
B (R) = 17
B (X) = 6
C (R) = 10^6

Benefit = 11×10^6 by (1) above.

2) For DOC relation, calculate the benefit of SELECTing over doctors with salaries > 20 000 (assume 10% meet this requirement)

Benefit = $0.9 \times 10^6 \times 17 = 15.3 \times 10^6$ by (2) above.

3) Calculate the benefit of semi-joining another relation CLIN (JOIN column A = dr-no) with relation DOC

Reduction in size of relation DOC as a result of SEMI-JOIN with CLIN on dr-no

Assume two different doctors in S (i.e. C (SA) = 2)
Assume six different doctors in R (i.e. C (RA) = 6)
Benefit is 4/6 × B (R) × C (R)
= 0.67 × 10^6 × 17 by (3) above.

5.5.2 Non-SEMI-JOIN methods

In R* the query execution strategy is generated at compilation time and it therefore uses a *static* optimization algorithm (see Section 5.6). Queries can be compiled during times when the system is slack and the optimal access plans for their execution are determined then. Frequently-used SQL queries clearly benefit, but since bindings are determined prior to execution time, compilation might have to be repeated from time to time. When a JOIN over several sites is required, a choice can be made of sites at which to carry out the JOINing, as for S-Js. There is also a choice between two techniques for transmitting relations between sites. We refer to these as 'fetch once' and 'fetch as required'.

The former method involves sending the *complete relation* as a stream of tuples to the other site, where it is either temporarily stored (at some I/O cost) for later execution of a JOIN, or a JOIN is executed tuple by tuple on arrival. In 'fetch as required' shipment the transfer of *individual tuples* is coordinated by the node executing the JOIN. For example, a message can be transmitted to the other node (the one sending the data) to indicate that tuples with a particular JOIN column value are expected, and actions are suspended at the receiving site until matching tuples are returned. This could mean re-fetching some tuples which are required more than once.

The nested loop and merge scan methods are used for the JOIN in R*. Recall that the nested-loop method scans one relation called the **outer relation** for each tuple of the other relation, called the **inner relation** with a matching JOIN value. One simple way of doing this is to scan the entire inner relation for each tuple (or maybe block) of the outer relation. The merge-scan method depends on the two operand relations being sorted on the JOIN attribute, and merging the two sorted relations produces the JOIN result. The choices of JOIN method, JOIN order, and access methods are all carried out as in the centralized System R optimizer. The efficiency of JOINing of several sub-query results usually depends on the order of access to the relations. (This is not true of the UNION of sub-query results, where each sub-query can be optimized optimally.)

Preceding query execution, four stages of 'query preparation' are completed in R*. They are

- analyse the SQL query and perform object name resolution;
- look up the catalog to check authorization (privilege) and view integration;
- plan the minimum cost access strategy (a string of relation accesses, PROJECTIONs, SELECTIONs, data communications transfers, SORTs and JOINs) for this global query;
- generate the access modules and store them at a master site.

The optimizer is invoked at the third stage.

A search tree is traversed to estimate the cost of each possible way of servicing the particular SQL query.

The published cost formulae include message, I/O and CPU contributions, calculated as follows:

$$\begin{aligned} \text{I/O} &= \text{pages fetched} \times \text{weight } C_p \\ \text{CPU} &= \text{tuples fetched} \times \text{weight } C_{cpu} \\ \text{message} &= \text{messages sent} \times \text{weight } C_m \end{aligned}$$

where the three weights Cp, Ccpu and Cm represent relative importance values distinguishing between I/O, CPU and messages respectively. More detailed formulae are presented at the end of this section. The ratios vary with the system of course.

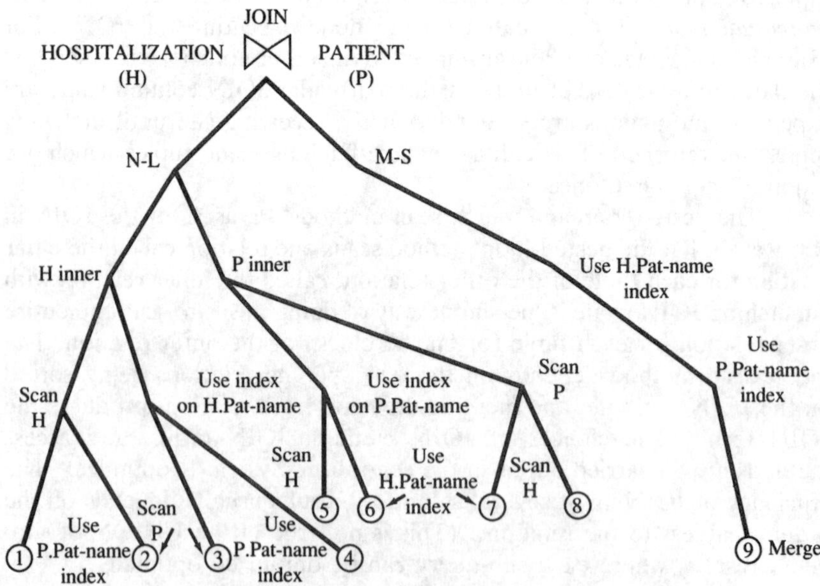

Figure 5.6 Tree for a JOIN using system R.

The criteria used for the partitioning of any relation are taken into account so that the costs of reconstituting it are kept low. The JOIN order and presentation order are considered in addition to the I/O, CPU and message factors above. This makes the fan-out of the search tree exceedingly large. Pruning heuristics for the centralized DBMS System R are used to reduce the space to be searched for an optimal plan. These are illustrated in Example 5.5, in which the published System R operation is 'interpreted' for clarity. The basic ideas behind the R* optimization method for non-nested queries are also illustrated in Example 5.5. This example serves to demonstrate the complexity of query optimization.

To find the optimal execution for a JOIN-based query like the one in this example, System R builds a decision tree of the strategies for executing the query. This tree has branches corresponding to operations such as sorts or index accesses on the relations and each leaf of the tree identifies a different way of executing the query expressed as the root of the tree (see Figure 5.6 for an illustration).

Heuristic rules are used to constrain the size of the tree. Some of the rules inspect the individual relations to discard unpromising strategies early (i.e. even before consideration of the JOIN method to be used). Exhaustive searching is then used to find the most efficient JOIN sequence, methods and sites. A well-known operations research technique called Dynamic Programming is used to speed up the search.

EXAMPLE 5.5

Consider a query on the relations of Example 5.1 which requires the 3 relations to be JOINed, ignoring any costs due to data transmission.

To illustrate the optimization technique used by System R, we define some indexes on the given relations. An index is said to be **clustered** if tuples with equal values of the indexed attribute are stored consecutively on the secondary storage devices. Unclustered indexes may require a particular page to be accessed many times for a single query, and so clustering has a potentially significant impact on efficiency. However, in order to highlight the essentials of the method, clustering is not considered in the following discussion.

There are indexes to HOSPITALIZATION on pat-name, admit and discharge. This means that there are four possible ways of accessing HOSPITALIZATION: by each of these indexes and by a serial scan.

Relation PATIENT also has an index on pat-name, so there are two possible ways of accessing it.

Relation SURVEY has no index on pat-name but has an index on type-of-work. System R's optimizer excludes all 'non-relevant' indexes (those not affecting the given query's efficiency) from consideration at this stage.

Given this information, we can limit the size of the query tree even before considering the JOIN orders. Look first at the HOSPITALIZATION relation and consider JOINing it with PATIENT. Assume that accessing a relation on any of the indexes presents the tuples in the corresponding order. We can use the admit index to restrict the HOSPITALIZATION relation before JOINing. However, the order of discharge and admit are not interesting orders (i.e. they are not used in a JOIN or specified in ORDER BY or GROUP BY clauses). A simple heuristic is to prune such 'uninteresting order' paths from further consideration for the JOIN tree. So we can discard the admit and discharge index accesses from the tree here.

Now assume that it is not possible to discard the serial scan method at this site. Note, however, that we discard it later, for illustration, using another heuristic, 'prune paths whose costs of execution are too great for some clear reason'.

Now look at the alternatives for executing these JOINs. They are: to use merge-scan, or to use one of the two nested-loop methods (HOSPITALIZATION inner and PATIENT inner respectively). Figure 5.6 shows the pruned query tree for this JOIN. For the merge scan method we assume the pat-name index on HOSPITALIZATION is the only contender because it is cheap and gives the correct JOIN order. One of the two possible methods of accessing PATIENT still remains, as shown.

Figure 5.6 shows nine possible routes, even having discarded the admit index and the discharge index. Suppose we prune the 'scan' branches because they take a much greater access time than the indexes, which are assumed here to be very selective. We are left with the following 'leaf' branches from above (all in pat-name order): {4, 6, 9}.

Consider now the second part of the evaluation path being considered in the JOIN order for this example. We need to find the effect of each of the access paths on the JOIN of the sub-result with SURVEY. In SURVEY (S) there is no index on pat-name and the index on type-of-work is not relevant in the sense above (although it could be used for restricting S). Probably a nested-loops JOIN would be chosen because the time to sort for the merge-sort would probably exclude it from consideration.

So in this case the cheapest of the three routes found earlier, {4, 6, 9}, would be chosen and the time or cost would be increased by that for the second part, in order to find the optimum strategy for the JOIN order being considered ((H $\bowtie$ P) $\bowtie$ S). This would then be compared with the other two possible JOIN orders to get the 'global' minimum.

A further simple heuristic, not illustrated in Example 5.5, is to reduce the order permutations for a JOIN by considering only orders having predicates which relate the inner relation to other relations already in the JOIN.

Selection of an execution strategy in the R* optimizer is carried out on the basis of the costs of the branches of the query tree. The cost of each branch is calculated by the system for each operation in terms of the expected number of tuples retrieved (giving the CPU cost), and the expected number of pages fetched from disk (giving the I/O cost), using formulae which depend on the access methods for the operand relations. The best root-to-leaf route is the one with lowest cost.

When the JOIN sites can vary in a DDB, there is clearly a significant increase in the number of alternative access plans to be considered. For one particular example the increase was found to be fourfold. When there are more than two relations, and more than two JOINs are encountered, the R* approach is to iteratively add a new relation to the corresponding previous $N-1$ relation plans (which is the cheapest for those relations), discarding plans which give the same {result, order and site} triple as some cheaper plan. The final choice of plan takes into account the cost of presenting the result in the user's requested order at the user's requested site.

At the site at which the query is submitted, the global parse tree and catalog information is used to generate a global execution plan. All intersite matters are decided here, but some can be overruled locally. Transfer strategies, JOIN orders and access methods are all decreed here, but they can, under some predefined conditions, be overruled at other sites for localized blocks of processing. An example is where sets of decisions are made globally which affect just one site.

As before, a Dynamic Programming method is used to complement the reduction in the search space obtained by using the pruning heuristics.

Some of the detailed cost formulae published for R* are presented below. Full details can be found in the R* papers listed in the references for this chapter.

Total cost

$$TC = (P \times C_p) + (R \times C_{cpu}) + M_c$$

where P is the number of pages fetched
R is the number of tuples fetched
M_c is the cost of messages
$(= C_{pm} + C_{mb} \times L)$
where L is the number of bytes transmitted

The C-factors are weights. C_p and C_{cpu} give the I/O and CPU weights respectively, as above. C_{pm} is the cost per message weight and C_{mb} is the cost per message byte.

Shipping cost

This gives the message cost for single relation access and is a component of JOIN costs.

$$S_c(R,L_r) = \text{Number of messages} \times C_{pm} + \text{size of relation} \times C_{mb}$$
$$= \text{CEIL}\ (R/\text{FLOOR}\ (L_{max}/L_r)) \times C_{pm} + R \times L_r \times C_{mb}$$

where L_{max} is maximum message length
L_r is the average record size
R is the cardinality of the single relation.

JOIN costs

Here we present the R* formula for NL for single site joins which is a component of total costs.

$$J_{css}(\text{R*}) = R_o \times (R_{io}) \times C_{cpu} + P_{io} \times C_p + O_{css}$$

where R_o is the cardinality of the outer relation
R_{io} is the average number of matching tuples in the inner relation
P_{io} is the average number of inner relation pages fetched for each outer relation tuple
O_{css} is the single site cost of accessing the outer table

$$J_c(\text{R*}) = J_{css}\ (\text{R*}) + R_o * [S_c(1,L_{ok}) + S_c\ (R_{io},L_i)]$$

where $S_c(1,L_{ok})$ is the cost of sending 1 record of length = (outer key length),
$S_c(R_{io},L_i)$ is the cost of sending R_{io} records of length. = (inner record length).

5.6 Some specific issues for modern query optimization

If a survey were made of the query optimization methods proposed in the literature in recent years, it would be found that there are many issues that have been addressed by researchers in query optimization. Idiosyncrasies which can be encountered include support of only relational views of the data, or prohibiting replication across sites, or broadcasting queries to all sites participating in the DDB. However, while these are clearly important questions in particular database applications, there is a set of issues which really helps to categorize the modern algorithms.

5.6.1 Is a static or a dynamic algorithm used?

This choice is clearly expressed by Nguyen and others. Static decomposition algorithms completely determine the processing of partial results before query execution.

The alternative approach, dynamic decomposition, is where not all the information for query execution is needed to start the execution but becomes available during the course of the evaluation. The dynamic approach is more appropriate for some of the modern classes of database systems, such as deductive database systems.

For static decomposition, actual result sizes are not available at optimization time and so estimation techniques are needed (see below). Errors in estimation are clearly propagated through the query tree. Dynamic decomposition frequently uses exact temporary file sizes and therefore seems to have an advantage.

Bodorik *et al.* have presented a method of query execution which aims to help correct inaccurate JOIN estimates at an intermediate stage of execution. As a query is executing, alternative strategies are evaluated using a sampling technique. The estimates are based on actual figures from a partially completed JOIN. If the new estimate is greater than the old one and one of the alternative strategies will reduce delay, then the new strategy is adopted forthwith.

Epstein has produced results backing up the conjecture that dynamic optimization would have a performance advantage, but the difference only averaged about 10% for his scenario, although there were some more significant differences. However, this modest overall average indicates that dynamic decomposition is only preferable if it comes very cheap, which is unlikely. This is because dynamic strategies need additional transmissions between sites to disseminate information on the actual sizes of the temporary relations and on the completion of subqueries.

5.6.2 Are independence and uniformity assumptions made?

If attributes in the relation(s) contributing to a JOIN or other operation are assumed to be independent and their values are assumed to be uniformly distributed, serious misestimation can result. Formulae making these assumptions are given by Chan and Naimir in a paper referenced below. The key papers on this subject were written by Christodoulakis. He showed that such assumptions often only provide upper bounds on the expected evaluation cost. He concludes that making these assumptions may result in poor strategies such as scanning or sorting being chosen more often than necessary.

Some early estimating techniques for intermediate relation sizes were extremely crude. For example, Wong and Youssefi used 'worst case' estimation. So the size of a JOIN result would be taken as the product of the cardinality of the contributing relations. Other researchers such as Selinger *et al.* suggest dividing this by, say, ten rather arbitrarily!

Epstein compared some of these estimation techniques and concluded that (worst case/2) and (worst case/10) were substantially superior, at least for exhaustive search, to (worst case). However such an arbitrary choice of divisor, while being simple to implement, is likely to be pessimistic in many cases and so is unacceptable for commercial systems.

A lot of work has still to be done on this issue. One promising technique referenced below is to use a 'piecewise uniform distribution' technique for characterizing attribute value distributions in a convenient and faithful way. Results obtained to date with this technique have been encouraging.

5.6.3 What JOIN method is used?

This issue was introduced in Section 5.5 and is very important since this is the costliest of the relational operations. An interesting additional method is that of BLOOM-JOINs. This method is based on a technique introduced by Bloom called Bloom filtering, and is really a bit-hashed SEMI-JOIN method. A Bloom filter is a large vector of bits which is initially zeroized. The outer relation's JOIN column is scanned and the value is hashed to a bit in this vector which is then set to 1. The completed bit vector is sent to the inner relation's site, where its JOIN column values are hashed. If there is a 1 in the bit vector, the corresponding tuple is sent to the first site, and the set of tuples arriving there is JOINed to the outer relation. The fact that the bit table is all that is shipped between sites makes this an efficient method as compared with conventional JOIN. In addition, at the inner site only a scan was needed to reduce the table and not another JOIN, as would be the case for SEMI-JOINs. Mackert and Lohmann showed that BLOOM-JOINs performed exceedingly well: over twice as fast as SEMI-JOIN for LANs for a variety of cardinalities of the relations, and even better for long haul networks.

Chen and Yu have explored the possibility of using JOINs as reducers in the same way as SEMI-JOINs (see Section 5.5). They show how the problem of determining a JOIN sequence can be mapped into the problem of finding sets of partitions of a graph, and they use this fact to obtain an efficient sequence of reductions by JOINing.

5.6.4 Is account taken of the effects of other system modules on optimization?

Conventional query optimizers tend to work independently of certain other system components which can in practice have a significant impact on the validity of the results of optimization. One example of this is seen in the interdependence between the buffer management module of a database system and the query optimizer. It has been pointed out by Cornell and Yu, for example, that query plans for a given query are affected to differing degrees by the sizes of available buffers. A plan which optimizes for one buffer size might not be the best choice when the size is changed. The reason for this is that the response time depends on the plan and the buffer allocation, but the buffer requirement depends also on the response time. A two-phase approach can be used to solve this problem for JOIN queries. The dependency is cycled by assuming a first-fix response time in the first phase in order to get the response time for the second phase using a queueing network model of the system. The new response times are used iteratively to improve the solution.

Other approaches to interfacing the query optimizer with the buffer manager are to use optimization results to help in buffer management, and to link information from these modules with index selection and data placement functions in a physical database design aid.

While most of the discussion by researchers studying these issues applies to centralized database systems, clearly they must also be considered in distributed systems.

5.6.5 Is simultaneous query traffic taken into account?

This is a neglected topic in the major prototypes which have appeared to date, but a little thought shows how important an issue it is. An early contribution on common expression analysis was presented by Finkelstein. A useful explanation of ways of exploiting global information on simultaneous queries is given by Kim, and Jarke, and a decisive approach to this specific issue was made by Satoh *et al*. They use 'global optimization' for multiple transactions and cluster and schedule commands by estimating the level of overlap between their results. This estimation is made by grouping transactions which reference the same relations and ordering the groups by time of entry of their transactions into the system, transaction class (read, write, etc.), and the number of relations referenced. A transaction-cluster analyser analyses these clusters one by one to determine transaction interrelationships and estimate result sizes. Using these results, a transaction execution scheduler determines an execution order for the transactions within clusters using three similar criteria as for clusters (the number of common relations accessed, transaction class and relations referenced). Similar processing is then carried out for commands within transactions to get command clusters, their execution orders and the ordering of commands within the clusters.

5.6.6 Is the search for an optimum exhaustive?

Exhaustive search (e.g. as discussed by Yao) involves sifting systematically through all possible query execution plans to find the optimum plan. This is not the normal approach taken because of the 'combinatorial explosion' of the time taken to execute such a search.

This problem is evident when we consider how the possible orders of operations increases as the query complexity increases. When it is also remembered that any site in the DDB network can be chosen for any partial execution, the difficulties with exhaustive searching are clear.

Number of variables	Number of plans examined
1	1
2	1
3	4
4	29
5	336
6	5687

So most algorithms seek to limit the choices considered in the search. For example at each step of the optimization the selection of the next step may be done on the basis of immediate advantage over the other contenders. A result of this is to monotonically increase the values of the objective function, but we may get stuck on a local optimum and hence produce a global choice which is sub-optimal.

5.6.7 Is any semantic query transformation carried out?

In order to help in the selection of 'non-brute-force' query evaluation techniques, various techniques of semantic query evaluation have appeared. This issue was first raised by King and by Hammer and Zdonik as outlined in Section 5.2. This approach uses knowledge of the semantics of the application addressing the database to get an equivalent transformation as defined earlier. The classical query optimization approaches consider only physical and syntactic matters when searching for an optimum.

In early methods, the selection of a new query with the same semantics as the original query but more efficient was based on heuristics concerning the file structures and the system's query processing methods. Such knowledge about the database is readily available from the database administrator. Another kind of information – on the data relationships – can also be provided. Suppose, for example, we know that there is a functional dependency in relation PATIENT: pat-name → GP. If in a particular query execution we need to get PATIENT (Bloggs, GP) and this requires a search of a large table, we can stop after the first occurrence of GP for Bloggs, thereby enhancing the query performance. This was generalized by Grant and Minker to account for more general constraints, such as 'a patient can only be on the lists of up to three doctors at one time'. Here the number of partial solutions is known or bounded above, and this is a case of semantic knowledge.

King used similar rules to eliminate unnecessary relations or to propagate constraints. In his case the rules governed classification of ships by weight range or linked attribute values such as maximum cargo and capacity. They were used to modify queries which were then processed by conventional optimizers.

5.6.8 Is the influence of heterogeneity considered?

Processing of queries in a heterogeneous DDB involves several problems in addition to those found in homogeneous systems:

(1) Data partitioned across several sites might be partially overlapping, and operations performed may vary between sites. For example, a CODASYL site may hold some accounts and a relational site hold the remainder;
(2) Local query processing costs may vary substantially between sites, for example, there are important differences between the level of control local systems allow data requests (e.g. compare relational and CODASYL systems);
(3) The ability to read records from external systems cannot be assumed at all sites (e.g. some DBMSs just do not provide a mechanism for this);
(4) Local operations may not be available to carry out the processing that would be specified by an optimizer for that site (e.g. a JOIN).

In the first case, Multibase solves the problem by allowing identifiers to be exchanged between sites before shipping large volumes of data. For example, to get the intersection in the customer account example, some possible strategies are:

- Ship all data from the two sites to the requestor site for the intersection to be performed;
- Exchange identifiers of customers between sites, and ship only the intersection data to the requestor site;
- Ship identifiers from one site (A) to the other (B), and at the same time ship all A's customer account data to the requestor site, to be intersected later with the relevant data from B (in the light of the identifiers received from A).

There are clear similarities to SEMI-JOIN methods here. The costs of strategies for (globally) processing data stored at heterogeneous sites will depend on the varying local querying costs, and so these will have to be supplied as parameters to the global query optimizer.

Sometimes rules of thumb can be used to circumvent the problem of accessing data from a remote site. If the amount of data that would be used is small, use "query modifications". For example a JOIN of 2 relations, one of which (R) has very small cardinality, can be replaced by a series of single relation queries with parameters representing the tuples from R.

SUMMARY

In this chapter we have explored the techniques that are available for obtaining executions of queries which are as fast or as cheap as possible.

We saw that changing the order of execution of relational operations such as JOINs has a profound effect on the efficiency of evaluation of queries. Moreover we saw that the methods chosen to access data and carry out the operations, notably the algorithms for performing JOINs, have an important impact on efficiency. Both of these factors are of even greater importance when the database is spread over distributed computing facilities.

An interesting feature of the chapter is the survey of some of the open questions facing researchers and developers concerned with query optimization. The variety and complexity of these issues demonstrates the fact that we have really only introduced what is a subject of great importance in present and future database systems.

EXERCISES

5.1 Derive an estimation formula for the size of the result of the JOIN of two relations of cardinalities c_1 and c_2 respectively, making the assumption that the values of the JOIN attributes are uniformly distributed. Assume that the relations have k_1 and k_2 distinct values of the JOIN attribute respectively, and that r of these keys are common to both relations.

5.2 (a) Devise some relational extensions which demonstrate formulae a(i) and b(ii) of Section 5.3.

(b) Illustrate that SELECT is distributive over JOIN provided that the SELECT condition over the JOIN is the intersection of the SELECT conditions over the individual relations.

5.3 Suppose that, for a given query, data from two relations EMP (10^3 tuples) and PROJ (10^2 tuples) at sites about 100 miles apart, must be concatenated (using a JOIN operation), and that there must be some way of screening out unwanted tuples. EMP shows employees' details and there is a tuple for each project they work on. PROJ gives details of the projects.

Table 5.1 Relations at sites 100 miles apart.

EMP (at Headquarters)

Emp-no	Emp-name	Spouse	Salary	Proj-no
1001	Arbuckle	ka	25 000	1
1001	Arbuckle	ka	25 000	9
1001	Arbuckle	ka	25 000	55
1002	Ling	sl	30 000	9
1002	Ling	sl	30 000	49
1003	McErlean	–	15 000	25
1003	McErlean	–	15 000	64
1004	Shao	ls	15 000	49
1016	Cai	–	15 000	16
1024	Young	ly	25 000	1

PROJ (at Branch)

Proj-no	Type	Leader	Status	Location	Phone-no
1	gov	Bell	O	J	253
9	gov	Hull	S	C	496
16	eec	Bell	O	C	253
25	loc	Ling	O	J	512
49	eec	Grimson	S	D	116

The rather redundant relations EMP (employee) and PROJ (project) are as follows:

```
EMP {employer-no, employee-name, spouse, salary,
     project-no. . .}
```

at headquarters

```
PROJ {project-no, type, leader, phone-no, status,
      location. . .}
```

at branch See Table 5.1.

Suppose that the following query, expressed in SQL, is addressed to the 'database' consisting of these two relations

```
SELECT spouse, leader
FROM EMP, PROJ
WHERE salary > 20000 and EMP.project-no =
PROJ.project-no.
```

That is, 'get the husbands or wives and project leaders of people earning more than £20 000'.

The common attribute 'project-no' is the JOIN column here. Suppose that the **join-factor** for this concatenation is ten (i.e. there is an average 'fan-out' of ten projects to each employee) and that 10% of the employees are paid more than 20 000. Show two alternative ways of evaluating the query, based on two alternative ways of transforming it (considering only the ordering of the relational operations and ignoring the final projection needed to get the two target attributes). This treatment therefore ignores the details of implementation which would of course add to the choices available.

5.4 Let A and B be two sites, headquarters and branch respectively, holding relations R_1 and R_2 respectively.
R_1 is EMP as defined in Exercise 5.3
R_2 is PROJ

```
A (Headquarters)
EMP (employee-no, employee-name, spouse, salary, project-no)

B (Branch)
PROJ (project-no, type, leader, phone-no, location, status)

C (Main)
JOIN site
```

Demonstrate the SEMI-JOIN procedure on the following query: 'get the employee and project details for all employees earning > 20 000'.

Suppose that the given selectivities are such that 10% of EMP qualify as before.

Suppose also that the result is required at site MAIN (=C).

5.5 Calculating beneficial SEMI-JOINS. Consider the data base:
EMP (employee-no, employee-name, salary),
PROJ(project-no, type, leader),
ASSIGN (employee-no, project-no, months)

and the query: 'For every employee earning more than 20 000, print the project-number and type for each project on which he/she worked, and the number of months he/she was assigned to it'.
Suppose we have the following extensions of the relations:

PROJ	project-no	type	leader
	1	Govt	Bell
	9	Govt	Hull
	16	EEC	Bell
	25	Local	Ewart
	49	EEC	Grimson

EMP	employee-no	employee-name	salary
	1001	Arbuckle	25 000
	1002	Burke	30 000
	1003	McErlean	15 000

ASSIGN	employee-no	project-no	months
	1001	1	8
	1001	9	4
	1003	25	6
	1004	16	5
	1004	49	5

Of the possible SEMI-JOINS here which are beneficial?

5.6 Using numbers and letters as attribute values and small cardinalities for relations based on the relations of Exercise 5.3, illustrate the reduction in *data traffic* obtained by using SEMI-JOINS for answering the query: 'Get all spouses and salaries of employees earning > 20 000, and the leaders and locations of *government* projects on which they work'.
Discuss the contribution made to the cost–benefit trade-off by the CPU concatenation costs for the JOINs. Does this have any implications for the accuracy of the SDD-1 method described in Section 5.5.1.?

5.7 Apply formula (3) of Section 5.5.1. to the query of Exercise 5.6 and to the database of Exercise 5.4 above, ignoring the effect of SELECTs on salary, and assuming attributes are six characters in length and that PROJ has six attributes, EMP five.

5.8 Can it be shown from the transformations in Figure 5.4 that:

$$\pi_{\text{Spouse, leader}}\ \sigma_{\substack{\text{type = government}\\ \text{salary > 20 000}}}\ (\text{EMP} \bowtie_{\text{project-no}} \text{DEPT}) =$$

$$\pi_{\text{spouse,leader}} \left\{ \left[\left[\pi_{\text{spouse, project-no}}\ \sigma_{\text{salary >20 000}}\ \text{EMP} \right] \bowtie_{\text{project-no}} \left[\pi_{\text{project-no, leader}}\ \sigma_{\text{type = government}}\ \text{PROJ} \right] \right] \right\}$$

Is this a beneficial transformation?

5.9 Discuss the question of efficiency of the query optimization process itself. Clearly if this process takes too long it defeats the whole purpose of the exercise!

5.10 Discuss the issue of static versus dynamic query optimization. Under what circumstances do you think dynamic optimizers would have the edge?

Bibliography

Beeri C., Fagin R., Maier D., Mendelzon A., Ullman J.D. and Yannakakis M. (1981). Properties of acyclic database schemes. In *Proc. 13th ACM Symposium on Theory of Computing*. Milwaukee, WC.

A particular problem dealt with here is that of converting cyclic queries to tree queries.

Bell D.A., Grimson J.B. and Ling D.H.O. (1986). Query optimisation for Multi-Star. *EEC Report 773 D7.1*, University of Ulster, N. Ireland.

Bell D.A., Ling D.H.O. and McClean S. (1989). Pragmatic estimation of join sizes and attribute correlations. In *Proc. 5th IEEE Data Engineering Conf.* Los Angeles.

This paper suggests a simple ten-parameter universal characterization of any distribution at any level of the execution hierarchy (see Section 5.6) which promises to give much superior estimates to those using the uniformity assumption.

Bernstein P.A. and Chiu D.M. (1981). Using semi-joins to solve relational queries. *J. ACM*, **28**(1), 25–40.

A treatment of SEMI-JOINs, as used on the SDD-prototype, is given. Object graphs are introduced.

Bernstein P. and Goodman N. (1981). The power of natural semi-joins, *SIAM J. Computing*, **10**(4), 751–71.

Bernstein P., Goodman N., Wong E., Reeve C.L. and Rothnie J.B. (1981). Query processing for a system of distributed databases. SDD-1. *ACM TODS*, **6**(4), 602–25.

This paper describes the CCA prototype DDB system called SDD-1. The paper gives a useful introduction to SEMI-JOINs.

Bloom B.H. (1970). Space/time trade-offs in hash coding with allowable errors. *Comm. ACM*, **13**(7), 422–26.

Bodorik P., Pyra J. and Riordon J.S. (1990). Correcting execution of distributed queries. In *Proc. 2nd IEEE Int. Symposium on Databases in Parallel and Distributed Systems*, Dublin, Ireland.

Cai F-F., Hull M.E.C. and Bell D.A. (1989). Design of a predictive buffering scheme for an experimental parallel database system. In *Computing and Information* (Janicki R. and Koczkodaj W.W., eds). pp. 291–99. Amsterdam: Elsevier.

Ceri S. (1984). Query optimization in relational database systems. In *Infotech State of the Art Report on "Database Performance"*, **12**(4) (Bell D.A., ed.). pp. 3–20. Oxford: Pergamon Infotech.

This paper gives a very clear overview of the issues of centralized and distributed query optimization, using a pedagogical approach similar to the one taken in this chapter.

Ceri S. and Pelagatti G. (1984). *Distributed Databases: Principles and Systems*. New York: McGraw-Hill.

The authors give a set of seven rules which can be used to define the results of applying relational algebra operations where qualifications may apply on local relations (for example, site 1 only stores tuples with 'Supplier' = 'London', whereas site 2 holds 'Supplier' = 'Edinburgh' tuples). There are also five criteria which can be applied to simplify the execution of queries. These are often simple, such as push SELECTIONs towards the leaves of the operator tree (e.g. distribute a SELECTION over a UNION).

Chan A. and Naimir B. (1982). On estimating cost of accessing records in blocked database organisations. *Computer J.*, **25**(3), 368–74.

Chan and Naimir present a formula for the expected number of pages holding records pertinent to a query. This formula can be approximated easily and accurately for fixed length records.

Christodoulakis S. (1983). Estimating block transfers and join sizes. In *Proc. ACM SIGMOD Conf.*, San Jose, California.

Christodoulakis shows how to obtain and use estimates of the number of pages moved across the 'storage gap' in hierarchical stores for the estimation of the sizes of JOINs (and SEMI-JOINs, where only one relation contributing to the JOIN is presented in the result) when the distribution of records to pages is non-uniform. Iterative formulae are developed for the calculation of the probability distributions of pages containing a given number of records.

Christodoulakis S. (1984). Query optimisation in relational databases using improved approximations of selectivities. In *Pergamon-Infotech State of the Art Report on "Database Performance"*: pp. 21–38. (Bell D.A., ed.).

Christodoulakis argues here that many common assumptions are unrealistic and presents estimates of the number of pages to be transferred across the storage gap for a query by generalizing some results for uniform distribution. He also derives formulae for the calculation of the probability distributions of pages containing a given number of records, which is perhaps less useful in practical systems.

Chen M.-S. and Yu P.S. (1990). Using join operations as reducers in distributed query processing. In *Proc. 2nd IEEE Int. Symposium on Databases in Parallel and Distributed Systems*, Dublin, Ireland.

Cornell D.W. and Yu P.S. (1989). Integration of buffer management and query optimisation in relational database environment. In *Proc. 15th Conf. on VLDB*, Amsterdam, Holland.

Daniels D., Selinger P.G., Haas L. *et al.* (1982). An introduction to distributed query compilation in R*. In *Distributed Databases* (Schneider H.-J., ed.), pp. 291–309. Amsterdam: North-Holland.

An excellent introduction to R*.

Epstein R. and Stonebraker M. (1980) Analysis of distributed database processing strategies. In *Proc. Sixth Int. Conf. on VLDB*, Montreal, Canada.

Finkelstein S. (1982). Common expression analysis in database applications. In *Proc. ACM SIGMOD Conf.*, Orlando, USA.

Goodman N. and Shmueli O. (1982). The tree property is fundamental for query processing (Extended Abstract). In *ACM SIGMOD Conf*, Orlando, USA.

This paper includes some help on converting cyclic queries to tree queries.

Grant J. and Minker J. (1981). Optimisation in deductive and conventional relational database systems. In *Advances in Database Theory* (Gallaire H., Minker J. and Nicolas J.M., eds.), pp. 195–234. New York: Plenum.

Hammer M. and Zdonik S.B. (1980). Knowledge-based query processing. In *Proc. Sixth Int. Conf. on VLDB*.

Hevner A.R. (1982). Methods for data retrieval in distributed systems. In *Proc. Eighth Conf. on VLDB*, Mexico City.

Jarke M. (1985). Common subexpression isolation in multiple query optimisation. In *Query Processing in Distributed Systems* (Kim W., Reiner D. and Batory D., eds.), pp. 191–205. Berlin: Springer-Verlag.

Jarke M. and Koch J. (1984). Query optimisation in database systems, *ACM Computing Surveys*, **16**(2), 111–52.

Transformation by ordering is called 'ameliorization' by Jarke and Koch. They identify two additional methods of transformation. One is 'simplification', which largely corresponds to identifying and capitalizing upon common expressions which appear in sub-queries (see Section 5.6). The other is termed 'standardization'. It is aimed at providing a means of optimizing and evaluating different components of a query separately through transforming the query to 'Prenex normal form' in Relational Calculus.

Kambayshi Y. and Yoshikawa M. (1983). Query processing using dependencies and horizontal decomposition. In *Proc. ACM SIGMOD Conf.*, San Jose, California.

Three procedures to convert a cyclic query into a tree query are analysed:

(1) Relation merging, which simply transforms a cycle into a tree by merging all relations in each cyclic part of the query;

(2) Tuple-wise processing, proposed originally by Wong and Youseffi (1976) is shown to be a special case of attribute addition.

(3) Attribute addition is a fast method. Decompositions are based on functional and multivalued dependencies.

Linear time algorithms for use during this process are presented. A good, more general discussion of several algorithms is presented by Sacco and Yao (see below).

Kiessling W. (1985). On semantic reefs and efficient processing of correlation queries with aggregates. In *Proc. 11th Conf. on VLDB*, Stockholm, Sweden.

Kim W. (1980). A new way to compute the product and join of relations. In *Proc. ACM SIGMOD Conf.*, Santa Monica, California.

This study shows how the number of page pairs to be considered in evaluating a JOIN can be reduced.

Kim W. (1982). On optimising an SQL-like query. *ACM Trans. on Database Systems*, 7(3), 443–96.

King J.J. (1981). QUIST: a system for semantic optimisation in relational databases. In *Proc. 7th Int. Conf. on VLDB*, Cannes, France.

An early semantic query optimizer called QUIST was designed in 1981. Substantial cost reductions are possible for a significant subset of the possible relational queries, namely those consisting of a Boolean combination of simple constraints on attributes, plus a list of attributes where values are desired. QUIST uses available knowledge of database structures and processing methods to select only the most appropriate transformations. Inference guiding heuristics are used to choose among the transformations permitted by the addition to the query of combinations of integrity constraints. These constraints often allow query terms to be pruned away or cycles in graphs to be avoided. See also Section 5.6.

Landers T. and Rosenberg R.L. (1982). An overview of Multibase. In *Distributed Databases* (Schneider H.J., ed.), pp. 153–84. Amsterdam: North-Holland.

Lohmann G.M., Mohan C., Haas L.M. et al. (1985). Query processing in R*. In *Query Processing in Database Systems*. (Kim W., Batory D. and Reiner D., eds), pp. 31–47. Berlin: Springer-Verlag.

Query plans for DDBs have to be chosen from a greater selection of possibilities than in centralized systems. It was found that for one particular case the number of access paths to be considered was four times that for the corresponding centralized system.

Mackert L.F. and Lohmann G.M. (1986). R* optimiser validation and performance evaluation for distributed queries. In *Proc. 12th Conf. on VLDB*, Kyoto, Japan.

Merrett T.H., Kambayshi Y. and Yasuura H. (1981). Scheduling of page-fetches in join operations. In *Proc. 7th Conf. on VLDB*, Cannes, France.

This paper discusses procedures to obtain a minimum cost schedule of JOIN operations in certain circumstances. The discussion is restricted to cases where only two relations are joined and the buffer manager permits a page from each relation to be buffered. More general situations can also be readily understood.

The computational complexity of deciding if a minimal cost solution is established along with some theoretical results on the conditions for such a solution are given. Heuristic procedures are given for obtaining good solutions. Sorting is the only means of improving performance and this work gives the designer of a query subsystem a means of stipulating when such rearrangement is necessary.

A simple procedure is presented to obtain a good schedule of page-fetches for a JOIN. 'Null' edges can be added to graphs having nodes which are pages of tuples from a relation, and edges which show an associativity between the pages. The algorithm for this has a linear time complexity function compared with the exponential order of computational time for the optimal solution, and gives a near optimum solution.

Nguyen G.T. (1981). Decentralised query decomposition for distributed database systems. In *Proc. 2nd Int. Conf. on Distributed Computing Systems*, Paris, France.

Rosenthal A. and Reiner D. (1982). An architecture for query decomposition. In *Proc. ACM SIGMOD Conf.*, Orlando, USA.

The authors have produced an experimental optimizer which incorporates a procedure for generating access plans to solve a wide class of conjunctive queries. It permits complex evaluations using a variety of physical access methods which are categorized according to the operations on them. Two types of (object) graphs are described: a graph of the possible JOINs, and a graph for each JOIN showing the alternative processing strategies. A concept of 'artificial joins' is used to help handle complex systems, and knowledge of strategies unlikely to be selected reduces the number of plans generated.

Rothnie, J.B. and Goodman N. Jr. (1977). A survey of research and development in distributed database management. In *Proc. 3rd Int. Conf. on VLDB*, Tokyo, Japan.

In this paper a good example of the impact of execution strategy on response time is presented. Two relations of sizes 10000 and 1000000 tuples are stored at one site, and a 100000 tuple relation is stored at another site. A simple query, involving the JOIN of all three relations and a SELECTION over the isolated relation and one of the other two, could be evaluated using at least six strategies, which are described. The network and communications details are given. Dramatic variances in responsiveness are demonstrated. For example, moving the isolated relation to the other site and processing everything there takes 16.7 min. Moving the other two relations to it, the execution would need 28 hr. Selecting qualified tuples in the isolated relation and checking for each if there is a matching tuple at the other site takes only 20 s. On the other hand, inverting this procedure by joining and selecting at the two-relation site and posting off individual tuples to be matched at the other site takes about 2.3 days! This is an excellent demonstration of the fact that even apparently plausible strategies can attract a tremendous performance penalty.

Sacco M.G. and Yao S.B. (1982). Query optimisation in distributed databases. In *Advances in Computers*, Vol. 21, (Rubinoff M. and Marshall C.Y., eds.), pp. 225–73. New York: Academic Press.

Satoh K., Tsuchida M., Nakamura F. and Oomachi K. (1985). Local and global query optimisation mechanisms for relational databases. In *Proc. 11th Conf. on VLDB*, Stockholm, Sweden.

Selinger P.G. and Adiba M. (1980). Access path selection in distributed database management systems. In *Proc. 1st Int. Conf. on Databases*, Aberdeen, Scotland.

This is a good introduction to System R.

Selinger P.G., Astrahan M.M., Chamberlain D.D., Lorie R.A. and Price T.G. (1979). Access path selection in a relational database management system. In *Proc. ACM SIGMOD Conf.*, Boston, Massachusetts.

An excellent introduction to System R's query strategies and decision procedures.

Stewart P.S., Bell D.A. and McErlean F. (1988). Some aspects of a physical database design and reorganisation tool, PDRT. *Data and Knowledge Engineering J.* **3**, 303–22.

Welty C. and Stemple D.W. (1981). Human factors comparison of query languages. *ACM Trans. on Database Systems*, **6**(4), 626–49.

In this paper the authors define a procedurality metric to determine the degree of procedurality

$$\mathrm{PM} = n_V/n_{V_O} + n_O/n_{O_O}$$

where n_V and n_O are the numbers of variable bindings and operations respectively, and n_{V_O} and n_{O_O} show the degree to which the variable bindings and operations respectively are ordered by the semantics of the language.

Wong E. and Youssefi K. (1976). Decomposition – a strategy for query processing. *ACM Trans. on Database Systems*, **1**(3), 223–41.

The nested iteration method for evaluation of JOINs can be found in this paper.

Yao S.B. (1979). Optimisation of query evaluation algorithms. *ACM Trans. on Database Systems*, **4** (2), 133–52.

In this paper the concept of operator graphs is introduced.

SOLUTIONS TO EXERCISES

5.1

Size is $r \times c_1c_2 \,/\, k_1k_2$

5.3

(a) (1) JOIN EMP AND PROJ at Branch site (i.e. after transmitting full EMP from headquarters) producing a temporary relation R of 10^3 tuples (note that each employee is associated with a number of tuples: one/project)

(2) SELECT THOSE WITH SALARY > 20 000 giving a result of (10% of EMP) = 100 tuples

(b) (1) SELECT FROM EMP TUPLES WITH SALARY > 20 000 at headquarters producing a temporary relation S of 100 tuples (10% of EMP)

(2) JOIN S WITH PROJ, at branch site (i.e. after transmitting S from headquarters) giving the same 100 tuples as in (a)

These figures can be verified by using a simple numerical example with the base 10 in the cardinalities being replaced by base 2; so that, for example EMP has 2^3 tuples and PROJ has 2^2 tuples.

In this example method (b) uses less CPU time than (a) because the JOIN is done between 10^2 and 10^2 relations rather than between 10^3 and 10^2 relations, and the SELECT is done on a 10^3 relation in each case. Fewer I/O operations are needed because the temporary relation S is smaller than the corresponding R.

If we assume that the query arises at the branch site and that the answer is required there, then the data transmission traffic is also smaller for (b): 10^2 tuples are sent from headquarters to branch in method (b) but the figure is 10^3 in method (a), because all EMP tuples are sent to the branch site. The message costs are ignored in this example, to clarify the point.

5.7

For EMP, as given $B(R) = 30$
$C(R) = 10^3$
$C(RA) = 100$ (10 projects/employee, and no SELECT on salary)
= (10 with SELECT on salary)
$C(SA) = 10$
So benefit = 27 000

For PROJ as given $B(R) = 36$
$C(R) = 10^2$
$C(RA) = 40$ (40% are government)
$C(SA) = 100$
So benefit = 0

Estimation is an imperfect science. Heuristics for pruning query trees in general have not yet been developed to the stage where everyone is happy with them.

Concurrency Control

6.1 Introduction

One of the most important characteristics of database management systems is that they should support multiuser access (i.e. several users 'simultaneously' reading and writing to the database). The problems associated with the provision of concurrent access, in particular to those writing to the database, are well known and have been the subject of extensive research both for centralized and distributed databases.

In this chapter, we will first introduce the notion of a **transaction** as the basic unit of work in a DBMS, and explain why control of concurrently executing transactions is required, by looking at the types of problems which can arise in the absence of any attempt at control. The module responsible for concurrency control in a DBMS is known as a **scheduler**, since its job is to schedule transactions correctly to avoid interference. Communication between application programs and the scheduler is via the **transaction manager**, which coordinates database operations on behalf of applications. The theory of **serializability** as the most common means of proving the correctness of these schedulers is then discussed. Having therefore established the background necessary to an understanding of concurrency control, the three principal methods of control, namely **locking, timestamping** and **optimistic methods**, are examined. The particular difficulties associated with replicated databases and multidatabases are discussed. Finally, some novel concurrency control methods are introduced, which are based on exploiting the semantics of transactions, and the chapter concludes with a brief description of some attempts to relax the strict serializability rule.

6.2 Transactions

6.2.1 Basic transaction concepts

Of fundamental importance to concurrency control is the notion of a *transaction*. A transaction is defined as a series of actions, carried out by a single user/application program, which must be treated as an indivisible unit. The transfer of funds from one account to another is an example of a transaction; either the entire operation is carried out (for example, one account is debited with an amount and the other account is credited with the same amount), or none of the operation is carried out.

Transactions transform the database from one consistent state to another consistent state, although consistency may be violated during transaction execution. In the funds transfer example, the database is in an inconsistent state during the period between the debiting of one account and the crediting of the second account. If a failure were to occur during this time, then the database could be inconsistent. It is the task of the **recovery manager** (see Chapter 7) of the DBMS to ensure that all transactions active at the time of failure are **rolled back**, or **undone**. The effect of the rollback operation is to restore the database to the state it was in prior to the start of the transaction and hence a consistent state. The four basic, or so-called **A.C.I.D.** properties of a transaction are:

(1) **atomicity** – the 'all or nothing' property; a transaction is an indivisible unit,

(2) **consistency** – transactions transform the DB from one consistent state to another consistent state,

(3) **independence** – transactions execute independently of one another (i.e. partial effects of incomplete transactions are not visible to other transactions),

(4) **durability** (also called **persistence**) – the effects of a successfully completed (committed) transaction are permanently recorded in the DB and cannot be undone.

The execution of an application program in a database environment can be viewed as a series of atomic transactions with non-database processing taking place in between as shown in Figure 6.1. It is the role of the transaction manager to oversee the execution of transactions and to coordinate database requests on behalf of the transaction. The scheduler, on the other hand, implements a particular strategy for transaction execution. The objective of the scheduler is to maximize concurrency without allowing concurrently executing transactions to interfere with one another and so compromise the integrity or consistency of the database. The transaction manager and scheduler are clearly very closely related and how a transaction manager responds to a database request from an application will depend on the scheduler being used.

Transactions issued by concurrent users/application programs can be interleaved in two ways: either they can execute end-to-end, in which case only one transaction can be active at a time, as shown in Figure 6.2(a), or they can execute concurrently, as shown in Figure 6.2(b).

The start of a transaction is signalled by a **begin transaction** command either explicitly by the user/application program or implicitly. The end of a transaction is signalled by either a **commit** command to the DBMS, indicating the successful completion of the transaction, or an **abort** command, indicating unsuccessful termination. Example 6.1 illustrates a fund transfer transaction T_1, in which £100 is transferred from account x to account y.

Balance$_x$ and balance$_y$ denote the values of the balance fields in accounts x and y respectively. If there are insufficient funds in account x, then the transaction is aborted and the user notified. The effect of aborting the transaction is to rollback the transaction and undo any updates which the transaction has made to the database. In this example, no changes will have been made to the DB before the transaction aborted, as the abort command would be executed *before* the first write to the DB.

Abnormal termination, signalled by the **abort transaction** command, can be brought about by the transaction itself, as in the example above, or by the DBMS as a result of the execution of the concurrency control algorithm.

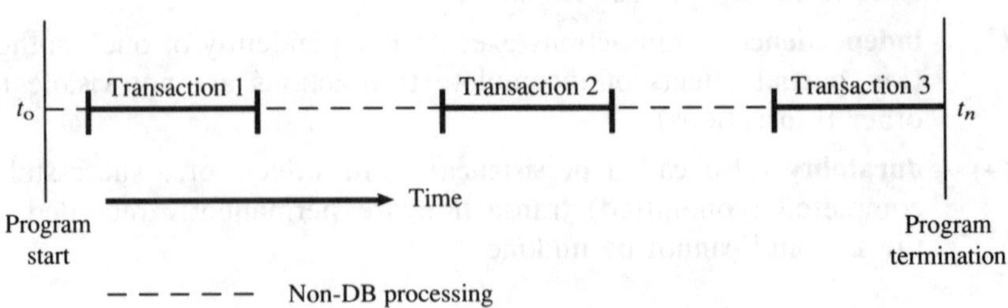

Figure 6.1 Program execution.

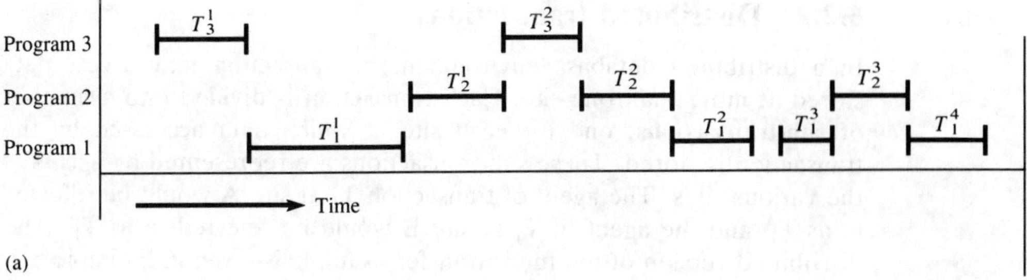

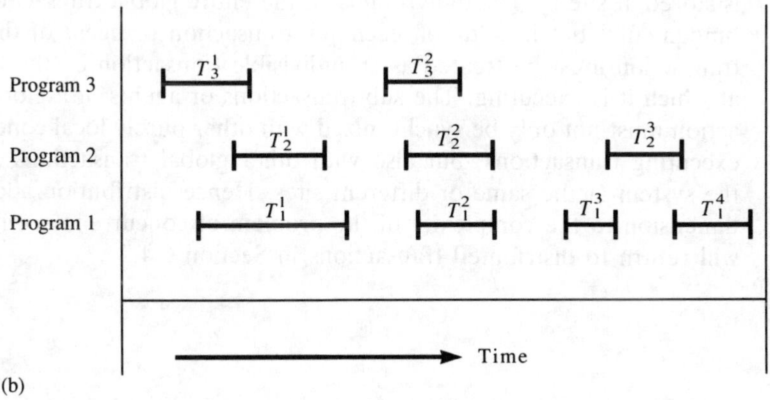

Figure 6.2 (a) End-to-end transaction execution. (b) Concurrently execution transactions.

Example 6.1 Transaction T_1: funds transfer.

```
begin transaction T1
  read balancex
  balancex = balancex - 100
  if balancex <0 then
     begin
        print'insufficient funds'
        abort T1
     end
  write balancex
  read balancey
  balancey = balancey + 100
  write balancey
commit T1
```

6.2.2 Distributed transactions

In a distributed database environment, a transaction may access data stored at more than one site. Each transaction is divided into a number of **sub-transactions**, one for each site at which data acccessed by the transaction is stored. These sub-transactions are represented by **agents** at the various sites. The agent of transaction T_1 at site A would be referred to as T_1^A and the agent of T_1 at site B would be referred to as T_1^B. The distributed version of the funds transfer example is given in Example 6.2, where one account, say x, is stored at site A, while the other account y, is stored at site B. The indivisibility of the entire *global* transaction is still fundamental but in addition each sub-transaction or *agent* of the global transaction must be treated as an indivisible transaction by the local site at which it is executing. The sub-transactions or agents of a global transaction must not only be synchronized with other purely local concurrently executing transactions, but also with other global transactions active in the system at the same or different sites. Hence distribution adds a new dimension to the complexity of the problem of concurrency control. We will return to distributed transactions in Section 6.4.2.

Example 6.2 Distributed version of funds transfer.

```
time begin transaction T1
  |
  |                     begin transaction T1^A
  |                       read balance_x
  |                       balance_x = balance_x - 100
  |                       if balance_x < 0 then
  |                         begin
  |                           print 'insufficientfunds'
  |                           abort T1^A
  |                         end
  |                       end-if
  |                       write balance_x
  |                     commit T1^A
  |
  |                     begin transaction T1^B
  |                       read balance_y
  |                       balance_y = balance_y + 100
  |                       write balance_y
  |                     commit T1^B
  v
     commit T1
```

6.3 Interference between concurrent transactions

There are many ways in which concurrently executing transactions can interfere with one another and so compromise the integrity and consistency of the database. We will look at three different examples of such interference:

(1) Lost update problem
(2) Violation of integrity constraints
(3) Inconsistent retrieval problem.

These problems are relevant to both the centralized and the distributed case, although for simplicity, we will discuss them in terms of *centralized* DBMSs.

6.3.1 The lost update problem

An apparently successfully completed update operation by one user can be overridden by another user. This is known as the *lost update problem* and an example is given in Example 6.3, in which transaction T_1 of Example 6.1 is executing concurrently in a centralized DBMS with transaction T_2, which is lodging £100 to account x.

Suppose that at the start of the two transactions T_1 and T_2, the balance of account x is £100. The increase of the balance to £200 by T_2will be overwritten by the decrement to £0 by T_1, thereby 'losing' £100.

Example 6.3 The lost update problem.

```
                                Value of balancex
                                     in DB
               T1                     100                     T2
                                       .
time                                   .             begin transaction T2
 |                                     .               read balancex
 |  begin transaction T1               .               balancex=balancex+100
 |    read balancex                   200              write balancex
 |    balancex=balancex-100            .             commit T2
 |    if balancex <0 then              .
 |    begin                            .
 v      print'insufficientfunds'
```

```
  abort T1                              .
end                                     .
write balancex                          0
read balancey
balancey=balancey+100
write balancey
commit T1
```

6.3.2 Violation of integrity constraints

A different type of problem, which results in the violation of the integrity constraints governing the database, can arise when two transactions are allowed to execute concurrently without being synchronized. Consider a hospital database containing two relations:

```
SCHEDULE (surgeon_name, operation, date)
SURGEON (surgeon_name, operation)
```

SCHEDULE specifies which surgeon (surgeon_name) is scheduled to perform a particular operation (operation) on a particular date (date). The SURGEON relation records the qualifications by operation (operation) for each surgeon (surgeon_name). An important integrity constraint for this DB is that surgeons must be qualified to perform the operations for which they are scheduled. The initial state of the DB is as shown in Table 6.1. Suppose there are two transactions, T_3 and T_4, which

Table 6.1 Initial state of operations database.

SCHEDULE

surgeon_name	operation	date
Mary	Tonsilectomy	04.04.91
⋮	⋮	⋮

SURGEON

surgeon_name	operation
Tom	Tonsilectomy
Mary	Tonsilectomy
Mary	Appendectomy
⋮	⋮

are concurrently accessing the DB, as shown in Example 6.4. Transaction T_3 changes the operation scheduled for 04.04.91 from a tonsillectomy to an appendectomy. In order to do this, it must first check that the surgeon scheduled on 04.04.91, namely Mary, is qualified to perform an appendectomy. Meanwhile independently it is discovered that Mary is unavailable on 04.04.91 so a second transaction, T_4, changes the surgeon assigned to 04.04.91 to Tom, after checking that Tom is qualified to perform the operation *currently* scheduled for 04.04.91, namely a tonsillectomy. The effect of these two transactions is to produce a database state which is inconsistent. Tom is now scheduled to operate on 04.04.91 and perform an appendectomy, which he is not qualified to do, as shown in Table 6.2, with potentially unfortunate results for the patient!

Note that neither transaction is aware of the action of the other transaction as they are updating different data.

Example 6.4 Violation of integrity constraints.

```
T3                                                  T4
begin transaction T3                                begin transaction T4
  read SCHEDULE where date = 04.04.91                 read SCHEDULE where date = 04.04.91
  read SURGEON where                                  read SURGEON where
      SURGEON.surgeon_name=SCHEDULE.surgeon_name          SURGEON.surgeon_name='Tom'
           and SURGEON.operation='appendectomy'       and SURGEON.operation=SCHEDULE.operation
  if not found then abort T3 (see note 1 below)
                                                    if not found then abort T4 (see note 2 below)
  SCHEDULE.operation='appendectomy'
                                                      SCHEDULE.surgeon_name='Tom'
commit T3                                           commit T4
```

1 indicates switch of operations not possible because surgeon scheduled on 04.04.91 is not qualified to perform new operation

2 indicates switch of surgeons not possible because new surgeon (Tom) is not qualified to perform operation scheduled

6.3.3. The inconsistent retrieval problem

Most of the concurrency control work concentrates on transactions which are updating the database since their interference can corrupt the database. However, transactions which are only reading the database can obtain inaccurate results if they are allowed to read partial results of incomplete transactions which are simultaneously updating the database. This is sometimes referred to as a **dirty read** or **unrepeatable read**. For example, a transaction which is summarizing data in a database (e.g.

Table 6.2 Final state of the operations database.

SCHEDULE

surgeon_name	operation	date
Tom	Appendectomy	04.04.91
:	:	:
:	:	:
:	:	:

SURGEON

surgeon_name	operation
Tom	Tonsilectomy
Mary	Tonsilectomy
Mary	Appendectomy
:	:
:	:
:	:

totalling credits or debits in a financial database) is going to obtain inaccurate results if, while it is executing, other transactions are updating the database. This is illustrated in Example 6.5, in which a summary transaction, T_5, is executing concurrently with transaction T_1. The wrong result (£100 too high) has been obtained.

Example 6.5 Incorrect summary problem.

```
time
|        T1                                      T5
|
|                                         begin transaction T5
|                                           sum = 0
|                                           do while not end-of-relation
|                                             read balance_a
|                                             sum = sum+balance_a
|                                             :
| begin transaction T1                        read balance_x
|   read balance_x                            sum = sum+balance_x
|   balance_x = balance_x - 100               :
|   if balance_x <0 then                      :
```

```
    begin                                  :
    print'insufficientfunds'               :
    abort T1                               :
    end                                    :
  write balancex                            :
  read balancey                            :
  balancey = balancey + 100                :
  write balancey                           :
commit T1                                  read balancey
                                           sum=sum+y
                                           :
                                           :
                                           :
                                         commit T5
```

6.4 Schedules and serialization

6.4.1 The centralized case

The principal problems associated with allowing transactions to execute concurrently have been shown above. The objective of the concurrency control algorithm used by the DBMS is to schedule the transactions in such a way as to avoid such interference. Clearly, if the DBMS allowed only one transaction to execute at a time (as in Figure 6.2(a)), then there would be no problem. One transaction would *commit* before the next transaction would be allowed to *begin*. However, the aim is also to maximize the degree of concurrency or parallelism in the system, thereby allowing transactions which can do so safely (i.e. without interfering with one another) to execute in parallel. For example, transactions which access totally disjoint portions of the database can be scheduled safety together. Finding the best way to maximize concurrency of transactions in a database system has been the objective of many research projects in the database community for many years.

A transaction consists of a sequence of reads and writes to the database. The entire sequence of reads and writes by all concurrent transactions in a database taken together is known as a **schedule**. A schedule S is generally written:

$$S = [O^1, O^2, O^3, \ldots O^m]$$

where O^i indicates either a read (R) or write (W) operation executed by a transaction on a data item. Furthermore O^1 precedes O^2, which in turn precedes O^3, and so on. This is generally denoted

$$O^1 < O^2 < O^3 < \ldots < O^m$$

Thus the schedule S for transactions T_1 and T_2 in Example 6.3 would be

$$S = [R_2(balance_x),\ R_1(balance_x),\ W_2(balance_x),\ W_1(balance_x),\ R_1(balance_y),\ W_1(balance_y)]$$

where R_i and W_i denote read and write operations respectively, by transaction T_i.

Note that most concurrency control algorithms assume that transactions read a data item *before* they update it (**constrained write rule**). That is

$$R_i\ (x_j) < W_i\ (x_j).$$

The order of interleaving of operations from different transactions is crucial to maintaining the consistency of the database. For example, if the order of execution of $R_1(balance_x)$ and $W_2(balance_x)$ were reversed, the effect on the database would be quite different. The objective of concurrency control algorithms is to generate schedules which are correct (i.e. leave the database in a consistent state). Of particular relevance in this regard are serial and serializable schedules.

A **serial** schedule is one in which all the reads and writes of each transaction are grouped together so that the transactions are run sequentially one after the other, as in Figure 6.2(a) above. A schedule, S, is said to be **serializable** if all the reads and writes of each transaction *can* be reordered in such a way that when they are grouped together as in a serial schedule the net effect of executing this reorganized schedule is the same as that of the original schedule S. This reorganised schedule is called the **equivalent serial schedule**. A serializable schedule will therefore be equivalent to and have the same effect on the DB as some serial schedule. We will give a more formal definition of serializability later.

Consider the example shown in Example 6.6 below. Chronologically, by start-time, the order of execution of transactions is T_7, then T_8 followed by T_6. T_7 is first (starts at t_1), followed by T_8 (starts at t_2) with T_6 last (starts at t_3). Logically however T_6 precedes T_7 which in turn precedes T_8, since T_6 reads the pre-T_7 value of y, while T_7 sees the pre-T_8 value of x (i.e. $T_6 < T_7 < T_8$) in spite of the fact that chronologically T_8 finishes before T_6 begins! Remember that the serializability of schedules is concerned with a total ordering across *all* transactions active in the system during the time period under consideration so T_6, T_7 and T_8 must be included.

The schedule S_1 for Example 6.6 is

$$S_1 = [R_7(x),\ R_8(x),\ W_8(x),\ R_6(y),\ W_6(y),\ R_7(y),\ W_7(y)]$$

and the equivalent serial schedule, SR_1 is

$$SR_1 = [R_6(y),\ W_6(y),\ R_7(x),\ R_7(y),\ W_7(y),\ R_8(x),\ W_8(x)]$$

Example 6.6 Serializable transactions.

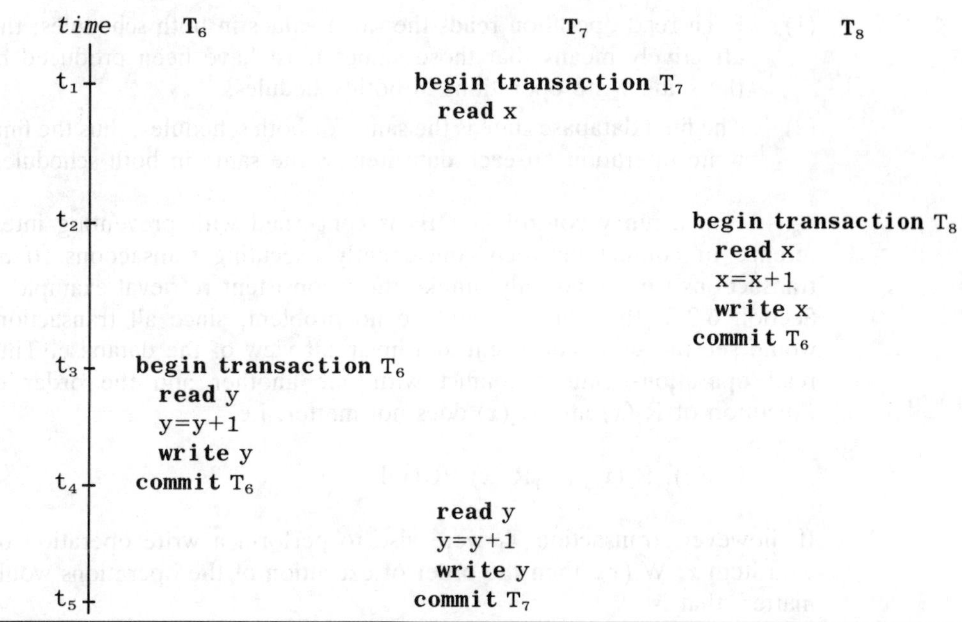

Note that a serializable schedule is *not* the same as a serial schedule. The objective of the concurrency control algorithm is to produce *correct* schedules so that the transactions are scheduled in such a way that they transform the DB from one consistent state to another consistent state and do not interfere with one another. Serializability is taken as proof of correctness. Thus, if a concurrency control algorithm generates serializable schedules, then these schedules are *guaranteed* to be correct. Deciding whether a schedule is equivalent to some serial schedule is difficult. In essence by applying the constrained write rule so that transactions must read a data object before they update it, the algorithm to determine serializability of a given schedule is of polynomial complexity. Without this rule, deciding serializability is an NP-complete problem.

Intuitively, we can say that two schedules, S_3 and S_4 are equivalent if their effect on the DB is the same. Thus each read operation on data item x in both of the schedules sees the same value for x and the final write operation on each data item be the same in both schedules.

Formally, we can state the rules for equivalence of schedules as:

(1) Each read operation reads the same values in both schedules; this effectively means that those values must have been produced by the same write operations in both schedules;

(2) The final database state is the same for both schedules; thus the final write operation on each data item is the same in both schedules.

Concurrency control in DBs is concerned with preventing interference or conflict between concurrently executing transactions. If *all* transactions were read only, unlike the inconsistent retrieval example in Section 6.3.3, then there would be no problem, since all transactions would see the same consistent and invariant view of the database. Thus read operations cannot conflict with one another and the order of execution of $R_1(x)$ and $R_2(x)$ does not matter, i.e.

$$[R_1(x), R_2(x)] \equiv [R_2(x), R_1(x)]$$

If, however, transaction T_1 were also to perform a write operation on data item x, $W_1(x)$, then the order of execution of the operations would matter, that is

$$[R_1(x), W_1(x), R_2(x)]$$

is not the same as

$$[R_1(x), R_2(x), W_1(x)]$$

since in the first case T_2 reads the post-T_1 value of data item x, whereas in the second it sees the pre-T_1 value of x. In general, $R_1(x)$ and $R_2(x)$ do not conflict, whereas $R_1(x)$ and $W_1(x)$ do conflict, as do $W_1(x)$ and $W_2(x)$. In terms of schedule equivalence, it is the ordering of **conflicting** operations which must be the same in both schedules. The conflict between a read and a write operation is called a **read–write conflict**, and a conflict between two write operations a **write–write conflict**.

6.4.2 Distributed serializability

The basic concept of serializability is the same for distributed DBMSs, but with the added complexity imposed by distribution. Consider the very simple example where two global transactions T_1 and T_2 each have two sub-transactions (agents) at sites A and B. Let T_1^A denote the agent of T_1 at A, T_1^B its agent at B, T_2^A the agent of T_2 at A and T_2^B its agent at B. Suppose that both transactions execute serially, but with T_1^A preceding

T_2^A at site A, and T_2^B preceding T_1^B at site B, as shown in Example 6.7. The schedules at site A and B, S^A and S^B are therefore

$$S^A = [R_1(x), W_1(x), R_2(x), W_2(x)] \Rightarrow T_1^A < T_2^A$$

$$S^B = [R_2(y), W_2(y), R_1(y), W_1(y)] \Rightarrow T_2^B < T_1^B$$

Thus, globally, the two transactions are not serializable even though their agents execute serially at each site. It is easy to envisage how such a situation could arise. For example, if the global transactions T_1 and T_2 were launched 'simultaneously' by different users at sites A and B, then the schedulers operating independently at each site could schedule them in this way. Hence, for distributed transactions, we require serializability of all local schedules (both purely local and local agents of global transactions) and global serializability for all global transactions. Effectively, this means that all sub-transactions of global transactions appear in the same order in the equivalent serial schedule at all sites, that is

if $T_i^A < T_j^A$
then $T_i^x < T_j^x$ for all sites K at which T_i and T_j have agents.

$T_1^K < T_2^K < T_3^K < T_4^K < \ldots < T_n^K$ is known as the **local** ordering for site K,
while

$T_1 < T_2 < T_3 < T_4 < \ldots < T_n$ is known as the **global ordering** for all sites.

Example 6.7 Globally unserializable transactions.

time

Site A	Site B
begin transaction T_1^A	**begin transaction** T_2^B
read x	**read** y
write	**write** y
commit T_1^A	**commit** T_2^B
begin transation T_2^A	**begin transaction** T_1^B
read x	**read** y
write x	**write** y
commit T_2^A	**commit** T_1^B

6.4.3 Distributed transaction processing

In a centralized DBMS, there is a single scheduler which is responsible for synchronizing transactions and for ensuring that only serializable and therefore correct schedules are generated. However, in a DDBMS, the

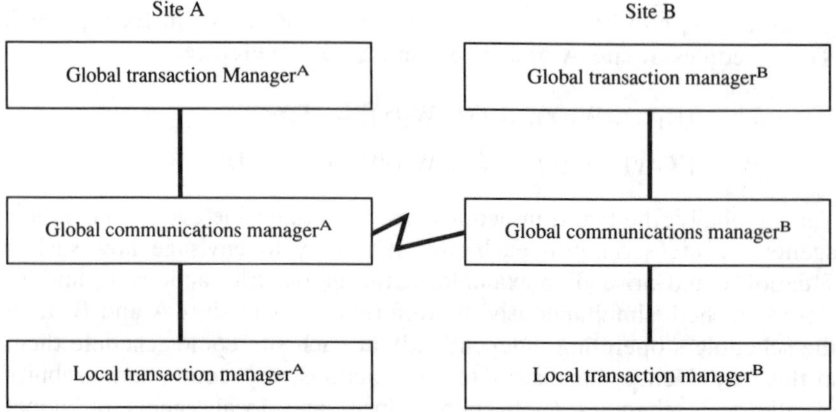

Figure 6.3 Transaction managers in a distributed environment.

schedulers and transaction managers themselves are distributed across the nodes in the network as shown in Figure 6.3. Generally speaking, the global transaction manager at the site where the global transaction is initiated, acts as **coordinator** for the transaction (distributed transaction control). The alternative is to appoint one site as coordinator for *all* global transactions. While the latter approach greatly simplifies many of the problems associated with concurrency control in distributed databases, it is an unrealistic solution since the site would quickly become a bottleneck. In the event of it failing, becoming overloaded or becoming disconnected from the network, no global transactions could be accepted anywhere in the system.

With distributed transaction control, the following sequence of steps is required to process a global transaction:

begin

Step 1: A global transaction is initiated at site A via the global transaction manager (GTM^A)

Step 2: Using information about the location of data (from the catalogue or data dictionary), the GTM^A divides the global transaction into a series of agents at each relevant site

Step 3: The global communications manager (GCM^A) at A sends these agents to the appropriate sites via the communications network

Step 4: Once all agents have completed, the results are communicated back to site A via the GCMs.

end

Note that agents do not normally communicate directly with each other, rather they communicate via the coordinator.

The above represents a somewhat simplified scenario and ignores many issues such as query decomposition and optimization. Each agent of the global transaction is itself an atomic transaction from the point of view of the local transaction manager (LTM) at which it is executing. It will terminate either with a commit or a rollback (abort) operation. However, the entire global transaction itself is also atomic, but it must wait until completion of all its agents before deciding whether to commit or rollback. As far as the global transaction is concerned, each agent represents only a *partial* transaction and hence cannot be made visible to other transactions or agents. Once an agent has completed, it goes into a wait state and sends a message to the coordinating GTM, indicating that it is ready to commit the sub-transaction or, in the case of failure, to rollback. The coordinating GTM analyses all the responses from the agents and then decides whether to abort (rollback) or commit the global transaction and hence all its agents. If the decision is to commit, then the instruction to commit is broadcast to all agent sites, which each perform their own commit processing and notify the requesting site that the commit has been successful. If the GTM decides to abort the global transaction, then abort messages are sent to all agents.

A number of decision strategies can be taken by the GTM. The simplest is **unanimity**: if all agents return a *commit*, then the global transaction is committed. If all agents return an *abort*, then the global transaction is aborted and all agents are rolled back. However, if only one agent returns an *abort* while all other agents return *commit*, the decision is not so straightforward. In this case, the safest and simplest approach is to abort the global transaction and therefore abort all sub-transactions and rollback at all sites. However, in the case of a highly replicated DDB, a **consensus** approach could be taken, whereby if the majority of sites involved 'vote' to commit, then the global transaction is committed and sites which had 'voted' to abort the transaction are notified and take appropriate action. For a fuller discussion of concurrency control issues in replicated databases see Section 6.6.

6.5 Concurrency control techniques

There are three basic concurrency control techniques which allow transactions to execute safely in parallel subject to certain constraints:

(1) Locking methods
(2) Timestamp methods
(3) Optimistic methods.

These methods have been mainly developed for centralized DBMSs and then extended for the distributed case. Both locking and timestamping are essentially **conservative** approaches in that they cause transactions to be delayed in case they may conflict with other transactions at some time in the future. **Optimistic** methods, are based on the premise that conflict is rare and allow transactions to proceed unsynchronized, and only check for conflicts at the end when a transaction commits.

6.5.1 Locking methods

Locking methods are the most widely used approach to handling concurrency control in DBMSs. There are several variations, but all share the same fundamental characteristic, namely that a transaction must claim a **read (shared)** or **write (exclusive) lock** on a data item prior to the execution of the corresponding read or write operation on that data item. Since read operations cannot conflict, it is permissible for more than one transaction to hold read locks simultaneously on the same data item. A write lock, on the other hand, gives a transaction exclusive access to that data item. Thus, as long as the transaction holds the write lock on the data item, no other transactions can read or update that data item. A transaction continues to hold a lock until it explicitly releases it and it is only when the write lock has been released that the effects of the write operation by that transaction will be made visible to other transactions. In summary, therefore, there can be any number of read locks at any one time on any one data item, but the existence of a single write lock on that data item precludes the existence of other simultaneously held write *or* read locks on that data item. In the case of Example 6.5, this would mean that the request by transaction T_1 for a write lock on $balance_x$ would be denied since T_5 already holds a read lock on $balance_x$.

Some systems allow upgrading and downgrading of locks. Thus, if a transaction holds a read lock on a data item, then it can **upgrade** that lock to a write lock, if it is the *only* transaction holding a read lock on that data item. This will effectively allow a transaction to examine the data first and *then* decide whether or not it wishes to update it. Where upgrading is not supported, a transaction must hold write-locks on *all* data items which it may subsequently decide to update at some time during the execution of the transaction, thereby potentially reducing the level of concurrency in the system. Also, if a transaction holds a write-lock on a data item, then it can downgrade that lock to a read lock, once it has finished updating the item. This will potentially allow greater concurrency.

The size or **granularity** of the data item which can be locked in a single operation will have a significant effect on the overall performance of the concurrency control algorithm. Consider a transaction which is simply updating a single tuple of a relation. At the one extreme, the concurrency control algorithm might allow the transaction to lock only that single tuple, while at the other, it might have to lock the entire database. In the first case the **granule size** for locking is a single tuple, while in the second it is the entire database, and would prevent any other transactions from executing until the lock is released; this would clearly be undesirable. On the other hand, if a transaction was updating 90% of the tuples in a relation, then it would be more efficient to allow it to lock the entire relation rather than forcing it to lock each individual tuple separately. Ideally, the DBMS should support mixed granularity with tuple, page and relation level locking. Many systems will automatically upgrade locks from tuple/page to relation if a particular transaction is locking more than a certain percentage of the tuples/pages in the relation.

The most common locking protocol is known as **two-phase locking** (2PL). 2PL is so-called because transactions which obey the 2PL protocol operate in two distinct phases: a **growing** phase during which the transaction acquires locks and a **shrinking** phase during which it releases those locks. The rules for transactions which obey 2PL are

(1) Transactions are well-formed, thus a transaction must acquire a lock on a data object *before* operating on it and all locks held by a transaction must be released when the transaction is finished;
(2) Compatibility rules for locking are observed, thus no conflicting locks are held (write-write and read-write conflicts are forbidden);
(3) Once the transaction has released a lock, no new locks are acquired;
(4) All write locks are released together when the transaction commits.

Condition 4 is necessary to ensure transaction atomicity, otherwise other transactions would be able to 'see' the partial uncommitted results of the transaction, but note that upgrading and downgrading of locks are possible under 2PL, with the restriction that downgrading is only permitted during the shrinking phase.

The fundamental goal of a scheduler is to produce correct schedules by allowing transaction operations to be interleaved in such a way that they do not interfere with one another and do not compromise the integrity of the DB. Serializability is taken as proof of correctness. However, because of the complexity of deciding whether or not a given schedule is serializable and therefore correct, it is preferable to design schedulers in such a way as to *guarantee* that they will only produce serializable schedules. A formal proof of the serializability of schedules produced by transactions which obey 2PL is to be found in Bernstein *et al*. (1986), to which the interested reader is referred.

The main problem with 2PL in a *distributed* environment, is the enormous message overhead incurred. Consider, for example, a global transaction which spawns agents at *n* sites. The successful execution of this transaction would require a minimum of 4*n* **messages**:

- n begin transaction messages from coordinator to agents,
- n (ready to) commit sub-transaction messages to the coordinator,
- n global commit transaction messages to agents,
- n local (sub-transaction) commit successful messages to the coordinator.

In fact, there are likely to be more than $4n$ messages exchanged because most messages normally require an acknowledgement of receipt to be sent from the receiver to the sender, effectively doubling the number of messages. If there are a lot of distributed transactions involving multiple sites, then this message overhead is likely to be unacceptable. Fortunately, however, an important objective for using distributed database technology in the first place is to store the data at the site where it is most frequently used. In other words, most of the updates will involve purely local data, making distributed 2PL a realistic proposition. Also all n messages in each of the four 'rounds' can generally be sent in parallel. Thus the distribution of data between sites is an important consideration.

It is necessary at this point to consider the impact of data replication across the DDB on 2PL concurrency control algorithms. If a data item is updated, then it is desirable that all copies of that data item be updated 'simultaneously'. Thus the update of a replicated data item becomes a global transaction whose purpose is to propagate an update to all sites which contain replicas of the item. In the case of locking protocols such as 2PL, each LTM must acquire a write lock on the copy of the data item stored at its site. A simpler and more efficient approach is to designate one copy as the **primary copy** for each replicated data item. All other replicas are referred to as **slave copies**. Thus it is only necessary to write-lock the master copy when the data item has to be updated. Once the master copy has been altered, the update can then be propagated to the slave copies. The propagation should be done as soon as possible to prevent transactions reading out-of-date versions. However, it does not have to be carried out as an atomic global transaction. Only the master copy is guaranteed to be up-to-date and consistent. So both transactions which wish to update the item and those which require an up-to-date and consistent copy, will direct their requests to the master copy anyway. See Section 6.6 for a more detailed discussion of concurrency control mechanisms for replicated databases.

6.5.2 Deadlock

A transaction T can be viewed as a sequence of read (R) and write (W) operations, which navigates through the database claiming read or write locks as it progresses. It can be represented by its schedule S_T where

$$S_T = [\mathrm{R}(x_1), \mathrm{R}(x_2), \mathrm{W}(x_1), \mathrm{R}(x_3), \mathrm{W}(x_3), \ldots \mathrm{R}(x_n), \mathrm{W}(x_n)]$$

If it obeys 2PL, then it will hold all write locks until commit. Imagine, however, that a transaction T_1 requests a write-lock on data item x_i, which is currently locked by another transaction, T_2. There are two possibilities:

(1) Place T_1 on a queue for x_i awaiting release of lock by T_2,

(2) Abort and rollback T_1.

In the case of the first option, T_1 retains all the locks it currently holds and just enters a wait state. In the case of the second option, however, T_1 must release all its locks and restart. For a complex transaction, particularly one that is distributed, the overhead of having to restart the entire transaction could be very high, as the rollback at one site will cause cascading rollback of all agents of that transaction at all other sites. A protocol which adopts this approach is referred to as a **deadlock prevention protocol** for reasons which will be clarified in the next paragraph.

Allowing a blocked transaction to retain all its locks while it waits for a lock to be released by another transaction can lead to **deadlock**. Deadlock occurs when one transaction is waiting for a lock to be released by a second transaction, which is in turn waiting for a lock currently held by the first transaction. Where there is a possibility of deadlock, a **deadlock detection protocol** is required, which will be invoked periodically to check if the system is deadlocked. Methods for detecting and resolving deadlock in both centralized and distributed DBMSs are discussed below. If, on the other hand, a transaction releases all its locks on becoming blocked, deadlock cannot occur; such protocols are therefore referred to as deadlock prevention protocols.

It is also possible in lock-based protocols for transactions to be repeatedly rolled back or to be left in a wait state indefinitely, unable to acquire their locks, even though the system is not deadlocked. Such a situation is referred to as **livelock**, since the transaction which is livelocked is blocked, yet all other transactions are 'live' and can continue normal operations. Consider, for example, a 'bed-state' transaction in a hospital which calculates the number of beds occupied at a particular time; this is a similar type of transaction to the summary transaction shown in Example 6.5. At the same time as this 'bed-state' transaction is executing, other transactions are admitting, discharging and transferring patients. The 'bed-state' transaction will therefore require read-locks on all in-patient records in order to get a consistent snapshot of the DB. However, in the presence of these other transactions, it may be very difficult for the 'bed-state' transaction to acquire its full lock-set. We say that the transaction is livelocked. To avoid livelock, most schedulers operate a priority system, whereby the longer a transaction has to wait, the higher its priority.

Deadlock in centralized DBMSs is generally detected by means of **wait-for** graphs. In a wait-for graph, transactions (or their agents in the distributed case) are represented by nodes and blocked requests for locks

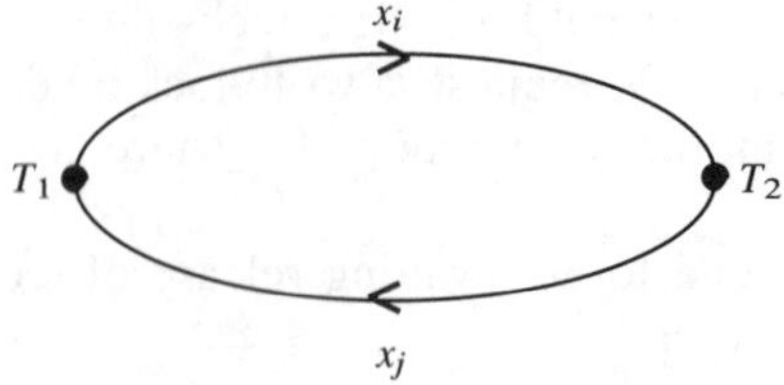

Figure 6.4 Simple deadlock.

are represented by edges. Figure 6.4 shows a wait-for graph in which there is deadlock between two transactions, T_1 and T_2. T_1 is waiting for a lock on data item x_i, which is currently held by transaction T_2, while T_2 is waiting for a lock on data item x_j, which is currently held by transaction T_2. The wait-for graph, G, can be represented diagrammatically as a directed graph as in Figure 6.4 or symbolically as

$$G = T_1 \rightarrow T_2 \rightarrow T_1$$

where $T_1 \rightarrow T_2$ indicates that transaction T_1 is waiting for transaction T_2; the $\rightarrow$ represents the wait-for relationship.

It is possible for deadlock to occur between two transactions indirectly via a chain of intermediate transactions as shown in Figure 6.5, that is

$$G' = T_1 \rightarrow T_2 \rightarrow T_3 \rightarrow T_4 \rightarrow T_5 \rightarrow T_1$$

Using wait-for graphs, detection of deadlock in *centralized* systems is straightforward; if the wait-for graph contains a cycle then there is deadlock. Deadlock must be resolved by pre-empting, that is, aborting or rolling back, one of the transactions; any one will do since this will always break the cycle. Generally speaking, the transaction which made the request which gave rise to the deadlock will be selected.

Deadlock detection in a *distributed* DBMS environment is more complex, since the chain of transactions, or transaction agents, can involve a number of different sites as shown in Figure 6.6.

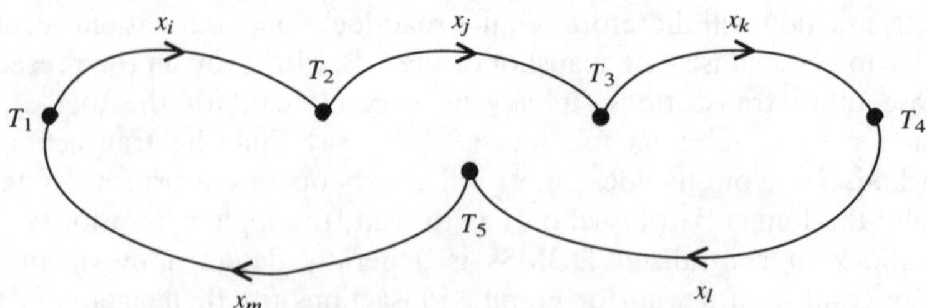

Figure 6.5 Chained deadlock.

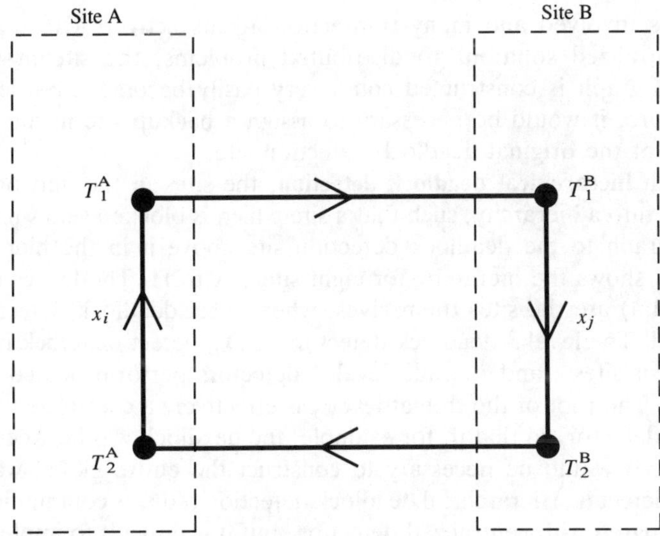

Figure 6.6 Distributed deadlock.

Additional arcs are inserted into the wait-for graph to represent the agent of a transaction waiting for completion of another agent of the same transaction at a different site. Thus, in Figure 6.6, transactions T_1 and T_2 are initiated at sites A and B respectively, where their agents are denoted as T_1^A and T_2^B. Each spawns an agent at another site: T_1 spawns T_1^B at site B, and T_2 spawns T_2^A at site A. In addition, T_2^A requests a lock on data item x_i currently held by T_1^A and the deadlock cycle is completed by T_1^B requesting a lock on data item x_j currently held by T_2^B. Symbolically, this deadlock would be represented by site A

$$G'' = T_1^A \rightarrow T_1^B \rightarrow T_2^B \rightarrow T_2^A \rightarrow T_1^A$$

Global deadlock cannot be detected with only local information using local wait-for graphs.

There are three approaches to detecting global deadlock in a distributed DBMS:

(1) centralized
(2) hierarchical
(3) distributed.

With **centralized deadlock detection**, all the local wait-for graphs are merged at one site, known as the **deadlock detection site**. The global graph is then examined for cycles. The communication overhead of constructing the global wait-for graph is potentially very high if there are many sites involved and many transaction agents active. Also, as with many centralized solutions to distributed problems, the site at which the global graph is constructed could very easily become a bottleneck. Furthermore, it would be necessary to assign a backup site in the event of failure of the original deadlock detection site.

With **hierarchical deadlock detection**, the sites in the network are organized into a hierarchy, such that a site which is blocked sends its local wait-for graph to the deadlock detection site above it in the hierarchy. Figure 6.7 shows the hierarchy for eight sites, A to H. The leaves of the tree (level 4) are the sites themselves, where local deadlock detection is performed. The level 3 deadlock detectors, DD_{ij}, detect deadlock involving pairs of sites i and j, while level 2 detectors perform detection for four sites. The root of the tree at level 1 is effectively a centralized global deadlock detector, so that if, for example, the deadlock was between sites A and G, it would be necessary to construct the entire global wait-for graph to detect it. Hierarchical deadlock detection reduces communication costs compared with centralized detection, but it is difficult to implement, especially in the face of site and communication failures.

There have been various proposals for **distributed deadlock detection** algorithms, which are potentially more robust than the hierarchical or centralized methods, but since no one site contains all the information necessary to detect deadlock, a lot of intersite communication may be required.

One of the most well-known distributed deadlock detection methods was developed by Obermarck, a variation of which was used in System

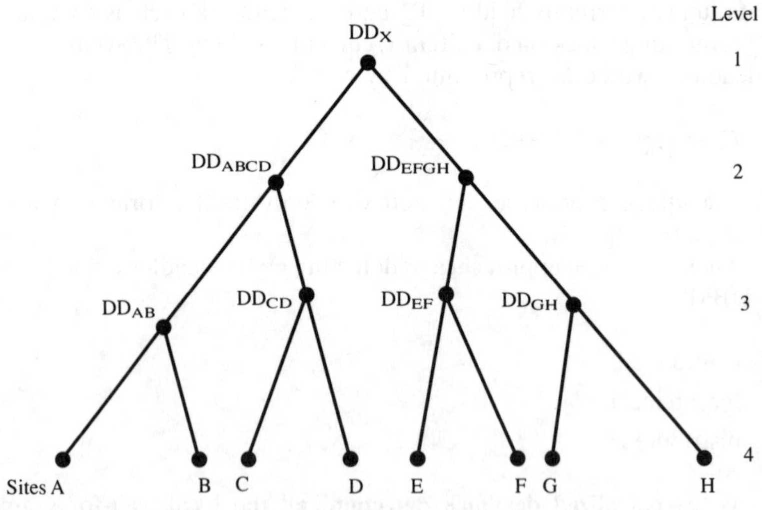

Figure 6.7 Hierarchical deadlock detector.

R*. Obermarck's method highlights one of the difficulties associated with global deadlock detection, namely how to prove that the methods developed are correct; that is, that all actual deadlocks will eventually be detected and that no **false deadlocks** are detected. Obermarck's method detects deadlocks which may include some which are false because it assumes a snapshot of the system's state is captured in the wait-for graph. For example, if transactions are allowed to abort spontaneously, that is, not as a result of concurrency control restrictions, false deadlocks are inevitable. An example of a spontaneous abort is to be found when there are 'insufficient funds' in Example 6.3.

Obermarck's method is as follows. An additional node, labelled EXT, is introduced into each local wait-for graph to indicate an agent at a remote site. Thus, when a transaction spawns an agent at another site, an EXT node is added to the graphs at both sites. The EXT node therefore represents links to and from a site. Thus the global wait-for graph shown in Figure 6.6 would be represented by the pair of wait-for graphs G^A at site A and G^B at site B, shown in Figure 6.8.

Note that the edges in the graph linking agents to EXT are labelled with the site involved. For example, the edge connecting T_1^A and EXT is labelled B, because this edge represents an agent spawned by T_1 at site B.

Both wait-for graphs in Figure 6.8 contain cycles:

$$G^A = EXT^A \rightarrow T_2^A \rightarrow T_1^A \rightarrow EXT^A$$
$$G^B = EXT^B \rightarrow T_1^B \rightarrow T_2^B \rightarrow EXT^B$$

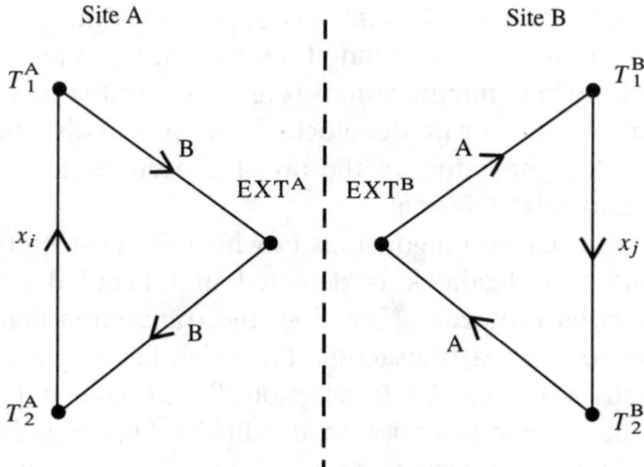

Figure 6.8 Global deadlock detection using nodes to represent external agents (EXT).

This does not necessarily imply that there is global deadlock since the EXT nodes could represent totally disjoint agents, but cycles of this form must appear in the graphs if there is a genuine deadlock. To determine whether or not there is in fact deadlock, it is necessary to merge the two graphs. Hence site A transmits its graph to B (or vice versa). The result, G^{AB}, will be the same as in Figure 6.6 and the cycle indicating actual deadlock will appear:

$$G^{AB} = T_1^A \rightarrow T_1^B \rightarrow T_2^B \rightarrow T_2^A \rightarrow T_1^A$$

In the general case, where a cycle involving the EXT node at site X appears in the wait-for graph, the wait-for graph for site X should be sent to site Y, for which X is waiting, where the two wait-for graphs are combined. If no cycle is detected then the process is continued with successive augmentation at each site of the wait-for graph. The process stops if either a cycle appears, in which case one transaction is rolled back and restarted together with all its agents, or the entire global wait-for graph is constructed and no cycle has been detected. In this case there is no deadlock in the system.

Even with the use of the external agent, represented by the addition of the EXT nodes to the local wait-for graphs, deadlock detection in a distributed system is still potentially a very costly exercise. It is difficult to decide at what point it is necessary to check for deadlock. It would be far too expensive to take the approach of centralized systems which generally test for deadlock every time a transaction has a lock request refused. It would probably also not be worthwhile checking for deadlock every time a cycle involving the external agent node appears in a local wait-for graph unless it is known that there is a lot of contention in the distributed system and that deadlock is likely to be present. One possible option is to use a time-out mechanism whereby deadlock detection is initiated only after the local node has apparently 'hung' for a certain period of time. However, distributed systems are prone to all sorts of delays, particularly in communications (e.g. heavy traffic on the network), which have nothing to do with deadlock. Time-outs in distributed systems are not as useful as indicators of the possible occurrence of deadlock as they are in a centralized system.

Concurrency control algorithms in which the possibility, as distinct from the reality, of deadlock is detected and avoided are known as **deadlock prevention protocols**. How does the transaction manager decide whether or not to allow a transaction T_1, which has requested a lock on data item x_i currently held by transaction T_2, to wait and to *guarantee* that this waiting *cannot* give rise to deadlock? One possible way is to order the data by forcing locks to be acquired in a certain data-dependent order. However, such an ordering would be virtually impossible to define, since users access the DB through non-disjoint user views which can be defined across any subset of the DB. A more realistic approach therefore is to impose an ordering on the transactions and ensure that all conflicting operations are executed in sequence according to this order. Deadlock is thus prevented by only allowing blocked transactions to wait under certain circumstances which will maintain this ordering.

The ordering mechanism is generally based on **timestamps**. The problems associated with defining unique timestamps in distributed systems will be discussed in Section 6.5.3. By assigning a unique timestamp to each transaction when it is launched, we can ensure that *either* older transactions wait for younger ones **(Wait-die)** *or* vice versa **(Wound-wait)**, as proposed by Rosenkrantz *et al.* Algorithm 6.1 is the algorithm for wait-die, while Algorithm 6.2 is the algorithm for wound-wait.

Note that if a transaction is rolled back, it retains its original timestamp, otherwise it could be repeatedly rolled back. Effectively, the timestamp mechanism supports a priority system by which older transactions have a higher priority than younger ones or vice versa. Note that the first part of the name of these protocols, wait- and wound-, describes what happens when T_1 is older than T_2, while the second part (die and wait) describes what happens if it is not. Wait-die and wound-wait use locks as the primary concurrency control mechanism and are therefore classified as **lock-based** rather than timestamp (see Section 6.5.3

Algorithm 6.1 Wait-die protocol.

```
begin
  T1 requests lock on data item currently held by T2
  if T1 is older than T2 i.e. ts(T1) < ts(T2)
    then T1 waits for T2 to commit or rollback
    else T1 is rolled back
  end-if
end
```

Algorithm 6.2 Wound-wait protocol.

```
begin
  T1 requests lock on data item currently held by T2
  if T1 is older than T2 i.e. ts(T1) < ts(T2)
    then T2 is rolled back
    else T1 waits for T2 to commit or rollback
  end-if
end
```

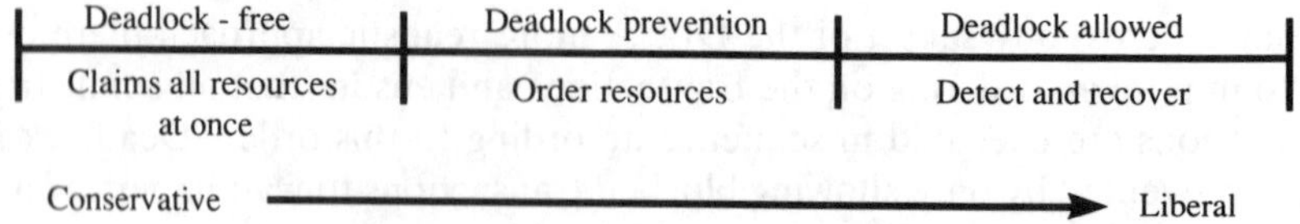

Figure 6.9 The deadlock spectrum.

below) protocols. The timestamps are used in a secondary role simply to order the transactions.

Wait-die and wound-wait are examples of deadlock prevention on the **'deadlock spectrum'**. At the one extreme of this spectrum, we have techniques which are **deadlock-free**, in which deadlocks are avoided altogether and can never occur, while at the other, we have techniques which *detect and recover* from deadlock. In the middle, lie the **deadlock prevention** methods, which essentially order the way in which transactions claim locks, thus preventing deadlock. This spectrum is illustrated in Figure 6.9. Deadlock-free protocols require no run-time support, whereas both deadlock prevention and detect and recover protocols do. Deadlock-free methods effectively require that all resources (data objects) required by a transaction are declared at the start. It is an all-or-nothing approach and there is no waiting. The advantage is that there will be no transaction restarts due to deadlock. The disadvantage is that the method results in reduced concurrency, so it is the preferred approach only in a few specialized cases, where there is a known structure to the transactions such as when all transactions access the data in a predefined order.

Deadlock prevention methods allow transactions to wait, under certain conditions, if the data object they require is locked by another transaction. Wound-wait and wait-die are the best known examples of this protocol. Timeout mechanisms can be used to abort transactions which are livelocked and have been waiting too long, although this could give rise to unnecessary restarts.

Finally, deadlock detection and recovery strategies potentially allow greater concurrency than either of the other two approaches, but at the expense of the overhead involved in actually detecting and recovering from the deadlock.

6.5.3. Timestamp methods

Timestamp methods of concurrency control are quite different from locking methods. No locks are involved and there can therefore be no deadlock. Locking methods generally involve transactions which make conflicting requests wait. With timestamp methods, on the other hand, there is no waiting; transactions involved in conflict are simply rolled back and restarted.

The fundamental goal of timestamping methods is to order transactions globally in such a way that older transactions, transactions with *smaller* timestamps, get priority in the event of conflict. If a transaction attempts to read or write a data item, then the read or write will only be allowed to proceed if the last update on that data item was carried out by an older transaction; otherwise the requesting transaction is restarted and given a new timestamp. Note that new timestamps must be assigned to restarted transactions to prevent them continually having their commit request denied. In the absence of new timestamps, a transaction with an old timestamp (either because it was genuinely long-lived or had been restarted many times) might not be able to commit due to younger transactions having already committed. *Timestamp methods produce serializable schedules, which are equivalent to the serial schedule defined by the timestamps of successfully committed transactions.*

Timestamps are used to order transactions with respect to each other. Each transaction is assigned a unique timestamp when it is launched, so no two transactions can have the same timestamp. In centralized DBMSs, they can be generated by simply using the system clock. Thus the timestamp of a transaction is simply the value of the system clock when the transaction is started. Alternatively, a simple global counter, or sequence number generator, can be used, which operates like a 'take-a-ticket' queueing mechanism. When a transaction is launched, it is assigned the next value from the transaction counter, which is then incremented. To avoid the generation of very large timestamp values the counter can be periodically reset to zero.

We now consider timestamps in a *distributed* environment. In a distributed system, there is no such thing as a central system clock (or a centralized counter), rather each node in the network has its own clock and there is no guarantee that these clocks are synchronized with each other. Moreover, in a centralized environment, two events cannot normally occur at the same time; in particular the transaction manager can only launch one transaction at a time. By contrast, in a distributed system, two (or more) transactions *can* start simultaneously at different sites in the network. Yet by using serializability as a guarantee of correctness of schedules, there must be some mechanism whereby these two 'simultaneous' events can be ordered with respect to one another.

A simple approach to supporting the notion of global time in a distributed system is to define **global time** as the concatenation of the local site clock time with the site identifier, that is

⟨site clock, site identifier⟩

Note that while it is easier to think of clocks in terms of physical system clocks, a global counter is generally used, which we can control. In particular, as we will see, it is sometimes necessary to advance a local clock to ensure that an event at one site occurs after an event at a different site, which would not be possible if we used the system clock! It is standard practice, however, to use the terms **clock** to refer to the global counter itself and **timestamp** to indicate the value of the counter when a particular event occurred.

The following rules are sufficient to ensure ordering of events both with respect to other local events and with respect to events occurring at other sites:

(1) The local site clock is advanced one unit for every event occurring at that site; the events of interest are transaction starts and the sending and receiving of messages;

(2) Intersite messages are timestamped by the sender; when site B receives a message from site A, B advances its local clock to

$$\text{max (message-timestamp, site-clock}^{B}\text{)},$$

where site-clock^{B} is the local clock value at site B.

Rule 1 ensures that if event e_i occurs before event e_j at site A, then

$$\text{ts}\ (e_i) < \text{ts}\ (e_j)$$

where ts (e_i) and ts (e_j) are the values of site-clock^{A} when events e_i and e_j respectively occurred. Rule 2 effectively maintains a degree of synchronization of local clocks between two communicating sites, such that if event e_i at site A is the sending of a message to site B occurring at time t_i, then we can ensure that event e_k, the receipt of the message at site B, occurs at t_k where $t_k > t_i$. If there is no communication between two sites then their clocks will drift apart, but this does not matter since, in the absence of such communication, there is no need for synchronization in the first place.

We must now consider the atomicity of transactions with timestamps. The purpose of the **commit** operation performed by a transaction is to make the updates performed by the transaction permanent and visible to other transactions (i.e. to ensure transaction atomicity and durability).

Transactions which have been committed can never be undone. With lock-based protocols, transaction atomicity is guaranteed by write-locking all records until commit-time and, with 2PL in particular, all locks are released together. With timestamp protocols, however, we do not have the possibility of preventing other transactions from seeing partial updates since there are no locks. Hence a different approach must be adopted which effectively hides the partial updates of transactions. This is done by using **pre-writes (deferred update)**. Updates of uncommitted transactions are not written out to the database, but instead are written to a set of buffers, which are only flushed out to the DB when the transaction commits. This approach has the advantage that when a transaction is aborted and restarted, no physical changes need to be made to the DB. Other methods of deferred updating are discussed further in the context of recovery in Chapter 7 (see Section 7.1.4).

6.5.4 Basic timestamping

To implement basic timestamping for both centralized and distributed DBMSs, the following variables are required:

- For each data item x
  ts (read x) = the timestamp of the transaction which last read data item x
  and
  ts (write x) = the timestamp of the transaction which last updated data item x
- For each transaction T_i
  ts (T_i) = the timestamp assigned to transaction T_i when it is launched

Since timestamping uses a system of pre-writes to ensure transaction atomicity, transactions actually issue pre-writes to buffers rather than writes to the DB. Physical writes to the DB are only performed at commit time. Furthermore, once it has been decided to commit a transaction, the system guarantees to execute the corresponding writes and they cannot be rejected.

Algorithm 6.3 Pre-write operation using basic timestamps.

```
begin
  Ti attempts to pre-write data item x
  if x has been read or written by a younger transaction i.e.
    ts(Ti) < ts(read x) or ts(Ti) < ts(write x)
    then reject Ti and restart Ti
    else accept pre-write: buffer (pre)write together with ts(T1)
  end-if
end
```

Algorithm 6.3 is the algorithm for the pre-write operation under basic timestamping:

It is possible that there could be a number of pre-writes pending in the buffer for any given data item and serializability demands that the corresponding writes take place in timestamp order. Hence when a transaction T_i attempts a write operation on data item x at commit, it must first check that there are no other writes on that data item by another older transaction T_j pending in the buffer. If one such transaction T_j is found, then T_i must wait until T_j has committed or has been restarted. The algorithm for the write operation under basic timestamping is as shown in Algorithm 6.4.

Similarly, in the case of a read operation by transaction T_i on data item x, the system must not only check that the data has *not* been updated by a younger transaction, but also that there are no writes pending in the buffer for that data item by some other older transaction T_j.

If the read operation by T_i were accepted, then ts (read x) would be updated to ts (T_i) and T_j's write operation would be invalid since data item x would have been read by a younger transaction, T_i. Hence, as in the case of the write operation, T_i must wait until T_j commits or is restarted. This is equivalent to applying exclusive locks on the data items between the pre-write and write operations. The algorithm for the read operation under basic timestamping is Algorithm 6.5.

Since all waits consists of younger transactions waiting for older transactions 'deadlock' is not possible.

6.5.5 Conservative timestamping

The main problem with basic timestamping is that the absence of delays due to locking is achieved at the expense of very costly restarts when conflicts are detected. A modification to basic timestamping, known as **conservative timestamping**, substantially reduces the degree of concurrency but eliminates the need for restarts. The basic approach is to make

Algorithm 6.4 Write operation using basic timestamping.

```
begin
  Ti attempts to update (write) data item x
  if there is an update pending on x by an older transaction, Tj
        i.e. for which ts(Tj) < ts(Ti)
    then Ti waits until Tj is committed or restarted
    else Ti commits update and sets ts(write x) = ts(Ti)
  end-if
end
```

Algorithm 6.5 Read operation using basic timestamping.

```
begin
  Ti attempts a read operation on data item x
  if x has been updated by a younger transaction
     i.e. ts(Ti) < write(x)
    then reject read operation and restart Tj
    else if there is an update pending on x by an older transaction,
       Tj i.e. ts(Tj) < ts(Ti)
      then Ti waits for Tj to commit or restart
      else accept read operation and
        set ts(read x) = max (ts(read x), ts(Ti))
    end-if
  end-if
end
```

transactions wait until the system knows it cannot receive a conflicting request from an older transaction. The method is fairly complex, but a description is included here since it is the method on which the concurrency control system of SDD-1 is based.

Each site maintains several pairs of queues, one read queue and one write queue for every site in the network. Each read queue contains requests for read operations on local data from transactions originating at a remote site, while each write queue maintains the same information for update requests. Individual read and update requests are labelled with the timestamp of the transaction which issued them. Furthermore, queues are maintained in increasing timestamp order (i.e. the oldest transaction is always at the head of each queue). The following rules apply:

(1) All sites guarantee to commit transactions at their own site in timestamp order;

(2) Transactions do not spawn agents at remote sites; they simply issue remote reads and writes;

(3) Read and write requests from site *M* to site *N* must arrive in timestamp order; this can be achieved by transactions completing all reads before any writes. So older transactions will issue their reads (writes) before younger transactions; if necessary younger transactions at site *M* will wait until all older reads (writes) have been sent to site *N*.

Note that rule 3 could also be satisfied by enforcing serial execution of transactions at each site, but such an approach could hardly be called a *concurrency* control method!

- Let RQ_A^B denote the read queue at site A of read requests from transactions originating at site B.
- Let UQ_A^B denote the write queue at site A of update requests from transactions originating at site B.
- Let ts (RQ_A^B) denote the timestamp of the read operation at the head of queue RQ_A^B; similarly for ts (UQ_A^B).
- Let r_A^B and u_A^B denote a read and an update request, respectively to site A from site B, with timestamp ts (r_A^B) and ts (u_A^B).

The algorithms for conservative timestamping for the read and write operations are given in Algorithms 6.6 and 6.7.

It is an essential requirement with this method that all queues are non-empty since if one queue, say, UQ_N^M is empty and an update request, u_N^K is received at site N from any other site K, there is no guarantee that site M could not at some time in the future issue a request, u_N^M, such that

$$\text{ts } (u_N^M < \text{ts } (u_N^K))$$

thereby invalidating the update operation.

Conservative timestamping relies on a lot of intersite traffic, otherwise an empty update queue at any site could cause that site to 'hang'. The designers proposed a simple solution to this problem which would involve site M sending site N periodic, timestamped null update requests, in the absence of genuine requests. The purpose of these null requests is to tell site N that site M guarantees not to send site N an update request

Algorithm 6.6 Read operation using conservative timestamping.

```
begin
  Site B issues a read request, r^B_A, for a data item stored at site A
  Insert r^B_A into appropriate place, according to its timestamp
  (ts(r^B_A)), in read queue, RQ^B_A
  Check that all update requests queued at A from all sites i are
  younger than r^B_A otherwise wait

  for all sites i
    do while ts (UQ^i_A) < ts(r^B_A)
      wait
    end-do
  end-for
  perform read r^B_A
end
```

Algorithm 6.7 Write operation using conservative timestamping.

```
begin
  Site B issues a write request, u^B_A, on a data item stored at site A
  Insert u^B_A into appropriate place, according to its timestamp
  ts(u^B_A), in update queue, UQ^B_A
  Check that all update queues at A from all sites i are non-empty

    for all sites i
    do while UQ^i_A = ∅
      wait
    end-do
  end-for
  Execute oldest update (i.e. update at the head of the queue) in UQ^B_A
  (not necessarily equal to u^B_A)
end
```

in the future with a timestamp less than the timestamp on the null request. Alternatively, a site which is currently blocked due to an empty queue could issue a specific request for such a null request.

6.5.6 Optimistic methods

Optimistic methods of concurrency control are based on the premise that conflict is rare and that the best approach is to allow transactions to proceed unimpeded by complex synchronization methods and without any waiting. When a transaction wishes to *commit*, the system then checks for conflicts and in the event of a conflict being detected restarts the transaction. So we optimistically allow transactions to proceed as far as possible. To ensure atomicity of transactions all updates are made to transaction-local copies of the data and are only propagated to the database at commit when no conflicts have been detected. In the event of conflict, the transaction is rolled back and restarted. The overhead involved in restarting a transaction is clearly considerable, since it effectively means redoing the entire transaction. It could only be tolerated if it happened very infrequently, in which case the majority of transactions will be processed without being subjected to any delays. Transactions are executed in three phases:

(1) Read phase: this phase represents the body of the transaction up to commit (no writes to the database during this phase);

(2) Validation: the results (updates) of the transaction are examined for conflicts;

(3) Write phase: if the transaction is validated, then the updates are propagated from the transaction-local copy to the database; if, during the validation phase, conflicts which would result in a loss of integrity are detected, then the transaction is rolled back and restarted.

Low-contention environments or environments where read-only transactions predominate make optimistic concurrency control attractive, since it allows the majority of transactions to proceed unhindered by synchronization overhead. However, none of the major DDB prototypes uses this method. IMS-Fast Path is one of the few centralized systems which uses a form of optimistic concurrency control. Furthermore, studies have shown that unless the level of contention in the system is extremely low, other concurrency control methods outperform optimistic methods by some margin. This is largely due to the enormous overhead (especially for distributed databases) involved in restarting a transaction which has reached commit.

The read and write phases of optimistic concurrency control methods are straightforward, except that the 'writes' during the read phase are internal to the transaction. The write phase involves the standard commit or rollback. The validation phase, however, is unique to this concurrency control method and we now discuss the algorithm proposed by Kung and Robinson for performing this validation.

Using this method, timestamps are assigned only to transactions. Timestamps take the form of an integer transaction number and are issued from a centralized counter, *tnc* (transaction number counter). Thus tn (T_i) represents the transaction number of transaction T_i. Validation for centralized DBMSs involves checking whether the schedule, produced by the transaction being validated is equivalent to a serial schedule *in timestamp order*. Moreover, all other transactions currently undergoing validation together with the schedule of 'all' (it is not in fact necessary to go back to the beginning of time!) other successfully committed transactions must be included.

When a transaction T_j is launched, it is timestamped with the current value of *tnc*; the value of the counter is also noted when the transaction completes its read phase and is therefore ready to validate. These timestamps, denoted stn(T_i) and ftn(T_i) for the start and finish of the read phase of T_i, are only provisional and are only used as part of the validation procedure. The definitive timestamps, which are denoted by tn (T_i), are not assigned to transactions until they have successfully committed, at which time the value of the counter is incremented. This is because, as with timestamp concurrency control methods, the schedule produced by this method is equivalent to the serial schedule produced by *successfully committed* transactions otherwise restarts would be included, which would lead to incorrect serialization. The set of data objects read by a transaction is called the transaction **readset**, while the set of data objects updated by a transaction is referred to as its **writeset**.

Thus to validate transaction T_j with transaction number tn(T_j), and for all transactions T_i where tn(T_i) < tn(T_j) one of the following conditions must hold:

(1) T_i completes its write phase before T_j starts its read phase; this effectively means that T_i has finished before T_j begins (condition 1 of Figure 6.10);

(2) Writeset (T_i) ∩ readset (T_j) = ∅ and T_i completes its write phase before T_j starts its write phase; this means that the set of data objects updated by T_i (writeset (T_i)) cannot affect the set of data objects read by T_j (readset T_j) and that T_i cannot overwrite T_j because it will have finished writing before T_j (condition 2 of Figure 6.10);

(3) Writeset (T_i) ∩ ((readset T_j) ∪ writeset (T_j)) = ∅ and T_i completes its read phase before T_j completes its read phase; this ensures that T_i does not affect either the read or write phase of T_j (condition 3 of Figure 6.10).

When a transaction T_j is ready to validate, having reached the end of its read phase (timestamp = ftn (T_j)), it must check that one of the three conditions listed above holds. Algorithm 6.8 illustrates this validation process for a centralized database.

A version of the this algorithm for use in distributed databases has been proposed by Ceri and Owicki. The transaction counter is global and

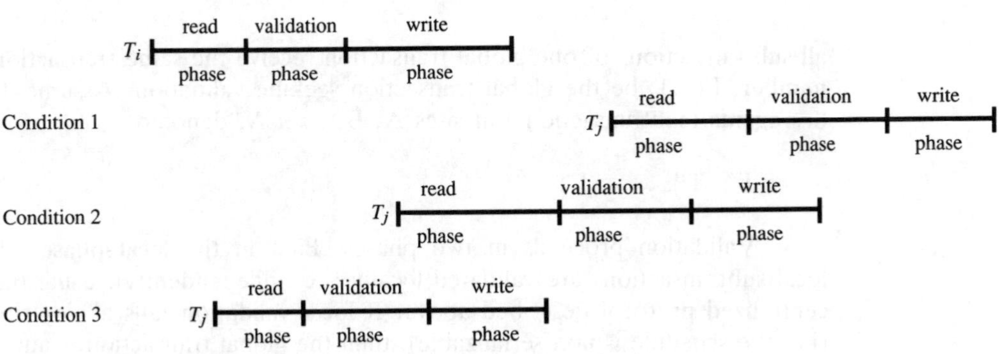

Figure 6.10 Classification of transactions for validation.

Algorithm 6.8 Validation using optimistic concurrency control for centralized DBMS.

```
begin
  Validate transaction Tj (transaction number tn(Tj) against all
  other older, committed transactions Ti)
  for all Ti where tn(Ti) < tn(Tj) do
  begin
    Condition 1: Ti has completed its write phase before Tj starts its
    read phase
    if tn(Ti) < stn(Tj)
      then return success
    end-if

    Condition 2: readset of Tj and writeset of Ti are disjoint, and Ti
    has completed its write phase before Tj starts its write phase
    if writeset (Ti) ∩ readset (Tj) = ∅
       and tn(Ti) < ftn(Tj)
       then return success
    end-if

    Condition 3: writeset of Ti does not intersect with either the
    readset of Tj or the writeset of Tj, and Ti completes its read
    phase before Tj completes its read phase
    if writeset (Ti) ∩ (readset (Tj) ∪ writeset (Tj)) = ∅
      and ftn(Ti) < ftn(Tj)
      then return success
    end-if
    All conditions fail, so validation fails
    return failure
  end-do
  No older transactions; return success
```

all subtransactions of one global transaction receive the same transaction number. Let T_j be the global transaction seeking validation. Assume T_j has agents (subtransactions) at sites A, B, . . ., N, denoted

$$T^A_j, T^B_j, \ldots, T^N_j$$

Validation proceeds in two phases. First in the **local phase**, all local subtransactions are validated locally (i.e. independently), using the centralized protocol described above. If local validation fails at any site (i.e. the schedule is non-serializable), then the global transaction is automatically aborted. If all local schedules are serializable, validation continues into the second phase, the **global phase**. The objective of the global validation phase is to ensure the *same* serialization at all sites. This is easily accomplished by ensuring that all subtransactions of global transactions which *precede* T_j in the global schedule have finished (i.e. completed or aborted). If any of these transactions have not finished, then validation of T_j is suspended until either they are all finished, or T_j times out and is therefore aborted. Timeout is necessary as the waiting could give rise to deadlock. This is shown in Algorithm 6.9.

When the global validation phase has been completed, the write phase can proceed using two-phase commit (see Section 7.4.1) and T_j can be aborted or committed, according to the result of the validation.

6.6 Concurrency in replicated databases

Replication of data within distributed databases is not uncommon for reasons of both performance and fault-tolerance. Performance is improved by storing data at all sites at which it is required rather than having to access it remotely across the network. Fault-tolerance is provided by replicated databases since copies of the data continue to be available to applications in the event of local site failure or network failure. Where a DDBMS supports replication, the system must ensure that all copies of the replicated data items are consistent. This can be done by treating the update of replicated data items as a distributed, atomic transaction, which can be handled by the scheduler in the normal way. Such an approach

Algorithm 6.9 Distributed validation under conservative timestamping.

Begin
Phase 1: All the local sub-transactions of T_j are validated independently as for centralized protocol.
Let the local schedule at site I, S^I be
$T^I_1, T^I_2, \ldots\ldots, T^I_j, \ldots\ldots T^I_m$
Note that this schedule contains local transactions as well as sub-transactions of global transactions. If any S^I is not serializable (validation fails) then global transaction T_j is aborted.

Phase 2: Assuming that all S^I are serializable, global validation of T_j proceeds as follows.
Check that all sub-transactions of global transactions which precede T^I_j, namely $T^I_1, T^I_2, \ldots T^I_{j-1}$ have finished, i.e. committed or aborted, otherwise suspend validation of T^I_j. T_j waits until either these sub-transactions finish, or T_j times out and is therefore aborted.
End

would require all sites at which replicas are stored to be operational and connected to the network. In the event of a network or site failure, it would not be possible to update such replicated data items at all. Clearly, such an approach would run counter to the fault-tolerant aims of replication. Hence, it is common to adopt a **consensus** approach, whereby if the majority of sites vote to accept the update of a replicated data item, then the global scheduler instructs all sites to update (commit). Sites which are inaccessible during the update due to local site or network failure could simply be notified of the update when they rejoin the network (see also Section 6.6.1).

One of the earliest optimistic methods of concurrency control for fully replicated databases was developed by Thomas. As with other optimistic methods for concurrency control, transactions execute in three phases: a **read phase** during which updates are made to local copies of the data only, a **validation phase** during which the proposed update is checked for conflicts at all sites and a **write phase** during which the transaction is committed. Thomas' validation method is based on data item and transaction timestamps for a fully replicated database. Transactions execute in their entirety at one site. Along with every copy of every data item is stored the timestamp of the transaction which last successfully updated that data item. Thus for global consistency the value of the timestamp should be the same for *all* copies of a given data item. In summary, the method proceeds as follows. On entering the validation phase at site S, transaction T_s sends details of its readsets, writesets and corresponding timestamps to all other sites. Each site then validates T_s against its local state and then votes to accept or reject it. If the majority vote 'accept' then T_s commits and all sites are notified. To validate T_s, site *I* checks the timestamps of the readset against the timestamps of the local copies of the corresponding data items. If these are the same, this indicates that if the updates performed by T_s were propagated to site *I*, no inconsistencies would result. If even one timestamp for a single data item is different, then this would indicate that T_s has read inconsistent data. It is also necessary for each site *I* to validate T_s against all other pending (concurrent) transactions at site *I*. If a pending transaction, T^I_j is found to conflict and is *younger* than T_s, then site *I* rejects T_s; if it is *older* then validation for T_s at I is deferred until the conflict request from T^I_j is resolved. This avoids deadlocks by ensuring that younger transactions always wait for older transactions. If the majority of the votes are 'accept', then T_s is accepted and validation succeeds, otherwise it is rejected and validation fails.

6.6.1 Effects of network partitioning

Some particular problems in replicated databases, which have been the subject of research, can arise due to network partitioning (see Chapter

2) following site or communication failure. Data in one partition could be updated by one transaction, while copies of the data in another partition may be subject to a totally different update by another transaction. These two transactions execute totally independently of one another since, due to the partitioning of the network, no communication between the two sites is possible. Hence versions of replicated data can diverge, resulting in consistency problems.

Methods for resolving inconsistencies when partitions are reunited fall into two groups: those which adopt an **optimistic** approach and those which adopt a **pessimistic** approach.

Optimistic methods, as with optimistic concurrency control generally (see Section 6.5.4) are based on the premise that conflicts are rare. Emphasis is placed on data availability at the expense of consistency. In the event of failure, updates are allowed to proceed independently in the various partitions. Very complex strategies are therefore required for detecting and resolving conflicts when the partitions are reunited. These will be discussed under recovery in Section 7.2.4.

Pessimistic methods for supporting update of replicated data during network partitioning adopt a conservative approach. They are based on the premise that data integrity is more important than data availability and that therefore conflict should be expected. Hence they sacrifice a degree of availability for the sake of guaranteeing consistency. They avoid the possibility of conflicts when partitions are reunited by confining updates during partition to a single **distinguished** or **majority** partition. Updates performed in the distinguished partition are simply propagated to other partitions when the network is reunited.

A number of options are available which limit update to a single partition:

(1) Every data item has one copy (at one site) designated as the **primary copy**; all other replicas are **slave copies**. Updates are directed to the primary copy only and then propagated to the slave copies. Also, all reads must first acquire a read lock on the primary copy before reading a slave copy. In the event of network partitioning, only primary copies are available, assuming of course that they are accessible. If the primary site itself fails, it is possible to promote one of the slave copies and designate it as the primary copy. This is generally accomplished using a **voting** strategy (see below), but this requires that the system can distinguish between site and network failures. A new primary copy cannot be elected if the network was partitioned due to communications failure, as the original primary site could still be operational but the system would have no way of knowing this;

(2) Under the **voting** (also called **quorum consensus**) strategy, a transaction is permitted to update a data item only if it has access to and can therefore lock a majority, of the copies of that data item. This majority is known as a **write quorum**. In the event of the transaction obtaining a majority, all copies are updated together as a single unit and the results are then propagated to other sites. A similar system, based on a **read quorum**, operates for reads to prevent transactions reading out-of-date versions of data items. If consistent reads are required, then the read quorum must also represent a majority. Hence it is often the case that the write quorum = read quorum. If, however, applications can tolerate versions of the data which are slightly out of date, then for the sake of higher data availability the read quorum can be reduced;

(3) While the voting strategy provides greater data availability than primary copy in the event of failure, this availability is achieved at the expense, during normal operation, of checking read or write quorums for every read or write operation. The **missing writes** strategy reverses this situation by involving much less overhead during normal operation at the expense of higher overhead when things go wrong. Under the missing writes strategy, transactions operate in one of two modes: normal mode when all copies are available, and failure mode when one or more sites may have failed. Timeouts are used to detect failures so that a transaction in normal mode, which issues a write to a site from which it fails to receive an acknowledgement, switches to failure mode. This switching can be made either dynamically, if possible, or else by rolling back and restarting the transaction in failure mode. During failure mode, the voting strategy outlined above is used.

(4) **Conflict class analysis** can be used as a general concurrency control strategy and is not restricted to replicated databases. It will therefore be discussed separately in Section 6.8.1.

6.7 Concurrency control in multidatabases

The foregoing discussion of methods for concurrency control in DDBs applies mainly to homogeneous distributed databases (see Section 2.4.1) in which the global transaction manager can synchronize all transactions in the system even though it is itself distributed. In a multidatabase, this is no longer the case. Multidatabases, or federated databases, integrate pre-existing, heterogeneous, autonomous databases as shown in Figure

2.15. Thus the concurrency control mechanism in a multidatabase has to be able to synchronize global transactions with purely local, autonomous transactions which are under the control of the local DBMS. Global transactions can be synchronized with respect to each other using any of the techniques already presented in this chapter. However, it is impossible to synchronize these global transactions with local transactions *and* preserve local autonomy. Once the global transaction submits a subtransaction to a local DBMS, it effectively relinquishes control over that transaction. The local DBMS will assume all responsibility and will decide, quite independently of other local agents of the global transaction, whether or not to commit or reject and rollback the transaction. Hence some local agents of a global transaction could commit, whereas other local agents of the same transaction could be aborted and rolled back, thereby destroying the atomicity of the global transaction and compromising the consistency of the distributed database.

The problems associated with the provision of general support for global transactions in the presence of local transactions can be summarized as follows:

(1) Maintaining global transaction atomicity *and* local subtransaction atomicity (see Section 6.2.2);

(2) Local and global serialization (see Section 6.4.1);

(3) Detection/prevention of global deadlock (see Section 6.5.2).

Most existing multidatabase prototypes support retrieval only; all update must be done locally. Even with this severe restriction, the problem of dirty or unrepeatable reads must be addressed (see Section 6.3.3). This means that read-only transactions which require a consistent view of the database (e.g. the summary transaction in Example 6.5) have to take into account that the database could be simultaneously updated by local transactions.

Consistent global update can be supported only if some of the constraints are relaxed, such as:

(1) Reducing the degree of nodal autonomy by introducing a degree of centralized control;

(2) Restricting the type of update that can be performed;

(3) Allowing only one global transaction in the system at a time, introducing centralized control;

(4) By relaxing the strict serializability requirement;

(5) By application-specific methods (see Section 6.8).

The problem of supporting updates in a multidatabase environment is similar in some ways to the problem of supporting updates through views in database systems. The global schema is effectively a relational view built on top of a collection of local relational schemas. However, while in a centralized database it is possible for the system to keep a user's view up-to-date automatically, a multidatabase system has no way of knowing what changes are being made to the local databases by non-global transactions.

It is unlikely that it is possible to develop a method to support *ad hoc* updates to multidatabases which does not represent some sort of compromise. The tradeoff is generally between preserving local autonomy and providing full functionality. Thus in order to support *ad hoc* updates without restriction, it is necessary to relinquish some nodal autonomy; typically this involves the transaction manager of the local database giving the GTM information about its local transaction processing such as in the form of a local wait-for graph. Alternatively, if nodal autonomy must be preserved then restrictions must be placed on the type of global transactions which are allowed (e.g. read-only, single site update, etc.). In fact this is often the only realistic course because the local nodes are managed by proprietary DBMSs whose internal transaction managers and schedulers cannot be altered.

6.7.1 Optimistic method based on global wait-for graph

Elmagarmid and Helal propose an optimistic method using a centralized control strategy. The algorithm is based on the integration of an optimistic concurrency control algorithm (see Section 6.5.6) and a deadlock prevention protocol. A global wait-for graph is constructed at the coordinating node. The nodes in this global wait-for graph, represent *sites* waiting for other *sites* rather than transaction *agents* waiting for other *agents*. Thus if transaction T_1 executing at site A, denoted T_1^A, spawns an agent at site B, denoted T_1^B, then an edge will be drawn in the global wait-for graph connecting node A, representing site A and node B representing site B. This coarser granularity makes the graph much quicker to construct, although because it contains less information the possibility of false deadlocks exists.

Each time a global transaction T is started, a check for cycles is made at the coordinating node in the graph. If a cycle is detected, transaction T's execution is delayed if necessary in order to avoid deadlock.

The following assumptions are made:

(1) No site, communications or transaction failures are accounted for; this simplifies the discussion and focuses attention on the concurrency control issues;

(2) The global DB is fully partitioned (i.e. there is no replicated data); this is probably a realistic assumption for many multidatabases which integrate pre-existing databases;

(3) Global transactions are restricted to those that do not write into the same site as they read from, with the exception of possibly one site; this restriction, which is fairly severe, is necessary because of the possibility of different local serialisations arising from the first and second writes at a site;

(4) A central coordinating node is used for the construction of the global wait-for graph; this node represents a potential bottleneck.

6.7.2 Integration of concurrency control methods

Some work has been done on the problems associated with integration of different concurrency control mechanisms. While the motivation for this work has in the main been the provision of *dynamic* concurrency control, the results are relevant to providing support for update in multidatabases.

Virtually all DBMSs, whether centralized or distributed, adopt a **static** approach to concurrency control: when the DBMS is being designed, a number of factors are taken into consideration and on the basis of this a single concurrency control method is adopted and built in the system. All transactions therefore use the same method. The sort of factors which would be relevant in a DDBMS include:

(1) Transaction arrival rate
(2) Transaction mix (reads versus writes and local versus global)
(3) Communication delays
(4) Size of readsets and writesets
(5) Cost of rollbacks and restarts
(6) Cost of deadlock detection.

The idea behind **dynamic** concurrency control is to allow the system to select, from among the methods available, the most appropriate scheduler for a particular transaction or class of transactions. For example, read-only transactions can be treated in quite a different way from update transactions. When there is little contention in the system, an optimistic method might be preferred to 2PL or timestamping, and so on. In the Oracle DBMS, for example, timestamping (called **multiversioning**) can be used for read-only transactions with conventional 2PL for other transactions. The read-only transactions can access timestamped before-images of data items which are currently locked by other transactions.

However, in order to support dynamic concurrency control, it is necessary to provide a method whereby the various concurrency control techniques can be integrated and synchronized and it is this aspect of the work that is particularly relevant to concurrency control in MDBMSs. In a multidatabase, there is no guarantee that the different local concurrency control mechanisms supported by the local DBMSs are the same; indeed it is highly probable that they are not. It is therefore worth examining the problems associated with integrating different concurrency control mechanisms with a view to converting them into some canonical form. Note that we are ignoring the issue of whether or not it is possible for the local transaction managers to make available information about their states for translation into such a canonical form.

Gligor and Popescu-Zeletin present the constraints for a global concurrency mechanism which is based on the concatenation of the local concurrency control mechanisms. These are summarized as follows:

(1) Local transaction managers must guarantee local atomicity for both purely local transactions and agents of global transactions;
(2) Local transaction managers must guarantee to preserve the order of execution of agents of local transactions determined by the global transaction manager;
(3) Each global transaction may spawn only *one* agent at a given site;
(4) The details of the readsets and writesets of all global transaction agents must be available to the global transaction manager;
(5) The global transaction manager must be able to detect and resolve global deadlocks; this means that local transaction managers must make the local wait-for graph available to the global transaction manager, which also must be able to view the local state.

Effectively, constraints (4) and (5) mean that synchronization information from local sites must be available to the global transaction manager, thereby compromising nodal autonomy.

6.8 Application-specific methods and quasi-serializability

The principal correctness criterion for concurrency control used by the methods discussed in this chapter is serializability. This is because the readsets and writesets of transactions are not known in advance and can only be constructed dynamically during transaction execution. If we knew *in advance* for every transaction exactly what data it would read and write in the database then we could produce an optimal interleaving of transactions in order to maximize the degree of concurrency and at the same time totally avoid conflicts. This idea has been investigated by a number of researchers and methods have been proposed which weaken the serializability criterion and so increase the degree of concurrency. This work exploits the fact that serializable schedules are actually a subset of the total set of correct schedules. Thus it is perfectly possible to have schedules which are unserializable, but which preserve DB consistency (see Exercise 6.8).

Global transactions are essentially hierarchical in nature (a global transaction is divided into many subtransactions) and this fact, taken in conjunction with the full local autonomy requirement, makes it very difficult to generate schedules which are globally serializable. Du and Elmagarmid propose a method based on **quasi-serializability** in which local and global transactions are treated differently. The method requires all global transactions to be submitted serially, while all local transactions execute in the normal way and are serializable. Local autonomy is maintained, but no global integrity constraints and no value dependencies (i.e. referential integrity) between different subtransactions of the same transaction are enforced by the method.

Application-specific methods allow transactions to be interleaved with other transactions subject to certain constraints. Hence rather than having to wait until a transaction has completed, these methods exploit advance knowledge about the transaction to allow other transactions to execute in parallel wherever possible. Transaction failure is handled by providing a **counterstep** for each step of the transaction. Garcia-Molina (1983) proposed a method for distributed databases which partitions transactions into disjoint sets. Transactions in one set are **compatible** and can be safely interleaved. Transactions in different sets are **incompatible** and cannot be interleaved. This approach has been developed further by Farrag and Oszu to support even greater concurrency. Rather than classifying transactions into compatible sets, transactions are themselves divided into a series of atomic steps divided by **breakpoints**. The breakpoints define points at which other transactions can be safely interleaved. The method is based on a new type of schedule called a **relatively consistent** schedule, which is non-serializable, but which guarantees consistency.

Garcia-Molina and Salem (1987) and Alonso *et al.* combine the notion of quasi-serializability with compensating transactions. Each global transaction, called a **saga**, is divided into a series of subtransactions which can execute concurrently without synchronization with other transactions. For example, a doctor might wish to order a series of tests T_1, T_2, T_3, . . . T_n on a patient. Assume that these tests must be carried out in a certain order, perhaps because test T_j depends on the result of test T_{j-1}. Assume furthermore that different sites in the hospital network are responsible for the scheduling and administration of each of the tests. It is perfectly admissible for each subtransaction scheduling a test to execute concurrently with other transactions. If, however, it is not possible to schedule one of the tests, T_i say, within a specified time period, then it is likely that the appointments for tests T_1, T_2, T_3, . . . T_{i-1} will have to be cancelled and rescheduled. This is done not by rolling back the corresponding transaction, but rather by applying a **compensating transaction**. In this example, this would mean executing a transaction which would cancel all the test appointments already made for that patient. The system guarantees 'semantic' atomicity of global transactions. Thus if any subtransaction fails, then any successfully committed subtransaction of that global transaction will be 'undone' by means of a compensating transaction. Of course, this approach presupposes that it is possible to define a compensating transaction for every transaction. Such compensating transactions are easier to define for the type of numerically based transactions in banking systems (funds transfer, debit, credit, etc.) than for non-financial systems. Even in financial systems, it may be difficult, if not impossible, to take into account the cascading effect on other transactions of 'undoing', by compensation, the effects of one transaction.

Because of the difficulties in developing satisfactory methods for concurrency control for MDBMSs, several researchers have investigated methods which are specifically designed for a particular application environment (i.e. they depend on the application context and semantics). A system, based on **S-transactions** (semantic transactions), has been specifically designed for a banking network. For every S-transaction, there is a corresponding compensating transaction, which undoes the effect of the original transaction (Eliassen *et al.*, 1988).

6.8.1 Transaction classes and conflict graph analysis

A simple mechanism for improving concurrency at little cost, is provided by the use of **transaction classes**, which were originally intended to be used in conjunction with conservative timestamping to prevent excessive restarts, but have since been shown to have wider applicability. Readsets and writesets are defined on the basis of transaction classes rather than individual transactions. A transaction T_i is assigned to a particular class, TC, if

$$\text{readset}\ (T_i) \subseteq \text{readset}\ (TC)$$

and

$$\text{writeset}\ (T_i) \subseteq \text{writeset}\ (TC)$$

Two transaction classes, TC_s and TC_t are said to be in conflict if

$$\text{writeset}\ (TC_s) \cap (\text{writeset}\ (TC_t) \cup \text{readset}\ (TC_t)) \neq \emptyset$$

or

$$\text{writeset}\ (TC_t) \cap (\text{writeset}\ (TC_s) \cup \text{readset}\ (TC_s)) \neq \emptyset$$

Transaction classes are generally used in conjunction with conflict graph analysis as this allows the optimum scheduling of transactions from the available information.

The objective of the graph is to identify which transactions need synchronization when executing in parallel with other transactions and which can safely proceed without any synchronization. A conflict graph consists of two sets of nodes: **read nodes** and **write nodes**, labelled R_i and W_i respectively, where R_i represents the readset of TC_i and W_i represents the writeset of TC_i. For convenience, the read node for TC_i is placed vertically above its corresponding write node. Edges are drawn between conflicting read and write sets.

A **vertical edge** $\langle R_i, W_i \rangle$ connects the readset and writeset of transaction class TC_i. Consider, for example, transaction T_1 which makes an appointment for patient P_a to attend an out-patient clinic, executing in parallel with transaction T_2 which is making an out-patient appointment for patient P_b. Both transactions T_1 and T_2 belong to the transaction class *make appointment*. If T_1 and T_2 execute concurrently without synchronization then it would be possible for the appointment made by one transaction to be overwritten by the other transaction (lost update problem, see Section 6.3.1). Hence transactions belonging to the same class clearly conflict, so there is always a vertical edge between every pair of read and write nodes, R_i and W_i.

A **horizontal edge** $\langle W_i, W_j \rangle$ connects two classes TC_i and TC_j whose writesets conflict. For example, transactions belonging to the *admit patient* transaction class would require synchronization with transactions belonging to the *transfer patient* class if the two were executing in parallel. Otherwise two patients could end up sharing the same bed or a bed could be left empty!

Finally, a **diagonal edge** $\langle W_i, R_j \rangle$ connects the two transactions classes when the writeset of W_i conflicts with the readset of R_j. An example of such a read–write conflict would be a '*bed-state*' transaction (see Section 6.5.2) which is counting the number of beds occupied and admit patient transaction class.

Consider the following example, which is illustrated in Figure 6.11. Assume that the readsets R_1 and R_2 and writesets W_1 and W_2 for two transaction classes TC_1 and TC_2 are the set of records (tuples) S, where

$$R_1 = W_1 = R_2 = W_2 = S$$

Furthermore, for a third transaction class, TC_3, let

$$R_3 = S \text{ and } W_3 = \emptyset$$

That is, TC_3 is a read-only transaction. Finally, let

$$R_4 = T \text{ and } W_4 = \emptyset$$

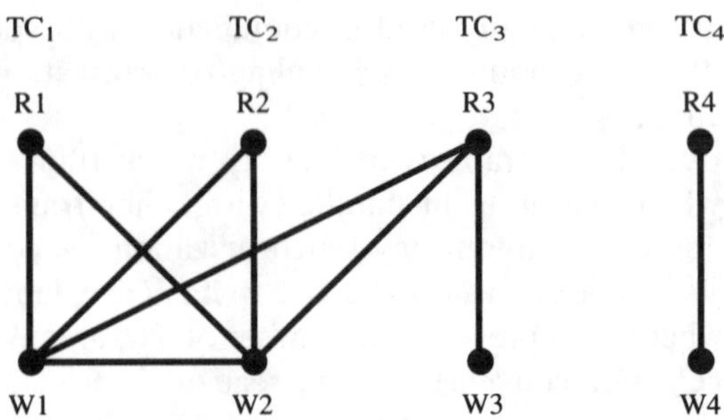

Figure 6.11 Conflict graph.

for transaction class TC_4. Note that

$$S \cap T = \varnothing$$

Two transactions are said to be **in conflict** if they are connected. The degree of synchronization required will depend on whether the two transactions are connected by a horizontal or a diagonal edge or lie on a cycle, such as TC_1 and TC_2 in Figure 6.11 ($\langle W_1, R_2, W_2, W_1 \rangle$). In the case of TC_4, however, no edges appear in the graph connecting it with any of the other transaction classes. This indicates that transactions belonging to TC_4 can be safely scheduled in parallel with transactions belonging to TC_1, TC_2 and TC_3 without synchronization and therefore with no delays or restarts.

Such an approach, when used in conjunction with conventional concurrency control techniques such as locking and timestamping, is very powerful and it is particularly useful in distributed systems, where the concurrency control overhead (the overhead due to locking etc.) can be very high. However, in the same way as the global wait-for graph to detect deadlock has to be constructed at a central site, the construction of the conflict graph would also have to be centralized. In both cases, the potential bottleneck at the chosen site is a major drawback of the method and is likely to make construction of the graph at run-time unrealistic. The solution adopted by SDD-1, which uses conservative timestamping coupled with transaction classes and conflict graph analysis, is to incorporate assignment of transactions to classes as part of the DDB design process. Hence transaction classes are predefined and transactions are assigned to those classes statically. The classes are then analysed and stored in a **protocol table**, which indicates for every pair of transaction classes (TC_i and TC_j) whether they require synchronization and, if so, at what level. The protocol table is stored as part of the system catalogue or data dictionary.

While such an approach might at first seem very inflexible, it is common practice in commercial data processing to optimize systems for so-called heavy-duty computing, for high volume transactions. The key issue therefore is to identify these transactions and optimize their processing and not worry too much about the rest. Under this scheme, transactions which have not been predefined (*ad hoc* updates) are scheduled conservatively in the normal way, whereas non-conflicting predefined transactions can be scheduled without synchronization and hence without being subject to unnecessary delays.

In summary, none of the solutions proposed to date completely solves the problem of supporting unconstrained (*ad hoc*) updates to multidatabases. However, from the results obtained so far it would appear that the adoption of consistency criteria which are weaker than serializability, coupled with exploitation of semantic information about the transactions is likely to prove the most useful (either by compensating transactions or by defining transaction classes). These methods should take into account that multidatabases are different in nature from homogeneous distributed databases. While it is theoretically possible that highly integrated global transactions involving many sites could be found in both systems, it is more likely that a much more limited form of global update will prove to be acceptable.

There are a number of issues yet to be resolved before the techniques discussed in this section can be applied with confidence to real systems. Examples are the handling of deadlock, transaction failure and definition of transaction countersteps. With the increasing focus on adding 'intelligence' to information systems by exploiting techniques for coupling artificial intelligence techniques with database technology, the advent of concurrency control mechanisms based on advanced knowledge of transactions can be expected.

SUMMARY

In this chapter, we have discussed the problems associated with and the solutions to the control of users who are concurrently accessing a DB. These problems are compounded in the DDB environment, where multiple local users accessing their own local DBs only, are combined with global users accessing data stored at different sites across the network.

We began with a review of the background. The transaction is the basic unit of work in a DBMS and has four A.C.I.D. properties, namely atomicity, consistency, independence and durability. In Section 6.3, the three classes of problems, lost updates, integrity constraint violation and incorrect summaries, which can arise when transactions are allowed to proceed without any attempt at synchronization, were discussed. This general background to concurrency control for both centralized and distributed DBs finished with a discussion of schedules and serialization. A schedule is the entire sequence in order of the reads and writes of all

concurrent transactions taken together. Concurrency control algorithms seek to allow the various read and write steps of a transaction to be interleaved with those of other concurrently executing transactions subject to certain constraints. Concurrency control algorithms therefore must produce correct schedules (i.e. schedules in which the read and write operations of a transaction are interleaved correctly, in which case consistency of both the transaction's view of the data and of the DB itself are guaranteed). Correct schedules are generally taken to be those which are serializable and are therefore equivalent and have the same overall effect as running the transactions sequentially one after the other. It is possible to have a correct schedule, which is not in fact serializable, but serializability is normally used as the correctness criterion, because it is better understood and easier to apply. Distributed serializability was discussed in Section 6.4.1.
The three principal methods for concurrency control are discussed in detail in Section 6.5.

- Locking
- Timestamping
- Optimistic methods

Deadlock and the particular problems associated with its detection and resolution in DDBs are covered as part of the section on locking methods (see Section 6.5.2).

The unique difficulties for transaction support and concurrency control posed by replicated DDBs in the face of network and/or site failure and network partitioning are outlined and various voting strategies are introduced which seek to allow the DDBMS to continue to provide the fullest possible service to users.

The majority of the methods for concurrency control discussed in this chapter assume either a homogeneous DDB or a major compromise with regard to nodal autonomy. The provision of full, unrestricted support for *ad hoc* updates in a multidatabase is still an open research issue. All existing approaches require a relaxation of some of the constraints. These include compromising nodal autonomy or relaxation of the strict serializability requirement. In addition, some application-specific proposals are presented which assume advance knowledge of the transactions.

EXERCISES

6.1 What are the four A.C.I.D. properties of a transaction and explain why they are necessary?

6.2 Two concurrent global transactions, T_1 and T_2, consist of the following:

$$T_1 = [r_1\ (x_1),\ w_1\ (x_1),\ r_1\ (x_3),\ w_1\ (x_3)]$$
$$T_2 = [r_2\ (x_2),\ w_2\ (x_2),\ r_2\ (x_4),\ w_2\ (x_4)]$$

where $r_i(x_j)$ and $w_i(x_j)$ denote a read and a write operation by transaction i on data item x_j. Data items x_1 and x_2 are stored at site A, while x_3 and x_4 are stored at site B. In addition, two local transactions, L_3 and L_4:

$$L_3 = [r_3(x_1), r_3(x_2)] \text{ at site A}$$
$$L_4 = [r_4(x_3), r_4(x_4)] \text{ at site B}$$

execute concurrently with T_1 and T_2.

Suppose that the schedules S^A and S^B produced by the local schedulers at site A and B respectively are as follows:

$$S^A = [r_3(x_1), r_1(x_1), w_1(x_1), r_2(x_2), w_2(x_2), r_3(x_2)]$$
$$S^B = [r_4(x_3), r_1(x_3), w_1(x_3), r_2(x_4), w_2(x_4), r_4(x_4)]$$

(a) Are these schedules locally serializable? If so, what are the equivalent local serial schedules?

(b) Are they globally serializable? If so, what is the equivalent global serial schedule?

6.3 Repeat Exercise 6.2, assuming that S^A is as before, but that the local scheduler at site B produces a different schedule, $S^{B'}$ where $S^{B'} = [r_1(x_3), w_1(x_3), r_2(x_4), r_4(x_3), r_4(x_4), w_2(x_4)]$

6.4 The diagram in Figure 6.12 shows the interleaved execution of three concurrent transactions, T_1, T_2 and T_3, with timestamps $ts(T_1) < ts(T_2) < ts(T_3)$

What would happen under each of the following protocols:

(a) 2PL with deadlock prevention
(b) 2PL with deadlock detection and recovery
(c) wait-die
(d) wound-wait?

6.5 The combined schedule of execution of transactions T_1, T_2, T_3, T_4, T_5 and T_6, is a follows:

$[r_6(l), r_2(y), r_5(m), r_1(z), r_1(x), r_4(b), r_3(a), r_6(n), r_3(c), r_5(a), r_1(y), r_3(x), r_6(m), r_2(b), r_4(n)]$

where $r_i(j)$ denotes a **read and lock** operation by transaction i on data object j.

Assume that the data is distributed across three sites A, B and C, of a network as follows:

x, *y*, *z* stored at site A
a, *b*, *c* stored at site B
l, *m*, *n* stored at site C

Draw the centralized global wait-for graph for transactions T_1 to T_6. Is there deadlock?

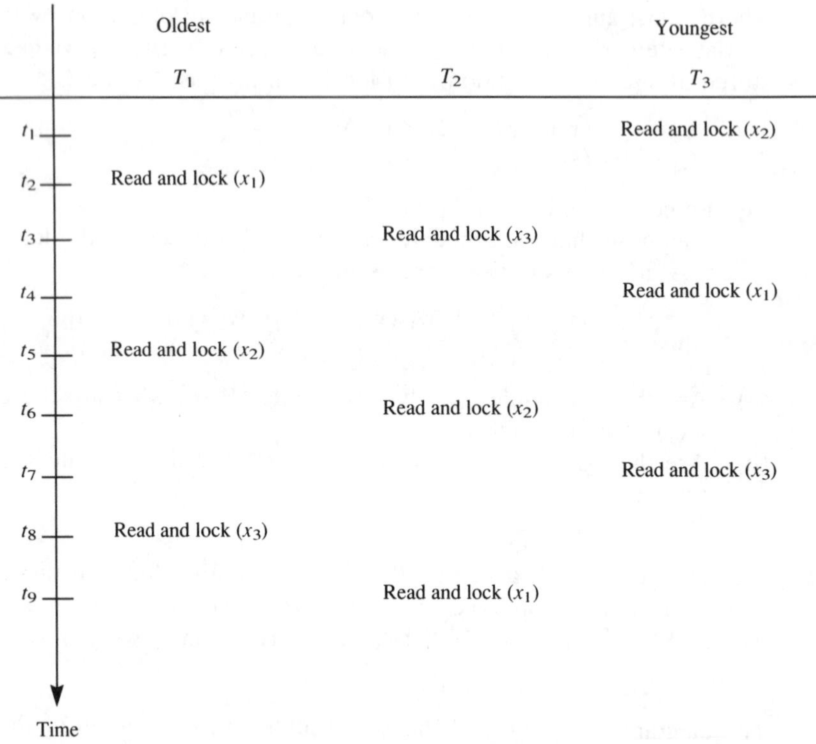

Figure 6.12 Interleaved execution of transaction T_1 and T_2 (Exercise 6.4).

6.6 Describe Obermarck's method for deadlock detection in a DDB. Redraw the global wait-for graph for Exercise 6.5 using Obermarck's method.

6.7 Why does Obermarck's method for deadlock detection in a DDB detect false deadlocks if transactions are allowed to abort spontaneously (e.g. to abort under application control (as in the 'insufficient funds' example in Example 6.1)) and not as a result of concurrency control?

6.8 Two transactions T_1 and T_2, execute as shown in Example 6.8. Account x is stored at site A and account y is stored at site B and transaction T_1 executes at site A and transaction T_2 at site B.

(a) In the absence of any attempt at synchronization, how many possible interleaved executions of these transactions are possible?
(b) Are any of them serializable?
(c) Are any of them correct but not serializable?

Example 6.8 Execution of two transactions (Exercise 6.8).

```
time
|            T1                              T2
|
|  begin transaction T1              begin transaction T2
|    read balance_x                    read balance_y
|    balance_x=balance_x-100           balance_y=balance_y-200
|    write balance_x                   write balance_y
|    read balance_y                    read balance_x
|    balance_y=balance_y+100           balance_x=balance_x+200
|    write balance_y                   write balance_x
v  commit T1                         commit T2
```

Bibliography

Agrawal R. and DeWitt D.J. (1985). Integrated concurrency control and recovery mechanisms: design and performance evaluation. *ACM TODS*, **10**(4), 529–64.

This paper presents an integrated study of concurrency control and recovery mechanisms for centralized DBs. It is particularly interesting because it considers both concurrency control and recovery, which are clearly intimately related, in a unified way. The model for analysing the relative costs of the various approaches is especially useful since it not only isolates the costs of the various components of a particular mechanism, but can also be used to identify why a particular mechanism is expensive and hence where improvements can be directed to greatest effect. See Section 6.7.2.

Alonso R., Garcia-Molina H. and Salem K. (1987). Concurrency control and recovery for global procedures in federated database systems. *Data Engineering*, **10**(3), 5–11.

Two approaches to synchronizing global transactions in an MDBS are discussed, namely sagas and altruistic locking (see Section 6.8).

Bernstein P.A. and Shipman D.W. (1980). The correctness of concurrency control mechanisms in a system for distributed databases (SDD-1). *ACM TODS*, **5**(1), 52–68.

Bernstein P.A., Shipman D.W. and Rothnie J.B. (1980). Concurrency control in a system for distributed databases (SDD-1). *ACM TODS*, **5**(1), 18–51.

These two papers give a comprehensive overview of the concurrency control and recovery mechanisms of the homogeneous DDBMS, SDD-1 (see Section 6.5.2.4).

Bernstein P.A. and Goodman N. (1981). Concurrency control in distributed database systems. *ACM Computing Surveys*, **13**(2), 185–222.

Bernstein P.A., Hadzilacos V. and Goodman N. (1987). *Concurrency control and recovery in database systems*. Wokingham: Addison-Wesley.

A comprehensive study of concurrency control and recovery issues for both centralized and distributed DBMSs.

Breitbart Y. and Silberschatz A. (1988). Multidatabase update issues. In *Proc. ACM SIGMOD Conf.* pp. 135–42. Chicago, Illinois.

Brodie M.L. (1989). Future intelligent information systems: AI and database technologies working together. In *Readings in Artificial Intelligence and Databases*. (Mylopoulos J. and Brodie M.L. eds.), 623–73. Morgan Kaufmann.

The next generation of computing, which will support intelligent information systems and will be based on distributed cooperative work, is discussed in this thought-provoking paper. The need for such systems, both in the long-term and short-term is presented, together with the results of a survey of 400 AI and DB researchers worldwide.

Buzzard J. (1990). *Database Server Evaluation Guide*, 3rd edn. San Francisco: Oracle Corporation.

The multiversioning approach to concurrency control for read-only transactions in Oracle is discussed (see Section 6.7.2).

Cellary W., Gelenbe E. and Morzy T. (1988). *Concurrency Control in Distributed Database Systems*. Amsterdam: North Holland.

A comprehensive study of concurrency control methods in DDBMSs.

Ceri S. and Owicki S. (1983). On the use of optimistic methods for concurrency control in distributed databases. In *Proc. 6th Int. Conf. on Distributed Data Management and Computer Networks*. Berkeley, California.

The distributed version of the validation algorithm for optimistic concurrency control, given in Section 6.5.4.1, is presented in this paper.

Ceri S. and Pelagatti G. (1984). *Distributed Databases: Principles & Systems*. New York: McGraw-Hill.

Du W. and Elmagarmid A. (1989). Quasi serializability: a correctness criterion for global concurrency control in InterBase. In *Proc. 15th Int. Conf. on Very Large Data Bases*, pp. 347–55, Amsterdam, Netherlands.

An altruistic locking scheme based on quasi-serializability is presented (see Section 6.8).

Eager D.L. and Sevcik K.C. (1983). Achieving robustness in distributed database systems, *ACM TODS*, **8**(3), 354–81.

This paper presents a fault-tolerant method of supporting updates in a DDB in the face of arbitrary site and network failures. In addition, the method also seeks to minimize the overhead involved in providing as high a degree of fault-tolerance (robustness) as possible, during normal operation in the absence of failures. The paper focuses on two important issues: network partitioning and dangling pre-commits. Dangling pre-commits (also known as missing writes) occur when sites fail or the network partitions after a site has received a pre-commit instruction, thereby leaving the site uncertain as to how to proceed.

Eliassen F., Veijalainen J. and Tirri H. (1988). Aspects of transaction modelling for interoperable information systems. In *Proc. EUTECO '88*, 1051–1067. Vienna, Austria.

This paper introduces the concept of the S-transaction discussed in Section 6.8.

Elmagarmid A.K. (1986). A survey of distributed deadlock detection algorithms. *ACM SIGMOD Record*, **15**(3), 37–45.

Elmagarmid A.K. and Helal A.A. (1988). Supporting updates in heterogeneous database systems. In *Proc. 4th Int.Conf. on Data Engineering*, 564–569. Los Angeles, California.

Eswaran K.P., Gray J.N., Lorie R.A. and Traiger I.L. (1976). The notions of consistency and predicate locks in a database system. *CACM*, **19**(11), 624–33.

Farrag A.A. and Özsu M.T. (1989). Using semantic knowledge of transactions to increase concurrency, *ACM TODS*, **14**(4), 503–25.

This is an interesting paper which introduces a novel type of schedule called a relatively consistent schedule. A precedence graph is used to show the ordering of steps within a transaction, as well as conflicts between steps of different transactions. The method guarantees that only acyclic graphs are created and that a correct schedule can be formed by ordering the nodes of the graph topologically. The method could be particularly useful for long-lived transactions and for supporting concurrency control in MDBMS.

Furtado A.L. and Casanova M.A. (1985). Updating relational views. In *Query Processing in Database Systems.* (Kim W., Reiner D. and Batory D., eds.), Berlin: Springer-Verlag.

Garcia-Molina H. (1983). Using semantic knowledge for transaction processing in a distributed database, *ACM TODS*, **8**(2), 186–213.

The method proposed in this paper, one of the early ones on exploiting application-specific knowledge for improving concurrency control, is discussed briefly in Section 6.8. In addition to pointing out the advantages of the approach, the paper also discussed its weaknesses.

Garcia-Molina H. (1991). Global consistency constraints considered harmful for heterogeneous database systems. In *Proc. 1st Int. Workshop on Interoperability in Multidatabase Systems*, Kyoto, Japan, April 1991, 248–250.

This paper argues that the existence of global integrity (consistency) constraints for MDBs is, by definition, a violation of nodal autonomy. The implication of the absence of such constraints for concurrency control is discussed; in particular MDBs and serializable schedules are seen as contradictory. The author argues in favour of the use of sagas to provide concurrency control for MDBs (see Section 6.8).

Garcia-Molina H. and Salem K. (1987). Sagas. In *ACM SIGMOD Conf.* May 1987, 249–259. San Francisco, California.

Sagas are long-lived transactions which can be written as a sequence of transactions which can be interleaved with other transactions (see Section 6.8).

Garcia-Molina H. and Wiederhold G. (1982). Read-only transactions in a distributed database, *ACM TODS*, **7**(2), 209–34.

A useful study of the requirements of read-only transactions (queries), which are likely to constitute a large part of transaction processing in a DDB environment. The requirements for queries are grouped under five headings: strong consistency (schedule of all update transactions and strong consistency queries must be consistent); weak consistency (only query's view of data has to be consistent); *t*-vintage query (requires a view of data as it existed at time *t*); *t*-bound query (requires data it reads to reflect all updates committed before time *t*); and latest-bound query (special case of *t*-bound query with *t*=current time, thereby giving latest versions of all data accessed by the query).

Gligor V.D. and Luckenbaugh G.L. (1984). Interconnecting heterogeneous database management systems. *IEEE Computer*, **17**(11), 33–43.

Gligor V.D. and Popescu-Zeletin R. (1985). Concurrency control issues in distributed heterogeneous database management systems. In *Distributed Data Sharing Systems* (Schreiber F.A. and Litwin W. (eds.), 43–56. Amsterdam: North Holland.

The requirements for global concurrency control mechanisms for MDBSs, based on the concatenation of local concurrency control mechanisms, are discussed.

Gligor V. and Popescu-Zeletin R. (1986). Transaction management in distributed heterogeneous database management systems. *Information Systems*, **11**(4), 287–97.

Gray J.N. (1978). Notes on database operating systems. In *Operating Systems – An Advanced Course*. Berlin: Springer-Verlag.

Grimson J.B., O'Sullivan D., Lawless P. *et al.* (1988). *Research Issues in*

Multidatabase Systems, Deliverable Report D8, CEC MAP Project 773B – Multistar, Trinity College, Dublin, Ireland.

This report discusses many open research issues in MDBMSs including the provision of support for *ad hoc* update transactions.

Jajodia S. and Mutchler D. (1990). Dynamic voting algorithms for maintaining consistency of a replicated database. *ACM TODS*, **15**(2), 230–80.

A method of voting (called dynamic voting) in the face of network partitioning is introduced, which permits updates in a partition provided it contains more than half of the up-to-date copies of the data object being updated.

Knapp E. (1987). Deadlock detection in distributed databases. *ACM Computing Surveys*, **19**(4), 303–28.

Kung H.T. and Robinson J.T. (1981). On optimistic methods for concurrency control. *ACM TODS*, **6**(2), 213–26.

This is one of the early papers on the subject of optimistic concurrency control (see Section 6.5.4).

Lamport L. (1978). Time, clocks and the ordering of events in a distributed system. *CACM*, **21**(7) 558–65.

This is the basic reference on the generation of timestamps in a distributed environment (see Section 6.5.3).

Lynch N. (1983). Multilevel atomicity – a new correctness criterion for database concurrency control. *ACM TODS*, **8**(4) 484–502.

An alternative to serialization as the correctness criterion, called multilevel atomicity, is presented. It appears to be especially useful for hierarchically structured transactions.

McGee W.C. (1977). The information management system IMS/VS Part V: Transaction processing facilities. *IBM Systems J.*, **16**(2), 148–68.

The concurrency control method used in IMS Fast Path is discussed (see Section 6.5.4).

Menasce D.A. and Muntz R.R. (1979). Locking and deadlock detection in distributed databases. *IEEE Trans. on Software Engineering*, **5**(3), 195–202.

Two protocols for the detection of deadlock in a DDBMS are presented, one hierarchical and the other distributed.

Menasce D.A., Popek G.J. and Muntz R.R. (1980). A locking protocol for resource coordination in distributed databases. *ACM TODS*, **5**(2), 103–38.

The locking protocol described in this paper uses a centralized controller with distributed recovery procedures.

Mitchell D.P. and Merritt M.J. (1984). A distributed algorithm for deadlock detection and resolution. In *Proc. ACM Symposium on Principles of Distributed Computing*, 282–84.

This paper presents an edge-chasing algorithm for distributed deadlock detection. It has the merit of being simple and straightforward to implement. It has also been proved that the algorithm will detect all deadlocks, but as with Obermarck's algorithm, there is also the possibility of false deadlocks being detected in the presence of spontaneous aborts. It can also be shown that the method will detect a deadlock only once, which makes resolution easier. Each transaction in the (virtual) wait-for graph is assigned two labels: a private label, which is always unique to that node, though its value can change, and a public label, which can be read by other transactions and is not unique. Initially, public and private labels are equal for each transaction. This algorithm is referred to as an edge-chasing algorithm, because the largest public label 'chases' along the edges of the wait-for graph in the opposite direction.

Obermarck R. (1982). Distributed deadlock detection algorithm. *ACM TODS*, **7**(2), 187–208.

This algorithm is discussed in Section 6.5.2.

Papadimitriou C.H. (1979). The serializability of concurrent database updates. *JACM*, **26**(4), 631–53.

This is the basic reference on the theory of serializability. It presents a formal proof that recognizing serializable schedules is an NP-complete problem. It shows that by restricting transactions to those which read before they write (the constrained write rule) deciding serializability is of polynomial complexity (see Section 6.4).

Rosenkrantz D.J., Stearns R.E. and Lewis P.M. II (1978). System level concurrency control for distributed database systems. *ACM TODS*, **3**(2), 178–98.

This paper presents the wound-wait and wait-die protocols for deadlock prevention discussed in Section 6.5.2.

Sheth A.P. and Larson J.A. (1990). Federated database systems for managing distributed, heterogeneous, and autonomous databases. *ACM Computing Surveys*, **22**(3), 183–236.

Singhal M. (1989). Deadlock detection in distributed systems. *IEEE Computer*, **22** (11), 37–48.

This paper contains a comprehensive review of a number of deadlock detection algorithms. It includes a good list of references.

Stonebraker M. (1979). Concurrency control and consistency of multiple copies of data in distributed INGRES. *IEEE Trans. on Software Engineering*, **5**(3), 188–194.

Tangney B. and O'Mahony D. (1988). *Local Area Networks and their Applications*. New York: Prentice Hall.

Thomas R.H. (1979). A majority consensus approach to concurrency control for multiple copy databases. *ACM TODS*, **4**(2), 180–209.

One of the earliest papers on concurrency control for fully replicated DBs. The method proposed (see Section 6.5) is an optimistic one using a majority consensus approach to voting and is deadlock free.

Walter B. (1982). Global recovery in a distributed database system. In *2nd International Symposium on Distributed Data Sharing Systems*. Amsterdam: North Holland.

Wang C.P. and Li V.O.K. (1987). The precedence-assignment model for distributed database concurrency control algorithms. In *Proc. 6th Symp. on Principles of Database Systems*, 119–128.

Wang C.P. and Li V.O.K. (1988). A unified concurrency control algorithm for distributed database systems. In *Proc. 4th Int. Conf. on Data Engineering*, 410–417. Los Angeles, California.

SOLUTIONS TO EXERCISES

6.2

(a) S^A is serializable:

L_3 sees x_1 in pre-T_1 version, $\therefore L_3 < T_1$

L_3 sees x_2 in post-T_2 version, $\therefore L_3 > T_2$

$\therefore T_2^A < L_3 < T_1^A$

$\therefore$ equivalent serial is

$SR^A = [r_2(x_2), w_2(x_2), r_3(x_1), r_3(x_2), r_1(x_1), w_1(x_1)]$

Similarly S^B is also serializable with:
$T_2^B < L_4^B < T_1^B$
∴ the equivalent serial schedule is
$SR^B = [r_2(x_4), w_2(x_4), r_4(x_3), r_4(x_3), r_1(x_1), w_1(x_1)]$

(b) Both T_1 and T_2 appear in the same order in both local schedules and hence the global schedule is also serializable with
$T_2 < T_1$
and the equivalent global serial schedule is
$SGR = [r_2(x_2), w_2(x_2), r_2(x_4), w_2(x_4), r_1(x_1), w_1(x_1), r_1(x_3), w_1(x_3)]$

6.3

(a) Both local schedules are serializable:
Site A as before, i.e. $T_2 < L_3 < T_1$
For site B $T_1 < L_4 < T_2$
∴ the equivalent serial schedule is
$SR^{B'} = [r_1(x_3), w_1(x_3), r_4(x_3), r_4(x_4), r_2(x_4), w_2(x_4)]$

(b) T_1 and T_2 appear in different orders in the local schedules and therefore the global schedule is not serializable.

6.4

(a) 2PL with deadlock prevention
t_4: T_3 is rolled back
t_6: T_2 is rolled back

(b) 2PL with deadlock detection and recovery
t_4: T_3 waits for T_1
t_5: T_1 waits for T_3
deadlock; T_1 (say) is rolled back so T_3 resumes executing
t_6: T_2 waits for T_3
t_7: T_3 waits for T_2
deadlock; T_3 (say) is rolled back so T_2 resumes executing

(c) Wait-die
t_4: T_1 is rolled back
t_6: T_2 waits
t_7: T_2 is rolled back

(d) Wound-wait
t_4: T_3 waits
t_5: T_3 is rolled back
t_6: T_2 waits
t_8: T_2 is rolled back

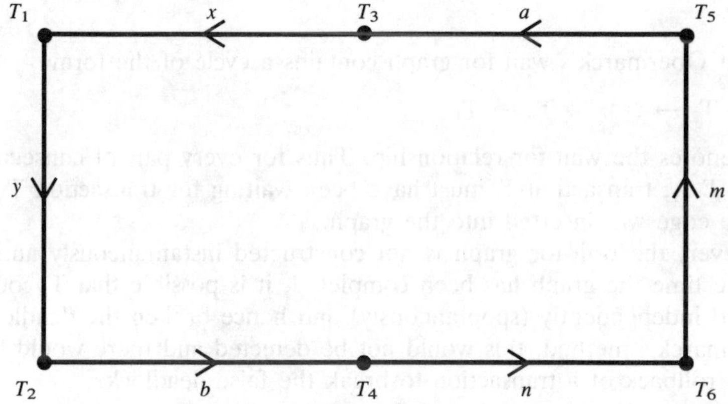

Figure 6.13 Global wait-for graph for Exercise 6.5.

6.5

See figure 6.13.
The global wait-for graph, G, contains a cycle and hence there is deadlock:

$$G = T_1 \rightarrow T_2 \rightarrow T_4 \rightarrow T_6 \rightarrow T_5 \rightarrow T_3 \rightarrow T_1$$

6.6

See Figure 6.14, which shows the final global wait-for graph:

$$G = T_1^A \rightarrow T_2^A \rightarrow T_2^B \rightarrow T_4^B \rightarrow T_4^C \rightarrow T_6^C \rightarrow T_5^C \rightarrow T_5^B \rightarrow T_3^B \rightarrow T_3^A \rightarrow T_1^A$$

Note that, for simplicity, the EXT nodes have been omitted.

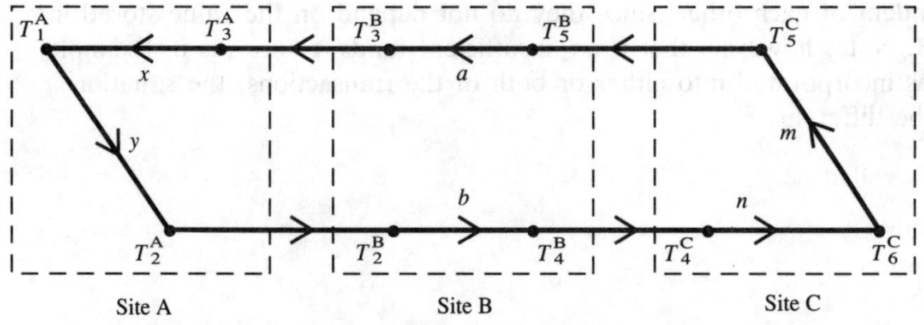

Figure 6.14 Global wait for graph (Obermarck's method) for Exercise 6.6.

6.7

Assume that Obermarck's wait-for graph contains a cycle of the form

$$T_1 \rightarrow T_2 \rightarrow \ldots \rightarrow T_n \rightarrow T_1$$

where $\rightarrow$ denotes the wait-for relationship. Thus for every pair of consecutive edges $T_i \rightarrow T_{i+1}$, transaction T_i must have been waiting for transaction T_{i+1} at the time the edge was inserted into the graph.

However, the wait-for graph is not constructed instantaneously and hence by the time the graph has been completed, it is possible that T_i could have aborted independently (spontaneously) and hence broken the deadlock. Using Obermarck's method, this would not be detected and there would be unnecessary rollback of a transaction to break the false deadlock.

6.8

(a) There are a total of eight operations to be performed (two reads and two writes by each transaction). They cannot be interleaved in any order; reads must precede writes and the decrement must precede the increment for each transaction. There are in fact a total of ${}^8C_4$ = 70 possible interleavings.

(b) Let $r_1(x)$ denote the read balance$_x$ operation by transaction T_1 and $w_1(x)$ denote the write balance$_x$ operation by T_1 (similarly for T_2)
Only 2 of the 70 schedules are serializable, namely
$S_1 = [r_1(x), w_1(x), r_1(y), w_1(y), r_2(y), w_2(y), r_2(x), w_2(x)]$
and
$S_2 = [r_2(y), w_2(y), r_2(x), w_2(x), r_1(x), w_1(x), r_1(y), w_1(y)]$
and both are in fact serial schedules with $T_1 < T_2$ in S_1 and $T_2 < T_1$ in S_2.

(c) All 70 schedules are correct and will leave the DB in a consistent state. This illustrates the point that serializable schedules form only a subset of correct schedules (i.e. those which guarantee the integrity of the DB). In this particular example, although T_1 and T_2 access the same data, they are independent of one another. The decrement and increment operations are also independent of each other, since they do not depend on the value stored in the DB. Note, however, that if an 'insufficient funds' clause (as in Example 6.1) was incorporated into either or both of the transactions, the situation would be different.

7 Recovery

7.1 Introduction

The ability to ensure the consistency of the DB in the presence of unpredictable failures of both hardware and software components is an essential feature of any DBMS. It is the role of the recovery manager of the DBMS to restore the DB to a consistent state following a failure which has rendered it either inconsistent or at least suspect.

In this chapter, we will introduce the background to recovery in DBMSs, both centralized and distributed. The fundamental role of transactions is discussed and the use of logs and the causes of failure are presented. An overview of recovery protocols for centralized DBMSs is then discussed in order to give a good understanding of the starting point for the development of recovery protocols for DDBMSs. The chapter ends with a brief discussion of the problems associated with recovery in MDBSs.

7.1.1 Transactions and recovery

Transactions represent the basic unit of recovery in a DBMS. It is the role of the recovery manager to guarantee two of the four A.C.I.D. properties of transactions (see Section 6.2.1), namely durability and atomicity, in the presence of unpredictable failures. Consistency and independence, the other two A.C.I.D. properties of transactions, are mainly the responsibility of the concurrency control module.

The recovery manager has to ensure that, on recovery from failure, either all the effects of a given transaction are permanently recorded in the DB or none of them. The situation is complicated by the fact that DB writing is not an atomic (single step) procedure, and it is therefore possible for a transaction to have committed, but for its effects not to have been permanently recorded in the DB simply because they had not yet reached the DB. When a transaction issues a write to the DB, the data is transferred from the local workspace to the transaction's DB buffers. The DB buffers occupy a special area in main (volatile) memory from which data is transferred to secondary storage and vice versa. Conceptually, these buffers operate like a volatile cache in which portions of the DB may reside temporarily. It is only once the buffer contents have been **flushed** to secondary storage that any update operations can be regarded as permanent. This flushing of the DB buffers to the DB can be triggered by a specific DBMS command (e.g. when a transaction is committed), or automatically when the buffers become full. The explicit emptying of the buffers is known as **force-writing**. If a failure occurs between the DB write to the buffers and the flushing of the buffers to secondary storage, the recovery manager must ascertain what the status of the transaction which performed the write was, at the time of failure. If it had issued its commit, then in order to ensure transaction durability, the recovery manager would have to **redo** its updates to the DB. If, on the other hand, the transaction was still active at the time of failure, then the recovery manager would have to **undo** any effects of that transaction on the DB in order to guarantee transaction atomicity. When only one transaction has to be undone, this is known as **partial undo**. A partial undo can be triggered by the transaction scheduler when a transaction is rolled back and restarted as a result of concurrency control restrictions (see Chapter 6). A transaction can also be aborted unilaterally as in the 'insufficient funds' example given in Example 6.1. When all active transactions have to be undone, this is known as **global undo**. To emphasize the permanency of the DB on secondary storage, it is often referred to as the **stable** or **persistent** DB because it persists after the power has been turned off. This differentiates it from portions of the DB which may be cached in main (volatile) memory in buffers and which will be lost in the event of a power failure.

Failure can range from simple failures which affect only one transaction to a power failure affecting all transactions at a site. Storage media can fail as a result of disk head crashes and, in a distributed environment, the network can fail, making communication between sites. We will discuss the various causes of failure in detail in Section 7.2, but first we will look at some of the relevant background to recovery.

The principal function of the recovery manager following failure is to identify which transactions have to be undone and which have to be redone, and then perform the necessary undo and redo operations. The DB **log** (also called **journal** or **audit trail**) plays an essential role in this recovery.

7.1.2 Log file

All operations on the DB carried out by all transactions are recorded in the log file. There is one log file for each DBMS which is shared by all transactions under the control of that DBMS. In a DDB environment, each site will have its own separate log. An entry is made in the local log file at a site each time one of the following commands is issued by a transaction (includes purely local transactions and sub-transactions of global transactions):

- begin transaction
- write (includes insert, delete and update)
- commit transaction
- abort transaction

Details of the meaning of these commands are given in Section 6.1. Note the log is often also used for purposes other than recovery (e.g. for performance monitoring and auditing). In this case, additional information may be recorded in the log (e.g. DB reads, user logons, logoffs, etc.) but these are not relevant to recovery and hence are omitted from this discussion. Each log record contains the following information, not all of which is required for all actions as indicated below:

(1) Transaction identifier (all operations);

(2) Type of log record, that is, which of the list of DB actions listed above it is recording (all operations);

(3) Identifier of data object affected by the DB action (insert, delete and update operations);

(4) Before-image of the data object, that is, its value before update (update and delete operations);

(5) After-image of the data object, that is, its value after update (update and insert operations);

(6) Log management information such as a pointer to previous log record for that transaction (all operations).

The log is vital to the recovery process and hence it is generally duplexed (i.e. two separate copies are maintained) so that if one copy is lost or damaged, the second one can be used (see Section 7.2.3 to see how this is achieved). Log files were traditionally stored on magnetic tape because tape was a more reliable form of stable storage than magnetic disk and was cheaper. However, the DBMSs of today are expected to be able to recover quickly from minor failures. This requires, as we shall see, that the log be stored on-line on a fast direct-access storage device. Moreover, the discs of today are, if anything, *more* reliable than tapes.

In systems with a high transaction rate, a huge amount of logging information will be generated every day ($> 10^7$ bytes daily is quite possible) so it is not realistic, or indeed useful, to hold *all* this data on-line all the time. The log is needed on-line for quick recovery after minor failures (e.g. rollback of a transaction following deadlock). Major failures, such as disk head crashes, obviously take longer to recover from and would almost certainly require access to a large part of the log. In such circumstances, it would be acceptable to wait until parts of the log on archival storage are transferred back to on-line storage.

A common approach to handling the archiving of the log, is to divide the on-line log into two separate direct access files. Log records are written to the first file until it is, say, 95% full. The logging system then opens the second file and writes all log records for *new* transactions to the second file. *Old* transactions continue to use the first file until they have finished, at which time the first file is transferred to archival storage. In this way, the set of log records for an individual transaction cannot be split between archival and on-line storage, making recovery of that transaction more straightforward.

The log is treated by the operating system as just another file on secondary storage. Hence log records must first be written into log buffers which are periodically flushed to secondary storage in the normal way. Logs can be written synchronously or asynchronously. With **synchronous** log-writing, every time a record is written to the log, it is forced out onto stable storage, while under **asynchronous** log-writing, the buffers are only flushed periodically (e.g. when a transaction commits) and/or when they become full. Synchronous writing imposes a delay on all transaction operations, which may well prove unacceptable. The log is a potential bottleneck in the overall DBMS and the speed of the write-log operation can be a crucial factor in determining the overall performance of the DBMS. However, the delay due to synchronous logging must be traded off against the obvious advantages of a more up-to-date log when it comes to recovery.

It is essential that log records (or at least certain parts of them) be written *before* the corresponding write to the DB. This is known as the **write-ahead log protocol**. If updates were made to the DB first and failure occurred before the log record was written, then the recovery manager would have no way of undoing (or redoing) the operation. Under the write-ahead log protocol, the recovery manager can safely assume that, if there is no commit transaction entry in the log for a particular transaction, then that transaction was still active at the time of failure and must therefore be undone.

Figure 7.1 shows the interaction between the local recovery manager, which oversees local recovery at that site, the buffer manager, which manages the buffers, the log buffers for communication to and from the log, and the DB buffers for communication to and from the DB and which at any time will contain cached portions of the DB.

7.1.3 Checkpointing

One of the difficulties facing the recovery manager, following major failure, is to know how far back in the log to go in order to identify transactions which might have to be redone (i.e. those which had commit-

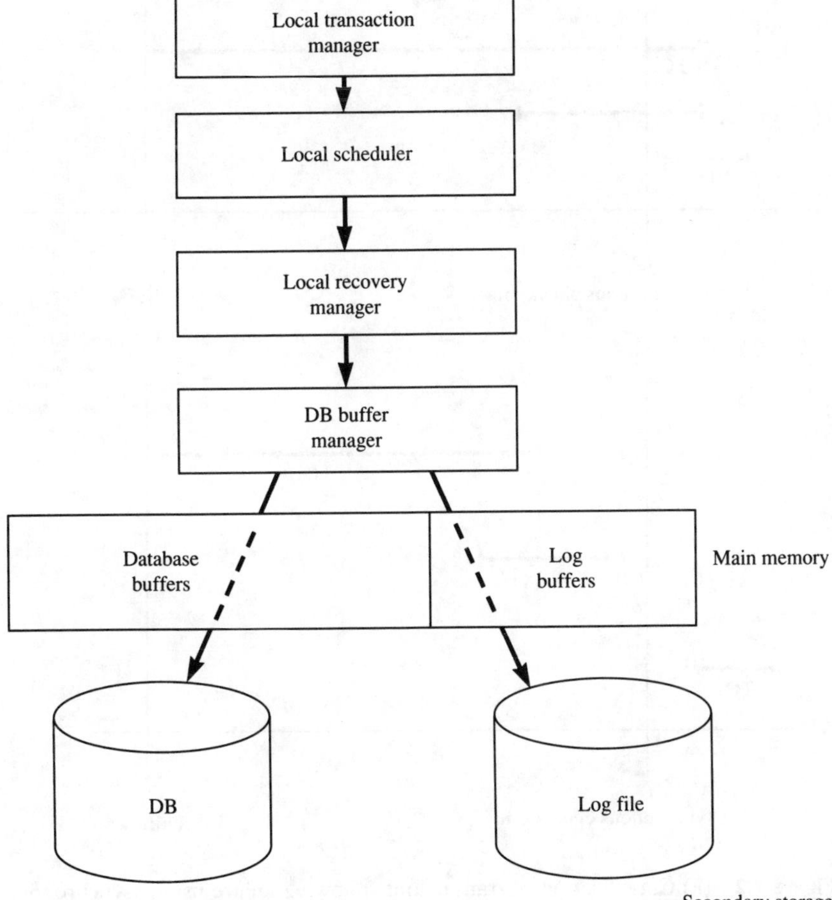

Figure 7.1 Local recovery manager and its interfaces.

ted prior failure) or undone (those which were active at the time of failure). To limit its search, the recovery manager takes periodic **checkpoints** and on recovery it only has to go back as far as the last checkpoint. There are two approaches to checkpointing, namely synchronous and asynchronous. With **asynchronous checkpointing**, system processing is allowed to continue uninterrupted by the checkpoint as shown in Figure 7.2(a). When a **synchronous checkpoint** is being taken, the system stops

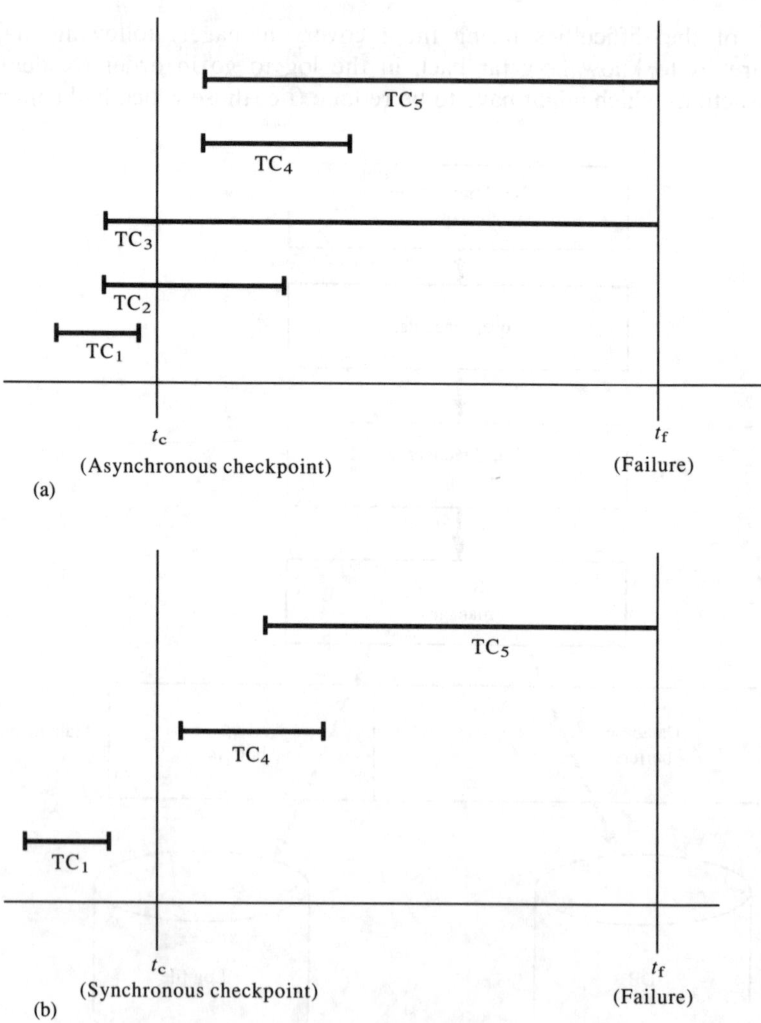

Figure 7.2 (a) Classification of transactions following failure using asynchronous checkpointing. (b) Classification of transaction following failure using synchronous checkpointing.

accepting any new transactions until all executing transactions have finished, as shown in Figure 7.2(b).

The following actions are carried out at an asynchronous checkpoint.

(1) A list of all transactions currently active in the system is written to the log; this information is available from the transaction manager as it is required for concurrency control (see Chapter 6);
(2) The address of the checkpoint record in the log is written to a special file known as the **restart file**;
(3) All buffers are forcewritten to both the log and the DB.

For synchronous checkpointing, action 1 is not required. The system is described as **quiescent** when no transactions are active. Synchronous checkpointing is recording the state of the system when it is quiescent. The actions required by the recovery manager are greatly simplified when synchronous checkpointing is used as transactions never have to be redone. However, this must be balanced against the overhead in delaying the start of new transactions until the checkpoint is complete.

7.1.4 Updating the DB

Most DBMSs use immediate or **in-place updating** (i.e. they write directly to the DB via the DB buffers). The advantage of this approach is that the updated pages are in place when the transaction commits and no further action is required. However, this approach suffers from the disadvantage that, in the event of transaction failure, updates may have to be undone. To avoid this, some systems use **shadow writing** or **differential files**.

With **shadow writing**, updates are written to a separate part of the DB on secondary storage and the DB indexes are not updated to point to the updated pages until the transaction commits. The old versions of the pages are then used for recovery and effectively become part of the log.

With differential files, the main DB is not updated at all; rather the changes effected by transactions are recorded in a separate part of the DB called the **differential file**. When the differential file becomes too large, resulting in a noticeable deterioration in overall performance, it can be merged with the read-only DB to produce a new read-only DB and an empty differential file.

The main DB is read-only, while the differential file is read-write. Stonebraker (1975) proposed that the differential file be divided into two distinct parts, D and I; deletions are stored in D and insertions are recorded separately in I. An update is treated as a deletion followed by an insertion. If the read-only DB is relational, then the entire logical DB can be considered as a view, LDB, defined as

$$LDB = (RDB \cup I) - D.$$

Agrawal and DeWitt carried out a detailed study of the performance of the various combinations of recovery (logging using in-place updating, differential files and shadows) with concurrency control (locking and optimistic) methods. They concluded that a combination of logging with in-place updating and a lock-based concurrency control technique gives the best overall performance for a mix of transactions of varying sizes. When there are only large transactions with a sequential access pattern, the use of shadow files combined with locking perform best, and if transactions are medium to large, then differential files combined with locking represent a viable alternative. Note that recovery and concurrency control are very closely related and transaction information which is required for one can also be used by the other. For example, optimistic concurrency control methods (see Section 6.5.6) require that all updates be made to transaction-local copies so there is no in-place updating until commit. Hence, if logging or shadowing is combined with an optimistic concurrency control method, the log records or shadows can double as the local copies for concurrency control. However, the above study showed that unless transactions are very short and there is a very low probability of conflict, optimistic methods, in general, are out-performed by logging plus locking.

7.2 Causes of failure

There are many different causes of failure, but for the purpose of this discussion on recovery in DDBMSs, we will classify them under four headings:

(1) Transaction-local failure
(2) Site failures
(3) Media failures
(4) Network failures.

The actions required by the recovery manager following each type of failure will be different and are discussed below. Note that in all cases we are assuming that systems are **fail-stop**; when failures or errors occur, they simply stop. We are therefore excluding hardware and software bugs which cause the system to behave inconsistently.

7.2.1 Transaction-local failure

The failure of an individual transaction can be brought about in a number of ways:

(1) **Transaction-induced abort**, as for example the 'insufficient funds' example shown in Example 6.1. In this case, the application programmer has written code to trap a particular error. The recovery manager is therefore explicitly told to rollback the transaction. No other transactions are affected.

(2) **Unforeseen transaction failure** arising from bugs in the application program (e.g. arithmetic errors such as division by zero). In this case, the system has to detect that the transaction has failed and then inform the recovery manager to rollback the transaction. Again no other transactions are affected.

(3) **System-induced abort** which occurs, for example, when the transaction manager explicitly aborts a transaction because it conflicts with another transaction, or to break a deadlock. Again the recovery manager is explicitly told to rollback the transaction and other transactions are not affected, apart from perhaps becoming unblocked.

In a centralized DBMS, transaction-local failure is a relatively straightforward operation, involving the undoing of any changes which the transaction has made to the DB on stable storage. This is done by restoring the before-images of the data objects updated by the transaction from the log. In a DDBMS, however, the failure of the local agent of a global transaction requires that all the other agents of that global transaction be aborted and rolled back in order to guarantee global atomicity. No other transactions, either global or local, will be affected.

7.2.2 Site failures

Site failures can occur as a result of failure of the local CPU or a power supply failure resulting in a system crash. All transactions on that machine are affected. The contents of main (volatile) memory including all buffers are lost. However, we assume that both the DB itself on persistent store and the log are undamaged.

In a DDB environment, since sites operate independently from each other, it is perfectly possible for some sites to be operational while others have failed. If all sites are down, this is called a **total failure**. If only some have failed, then it is referred to as a **partial failure**. The main difficulty with partial failures is for sites which are working to know the status of other sites (i.e. whether they have failed or are operational). Also, as a result of partial failure, it is possible for sites to become **blocked** and therefore unable to proceed. This can happen when a site executing the agent of a global transaction fails in mid-transaction. Other agents of that global transaction may be uncertain as to whether to commit or rollback. It should be remembered that one of the significant advantages of the distributed approach to data management is that the data (or most of it) continues to be available to users even in the event of local site failures. It is therefore of paramount importance that such local failures do not cause operational sites to become blocked. We will return to this subject later as we look at the various recovery protocols.

In order to recover from such a site failure, the local recovery manager first of all has to find out the state of the local system at the time of failure – in particular, what transactions were active. The objective is to restore the DB to a consistent state by undoing or redoing transactions according to their status at the time of failure by applying the before- and after-images, respectively, from the log. The last known state is recorded in the last checkpoint. If synchronous checkpointing is used, then the last checkpoint will mark a consistent state. If asynchronous checkpointing has been used, then the last checkpoint will mark a *known*, but not necessarily consistent, state.

When the site is restored following a failure, control is passed to the recovery manager to execute the **recovery** or **restart procedure**. During this procedure, no transactions are accepted by the DBMS until the DB has been repaired. The recovery manager's first task is to locate the last checkpoint record in the log. This information is stored in the **restart file** (see Section 7.1.2). The recovery manager, using the list of active transactions in the checkpoint record, works through the log building up a list of transactions which have to be undone and another for those which have to be redone. Details of how the recovery manager classifies transactions are to be found in Section 7.3.2.

The type of restart following system failure which we have described above is known as an **emergency restart**. An emergency restart follows when a system fails without warning (e.g. due to a sudden power failure). Other types of restarts are possible, depending on how the system stopped.

With a **cold start** the system is restarted from archive when the log and/or restart file has become corrupted following a major, catastrophic failure. Remember that both the restart and log files are duplexed or triplexed so the chances of losing all copies are very small. All updates performed since the archive copy was made will probably be lost. A cold start is also required when the system is initialized.

A **warm start**, on the other hand, follows controlled shutdown of the system. The system manager issues a SHUTDOWN command, after which no *new* transactions are started. The system then waits until all transactions active at the time of shutdown have finished completely, flushes all the log and DB buffers to stable storage, and then terminates itself. At that point there is no activity in the system, so there is no need for the recovery manager to do anything on restart.

7.2.3 Media failures

A media failure is a failure which results in some portion of the stable DB being corrupted. A common cause of such failure is a disk head crash. The objective of the recovery manager following media failure is to restore the last committed values of all data objects. There are two possible approaches: **archiving** and **mirroring**, which are explained below.

It is common practice in all data processing installations, from small single-user PCs to large multi-user systems to take periodic backups of stable storage. These backups form the DB **archive**. Traditionally DBs were archived to magnetic tape because it was a cheap medium and was easy to store. Larger installations today are moving to optical disks as they provide a more efficient and compact alternative.

It is desirable that the backup copy is made when the system is quiescent, otherwise the backup may contain partial updates which would complicate its use for recovery. Hence such backup copies are taken infrequently at carefully chosen times such as following DB reorganization or following a controlled system shutdown (see Section 7.2.2). To recover using the archive, the recovery manager loads the DB from the most recent archive copy and then redoes all committed transactions from the log. This could be a very long process if the last backup was made some time previously.

In many DB environments, it would take too long to backup the entire DB. Hence some systems allow backups to be taken of some portions only of the DB, while allowing other parts to remain on-line during the archiving procedure. Other systems support **incremental dumping** whereby the only changes recorded are those which have been made to the DB since the last backup. Both these approaches are particularly useful in the commonly occurring scenario where some portions of the DB are much more frequently accessed than others and should therefore be backed up more frequently.

In environments where non-stop, fault-tolerant operation is important, **mirroring** can be used. This allows two complete copies of the DB to be maintained on-line on different stable storage devices. For added security, the devices should be attached to different disc controllers (see Figure 7.3(a)) and located in different rooms. Reads can therefore be directed to either disk, but writes must be applied to both. If one disk fails, then all reads and writes are directed to the mirror copy and the system can continue operating without interruption. Once the failure has been repaired, the updated DB must be copied across to the repaired disk.

An alternative approach which provides the same degree of reliability is to divide each disk into two partitions: the **primary area** and the **fallback area**, as shown in Figure 7.3(b). The DB itself is then distributed across all the primary partitions and the mirror copy across

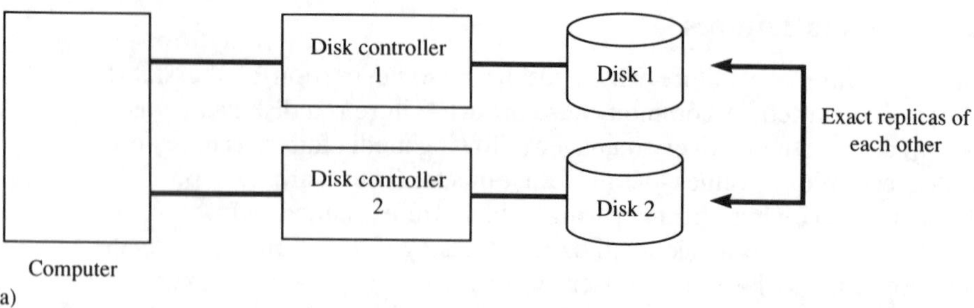

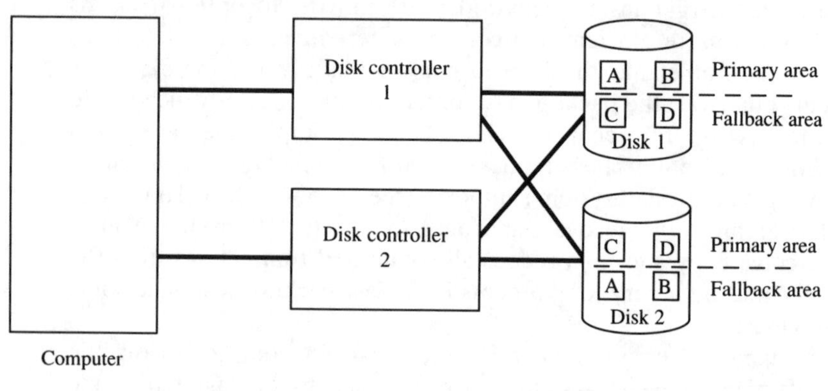

Figure 7.3 (a) Mirroring. (b) Mirroring using primary and fallback partitions.

the fallback partitions, such that the same segment of the DB is stored on different discs. Thus if segments A and B are stored in the primary area on disk 1, then their mirrors will be stored in the fallback area of disk 2 and vice versa. The disc controllers are multiply connected to the discs. This approach is used in the Teradata DBC/1012 Database Machine, although for added reliability there are multiple processors and duplicated communication buses. In normal operation, the DBMS uses both disk controllers to search disks in parallel, whereas such parallelism is not possible with standard mirroring.

7.2.4 Network failures

DDBMSs depend for their successful operation on the ability of all sites in the network to be able to communicate reliably with one another. Most networks today are very reliable. The protocols guarantee correct transmission of messages in the correct order. In the event of line failures, many networks support automatic rerouting of messages. However, communications failures can still occur. Such a failure can result in the network being **partitioned** into two or more sub-networks. Sites within the same partition can communicate with one another, but not with sites in other partitions. In Figure 7.4, following the failure of the line connecting sites C and E, sites {A,B,C} in one partition are isolated from sites {D,E,F} in the other partition. One of the difficulties of operating in a distributed environment is knowing when and where a site or communication failure has occurred. For example, suppose site C in Figure 7.4 sends site E a message which E then fails to acknowledge within a certain time period called a **timeout**. How can C decide whether E has failed or whether the network has been partitioned due to communication failure in such a way that C and E are in separate partitions and hence cannot communicate with one another? In fact, all that C can conclude from E's failure to respond, is that it is unable to send and receive messages to and from E. Choosing the correct value for the timeout which will trigger this conclusion is difficult. It has to be at least equal to the maximum possible time for the round-trip of message plus acknowledgement plus the processing time at E.

If agents of the same global transaction are active at both C and E and a network failure occurs which puts C and E in different partitions, then it is possible for C and other sites in the same partition, to decide to commit the global transaction, while E and other sites in its partition, decides to abort it. Such an occurrence violates global transaction atomicity.

In general, it is not possible to design a non-blocking atomic commitment protocol for arbitrarily partitioned networks. A **non-blocking protocol** is one which does not block operational sites in the event of failure. Sites which are still capable of processing should be allowed to do so, without having to wait for failed sites to recover. Since recovery

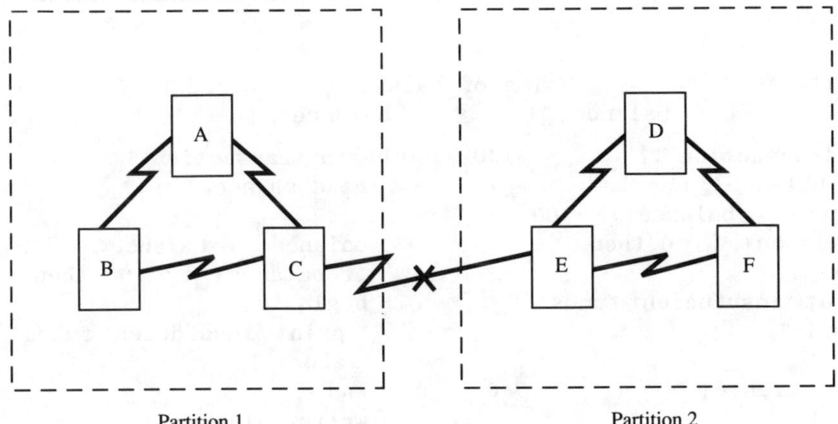

Figure 7.4 Partitioning of a network.

and concurrency control are so closely related, the recovery techniques which will be used following network partitioning will depend on the particular concurrency control strategy being used, as discussed in Section 6.6. Methods are classified as either optimistic or pessimistic.

Optimistic commit protocols choose availability at the expense of consistency and go with the optimistic approach to concurrency control for partitioned networks described in Section 6.6.1, in which updates are allowed to proceed independently in the various partitions. Hence, on recovery, when sites are reconnected, inconsistencies are likely. Since the resolution of these inconsistencies depends in large measure on the semantics of the transactions, it is generally not possible for the recovery manager to re-establish consistency without assistance from the user.

For example, imagine the situation where two identical transactions, T_A and T_B, are executing in two network partitions, A and B, as shown in Example 7.1. Assume that at the start, the database was consistent; the balance of account x was the same and equal to £100 throughout the database. Both T_A and T_B would commit successfully and the balance for the account would be set to zero at both sites. A superficial check when the partitions are reunited would indicate no inconsistencies between the two accounts, but in reality the account is £100 overdrawn! Now if the two replicas contained different values, at least the system would know immediately that there was a problem. However, for the system to discover the nature of the problem and devise a solution requires an understanding of the semantics of transactions. As this example suggests, there is a possibility that the action of every transaction must be scrutinized.

Having discovered, by whatever means, that there is a consistency problem, the system is faced with three possibilities:

Example 7.1 Parallel execution of identical transactions in different network partitions.

```
time
|      Site A                    Value of balance              Site B
|                           balance(xA)          balance(xB)
|  begin transaction TA              100    100 begin transaction TB
|    read balance(xB)                  .      .    read balance(xB)
|    balance(xA)=balance(xA)-100       .      .
|    if balance(xA) <0 then            .      .    balance(xB)=balance(xB)-100
|    begin                             .      .    if balance(xB) <100 then
|      print 'insufficient funds'      .      .    begin
|      abort TA                        .      .      print 'insufficient funds'
|    end                               .      .      abort TB
|    write balance(xA)                 0      0    end
v  commit TA                                       write balance(xB)
                                                 commit TB
```

(1) Undo one (or more) of the offending transactions – this could have a cascading effect on other transactions in the same partition;

(2) Apply a **compensating transaction**, which involves undoing one of the transactions and notifying any affected external agent that the correction has been made; in the above example, this would not only involve undoing the effect of one of the transactions (T_A or T_B) but also asking the customer to return the £100!

(3) Apply a **correcting transaction**, which involves correcting the database to reflect all the updates; in our example this would mean amending the balance of the account to reflect both withdrawals, thus setting the account balance to −£100 and applying an overdrawn interest charge.

Clearly, option 1 is only viable if the database merely has to be internally consistent (i.e. as long as the balance 'on paper' is correct). In reality, of course, databases not only have to be internally consistent but they must also be consistent with the real world which they model. Options 2 and 3, on the other hand, take into account the semantics of the transactions involved in relation to the real world actions which they represent. It is likely that certain types of transactions will favour compensation, while other will favour correction. In the above example, the bank would probably prefer to apply a correcting transaction!

Pessimistic merge protocols choose consistency over availability and go with the pessimistic approach to concurrency control in partitioned networks discussed in Section 6.6.1. Recovery using this approach is much more straightforward, since updates would have been confined to a single, distinguished partition. Recovery or reconnection of the network simply involves propagating all the updates to all other sites.

7.3 Local recovery protocols

In a DDBMS, we have to consider both local and global atomicity and durability of transactions. We will first examine the commonly used protocols for local recovery as in a centralized DBMS, and then see how these fit into the distributed scenario.

We have discussed a number of general issues relating to the recovery manager in Section 7.1; not all the functions described are needed by every recovery manager. These depend on the particular algorithm used by an individual recovery manager. There are four principal algorithms:

(1) Undo/redo
(2) Undo/no-redo

(3) No-undo/redo
(4) no-undo/no-redo.

Each of these will be described below. The four algorithms specify how the recovery manager handles each of the different transaction operations:

- begin transaction
- read
- write
- commit
- abort

and an additional operation which is invoked on recovery

- restart.

As is apparent from the titles of the four algorithms, they differ according to whether or not they require changes made in the DB to be undone and/or redone following failure. This decision depends on when the DB buffers are flushed to stable storage. As previously explained, if they are flushed synchronously *during transaction execution*, then changes may have to be undone. If, on the other hand, buffers are only flushed following a specific force-write from the recovery manager, then undoing may not be necessary. Whether or not redoing of a transaction is required depends on whether or not buffer pages are flushed synchronously at commit, when no redo is required, or asynchronously according to the needs of the buffer manager where a redo may be required.

7.3.1 Undo/redo

Recovery managers based on the undo/redo algorithm are the most complex since they involve both undoing and redoing of transactions following failure. However, this approach has the advantage of allowing the buffer manager to decide when to flush the buffers, hence reducing I/O overhead. Its overall effect is to provide maximum efficiency during normal operation (i.e. in the absence of transaction aborts and failures) at the expense of greater overhead at recovery. The actions of the recovery manager in response to the various operations are as follows:

Begin transaction: this triggers some DBMS management functions such as adding the new transaction to the list of currently active transactions. Conceptually also an entry is made in the log, although, for efficiency reasons, this can safely be postponed until the transaction issues its first write.

Read: the data object requested in the read command will either be read from the DB buffers (cache) belonging to the transaction, if the data object is there, or, following a fetch instruction, from the DB into its buffers, if it is not. A read does not generally require an entry to be made in the log for recovery purposes, but an entry may be made at this point for other reasons, as explained in Section 7.1.2.

Write: as for as the read operation, the data object will be updated in the transaction's buffers, if it is in the buffers or else it will be fetched from the DB and then updated. Both the before- and after-images of the data object will be written to the log.

commit: a commit transaction record is written to the log.

abort: the recovery manager must undo the transaction (i.e. partial undo); if in-place updating is being used, then the recovery manager has to read the updated pages into the DB buffers and restore the original values from the before-images on the log.

restart: the recovery manager works through the log redoing all transactions which have committed (i.e. those transactions for which there is *both* a begin transaction *and* a commit transaction entry) and undoing those for which there is no corresponding commit transaction. Recall that redoing is necessary because the changes made by committed transactions after the last checkpoint may not have reached the DB. The algorithm classifying transactions as requiring either to be undone or redone is given below. Note that this process could theoretically involve going through the entire log, but the use of checkpointing (see Section 7.1.3 above) means that it is only necessary to go back as far as the last checkpoint.

A variation on undo/redo is for the recovery manager to keep an active-list, an abort-list and a commit-list. A transaction is added to the active-list when it issues a *begin transaction*. The abort-list contains a list of all transactions aborted, while the commit-list contains a list of all committed transactions. All that is required when a transaction aborts is to add the transaction identifier to the abort-list and similarly for commit. On restart, the recovery manager simply uses those lists to decide which transactions have to be undone (abort-list) and which redone (commit-list), rather than having to go through the building up of a redo list and an undo list. Clearly, for recoverability, these lists have to be kept on stable storage and generally form part of the log.

Transactions fall into five classes as shown in Figure 7.2(a), where t_c is the time of the last checkpoint and t_f the time at which failure occurs ($t_c < t_f$). Let TC_i (start) denote the start time of transaction class i (i.e. when the begin transaction entry was made on the log) and TC_i (end) its finishing time (i.e. when the commit or abort entry was written to the log). Remember that, for performance reasons, the actual *begin transaction* entry may not be made in the log until the transaction performs its first write operation. Referring to Figure 7.2(a):

TC_1: Transactions belonging to class TC_1 started and finished (committed or aborted) prior to the last checkpoint,

$$TC_1 \text{ (start)} < t_c \text{ and } TC_1 \text{ (end)} < t_c.$$

The action of taking the checkpoint at t_c has ensured that all changes made by such transactions will have been permanently recorded in the DB (durability).

TC_2: Transactions belonging to this class started before the last checkpoint and finished before the failure occurred,

$$TC_2\text{(start)} < t_c \text{ and } TC_2\text{(end)} < t_f.$$

These transactions have completed, but may have to be redone because the data objects of the DB they updated could have still been in the DB buffers at t_f and hence would have been lost. The redo operation uses the after-images recorded on the log to restore the DB.

TC_3: Transactions belonging to this class began before the checkpoint and were still executing at t_f,

$$TC_3\text{(start)} < t_c \text{ and } TC_3\text{(end)} = \text{undefined}.$$

These transactions must be undone by applying the before-images recorded in the log for the transaction.

TC_4: Transactions of this class began after the checkpoint and finished before the failure,

$$TC_4\text{(start)} > t_c \text{ and } TC_4\text{(end)} < t_f.$$

Hence they are treated like transactions of class TC_2.

TC_5: The final class of transactions began after the last checkpoint was taken but were still active at the time of failure,

$$TC_5 \text{ (start)} > t_c \text{ and } TC_5 \text{ (end)} = \text{undefined}.$$

The log for this transaction class contains *begin transaction* and possibly before- and after-images for data objects updated by the transaction, but no corresponding *commit transaction*. As with transactions of class TC_3, transactions in class TC_5 must be undone.

Algorithm 7.1. outlines the restart procedure under the undo/redo protocol. Note that the situation is somewhat simplified if checkpoints are taken at quiescent points (synchronous checkpointing), as only transactions of classes TC_1, TC_4 and TC_5 would have to be considered, as shown in Figure 7.2(b). Recovery procedures for these three classes are the same as for asynchronous checkpointing.

When the recovery manager encounters an *abort transaction* command on the log, it adds the transaction to the undo-list. If a failure occurs during the recovery procedure, on restart the recovery manager must continue repairing the DB. It is therefore essential that the effect of undoing or redoing an operation any number of times, will be the same

Algorithm 7.1 Restart procedure for undo/no-redo protocol.

```
begin

STEP 1 LOCATE LAST CHECKPOINT RECORD
  read address of last checkpoint record from RESTART file
  read checkpoint record
  undo-list = list of transactions from checkpoint record
  redo-list = empty

STEP 2 CLASSIFY
  do while not end-of-log
    read next entry from log into log-record
    if log-record type = 'begin transaction' or 'abort transaction'
      then add transaction identifier for log record into undo-list
      else if log-record type = 'commit transaction'
        then move transaction identifier for log record from undo-list
          to redo-list
        end-if
    end-if
  end-do

  do while not end-of-undo list (working backwards)
     undo transaction
  end-do
  do while not end-of-redo-list (working forwards)
     redo transaction
  end-do
end
```

as undoing it or redoing it only once. Formally, both undo and redo must be **idempotent**, that is

$$\text{UNDO}(\text{UNDO}(\text{UNDO}(\ldots O_i))) = \text{UNDO}(O_i)$$

and

$$\text{REDO}(\text{REDO}(\text{REDO}(\ldots O_i))) = \text{REDO}(O_i)$$

for all operations O_i.

7.3.2 Undo/no-redo

Using the undo/no-redo algorithm, the DB buffers are flushed at commit so there will never be any need to redo transactions on restart, and hence there is no need to store after-images on the log. Referring to Figure 7.2(a), the recovery manager only has to concern itself with transactions active at the time of failure (i.e. transactions belonging to classes TC_3 and TC_5) which will have to be undone. The detailed actions are as follows:

begin transaction, read, write and *abort* as for undo/redo.

commit: all DB buffers are flushed and a commit record is written to the log. Alternatively, if a commit list is being used, then the transaction identifier is simply added to the list.

restart: the recovery manager must perform a global undo.

Algorithm 7.2 below outlines the procedure for restart following site failure under the undo/no-redo protocol.

7.3.3 No-undo/redo

Using the no-undo/redo algorithm, the recovery manager does not write uncommitted transactions to the stable DB. The buffer manager is forced to retain the records in main memory in the DB buffers until *commit* and this is known as **pinning** the buffers. Alternatively, updates can be written to the log instead of the DB buffers or shadowing can be used. Referring to Figure 7.2(a), the recovery manager only has to handle transactions of classes TC_2 and TC_4, which will have to be redone. No writes by transactions of classes TC_3 and TC_5 will have reached stable storage. Details of the actions required are as follows:

begin transaction and *read* as for undo/redo.

write: if the log is being used to record updates, then on receiving a write from a transaction, the recovery manager adds the after-image of the record/page to the log.

Algorithm 7.2 Restart procedure for undo/no-redo protocol.

```
begin

STEP 1 LOCATE LAST CHECKPOINT RECORD
  read address if last checkpoint record from RESTART file
  read checkpoint record
  undo-list = list of transactions from checkpoint record

STEP 2 CLASSIFY
  do while not end-of-log
    read next entry from log into log-record
    if log-record type = 'begin transaction' or 'abort transaction'
      then add transaction identifier for log-record into undo-list
      else if log-record type = 'commit transaction'
        then remove transaction identifier for log record from
             undo-list
      end-if
    end-if
  end-do

STEP 3 RECOVER
  do while not end-of-undo-list (working backwards)
     undo transaction
  end-do
end
```

commit: either the buffer manager is told it may flush the DB buffers or, where updates have been written to the log, the after-images of updated records are transferred to the DB via the buffers. A commit record is written to the log, or the transaction identifier is added to the commit-list, if one is being used.

abort: if updates are being written to the log, then the recovery manager simply writes an abort record to the log or adds the transaction identifier to the abort-list; strictly speaking, neither of these operations is necessary, but they represent good housekeeping and facilitate subsequent garbage collection in the log. If the updates are in the DB buffers, then they are erased and an abort record added to the log or abort-list.

restart: the recovery manager must perform global undo.

Algorithm 7.3 outlines the procedure for restart under the no-undo/redo protocol.

Algorithm 7.3 Restart procedure following site failure for no-undo/redo protocol.

```
begin

STEP 1 LOCATE LAST CHECKPOINT RECORD
  read address of last checkpoint record from RESTART file
  read checkpoint record
  redo-list = empty

STEP 2 CLASSIFY
  do until checkpoint record in log is reached (working backwards)
    read next entry from log into log-record
    if log-record type = 'commit transaction'
      then add transaction identifier for log-record into redo-list
    end-if

  end-do

STEP 3 RECOVER
  do while not end-of-redo-list (working forwards)
     redo transaction
  end-do
end
```

7.3.4 No-undo/no-redo

In order to avoid having to undo transactions, the recovery manager has to ensure that no updates of transactions are written to the stable DB prior to commit, whereas to avoid having to redo transactions, the recovery manager requires that all updates have been written to the stable DB prior to commit. This apparent paradox can be resolved by writing to the stable DB in a single atomic action at *commit*. To do this, the system uses shadowing as described in Section 7.1.4. Updates are written directly via the buffers to stable storage (as for in-place updating) but to a *separate* part of the stable DB. Addresses are recorded in a shadow address list. All that is then required at *commit* is to update the DB indexes to point to the new area using the shadow address list. This can be implemented as an atomic operation. No action is required on *restart* since the stable DB is guaranteed to reflect the effects of all committed transactions and none of the uncommitted ones. The before- and after-images of data objects, which are normally recorded in the log, are provided during transaction execution by the DB itself and the shadow area, respectively. A separate log is no longer required for recovery, although, as was indicated previously, a log may be maintained for other purposes. The details of no-undo/no-redo actions are as follows:

begin transaction and *read* as for undo/redo.

write: updates, via the DB buffers, are written to an unused location on stable storage and their addresses recorded in a *shadow address list*.

commit: the DB buffers are flushed to the shadow section of the stable DB, the DB indexes are updated to point to the shadow area and a *commit* record is added to the log, or the transaction identifier is added to the commit-list.

abort: the transaction is removed from the shadow address list, making the updates of the transaction effectively unreachable. As in the case of no-undo/redo, an abort record is written to the log or added to the abort-list for book-keeping purposes.

restart: the shadow address list, which contains all transactions active at the time of failure, is garbage collected, thereby leaving the DB indexes as they were.

7.4 Distributed recovery protocols

Recovery in a distributed system is complicated by the fact that atomicity is required for both the local sub-transactions for global transactions, and for the global transactions themselves. The techniques described in Section 7.3 will guarantee the atomicity of sub-transactions, but for ensuring global transaction atomicity, additional actions are required. It is necessary to modify the commit and abort processing so that a global transaction will not commit or abort until all its sub-transactions have successfully committed or aborted. The possibility of site and data communication failures further complicates the situation. An important aim of recovery techniques for DDBMSs is that the failure of one site should not affect processing at another site. In other words, operational sites should not be left blocked. Protocols which obey this are referred to as **non-blocking** protocols.

In this section, we will review two common commit protocols suitable for the DDB environment, namely

(1) Two-phase commit (2PC)
(2) Three-phase commit (3PC).

We assume that every global transaction has one site which will act as **coordinator** for that transaction. This will generally be the site at which the transaction was submitted. Sites at which the global transaction has agents are referred to as **participants**. The assumption is that the coordinator knows the identity of all participants, and each participant knows the identity of the coordinator but not necessarily of each other.

7.4.1 Two-phase commit (2PC)

As the name implies, 2PC operates in two phases: a **voting phase** and a **decision phase**. The basic idea is that all participants are asked by the coordinator whether or not they are prepared to commit the transaction. If one participant votes to abort, or fails to respond within the timeout period, then the coordinator instructs all participants to abort the transaction. If all vote to commit, then all participants are told to commit the transaction. This protocol assumes that each site has its own local log and can therefore rollback or commit the transaction reliably.

The voting rules are as follows:

(1) Each participant has one vote which can be either 'commit' or 'abort';

(2) Having voted, a participant cannot change its vote;

(3) If a participant votes 'abort' then it is free to abort the transaction immediately; any site is in fact free to abort a transaction at any time up until it records a 'commit' vote. Such a transaction abort is known as a **unilateral abort**.

(4) If a participant votes 'commit', then it must wait for the coordinator to broadcast either the 'global-commit' or 'global-abort' message;

(5) If all participants vote 'commit' then the global decision by the coordinator must be 'commit';

(6) The global decision must be adopted by all participants.

Algorithm 7.4 (a) 2PC coordinator algorithm. (b) 2PC participants algorithm.

```
(a)  begin

     STEP C1  VOTE INSTRUCTION
       write 'begin global commit' message to log
       send 'vote' message to all participants
       do until votes received from all participants
         wait
         on timeout go to STEP C2b
       end-do

     STEP C2a  GLOBAL COMMIT
       if all votes are 'commit'
```

```
    then begin
      write 'global commit' record to log
      send 'global commit' to all participants
     end

STEP C2b  GLOBAL ABORT
    at least one participant has voted abort or coordinator has timed
    out
    else begin
      write 'global abort' record to log
      send 'global abort' to all participants
     end
  end-if

STEP C3  TERMINATION
    do until acknowledgement received from all participants
     wait
    end-do
    write 'end global transaction record' to log
    finish
end
```

(b)
```
begin

STEP P0  WAIT FOR VOTE INSTRUCTION
  do until 'vote' instruction received from coordinator
    wait
  end-do

STEP P1  VOTE
  if vote = 'commit' then send 'commit' to coordinator
  else send 'abort' and go to STEP P2b
  do until global vote received from coordinator
    wait
  end-do

STEP P2a  COMMIT
  if global vote = 'commit'
    then perform local commit processing

STEP P2b  ABORT
    at least one participant has voted abort
    else perform local abort processing
  end-if

STEP P3  TERMINATION
    send acknolwedgement to coordinator
    finish
end
```

Figure 7.5 (a) Global commit stages under 2PC.

The stages of 2PC for global commit and global abort are shown diagrammatically in Figures 7.5(a) and (b) respectively, while details of the algorithm are given in Algorithm 7.4(a) for the coordinator and in Algorithm 7.4(b) for the participants.

2PC involves processes waiting for messages from other sites. To avoid processes being blocked unnecessarily, a system of timeouts is used. Timeouts in a distributed system have to be fairly accommodating due to possible queues at computing facilities and network delays!

At the start (STEP P0 of Algorithm 7.4(b)), the participant waits for the 'vote' instruction from the coordinator. Since unilateral aborts are allowed, the participant is free to abort at any time until it actually casts its vote. Hence, if it fails to receive a vote instruction from the coordinator,

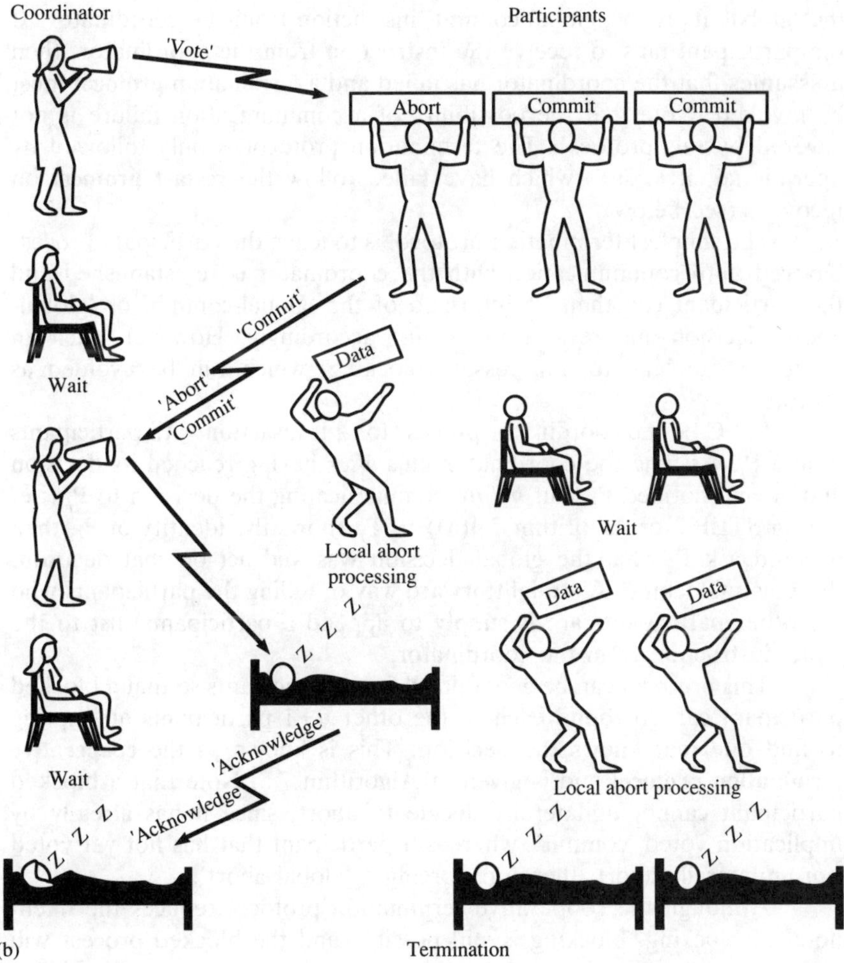

Figure 7.5 (b) Global abort steps under 2PC.

a participant simply times out and aborts. Hence a participant could in fact already have aborted, *and* performed local abort processing, prior to voting.

At step C1 (Algorithm 7.4(a)), the coordinator must wait until it has received the votes from all participants. If a site fails to vote, then the default vote of 'abort' is assumed by the coordinator and a 'global-abort' message is broadcast to all participants. The issue of what happens to the failed participant on restart will be discussed later. Since it takes only one 'abort' vote to cause a global abort, it is not necessary for the coordinator to send a 'global-abort' message to any site which voted 'abort'.

At step P1 (Algorithm 7.4(b)), the participant has to wait for either the 'global-abort' or 'global-commit' instruction from the coordinator. If the participant fails to receive the instruction from the coordinator, then it assumes that the coordinator has failed and a **termination protocol** must be invoked. Note that the possibility of a communication failure is not covered by this protocol. The termination protocol is only followed by operational sites; sites which have failed follow the **restart protocol** on recovery (see below).

The simplest termination protocol is to leave the participant process blocked until communication with the coordinator is re-established and the participant can then be informed of the 'global-commit' or 'global-abort' decision and resume processing accordingly. However, such an approach can lead to unnecessary blocking, which can be avoided as follows.

Let C be the coordinator process for a transaction with participants P_i and P_j. Assume the coordinator fails *after* having reached its decision and having notified P_i, but *before* communicating the decision to P_j (i.e. during STEP 2 of Algorithm 7.4(a)). If P_j knows the identity of P_i, then it could ask P_i what the global decision was and act on that decision, thereby unblocking. A straightforward way of telling the participants who the other participants are is simply to append a participants' list to the 'vote' instruction from the coordinator.

This protocol can be generalized for n participants so that a blocked participant can go round each of the other $n-1$ participants attempting to find one that knows the decision. This is known as the **cooperative termination protocol** and is given in Algorithm 7.5. Note that a blocked participant cannot unilaterally decide to abort, since it has already by implication voted 'commit', whereas a participant that has not yet voted *can* unilaterally abort, therefore forcing a 'global abort'.

Although the cooperative termination protocol reduces the likelihood of blocking, blocking is still possible and the blocked process will just have to keep on trying to unblock as failures are repaired. If it is only the coordinator which has failed and all participants detect this as a result of executing the termination protocol, then they can elect a new coordinator and so unblock.

The **election protocol** is straightforward. All sites involved in the election (i.e. all those which are operational) agree on a linear ordering of sites and the first site in this ordering is elected as the new coordinator. Site identifiers provide a simple way of determining this ordering. Note that it is possible for a participant which happens to be *first* in this ordering to time out, and therefore invoke the election protocol, and elect itself as coordinator.

The action on restart required by a participant following failure depends on what stage it had reached in its processing at the time of failure. The state of a participant process can be determined by examining the local log. The objective is to ensure that a participant process on

Algorithm 7.5 Cooperative termination protocol for 2PC.

```
begin
  do while P0 is blocked

STEP 1 HELP REQUESTED FROM Pi
    P0 sends a message to Pi asking for help to un-block
    if Pi knows the decision (Pi received global commit/abort or Pi
    unilaterally aborted)
      then begin
          Pi conveys decision to P0
          P0 unblocks and finishes
      end
    end-if

STEP 2 HAS Pi VOTED?
    if Pi has not voted
      then begin
          Pi unilaterally aborts
          P0 told to abort
          P0 unblocks and finishes
      end
    end-if

STEP 3 Pi CANNOT HELP; TRY Pi+1
    next Pi
  end-do
end
```

restart performs the same action as all other participants and that this restarting can be done independently (i.e. without the need to consult either the coordinator or the other participants).

Let P_r be the participant process which is attempting to restart following failure. If P_r had not voted prior to failure, then it can safely abort unilaterally and recover independently. It can also recover independently if it had received the global decision (global-commit or global-abort) prior to failure. If, however, P_r had voted 'commit' and had not been informed of the global decision prior to failure, then it cannot recover independently. It must therefore ask the coordinator (or other participants) what the global decision was. Algorithm 7.6 shows the restart protocol.

A number of improvements to the centralized 2PC protocol have been proposed which attempt to improve its overall performance, either by reducing the number of messages which need to be exchanged, or by speeding up the decision making process. These improvements depend on adopting different ways of exchanging messages, or **communication**

Algorithm 7.6 2PC participant restart following failure.

```
begin
  do while Pr is blocked

STEP 1  ASCERTAIN STATUS OF Pr IMMEDIATELY PRIOR TO FAILURE
    if Pr voted 'commit'
      then go to STEP 2
      else begin
        Pr voted 'abort' prior to failure or had not voted
        Pr aborts unilaterally
        Pr recovers independently and finishes
        end
    end-if

STEP 2  IS GLOBAL DECISION KNOWN?
    if Pr knows global decision
      then begin
        Pr takes action in accordance with global decision
        Pr recovers independently and finishes
        end
    end-if

STEP 3  Pr CANNOT RECOVER INDEPENDENTLY AND ASKS FOR HELP
    Pr asks for help from participant Pr+1 using the cooperative
    termination protocol
  end-do
end
```

topologies. The communication topology for **centralized 2PC** is shown in Figure 7.6(a). All communication is funnelled through the coordinator.

An alternative is to use the linear topology shown in Figure 7.6(b) giving **linear 2PC**. In linear 2PC, sites are ordered 1, 2, . . . , N, where site 1 is the coordinator and site 2, 3, . . . , N are the participants. The coordinator passes the 'vote' instruction to site 2, which votes and then passes its vote to site 3. Site 3 then combines its vote with that of site 2 and transmits the combined vote to site 4, and so on. Thus each participant process receives the vote of its neighbour to the left and then combines it with its own vote to produce an overall result to pass on to the participant to its right. If the vote from participant $i-1$ to i is 'commit' and i votes 'commit' then process i sends 'commit' to $i+1$. An 'abort' vote by any process will cause an 'abort' to be propagated. Having reached the end, the Nth participant adds its vote to reach the final global decision which is then passed to process $N-1$, $N-2$, . . . and so on back to the coordinator. While this procedure certainly reduces the number of messages involved in the centralized 2PC protocol, it allows no parallelism. It

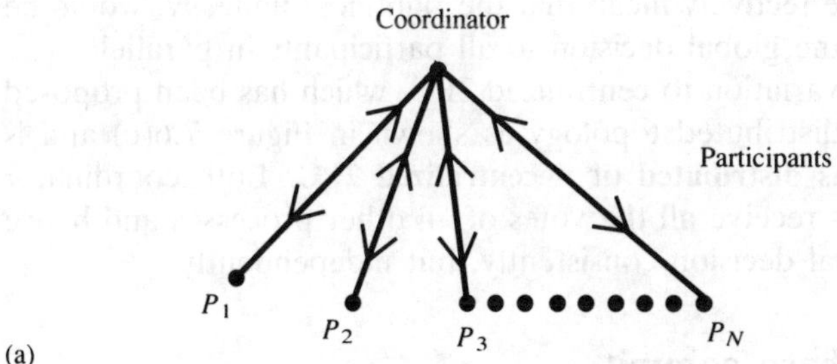

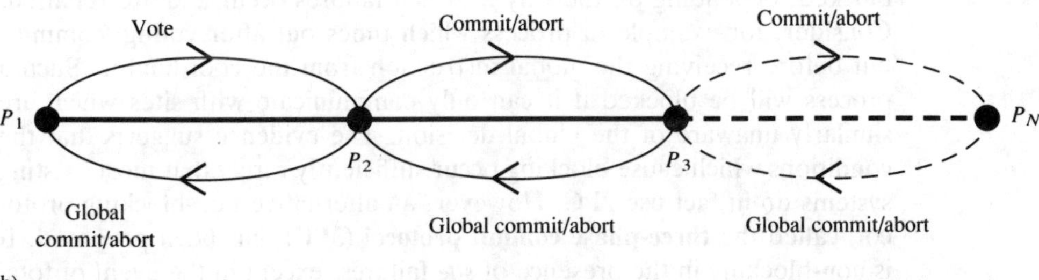

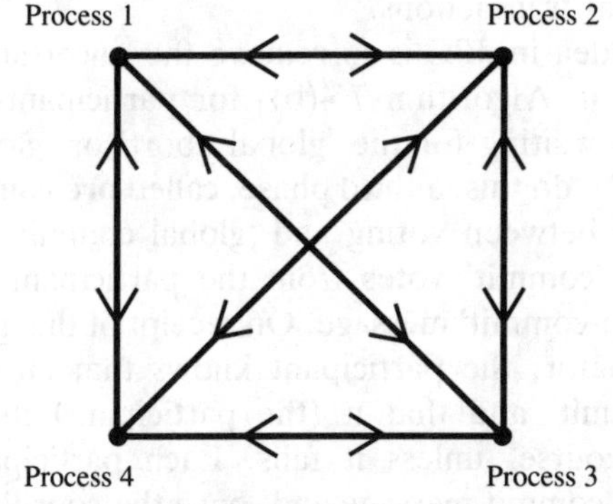

Figure 7.6 (a) Centralized 2PC topology. (b) Linear 2PC topology. (c) Distributed (decentralized) 2PC with four processes.

might suit a geographically distributed system in which distance between the source and destination plays a major role in determining the cost of sending messages.

Bernstein *et al.* (1987) suggest that linear 2PC could be improved if the voting process adopts the linear topology shown in Algorithm 7.4(b), while the decision process adopts the centralized topology of Algorithm

7.4(a); this would effectively mean that the rightmost node, *N*, would be able to broadcast the global decision to all participants in parallel.

The second variation to centralized 2PC, which has been proposed by Skeen, uses a distributed topology as shown in Figure 7.6(c) and is therefore known as **distributed** or **decentralized 2PC**. Both coordinator and all participants receive all the votes of all other processes and hence can make the global decision consistently, but independently.

7.4.2 Three-phase commit

2PC is *not* a non-blocking protocol since it is possible for sites to become blocked, depending on the way in which failures occur and are repaired. Consider, for example, a process which times out after voting 'commit', but before receiving the global instruction from the coordinator. Such a process will be blocked if it can only communicate with sites which are similarly unaware of the global decision. The evidence suggests that the conditions which cause blocking occur sufficiently rarely that most existing systems do in fact use 2PC. However, an alternative non-blocking protocol, called the **three-phase commit protocol (3PC)**, has been proposed. It is non-blocking in the presence of *site* failures, except in the event of total site failure (i.e. failure of all sites). Communication failures can, however, result in different sites reaching different decisions, thereby violating the atomicity of global transactions.

The basic idea in 3PC is to remove the uncertainty period (at the end of STEP P1 in Algorithm 7.4(b)) for participants who have voted 'commit' and are waiting for the 'global abort' or 'global commit' from the coordinator. To do this, a third phase, called **pre-commit**, is introduced into the protocol between voting and 'global commit' or 'global abort'. On receiving all 'commit' votes from the participants, the coordinator sends a 'global pre-commit' message. On receipt of the 'global pre-commit' from the coordinator, the participant knows that all other participants have voted 'commit' and that it (the participant) itself will definitely commit in due course, unless it fails. Each participant acknowledges receipt of the pre-commit message and, once the coordinator has received all the acknowledgements, it then issues the 'global commit'. The stages for global commit and global abort are given in Figures 7.7(a) and (b) respectively, while the detailed algorithms are presented in Algorithm 7.7(a) for the coordinator and Algorithm 7.7(b) for the participant. Note that an 'abort' vote from a participant is handled in exactly the same way as under 2PC.

We now consider timeouts under 3PC. Both participant and coordinator still have periods of waiting but the important feature is that all *operational* processes have been informed of a global decision to commit by the 'pre-commit' message *prior* to the first process committing and can therefore act independently in the event of failure.

Algorithm 7.7 (a) 3PC termination co-ordinator algorithm. (b) 3PC participants' algorithm.

```
(a) begin

    STEP C1  VOTE
      write 'begin transaction' in log
      send 'vote' instruction to all participants
      do until all votes received
        wait
        on timeout go to STEP C2b
      end-do

    STEP C2a  PRE-COMMIT
      if all votes are 'commit'
        then begin
            write 'pre-commit' message to log
            send 'pre-commit' message to all participants
          end

    STEP C2b  GLOBAL ABORT
        at least one participant voted 'abort' or coordinator timed out
        else begin
            write 'global abort' message in log
            send 'global abort' message to all participants
            go to STEP C4
          end
      end-if

    STEP C3  GLOBAL COMMIT
      do until all (pre-commit) acknowledgements received
        wait
      end-do
      write 'global commit' to log
      send 'global commit' to all participants

    STEP C4  TERMINATION
      do until acknowledgements received from all participants
        wait
      end-do
      write 'end transaction' entry in log
      finish
    end

(b) begin

    STEP P0  WAIT FOR VOTE INSTRUCTION
      do until 'vote' instruction received from coordinator
        wait
      end-do
```

```
STEP P1  VOTE
  if participant is prepared to commit
    then send 'commit' message to coordinator
    else send 'abort' message to coordinator and go to STEP P2b
  do until global instruction received from coordinator
    wait
  end-do

STEP P2a  PRE-COMMIT
  if global instruction = 'pre-commit'
    then go to STEP P3 (and wait for global commit)
  end-if

STEP P2b  ABORT
  at least one participant voted 'abort'
  perform local abort processing
  go to STEP P4

STEP P3  COMMIT
  do until 'global commit' instruction received from coordinator
    wait
  end-do
  perform local commit processing

STEP P4  TERMINATION
  send acknowledgement to coordinator
  finish
end
```

At the very beginning (STEP P0 of Algorithm 7.7(b)), participants wait for the 'vote' instruction from the coordinator and at the end of STEP C1 (Algorithm 7.8(a)), the coordinator waits for the votes to come in from the participants. Both these 'waits' timeout in the same way as for 2PC (i.e. unilateral abort for participant at step 0 and global-abort for the coordinator at step 1).

At the end of STEP P1 (Algorithm 7.7(b)), the participant is waiting for the 'pre-commit' or 'global abort' message from the coordinator, while at STEP P3, it is waiting for a 'global commit'. In both cases, since the participant has already voted 'commit' (otherwise it would have already unilaterally aborted), it cannot act independently and must communicate with other processes before acting. If no message has been received within the timeout limit, the participant assumes that the coordinator has failed. As for 2PC, a termination protocol for operational processes only must be invoked using an **election protocol**, such as the one described in Section 7.4.1, to elect a new coordinator.

For the 3PC termination protocol, the action required by each participant depends on the state of the participant, whether it has voted and how. The termination protocol proceeds as follows.

The first action of the new coordinator is to find out the state of each participant at the time of failure of the old coordinator. The protocol assumes that the participants all know the identity of all other participants. The new coordinator sends a 'request state' message to each participant. It then examines the information returned by the participants and makes the appropriate global decision consistent with any local decisions which have already been made. Algorithm 7.8(a) shows how the new coordinator reaches this decision, the termination protocol for the coordinator, and Algorithm 7.8(b) shows the termination protocol for the participant.

If a participant informs the new coordinator that it has already committed, because it had received a 'global commit' from the old coordinator prior to the latter's failure, then this forces the new coordinator to decide on a 'global commit'. Similarly, if a participant had received a 'global pre-commit' message from the old coordinator, then the new coordinator (re)issues the 'global pre-commit' message to all participants. Finally, if any participant had already received a 'global abort' from the old coordinator, or had unilaterally aborted, then the new coordinator must instruct all other participants to perform a global abort by issuing a 'global abort' instruction.

The new coordinator can safely ignore participants who do not respond; the protocol is concerned only with consistency among *operational* sites. How then does the protocol guarantee that the operational sites do not reach a decision to commit or abort a transaction, which is inconsistent with a decision which has already been made by a now-failed site, but which failed before it could communicate its decision to the coordinator? To answer this question we will discuss each of the two possibilities:

(1) Global decision to abort but failed participant had committed,

(2) Global decision to commit but failed participant had aborted.

In the first case, a failed participant could only have committed if it had received a 'global commit' from the coordinator. But such a message could only have been received by the failed participant if all other operational participants had received and acknowledged 'global pre-commit' messages in which case the global decision could not have been to abort.

In the second case, in order to have reached a decision to abort, the failed participant must have aborted unilaterally prior to voting (and hence voted 'abort') or received a 'global abort' message prior to failure. If it had voted 'commit' and had received a 'global abort' then the global decision could not have been commit. If, on the other hand, it had aborted

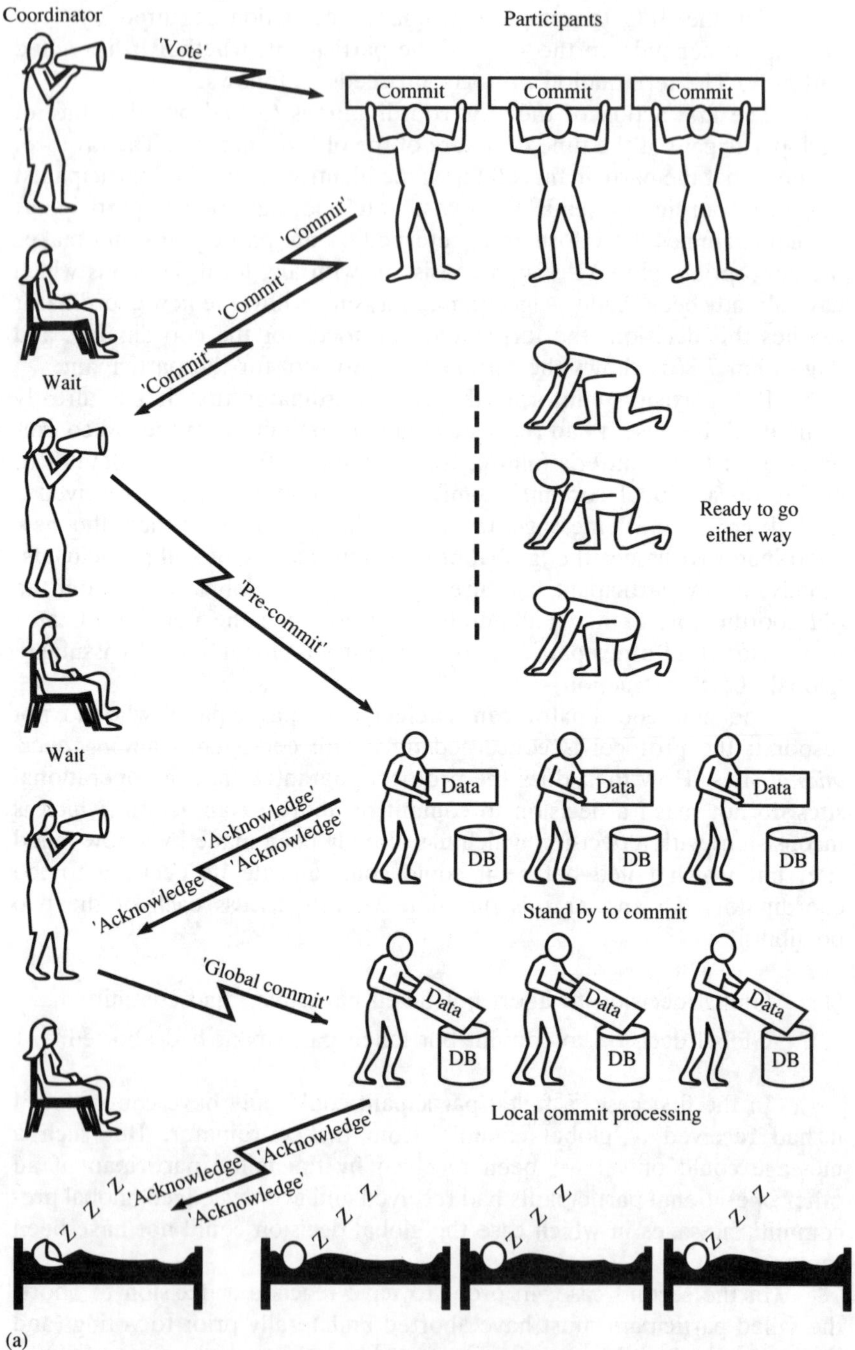

Figure 7.7 (a) Global commit stages under 3PC.

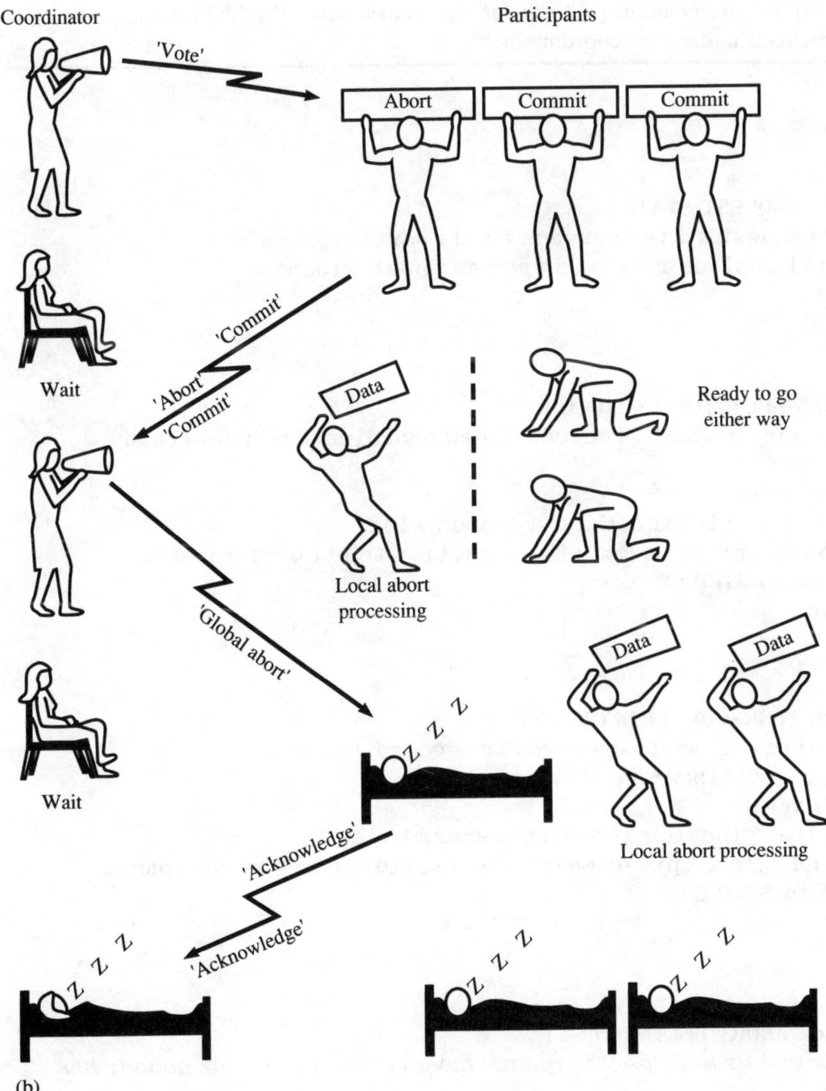

Figure 7.7 (b) Global abort steps under 3PC.

unilaterally, then there could not have been a 'global pre-commit' and hence the global decision again could not have been commit. A more rigorous proof of the correctness of 3PC and non-blocking nature of 3PC has been given by Bernstein *et al*. (1987).

On restart, a process must first ascertain what state it was in prior to failure, which it does by examining its log. As with 2PC, if it had failed prior to voting or had unilaterally aborted, then, on restart, it can safely

Algorithm 7.8 (a) 3PC termination protocol for new coordinator. (b) 3PC termination protocol for participant under new coordinator.

```
(a)  begin

     STEP C1  REQUEST STATE
       send 'request state' message to all participants
       do until replies received from all participants
         wait
       end-do

     STEP C2a  DECISION IS COMMIT
       if any participant (including new coordinator) has already
       committed
         then begin
             write 'global commit' record to log
             send 'global commit' instruction to all participants
             go to STEP C3
           end
       end-if

     STEP C2b  PRE-COMMIT DECISION
       'global pre-commit' received from coordinator
       if any participant is ready to commit
         then begin
           write 'global pre-commit' record to log
           send 'global pre-commit' instruction to all participants
           go to STEP C3
         end
       end-if

     STEP C2c  ABORT DECISION
       Either one or more participants have voted 'abort' or nobody has
       voted
       write 'global abort' record to log
       send 'global abort' instruction to all participants

     STEP C3  TERMINATION
         do until acknowledgements received from all participants
           wait
         end-do
         write 'end transaction' record to log
         finish
     end
```

```
(b) begin
    STEP P1 NEW CO-ORDINATOR REQUIRED?
     do until 'request state' message received from new co-ordinator
       wait
       if timeout then go to STEP P2
     end-do
     go to STEP P3

    STEP P2 ELECTION OF NEW COORDINATOR
     Follow election protocol
     if this participant elected
       then begin
          execute new coordinator's termination algorithm
          finish
        end
       else go to STEP P1

    STEP P3 SEND STATE TO NEW COORDINATOR
     if participant voted 'abort' or received a 'global abort' message
       then state = 'abort'
       else if participant received 'global commit'
          then state = 'committed'
          else if participant received 'global pre-commit' message
            then state = 'ready to commit'
            else state = 'don't know'
          end-if
        end-if
     end-if

    STEP P4 AWAIT INSTRUCTION FROM NEW COORDINATOR
     do until instruction received from new coordinator
       wait
       if timeout then go to STEP P1
     end-do

    STEP P5 TERMINATION
     Execute standard participant's 3PC algorithm with new coordinator
     finish
    end
```

unilaterally abort and so recover independently. It can also recover independently if it had already received a 'global commit' or 'global abort' from the coordinator prior to failure. The only difficulty therefore is if the participant had received a 'pre-commit' message prior to failure. It is possible, due to the way in which failures occur, that the global decision is 'abort'. Consider, for example, four participant sites, P_1, P_2, P_3 and P_4, and a coordinator site, C. Assume P_1 received a pre-commit message from C prior to P_1's failure. Assume then that before sending pre-commit messages to P_2, P_3 and P_4, C also fails. Following an election, one of the three operational sites left, say P_3, is elected the new coordinator. The result of the termination protocol, since none of the *operational* sites had received a global pre-commit instruction from the old coordinator, will be global-abort. Hence a participant such as P_1 which received a global pre-commit prior to failure cannot recover independently and must on restart therefore consult other sites. It seeks help in deciding how to terminate and it can still process a 'global abort' decision correctly since it has not actually committed the transaction.

In the case of total failure, each participant will attempt to recover independently and then communicate its decision to all other participants. If none can recover independently, then the last participant site to fail applies the termination protocol. How a site knows that it was the last site to fail is discussed in the next two paragraphs. Note that the termination protocol is *normally* only invoked by operational sites.

Once total site failure has occurred, the termination protocol may only be invoked by the last site to fail, otherwise a decision could be taken to commit or abort a transaction which is inconsistent with the action already taken by the now-failed last process. Assume that each site, I, maintains a list of operational sites, OP_I. This can easily be accomplished by appending a list of participants to the vote instruction from the coordinator, as suggested above. These lists are updated by sites as failures are detected. As sites recover from total failure, they can invoke the termination protocol if and only if the set of recovered operational sites, RS, includes the last process to fail. This condition can be easily verified, as the last site to fail must be common to each OP_I. Hence, for the set of sites, RS, to ensure consistent recovery, RS must contain all those common sites, i.e.

$$RS \supseteq \bigcap_{I \in S} OP_I$$

where S is the set of *all* sites in the network.

This protocol depends on the availability of all the OP_I on restart, which can be accomplished by storing them on stable storage, perhaps as part of the log. It does not matter if the lists are slightly out-of-date (i.e. they include sites as operational which have failed) since an out-of-date list will always be a superset (never a subset) of the operational sites.

The basic 3PC protocol outlined above can give rise to inconsistencies in the event of communications failures, whereby sites in one partition decide to commit a transaction, while those in another decide to abort the transaction. A modification has been suggested which overcomes this problem by essentially ensuring, as part of the termination protocol, that a coordinator cannot decide to commit or abort a transaction unless it can communicate with a majority of the sites.

To implement this modification to 3PC, we must introduce a new state, the 'ready to abort' state. This is the abort equivalent to the 'ready to commit' state, which a process under normal 3PC assumes when it receives a global pre-commit message from the coordinator. Thus before a coordinator issues a 'global abort' instruction, a majority of sites must have acknowledged a pre-abort or have committed; similarly, for global abort command and are therefore in the 'ready to abort' state. Note that if any one site has actually aborted, it is not possible for one coordinator in one partition to have a majority for abort (and therefore decides to abort), while another coordinator in a different partition has a majority for commit (and decides commit).

7.5 Recovery in multidatabases

It was pointed out in Section 6.6 that it is not possible to design a consistent concurrency control algorithm which supports *ad hoc* updates to a multidatabase and at the same time guarantee nodal autonomy. The global transaction manager must have information about local transactions in order to produce globally serializable schedules. The same problem arises with recovery protocols. All the protocols described in Section 7.4 depend on sites cooperating; in particular, delaying committing until receiving a 'global commit'. In the face of full nodal autonomy, such cooperation cannot be assumed and hence global atomicity cannot be ensured. In fact, the problem for multidatabases is almost equivalent to fully partitioned networks in which each site runs in an independent partition. This is of course a bit of an overstatement, since in the absence of communication failures, the sites in the multidatabase *can* communicate with one another. However, the lack of global control over the actions of individual sites poses the same problems for the recovery manager as with full partitioning.

SUMMARY

The ability of a (D)DBMS to be able to recover automatically, without user intervention, from unpredictable hardware and software failures is difficult and expensive to achieve. This job is the responsibility of the recovery manager. It is estimated, for example, that some 10% of the code in System R was devoted to recovery and furthermore this particular 10% of code was some of the most complex in the whole system. The recovery manager has to cater for a wide range of failures from a user-induced transaction rollback to a total failure of the entire system.

It is the objective of the recovery manager to ensure and, if necessary, restore the (D)DB to a consistent state following failure. By consistency, we mean ensuring that the acid properties of transaction atomicity and durability have been observed. To be able to perform this restoration, the recovery manager depends on information which is stored redundantly somewhere else in the system. Indeed it is this principle of built-in **redundancy**, which is fundamental to recovery. In this chapter, we have seen the importance of the log as the principal means of storing this redundant information. In order to speed up the recovery process and avoid having to go through the entire log, checkpoints are used. When a checkpoint is taken, the state of the system is recorded in the log, so that on recovery we only need to go back as far as the last checkpoint. As far as the recovery manager is concerned, the state of the system is expressed in terms of active transactions.

In a DDBMS, we have to rely on the services of the local DBMSs to perform recovery at the local level. However, the whole activity must be coordinated at the global level so that either *all* sub-transactions of a global transaction are committed or aborted. For each global transaction, one node is designated as the coordinator and is generally the site at which the transaction was submitted. All other sites involved are called participants. We discussed two protocols, known as two-phase commit and three-phase commit and examined the behaviour of both the coordinator and participant under each protocol.

These protocols depend upon a lot of communication between coordinator and participant and also on the ability of local sites to delay committing a sub-transaction until instructed by the coordinator to do so. Such a scenario is unrealistic in an MDBS environment with full nodal autonomy. It is unlikely that a general recovery protocol for MDBSs, which does not require relaxation of nodal autonomy, exists. Solutions are likely to be centred around application-specific approaches, such as those described in Section 6.8 for concurrency control.

EXERCISES

7.1 List the main causes of failure in a DDBMS and describe *briefly* what action the recovery manager must take to recover in each case.

7.2 Write algorithms for restart under the following recovery protocols
(a) undo/redo
(b) no-undo/redo
(c) undo/no-redo
(d) no-undo/no-redo.

7.3 Explain in detail the 2PC protocol.

7.4 Explain in detail the 3PC protocol.

7.5 What advantages does 3PC have over 2PC?

7.6 Why is it difficult for the DDBMS to distinguish between network and site failures and why is this distinction important?

7.7 Design coordinator's and participants' algorithms for distributed 2PC (i.e. 2PC using a distributed communication protocol).

7.8 What are the implications of synchronous logging under the undo/redo protocol?

7.9 How many messages and rounds are required for *n* participants plus one coordinator (i.e. $n+1$ sites), in the absence of failures, for each of the following protocols:
(a) centralized 2PC
(b) distributed 2PC
(c) linear 2PC
(d) 3PC.

7.10 Explain, by example, how communication failures can cause sites in different partitions to make inconsistent decisions (i.e. sites in one partition abort a transaction, while sites in a different partition commit the transaction) under 3PC.

7.11 Given the network topology shown in Figure 7.8:
(a) Which failures of a single communication link would cause the network to partition; for each failure, indicate the site membership of each partition?
(b) What is the minimum set of such failures which would have to occur for the network to be divided into three separate partitions {A, B, F}, {D, E, G, C} and {H}?

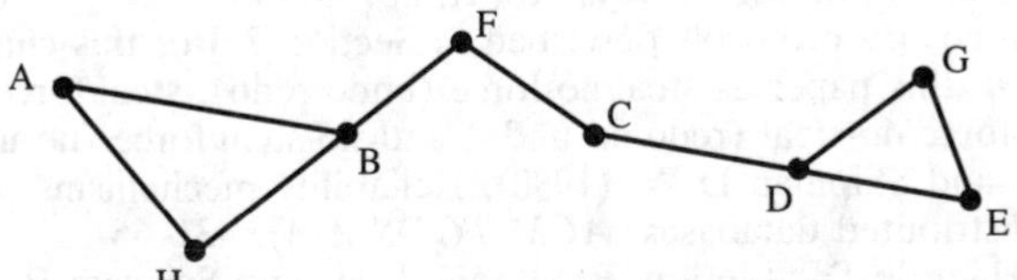

Figure 7.8 Network topology for Exercise 7.11.

Bibliography

Agrawal R. and DeWitt D.J. (1985). Integrated concurrency control and recovery mechanisms: design and performance evaluation. *ACM TODS*, **10**(4), 529–64.

This paper provides a comprehensive study of various combinations of concurrency control and recovery techniques (see Section 7.1.3).

Bernstein P.A. and Goodman N. (1984). An algorithm for concurrency control and recovery in replicated distributed databases. *ACM TODS*, **9**(4), 596–615.

The 'available copies' algorithm described in this paper assumes that site failures are detectable and that the network does not partition. On restart, a failed site must do a lot of work which means that 'missing write' or 'quorum consensus' may be preferable if there are a lot of site failures (see Section 6.6.3).

Bernstein P.A., Hadzilacos V. and Goodman N. (1987). *Concurrency Control and Recovery in Database Systems*. Wokingham: Addison-Wesley.

A comprehensive study of recovery in both DBMS and DDBMS.

Chin F. and Ramarao K.V.S. (1983). Optimal termination protocols for network partitioning. In *Proc. 2nd ACM SIGACT-SIGMOD Symp. on Principles of Database Systems*, 25–35. Atlanta, USA.

Discusses site-failure-tolerant termination protocols (see Section 7.4.2.5).

Christodoulakis S. and Ford D.A. (1989). Retrieval performance versus disc space utilization on WORM optical discs. In *Proc. SIGMOD 89*, 306–315. Portland, Oregon.

Christodoulakis S. (1987). Analysis of retrieval performance for records and objects using optical disc technology. *ACM TODS*, **12**(2), 137–169.

The above two references discuss the issues involved in archiving (see Section 7.2.3).

Date C.J. (1982). *An Introduction to Database Systems*. Vol. II, Wokingham: Addison-Wesley.

Chapter 1 of this book gives a good, clear overview of the issues involved in recovery in centralized DBMS. The importance of built-in redundancy as the key underlying principle of recovery is stressed.

Gray J.N. (1979). Notes on Database Operating Systems. In *Operating Systems: An Advanced Course*, Lecture Notes in Computer Science (60). 393–481. New York: Springer-Verlag.

A comprehensive overview of transaction management in DBMSs covering both recovery and concurrency control. The 2PC algorithm discussed in Section 7.4.1 was first proposed in this paper. Although published some time ago, much of the material is still relevant today.

Harder T. and Reuter A. (1983). Principles of transaction-oriented database recovery. *ACM Computing Surveys*, **15**(4), 287–318.

The four recovery protocols described in Section 7.3 of this chapter are presented in this paper as steal/no-force (undo/redo), steal/force (undo/no-redo), no-force/no-steal (redo/no-undo) and no-steal/force (no-undo/no-redo).

Hammer M. and Shipman D.W. (1980). Reliability mechanisms from SDD-1: a system for distributed databases. *ACM TODS*, **5**(4), 431–66.

Mohan C., Haderle D., Lindsay B., Pirahesh H. and Schwarz P. (1989). ARIES: A Transaction Recovery Method Supporting Fine-Granularity Locking and Partial Rollbacks Using Write-Ahead Logging. *IBM Research Report RJ6649*, Almaden Research Center.

ARIES (Algorithm for Recovery and Isolation Exploiting Semantics), developed at IBM's Almaden Research Center, is a recovery method which supports partial rollbacks of transactions, multiple-level locking and the write-ahead logging protocol. It is aimed at providing highly efficient recovery with minimum overhead (see also Rothnel and Mohan, 1989).

Oszu M.T. and Valduriez P. (1991). *Principles of Distributed Database Systems*, New York: Prentice Hall.

The four recovery protocols presented in Section 7.3 are classified in this book as no-fix/no-flush (undo/redo), no-fix/flush (undo/no-redo), fix/no-flush

(redo/no-undo) and fix/flush (no-undo/no-redo).
Patterson D.A., Gibson G. and Katz R.H. (1988). A case for redundant arrays of inexpensive disks (RAID). In *ACM SIGMOD Conf.*, 109–116. Chicago, Illinois.
This paper presents an interesting proposals for increasing reliability of secondary storage by mirroring the data across an array of inexpensive disks of the type normally used with personal computers. The benefits include a much longer mean-time-to-failure, better performance, lower power consumption and scalability, than the use of conventional large single disks.
Rothnel K. and Mohan C. (1989). ARIES/NT: A Recovery Method Based on Write-Ahead Logging for Nested Transactions. *IBM Research Report RJ 6650*, Almaden Research Centre.
This report describes an extension to the ARIES recovery system to support nested transactions. The approach is particularly applicable to DDBMSs (see also Mohan *et al.*, 1989).
Severance D.G. and Lohman G.M. (1976). Differential files: their application to the maintenance of large databases. *ACM TODS*, **1**(3), 256–61.
An early paper on the use of differential files (see Section 7.1.4).
Skeen D. (1982). Non-blocking commit protocols. In *Proc. ACM SIGMOD Conf.*, Orlando, Florida.
The distributed 2PC communication topology discussed in Section 7.4.1 and the 3PC protocol presented in Section 7.4.2 are described in this paper.
Skeen D. (1985). Determining the last process to fail. *ACM TOCS*, **3**(1), 15–30.
Stonebraker M.R. (1975). Implementation of integrity constraints and views by query modification. In *Proc. ACM SIGMOD Conf.*, San José, California, 65–78.
As part of a broad discussion of integrity constraints, this paper proposes a modification to differential files in which insertions and deletions are stored separately (see Section 7.1.4).
Teradata Corporation (1990). *DBC/1012 Data Base Computer Concepts and Facilities*. Teradata Corporation.

SOLUTIONS TO EXERCISES

7.7

Algorithm 7.9 (a) Coordinator's algorithm for distributed 2PC (Exercise 7.7). (b) Participants' algorithm for distributed 2PC (Exercise 7.7).

```
(a) begin

    STEP C1  VOTE INSTRUCTION
      write 'begin global commit' message to log
      send 'vote' message to all participants
      do until votes received from all participants
        wait
        on timeout go to STEP C2b
      end-do

    STEP C2a  GLOBAL COMMIT
      if all votes are 'commit'
```

```
    then begin
       write 'global commit' record to log
      end

STEP C2b  GLOBAL ABORT
    at least one participant has voted abort or coordinator has timed
    out
    else begin
       write 'global abort' record to log
      end
  end-if

STEP C3  TERMINATION
    write 'end global transaction record' to log
    finish
end
```

(b)

```
begin

STEP P0  WAIT FOR VOTE INSTRUCTION
  do until 'vote' instruction received from co-ordinator
    wait
  end-do

STEP P1  VOTE
  if vote = 'commit' then send 'commit' to coordinator
  else send 'abort' and go to STEP P2b
  do until global vote received from co-ordinator
    wait
  end-do

STEP P2a  COMMIT
  if all votes = 'commit'
    then perform local commit processing

STEP P2b  ABORT
    at least one participant has voted abort
    else perform local abort processing
  end-if

STEP P3  TERMINATION
    finish
end
```

7.8

Fewer redos would be needed.

7.9

(a) Centralized 2PC
Three rounds: (1) coordinator issues vote instruction
(2) participants cast their votes
(3) coordinator broadcasts the decision.
$3n$ messages: n per round.

(b) Distributed 2PC
Two rounds: (1) coordinator broadcasts its vote
(2) participants vote.
$n + n^2$ messages: n for round 1 and n^2 for round 2.

(c) Linear 2PC
$2n$ rounds: (1) to pass vote instruction and decision to each participant (no broadcasting of messages in parallel).
$2n$ messages: one per round.

(d) 3PC
Five rounds:
(1) coordinator issues vote instruction
(2) participants cast their votes
(3) coordinator broadcasts pre-commit
(4) participants acknowledge pre-commit
(5) coordinator broadcasts global commit.
$5n$ messages: n per round.

7.10

Suppose that a communications failure has resulted in sites being partitioned into two separate partitions, P_1 and P_2. It is possible for all sites in P_1 to be ready to commit (i.e. they have received the pre-commit instruction), while sites in P_2 are uncertain by virtue of the fact that the network partitioned before they received the pre-commit instruction. According to the 3PC termination protocol, sites in P_1 will commit, while those in P_2 will abort.

7.11

(a) Failure of ⟨B, F⟩ would result in two partitions:
{F, C, D, E, G} and {A, B, H}
Failure of ⟨F, C⟩ would result in two partitions:
{C, G, D, E} and {A, B, H, F}
Failure of ⟨C, D⟩ would result in two partitions:
{D, E, G} and {A, B, H, F, C}

(b) ⟨B, H⟩, ⟨A, H⟩ and ⟨F, C⟩

Integrity and Security

8.1 Introduction

The **integrity** of a DB is concerned with its consistency, correctness, validity and accuracy. DBs generally model real-world organizations such as banks, insurance companies and hospitals, and the state of the DB, if it were to be frozen at a particular point in time, should accurately reflect a real-world state. This freezing must be done when the DB is quiescent (i.e. no transactions active). Since we are not talking about real-time systems, we cannot say that the state of the DB corresponds *exactly* to a real-world state at a given point in time. We are concerned with integrity of the DB at a higher level. Looking at it in another way, we can say that DB integrity is concerned with whether or not the state of the DB obeys the rules of the organization it models. These rules, called **integrity rules** or **integrity constraints**, take the form of general statements governing the way the organization works.

Integrity can be viewed as addressing the issue of *accidental* corruption of the DB, for example, by inserting an invalid patient#, by failure of a concurrency control algorithm to generate serializable schedules, or the recovery manager not restoring the DB correctly following failure. **Security**, on the other hand, is concerned with *deliberate* attempts to gain unauthorized access to the data and possibly alter it in some way. This chapter reviews DB integrity issues for centralized DBMSs and then outlines how these methods can be transferred to DDBs. This is followed by a similar overview of security in centralized DBMSs. Security is concerned with ensuring that the only operations which are accepted by the (D)DBMS are from users who are authorized to perform those operations on the data in question. For example, in a university DB, a student would normally be allowed to *read* their own record in its entirety, but only the lecturer on a particular course would be allowed to *alter* the student's grade in that course. Thus while the motivations for DB integrity and security are quite different, similar techniques can be used to assist in safeguarding both.

The chapter ends with a section on security in DDBMSs, where the existence of the underlying network must be taken into consideration.

8.2 Integrity in centralized databases

8.2.1 Basic integrity concepts

DB integrity is concerned with trying to reflect in the DB the rules governing the organization which the DB is modelling. For example, consider the hospital relations which were introduced in Section 2.2.4:

```
INPATIENT(patient#, name, date_of_birth, address,
          sex, gp)
LABREQ (patient#, test-type, date, reqdr)
```

Examples of integrity rules which could be specified are:

(1) A laboratory test cannot be requested for a non-existent patient,
(2) Every patient must have a unique patient number,
(3) Patient numbers are integers in the range 1 to 99999.

These real-world rules are implemented as **integrity constraints** in the DB. For example, rule 1 could be expressed in DB terms as 'No tuple may be inserted into the LABREQ relation unless there is a corresponding tuple in the INPATIENT relation with the same value for patient#'.

There is an example of a particularly important type of integrity constraint called a **referential integrity constraint**, which will be discussed later in Section 8.2.3.

Rule 2 could be simply expressed by defining patient# as the primary key for INPATIENT. By making patient# the primary key of the relation, we have automatically guaranteed its uniqueness property and no two patients will have the same patient#. Such a constraint is called a **relation constraint**.

Finally, Rule 3 could be specified as 'patient # is an integer in the range 1 to 99999'. This is an example of a **domain constraint**.

There are a number of different aspects to integrity in addition to domain, relational and referential integrity. Concurrency control and recovery are very much concerned with ensuring the integrity of the DB through transaction atomicity and durability. However, these topics have already been discussed in detail in Chapters 6 and 7 and this chapter will therefore concentrate on other integrity issues.

8.2.2 Integrity constraints

There are basically four types of integrity constraints:

(1) Domain
(2) Relation
(3) Referential
(4) Explicit.

The first three are often grouped together and referred to as **implicit constraints** because they are an integral part of the relational data model. Relation constraints simply define the relation and its attributes and are supported by all RDBMSs. Domain constraints define the underlying domains on which individual attributes are defined and these are not explicitly supported by all RDBMSs, although they should be. Referential integrity constraints (see Section 2.2.4) are also not universally supported, although most vendors of RDBMSs promise to provide such support in their next release! Only a few systems, mainly research prototypes, support the specification of explicit constraints and usually only in a limited way. Generally, explicit constraints are imposed by the rules of the real world and are not directly related to the relational model itself. For example, in a banking system the accounts of customers with a poor credit rating are not allowed to be overdrawn. Such explicit constraints can also be used to trigger a specific action. For example, if a stock level falls below the reorder level, then an order is automatically produced. We will see examples of different types of integrity constraints later.

The **integrity subsystem** of the DBMS is conceptually responsible for enforcing integrity constraints. It has to detect violations and, in the event of a violation, take appropriate action. Since in the absence of failures and assuming correct concurrency control, the only way in which the integrity of a DB can be compromised is as a result of an update operation. The integrity subsystem must therefore monitor all update operations. In a large multi-user DB environment, data will be updated by many different applications. For example, patient tuples could be entered into the INPATIENT relation by personnel in both the admissions office and in the casualty department. Hence the check on validity of patient# (uniqueness and range) would have to be made for both routine admission transactions through the admissions office and casualty admission transactions through the casualty department. To duplicate the code is not only wasteful, but also error-prone. It is preferable to store all integrity constraints together in one place and the obvious choice is to use the system catalogue. The same integrity rules are therefore shared by all applications. With domain, relation and referential integrity rules, this is straightforward since they are specified in the data definition language and are therefore automatically stored in the system catalogue. It is important that explicit constraints be treated in the same way.

8.2.3 Relation constraints

Relation constraints are simply the method used to define relations. In SQL, relations and their attributes are defined using the CREATE command. For example, to define the INPATIENT relation:

```
CREATE TABLE INPATIENT  (patient#        INTEGER        NOT NULL,
                         name            VARCHAR(20)    NOT NULL,
                         date_of_birth   CHAR(8),
                         address         VARCHAR(20),
                         sex             CHAR(1),
                         gpn             VARCHAR(20),
  PRIMARY KEY patient# );
```

The CREATE command gives the relation a name, INPATIENT, and then lists the attributes of the relation and their type. The specification that attributes (patient# and name) are not allowed to be null (NOT NULL) means that every time a new tuple is inserted into the INPATIENT relation, values must be given for both of these attributes. Of course, primary keys must always be defined as NOT NULL. Although there is an ANSI standard for SQL, most relational DBMSs do not adhere rigidly to it; many incorporate additional features of their own and/or omit other features. The examples given here are not in any particular dialect of SQL; they should be viewed as a form of 'pseudo-SQL' serving to illustrate concepts rather than give a precise syntax for commands. For example, in the definition of the INPATIENT relation, we have explicitly defined patient# as the primary key. Some versions of SQL do not support the concept of primary keys directly; users are required to declare the primary key as NOT NULL *and* explicitly create an index on that attribute. However, since primary keys are so fundamental to the relational model, it would seem preferable to provide explicit support for them.

8.2.4 Domain constraints

The example of a relation definition given above does not show underlying domains. Attributes are just defined to be of a particular built-in type (e.g. INTEGER, VARCHAR, CHAR, DATE†, etc.). However, just as primary keys are fundamental to the relational model, domains are equally important, since it is through attributes defined over common domains that relationships between tuples belonging to different relations can be defined. An alternative definition of INPATIENT, showing domains explicitly, is as follows:

```
CREATE TABLE INPATIENT (patient#       DOMAIN(patient#)    NOT NULL,
                        name           DOMAIN(name)        NOT NULL,
                        date of_birth  DOMAIN(dob),
                        address        DOMAIN(address)
                        sex            DOMAIN(sex),
                        gpn            DOMAIN(name),
PRIMARY KEY patient# );

CREATE DOMAIN           patient#                 INTEGER
                        patient# > 0             AND
                        patient# < 10000;
CREATE DOMAIN           name                     VARCHAR(20);
CREATE DOMAIN           dob                      DATE;
CREATE DOMAIN           address                  VARCHAR(20);
CREATE DOMAIN           sex                      CHAR(1) in ('M', 'F');
```

Apart from the advantages of explicit domain definition for showing interrelation relationships, it also has the advantage of ensuring consistency in typing. Thus, for example, all names have the same type definition.

8.2.5 Referential integrity

In Section 2.2.4, the notion of foreign keys was introduced as a means of expressing referential integrity constraints. Formally, we can define a foreign key as a (composite) attribute FK = $\{a_1, a_2, a_3, \ldots, a_n\}$, where $a_1, a_2, a_3, \ldots, a_n$ are attributes of relation R if it satisfies the following conditions:

(1) Either $a_i \neq \varnothing$ for all i or $a_i = \varnothing$ for all i (i.e. all parts of a composite foreign key are either null or all parts are non-null).

(2) There exists another relation S which has primary key PK = $\{b_1, b_2, b_3, \ldots, b_n\}$ such that

† Most systems provide a number of DATE data types.

$\{a_1, a_2, a_3, \ldots, a_n\} = \{b_1, b_2, b_3, \ldots, b_n\} \neq \emptyset$
(i.e. every non-null foreign key value in R is identical to a corresponding primary key in relation S).

Recall that while primary keys, or parts thereof, are not allowed to be null, foreign keys may be null. Whether it makes sense to allow null foreign keys will depend on the rules governing the application. For example, patient# in the LABREQ relation is a foreign key of the INPATIENT relation, but it would not make sense to have a null value for patient# in LABREQ, since we would have no way of telling for which patient the test had been ordered. Of course, in this particular case, patient# in LABREQ is in fact part of a composite primary key {patient#, test_type} of LABREQ and hence by definition is not allowed to be null. Assume in addition to the INPATIENT relation

INPATIENT (patient#, name, date_of_birth, address, sex, gpn)

there is a second relation containing information about GPs:

GPLIST (gpname, gpaddress, gptelno)

gpn in the INPATIENT relation is a foreign key of GPLIST. We have assumed, for simplicity, that GP names are unique. In this case it would be acceptable to allow gpn in INPATIENT to assume null values when the patient either does not have a GP (inapplicable) or cannot remember their GP's name (not known).

Having defined foreign keys, we can now define **referential integrity** in terms of foreign keys as follows: the database must not contain any unmatched foreign keys.

This rule has consequences for updates to and deletions of the target or referenced primary key. In both cases, there are a number of possibilies. Consider the case of the deletion of a primary key which is referenced by a foreign key in another relation. For example, what should happen to tuples in the INPATIENT relation which have gpn='John Doe' if we delete John Doe from GPLIST? Remember that deletion of the primary key automatically implies deletion of the entire tuple. In this case, a logical solution would probably be to set the gpn value in the referenced tuples in INPATIENT to null. In general, however, there are three possibilities:

(1) Disallow the deletion of primary keys as long as there are foreign keys referencing that primary key (RESTRICTED);

(2) Deletion of the primary key has a cascading effect on all tuples whose foreign key references that primary key, and they too are deleted (CASCADES);

(3) Deletion of the primary key results in the referencing foreign keys being set to null (NULLIFIES).

In the case of updates to the primary key, the same three possibilities exist, although the results are slightly different:

(1) Disallow the update as long as there are foreign keys referencing the primary key (RESTRICTED);
(2) Update of the primary key cascades to the corresponding foreign keys, which are also updates (CASCADES);
(3) Update of the primary key results in the referencing foreign keys being set to null (NULLIFIES).

The choice of which of the three approaches for both update and deletion is appropriate will depend on the application, and it is likely that different options will be specified for different foreign keys in the same DB. For example, to our definition of the INPATIENT relation, we could add the following foreign key definition:

```
FOREIGN KEY gpn REFERENCES gpname OF TABLE GPLIST
  NULLS ALLOWED
  DELETION NULLIFIES
  UPDATE CASCADES;
```

8.2.6 Explicit constraints

Most RDBMS provide only very limited support for explicit (also called **semantic** constraints). SQL provides an ASSERT command for specifying such constraints, although it is not implemented in many systems. To illustrate the use of explicit constraints, consider a banking DB with two relations

```
CUSTOMER (cust#, name, address, telno,
          credit_rating)
ACCOUNT (acc#, cust#, acctype, balance)
```

We wish to specify the integrity constraint that accounts of customers with a poor credit rating are not allowed to be overdrawn. This could be specified as:

```
ASSERT OVERDRAFT_CONSTRAINT ON CUSTOMER, ACCOUNT:
ACCOUNT.balance>0 AND
ACCOUNT.acc# = CUSTOMER.cust# AND
CUSTOMER.credit_rating='poor';
```

The general format of the ASSERT command is

```
ASSERT constraint-name
        ON relations-names: condition
```

The condition is evaluated by the integrity subsystem and if it evaluates to false then the constraint is said to be violated. Thus, if an attempt is made to withdraw money from the account of a customer with a poor credit rating which would result in the account being overdrawn, the ASSERT condition would evaluate to false and the update would therefore be rejected. The ASSERT command effectively defines valid states of the DB.

The second type of explicit constraint specifies an action to be taken in response to a certain state of the DB. Such constraints are known as **trigger constraints** because they trigger certain actions. For example in a stock control system with a relation:

STOCK (<u>part#</u>, no_in_stock, re_order_level)

we could specify that a procedure called ORDER_PROC should be triggered when the no_in_stock falls below the re_order_level:

```
DEFINE TRIGGER REORDER_CONSTRAINT
ON STOCK:
no_in_stock < re_order_level
ACTION ORDER_PROC(part#);
```

The general format of DEFINE TRIGGER is

```
DEFINE TRIGGER trigger_constraint_name
ON relation_names:
trigger_condition
ACTION trigger_procedure_name(parameter_list);
```

If the trigger_condition is detected, then trigger_procedure_name is called with parameters parameter_list. Note that the ASSERT command is used to *avoid* a certain DB state which violates an integrity condition and hence must be applied *before* the update takes place. Trigger conditions, on the other hand, are evaluated *after* the update.

8.2.7 Static and dynamic constraints

So far we have classified integrity constraints as either **implicit** (domain, relation and referential) or **explicit**. They can also be classified as either **static** (or **state**) or **dynamic** (or **transition**) constraints. Static constraints specify legal DB states, whereas dynamic constraints describe legitimate transitions of the DB from one state to another. For example, a salary might only be allowed to increase, which could be specified for the relation

```
EMPLOYEE (emp#, name, address, dept, jobtitle,
          salary)
```

as

```
ASSERT PAYRISE_CONSTRAINT ON UPDATE OF EMPLOYEE:
    NEW salary > OLD salary;
```

We have added the additional keywords of UPDATE OF, OLD and NEW to the syntax of the ASSERT statement introduced above in Section 8.2.6. UPDATE indicates that the integrity constraint is to be checked prior to update. It is more sensible to do the check first than to go ahead and perform the update, which could involve a write to the DB, only to have to undo it if the constraint is violated as a result of the update. NEW and OLD obviously refer to the new (after update) value of the data item to which the constraint is applied and OLD refers to its value before update.

8.3 Integrity issues in distributed databases

Apart from concurrency control and recovery, which have already been discussed in Chapters 6 and 7 respectively, very little research has been carried out on integrity issues for distributed databases, especially for multidatabases. In the case of homogeneous distributed databases, which have been designed 'top–down', there is generally no problem. Explicit and implicit integrity constraints can be defined at DDB design time and incorporated into the integrity subsystems of each of the local DBMSs in a consistent manner. However, the division into global and local levels in multidatabases makes consistent support for integrity constraints much more difficult. We can divide the problems into three main groups:

(1) Inconsistencies between local integrity constraints,
(2) Difficulties in specifying global integrity constraints,
(3) Inconsistencies between local and global constraints.

8.3.1 Local integrity constraints

Local integrity constraints are specified and enforced by the local DBMS and nodal autonomy requires that these should not be changed just because that node participates in a multidatabase. At the organizational level, different rules could apply at different nodes. For example, one hospital might insist on a date of birth being entered for all inpatients, while another does not. This was a common requirement of manual hospital record systems, where patient records were sometimes filed by date of birth. One faculty in a university might require students to take a minimum of five courses a year, whereas another might require six. From the local DBMS point of view, this does not pose any particular problem, since it simply enforces its own integrity rules for its own local DB. However, for the global user these differences cause confusion. For example, a global user might ask for the total marks a student had gained in their end-of-year examinations with a view to calculating an average. To calculate the average correctly, the user must know that the divisor for one faculty is 5 and for the other 6.

Taking this example one step further, what do we do if the student takes some courses in one faculty and some from another? This is of course an organizational issue but one which places demands on the DDBMS to support integrity constraints at the global as well as the local level.

8.3.2 Global integrity constraints

As the example above illustrates, it is quite possible to envisage the need for global integrity constraints. Consider a large organization with several semi-autonomous departments, each one running its own DBMS managing its own employee DB. Suppose an individual works part-time for more than one department and that, in order to maintain their part-time status, this employee must not work more than 20 hours per week. It is obviously not sufficient to apply a local constraint at both sites, which does not allow the number of hours worked to go above 20, since this could allow the global figure to exceed 20. Also, it is unlikely to be logical to simply set the upper limit to 10 hours per week at each site, as this would create unnecessary inflexibility for the employee and the departments. Presumably the departments wish to be free to move the employee around freely wherever the demand for their services is greatest. Hence it is quite conceivable that the employee could work 20 hours in any one week in one department and no hours in the other. It is clear from this example, that global constraints may be necessary.

It is also possible to envisage global referential integrity constraints. For example, the INPATIENT relation might be stored at one site and the GPLIST at another with INPATIENT.gpn being a foreign key of GPLIST. Such a constraint could only be enforced at a global level. Global integrity constraints can be stored in the global system catalogue (see Chapter 9) and applied at the global level to global transactions. The problem of resolving inconsistencies between local and global constraints is discussed below in Section 8.3.3.

8.3.3 Inconsistencies between local and global integrity constraints

If both local and global constraints are permitted, then there must be a way of resolving inconsistencies between them. In the case of the employee example above, assume that the local DBs and the global DDB have specified an upper limit of 20 hours. What do we do when one local DB, LDB_1, has entered a value of 15 for number_of_hours_worked for employee x, and the other local DB, LDB_2, wants to enter a value of 10 for number_of_hours_worked for the same employee in the same week. If we reject LDB_2's transaction, we are violating its autonomy, but if we accept it we are violating the global integrity constraint. Presumably if such a situation actually occurred in the real world, both departments would be notified and take some corrective action together. In a multidatabase environment, therefore, we need a facility for defining a global trigger procedure which might allow LDB_2's update to be made, but notifies both LDB_1 and LDB_2.

The resolution of conflicting global and local integrity constraints will depend in the main on the degree of integration between the various sites participating in the DDB. If there is strong global control, then it is likely that global constraints will have priority over local constraints. On the other hand, if the DBs are just participating in a loose federation with virtually no global control, then local integrity constraints will dominate over global constraints.

8.3.4 Summary of integrity issues

The above discussion has clearly shown the need for both local and global integrity constraints in DDBMSs. The design of these global integrity constraints will form an important part of schema integration, which is discussed in Chapter 9. In the case of multidatabases, issues such as checking that the current state of the underlying local DBs does not violate a newly specified global integrity constraint must be addressed at the management policy level. In centralized DBMSs, the addition of a new integrity constraint to the system catalogue will be rejected by the integrity subsystem if the state of the DB at that time violates the constraint. Even in a centralized DBMS with a centralized system catalogue, such checking can be costly. But in a multidatabase with strong global control, it would be essential to check the current state of all the local DBs involved and the local system catalogues. This is necessary in order to make sure that the new global constraint does not conflict directly with an existing local constraint or local state. In fact, only those sites whose data is included in the integrity constraints would have to be checked. In a loose federation, it is unlikely that such checking would be done.

8.4 Security in centralized DBMSs

Ensuring the security of data in large DBs is a difficult task and imposes an access overhead on users of the DB. The level of security installed will depend on how valuable or sensitive the data is. This is exactly the same with physical security: £1,000,000 would be guarded more carefully than £1. Thus when deciding on the level of security to impose on a DB, it is necessary to consider the implications of a security violation for the organization which owns the data. If, for example, criminals gained access to a police computer system in which details of surveillance operations and suchlike were stored, the consequences could be serious. Although most of the advances in the development of secure computer systems have come from military applications, many other organizations also require security, if only to avoid competitors gaining inside knowledge about the company or to prevent fraud being perpetrated by employees.

8.4.1 DB security issues

There are many different aspects to security in organizations, from the legal, social and ethical issues to how often passwords should be changed. Most countries now have data protection legislation which, among other things, requires owners of DBs containing personal information about individuals to take reasonable precautions to ensure that unauthorized people do not gain access to it. Most of these issues have nothing to do with the DBMS itself and are in fact totally outside the control of the DBMS. They are part of the general **security policy** of the organization. The basic security mechanism provided by a DBMS is control of access to data objects. For example, a user may be allowed to read two relations but only to update one of them.

One fundamental decision which must be made is the basic unit or **granule** to which security control can be applied. The **granularity** of the data object can range from an individual attribute within a tuple of a relation to a whole relation or even the entire DB. The finer the granularity of data objects supported by the system, the more precise can be the access rights. Generally speaking, a fine granularity system will incur a much higher administration overhead than a coarse granularity system. For example, if the granule is in fact the whole DB, then virtually all that we need to do is to maintain a list of authorized users for that DB, indicating what type of access rights the users have (read, update, insert, delete). At the other extreme, if the data granule is an individual attribute, then we have to store the same information for each attribute. Of course, defaults will operate depending on the security policy of the organization.

There are four main types of security policies for control of access within organizations:

(1) Need to know
(2) Maximized sharing
(3) Open systems
(4) Closed systems.

Many organizations adopt a policy which restricts access to information on a **need to know** basis. Thus, if a user requires read (write) access to a particular set of data objects, then they are granted the appropriate rights to those objects and those objects alone. For example, if security controls are placed at the relation level (i.e. the granule is a relation), then once a user has access to any part of a relation, they have automatic access to all attributes of all tuples within that relation. If the granule is the individual attribute then it is possible to implement a very precise need to know system.

However, while a need to know security policy might well be appropriate for military and high security applications, it is generally not appropriate for normal commercial information processing environments where *data sharing* is an important and fundamental goal of the DB approach. At the other end of the security policy spectrum from need to know, we have a policy of **maximized sharing** in which the objective is to facilitate as much data sharing as possible. Maximized sharing does not mean that all users have full access rights to all the data in the DB; only those parts of the DB which really need to be protected are protected. For example, those who are using a patient DB for epidemiological research need full access to all the clinical information about the patients, plus probably data such as the patient's age, sex, occupation, etc. They do not, however, need access to personal identification information such as names. The problem of providing security in DBs which are used in this way (statistical DBs) will be discussed in detail in Section 8.4.5.

An **open policy** for access control means that the default is that users have full access to the data, unless access is *explicitly* forbidden. Such an approach facilitates data sharing, but has the disadvantage that the omission or accidental deletion of an access rule results in data being accessible to all users, and could lead to confidential data being made public.

In a **closed policy**, on the other hand, access to all data is implicitly forbidden, unless access privileges to that data are explicitly granted. Such a policy is used by organizations that follow the need to know approach. Closed systems are obviously more secure than open systems. Moreover, since the default is to forbid access, errors in the rules will restrict rather than open up access.

Information on access privileges is called a **user profile**, which describes an individual user's access rights to data objects in the system.

User profiles are generally represented in the form of an **authorization matrix** in which the users (or user groups) form the rows of the matrix, and the data objects the columns. Each entry in the authorisation matrix, A[*i*,*j*], specifies the set of operations which user *i* is allowed to perform on data object *j*. An example is given in Table 8.1

8.4.2 Types of access control

In Section 8.4.1 we looked at the various policies for access control at the organizational level. In this section we will look at the access control at the DB level. Four main types of controls can be identified:

(1) Content independent
(2) Content dependent
(3) Statistical control
(4) Context dependent.

With **content-independent control**, a user is allowed/not allowed to access a particular data object irrespective of the content of the data object. An example of a content-independent access control would be: 'user A is allowed read access to the employee relation'. Checking can be done at compile time, since the actual value of the data object does not have to be examined.

With **content-dependent control**, access to a data object by an individual user depends on the content of the DB and hence can only be checked at run-time. This clearly involves a greater overhead than content-independent control. An example of a content-dependent access control

Table 8.1 Authorization matrix.

	DATA OBJECTS			
USERS	R_1	R_2	R_3	R_4
A	All	All	All	All
B	Select Update	Select	Select Delete	All
C	All	Select	Select Update	Select
D	Select	None	All	Select
E	All	None	Select Insert	Select Delete

would be: 'Employee x is allowed to update the salary field of an employee provided the current salary is less than £15,000'.

Under **statistical control** the user is permitted to perform statistical operations such as SUM, AVERAGE, and so on, on the data but is not allowed to access individual records. For example, a user might be allowed to count the number of patients in the DB suffering from a particular disease, but is not allowed to see the diagnosis of an individual patient. The provision of security for statistical DBs is complex and will be discussed separately in Section 8.4.5.

With **context-dependent control**, the user's access privileges depend on the context in which the request is being made. For example, a user may only be allowed to modify a student's grade in a course if the user is the course lecturer. A user in the personnel department may be allowed to update an employee's salary, but only between 9 a.m. and 5 p.m.

8.4.3 Multilevel security

It is common practice in military organizations to classify information according to various levels (e.g. top-secret, secret, confidential and unclassified) and to assign an appropriate security clearance level to each user. Thus a user with confidential security clearance is allowed to see material with *both* a confidential *and* unclassified security level. This approach has been copied in the development of security systems for computer software, especially operating systems. A security **classification level** is assigned to objects (data, files, etc) and a **clearance level** to users. The classification and clearance levels are ordered

top secret > secret > confidential > unclassified

The rules governing this multilevel security model, where clearance (A) is the clearance level of user A and classification (x) is the classification level of object x are

(1) User A can read object x if and only if clearance (A) $\geqslant$ classification (x),

(2) User A can update object x if and only if clearance (A) = classification (x).

One of the advantages of the multilevel model is that it not only supports powerful content-independent access controls, but also restricts the flow of information by ensuring that information can only flow upwards through the model. It is not possible for a user with a particular clearance level to copy data, and thereby make it accessible to other users with a lower clearance level.

In order to develop a multilevel security policy for a DBMS, it is generally assumed that the operating system on which the DBMS is built also has a multilevel security policy in operation at the file level. Such operating systems make use of a **reference monitor** which has the following characteristics:

(1) It is called every time a user requests access to an object,

(2) It supports a multilevel security policy,

(3) It is tamper-proof,

(4) It is sufficiently small that it can be thoroughly tested and the code formally verified as correct.

Thus DBMSs built on top of such systems normally use the operating system's reference monitor by careful mapping of the DB objects (relations, tuples, attributes) onto files. The simplest approach is to use the relation as the security granule (i.e. the basic unit of data to which security controls can be applied). Thus all tuples in a relation will be at the same classification level and the relation is then mapped directly onto an operating system file. If rows (or columns) of a relation have different security classifications, then the relation must be divided into units of the same classification level which can then be mapped onto individual files. With horizontal fragmentation by row, the original relation can be reconstituted by applying the set UNION operator to the fragments. With vertical partitioning by column, it is necessary to repeat the primary key in each partition and reconstitution is carried out by performing a relational JOIN on the fragments.

If content-dependent control is required, then the services of the operating system cannot be used and hence security would have to be provided by the DBMS directly. In this case, the DBMS would therefore require its own reference monitor.

Work on reference monitors has led to the development of secure operating systems based on a **trusted kernel**, containing all the security-related functions. One of the problems with many security techniques is that code concerned with authorization checks and security related issues is scattered throughout the system (query interface, system catalogue, etc.). The objective of the trusted kernel approach is to centralize all security-related information and processes in the kernel. In a multilevel security system, the reference monitor corresponds directly to the trusted kernel.

The level of security provided by commercial RDBMSs is insufficient for applications which require very tight security; such systems need to make use of trusted kernels. However, with current research into the development of secure versions of UNIX and other common operating systems coupled with growing interest by the information technology industry in security-related issues, it seems probable that some of the high security features normally associated with military systems will gradually find their way into commercial RDBMSs.

8.4.4 Security facilities in SQL

In this section we will review the basic security features provided through SQL for RDBs. These features are provided in two quite different ways:

(1) View mechanism
(2) Authorization rules.

The ANSI–SPARC division of the architecture of DBMSs into three levels, conceptual, internal and external, was motivated mainly by the need to provide data independence (see Section 2.2). Users access the DB through a logical external schema or user view (external level), which is mapped onto the global logical schema (conceptual level), which is then mapped onto physical storage (internal level). Data independence insulates applications using different views from each other, and from the underlying details of physical storage. Views also provide users with a means of logically structuring the data in a way which is meaningful to them, and of filtering out data which is not relevant. An important and very useful byproduct of the view mechanism is the security that it provides. Users can only access data through views and hence are automatically prevented from accessing data which is not contained in their own view.

The SQL view definition facility allows users to create views which combine data from any number of relations. The original relations of the conceptual schema on which views are defined are referred to as **base relations** or **base tables**. Effectively, the view mechanism creates a virtual table, against which the user can issue queries in just the same way as against a base table. For example, using the relation

```
INPATIENT (patient#, name, date_of_birth, address,
           sex, gpn)
```

we can define a view which gives only Dr Haughey's patients as follows:

```
CREATE  VIEW  HAUGHEY_PATS
        AS    SELECT  patient#, name,
                      date_of_birth, address, sex
              FROM    INPATIENT
              WHERE   gpn = 'Dr Haughey';
```

Users accessing the DB through the view will have access only to a value-dependent horizontal subset of the original relation.

Similarly, if the INPATIENT relation is being used for statistical analysis, then users would not be allowed to see individual patients' names and hence could access the DB through the following view:

```
CREATE   VIEW   INPAT_STAT
         AS     SELECT  patient#, date_of_birth, sex
                FROM    INPATIENT;
```

Tuples in the INPAT_STAT virtual relation are a vertical, value-independent subset of the original INPATIENT table.

Views can also be defined across two or more tables. For example, consider the relations

```
STUDENT (student#, name, address)
RESULT (student#, course#, grade)
```

We wish to form a view over these two relations which contains the names and addresses of all students who passed course 1BA1 in 1990. This can be accomplished using the following CREATE command:

```
CREATE   VIEW   PASS_1BA1
         AS     SELECT     student#, name, grade
         FROM STUDENT, RESULT
         WHERE STUDENT.student# =
                RESULT.student#
                AND RESULT.course# = '1BA1'
                AND RESULT.grade ≠ 'FAIL'
                AND RESULT.date = '1990';
```

Views therefore provide a very valuable and efficient security feature at no extra cost since they are provided already as part of the 3-level architecture.

In addition to the view mechanism, SQL also provides facilities for **authorization rules**, via the GRANT command which allows users to define authorisation matrices as shown in Table 8.1. The GRANT command has the general form

```
GRANT operation ON relation-or-view-name TO user
```

where operation can be SELECT, INSERT, DELETE or UPDATE. Examples of the use of the command are

```
GRANT SELECT ON INPAT-STAT TO USER-1;
GRANT ALL ON RESULT TO USER2;
GRANT SELECT ON STUDENT TO PUBLIC;
```

ALL and PUBLIC are keywords indicating all DB operations (SELECT, INSERT, DELETE AND UPDATE) and all users, respectively.

SQL also allows users to propagate privileges to other users by including the WITH GRANT OPTION in the original command. For example,

```
GRANT SELECT ON INPAT_STAT TO USER-4 WITH GRANT
OPTION;
```

would allow USER-4 to propagate the select privilege to another user by issuing the following command:

```
GRANT SELECT ON INPAT_STAT TO USER_5;
```

The corresponding SQL command for withdrawing access privileges is REVOKE:

```
REVOKE operation ON relation-or-view-name FROM
user;
```

For example:

```
REVOKE SELECT ON INPAT_STAT FROM USER-4;
```

If USER-4 had propagated this privilege to USER-5, as shown above, then this REVOKE command on USER-4 would automatically cascade to USER-5 who would no longer have SELECT privilege on INPAT_STAT.

To avoid specifying vast numbers of authorization rules, it is possible to establish a set of defaults, which obviate the necessity of defining every possible combination of privileges for all users. Thus, for example, a user who is allowed to update a relation would normally be allowed to read it, without explicitly having been granted SELECT privilege on that relation.

The INGRES RDBMS, through its query language QUEL, adopts a slightly different approach and allows users to specify additional access constraints on the basis of the time of day, the day of the week and the particular terminal(s) from which the request is being made (i.e. context-dependent controls, see Section 8.4.2). In addition INGRES uses **dynamic query modification**. Consider the QUEL specification of the INPAT_STAT view given above:

```
DEFINE PERMIT ON INPATIENT (patient#, date_of_birth,
                           sex) TO USER-6
```

If USER-6 then issues a query to list all the female patients of the INPATIENT relation in QUEL, that is

```
RETRIEVE (INPATIENT.ALL)
    WHERE sex = 'F'
```

INGRES will dynamically modify this query before executing it as follows:

```
RETRIEVE (patient#, date of birth, sex)
    WHERE sex = 'F'
```

RETRIEVE is the QUEL equivalent of SQL SELECT, and ALL is equivalent to SQL*, indicating all attributes of the referenced table.

8.4.5 Statistical databases

Statistical databases present particular security problems, which are difficult to overcome. A **statistical database** is one which generally contains information about individuals in a population and is used primarily for producing statistics on that population (e.g. for census purposes or epidemiological research). Users of such DBs are only allowed to perform statistical operations on the DB such as SUM, COUNT and AVERAGE.

Consider a census DB containing the following relation:

```
PERSON (census#, name, address, dob, sex,
        profession, income)
```

Suppose a user knows an individual's name ('Patrick Murphy') and his address ('22 Rowan Heights') and wants to find out his salary. An SQL query of the following form is not permitted:

```
SELECT    salary       FROM PERSON
          WHERE        name='Patrick Murphy'
          AND          address = '22 Rowan
                       Heights';
```

Instead the user issues the following legitimate query:

```
SELECT    COUNT(*)     FROM PERSON
          WHERE        name = 'PatrickMurphy'
          AND          address = '22 Rowan
                       Heights';
```

The SQL COUNT function returns the number of tuples in the referenced relation. Suppose then that there is only a single tuple in the PERSON relation satisfying the search predicate so the system will respond:

```
Number of tuples found = 1.
```

Having located Patrick Murphy's tuple in the relation, the user can then issue the following legitimate query to obtain the income:

```
SELECT   SUM (income) FROM PERSON
         WHERE        name = 'PatrickMurphy'
         AND          address = '22 Rowan
                      Heights';
```

The SQL SUM function calculates the sum of the values in a given column of a relation.

Of course it is unlikely that users would be allowed to issue search predicates involving names of individuals in such an application. However, if the user knows something about an individual, such as their profession or their date of birth, it is possible for the user to experiment with different search predicates until eventually locating a single tuple. Such a search predicate is known as a **single tracker** because it enables the user to track down an individual tuple. The existence of a single tracker potentially compromises the security of the DB.

A detailed discussion of statistical DBs is beyond the scope of this book, and for further information, the reader is referred to Date (1982) and Fernández *et al.* (1981), and for a discussion on trackers to Denning *et al.* (1979). As yet the security problems associated with statistical DBs have not been fully and satisfactorily solved. Although this might seem like a peripheral and rather specialized issue, our research has shown that there is great potential for the use of multidatabase technology in the medical domain, specifically for the purpose of building large statistical DBs for epidemiological research.

8.5 Security issues in distributed databases

In a DDB with nodal autonomy, security of data will ultimately be the responsibility of the local DBMS. However, once a remote user has been granted permission to access local data, the local site no longer has any means of further ensuring the security of that data. This is because such access implies copying the data across the network. Issues such as the relative security level of the receiving site and the security of the network have to be taken into account. There is no point in a secure site sending confidential data over an insecure communications link or sending it to an insecure site. In this section, we will look at four additional security issues which are peculiar to DDBs.

Remember that the local DBMS is assumed to take responsibility for its own data at its own site. The four issues which we will consider are

(1) Identification and authentication
(2) Distribution of authorization rules
(3) Encryption
(4) Global view mechanism.

8.5.1 Identification and authentication

When a user attempts to access any computer system, they must first identify themselves (e.g. by giving a name), and then authenticate that identification (e.g. by typing a password). In order to allow users to access data at remote sites in a DDB, it would be necessary to store their user names (identification information) and passwords (authentication information) at *all* sites. This duplication of essential security information is in itself a security risk, even though the passwords are always stored in encrypted form.

A better approach which avoids duplication, is to allow users to identify themselves at one site, called their **home site**, and for that site to perform the authentication. Once that user has been admitted by the DDBMS at their own site, all other sites will accept the user as a *bona fide* user. This does not of course mean that the user now has unlimited access to all data in the DDB, as they would still have to satisfy local access controls on the data. Naturally such a system depends on sites being able to satisfactorily identify themselves to one another first, and this can be done in exactly the same way as for users by giving a site identifier followed by a password.

8.5.2 Distribution of authorization rules

Since the data itself is distributed, it is logical to store authorization rules for access to a data object at the site at which that data object is stored. The alternative is to replicate all rules fully at all sites. This would enable authorization checks to be performed at compilation time for content-independent control and at the beginning of execution for content-dependent controls. However, this early validation of access rights to remote objects has to be offset against the cost of maintaining fully replicated rules.

8.5.3 Encryption

Encryption is intended to overcome the problem of people who bypass the security controls of the DBMS and gain direct access to the DB or who tap the communication lines. It is standard practice to encrypt passwords, but it is possible also to encrypt data and messages, and this may well be desirable in a DDB environment. The original data or message, referred to as **plaintext**, is subjected to an **encryption algorithm**, which scrambles the plaintext into **ciphertext** using an **encryption key**. Unless the recipient knows the encryption key, it will be virtually impossible to decipher the ciphertext. In fact, the dominating issue is not the difficulty of breaking the code, but rather the security of the encryption keys.

There are two principal methods of encryption, the Data Encryption Standard and Public Key Encryption. The **Data Encryption Standard (DES)** was adopted by the National Bureau of Standards in 1977 and is widely used. DES uses a 64-bit key and the algorithm is available on an LSI chip which is capable of processing text at a rate of over one megabit per second.

An alternative approach is provided by **public key cryptosystems**. Here the idea is to assign two keys to each user: an **encryption key** for encrypting plaintext, and a **decryption key** for deciphering ciphertext. A user's encryption key is published in much the same way as a telephone number so that anyone can send coded messages, but only the person who holds the corresponding decryption key can decipher the message. It is effectively impossible to deduce the decryption key from the encryption key.

A useful feature of public key cryptosystems is that it is possible to use the system for appending digital signatures to messages, thereby authenticating the identity of the sender to the recipient. A **digital signature** is the computer equivalent of a handwritten signature, except perhaps that they are harder to forge! The ability to sign a message using public encryption depends on the fact that the encryption and decryption algorithms are the inverse of one another, that is

$$p = d(e(p))$$

where p = Plaintext, e = Encryption procedure based on encryption key and d = Deciphering procedure based on decryption key.

The encryption procedure is public, whereas the deciphering procedure is not by virtue of the fact that the deciphering key is private. Let e_A and d_A be the encryption and deciphering procedures respectively of user A, and e_B and d_B be the encryption and deciphering procedures respectively of user B. For A to send a message, m, to B, A simply encrypts the message using B's encryption key, $e_B(m)$ and sends the encrypted message to B. B then deciphers the message,

$$d_B(e_B(m)) = m$$

Using this system, it is possible for another user to masquerade as user A and send a message to B; the message could in fact have been sent by anyone since everyone has access to e_B. Thus instead of simply encrypting the message, A first of all applies its own private deciphering algorithm to the message, then encrypts it using B's encryption procedure and sends it to B, that is e_B (d_A (m)). By applying the inverse functions to the message, B can not only decipher the message but also be certain that A sent it since only A knows d_A. B first applies the deciphering procedure, d_B, to 'undo' the effect of A's e_B, and then 'undoes' the effect of A's d_A by applying the public procedure e_A to yield the message m. Simply stated

$$\begin{aligned} & e_A\ (d_B\ ([e_B\ (d_A(m))])) \\ = \ & e_A\ (d_A(m)) \\ = \ & m \end{aligned}$$

Effectively, the deciphering procedure, d_A, constitutes the digital signature of the sender A.

8.5.4 Global view mechanism

It is relatively straightforward to provide support for views in the DDB environment, the views themselves being defined in the normal way on top of global relations.

Indeed both from the point of view of data independence and security the view mechanism is, if anything, even more useful in a distributed environment. DDBs are typically much larger and more complex than centralised DBs and views provide an excellent means of providing users with only relevant data. Moreover, from the security point of view, there are likely to be many more users in the distributed environment and views enable users to be classified into groups. However, complex views, especially those requiring joins across several tables, can be very expensive to materialize. For a DDBMS, which allows fragmentation and partitioning of global relations, the performance penalty is likely to be quite high. Fortunately, however, the use of powerful query optimizers, as discussed in Chapter 5, can help by combining the view definition with the global query and optimize the whole process of view materialization and query against the view as a unit.

SUMMARY

In this chapter, we have reviewed the basic concepts and issues relating to both integrity and security. Under the heading of integrity, we have seen how integrity constraints are used to implement the rules of the real-world organization which the DB is modelling. The transfer of these ideas to homogeneous DDBMSs presents few problems, since the constraints can always be incorporated into the system catalogue in just the same way as for centralized DBMSs. The specification and enforcement of integrity constraints for MDBMSs with local autonomy is still, however, an open research issue. We looked at a number of problems including, inconsistencies between local constraints, the specification of global constraints, and inconsistencies between local and global constraints. Existing centralized DBMSs generally fall far short of providing full integrity support, and in the case of MDBMS, there is virtually no support at all. Enforcement of integrity is left to the application programmers, who have to 'hardcode' the constraints and their enforcement into the application programs. The run-time checking of integrity constraints imposes an additional overhead on normal update operations, but it is generally more efficient to allow the system to do the checking, when the process can be optimized, than to leave it to the programmer. In a centralized DBMS, a new integrity constraint will only be accepted if the current DB state does not violate the new constraint and does not contradict any existing constraints. For example, if a constraint was specified that limited the maximum number of hours an employee could work in one week to, say 60 hours, then prior to inserting this constraint into the system catalogue thereby activating it, the integrity checker will first verify that no current employee has worked more than 60 hours in a week. If such an employee is found, then the new constraint will be rejected. Even in a centralized system, such checking of new constraints could be tedious and time-consuming. In a large, distributed DB, this checking would involve validation against local integrity constraints and local DB states across several sites. So it is easy to see why the provision of integrity in MDBMSs at the global level is still an open issue.

Integrity and security are related – the former is concerned with accidental corruption of the DB leading to inconsistencies, while the latter is concerned with deliberate tampering with, or unauthorized access to, the data. DDBMSs rely, in the main, on the local security facilities, both organizational through a security policy, and technical through access controls on the data. Distribution adds a new dimension in that data must be transmitted across potentially insecure networks. The most widespread technical solution to this problem is to use encryption. As has been indicated in this chapter, it is possible to develop quite elaborate security measures at the local level, but if all sites in the network do not enforce the same level of security, then security will inevitably be compromised. As with integrity, security in MDBMSs with full nodal autonomy for security policy is still an open, unresolved issue.

EXERCISES

8.1 A simple student DB is being established containing information about students and the courses they are taking. The following information is to be stored:

For each student: Student number (unique), name, address together with a list of the courses being taken by the student and the grades obtained.

For each course: Course number (unique), title and lecturer.

Design a plausible set of domain, relation and referential constraints for this DB.

8.2 For the DB given in Exercise 8.1, define a trigger constraint which will notify a student if they have failed a course (grade = 'F').

8.3 Discuss the problems associated with specifying and enforcing global integrity constraints for MDBMSs.

8.4 Discuss the four main types of security policies for access control within organizations.

8.5 (a) What is an authorization matrix.

(b) Specify the following access constraints in the form of an authorization matrix:

User Jones is allowed to read relation STUDENT.
User Smith is allowed to read and update and delete relation COURSE.
User Jones is allowed to read, update relation RESULT.
User Brown is allowed to read and update relation RESULT.
User Murphy is allowed to perform all operations on all three relations.
See Table 8.3.

8.6 Give examples of the four main types of access control to DBs.

8.7 What advantages does the view mechanism have over the authorization matrix approach as a security measure?

8.8 Queries on the statistical DB, STATDB, shown in Table 8.2 are restricted to COUNT and SUM. COUNT returns the cardinality (number of tuples) of the result of a query and SUM returns the arithmetic sum of the values of an attribute (or set of attributes) satifying the query. As an added security measure, only queries where the cardinality of the result is greater than 2 and less than 8 are allowed. The intention of this constraint is to prevent users from identifying small subsets of records. Devise a series of statistical SQL queries, using only COUNT and SUM, which will disclose Murphy's salary, given that the user knows that Murphy is a programmer and lives in Dublin.

Table 8.2 STATDB for Exercise 8.8.

STATDB

Name	Address	Job	Salary
O'Sullivan	Athlone	Programmer	14 000
O'Hegarty	Cork	Analyst	16 000
Hurley	Dublin	Engineer	18 500
MacDonagh	Galway	Clerk	7 000
Murphy	Dublin	Programmer	20 000
Slattery	Sligo	Clerk	10 000
O'Donnell	Dublin	Engineer	17 300
Hughes	Cork	Programmer	15 200
Mulvaney	Galway	Programmer	13 700

8.9 What is meant by the terms
(a) authentication
(b) identification?

8.10 What advantages do public key cryptosystems have over the Data Encryption Standard?

8.11 A DDB consists of the following relations:

```
PATIENT (patient#, name, address, dob, sex, diagnosis, gpn)
GP (gpname, address, telno)
```

PATIENT contains information about patients, including the name of their GP (gpn), while the GP relation contains information about the GPs. gpn is a foreign key of GP.

Write an SQL view definition which contains the patient#, name, dob, gpn and the telno of their GP for all male patients who have been diagnosed as having haemophilia.

Bibliography

ANSI (1986). *American National Standard for Information Systems, Database Language-SQL*, ANSI X3.135-1986.

Date C.J. (1982). *An Introduction to Database Systems*. Vol. II. Wokingham: Addison-Wesley.

Chapter 4 of this book contains an overview of security issues for centralized DBs.

Date C.J. (1990). *A Guide to the SQL Standard*, 2nd edn. Reading, MA: Addison-Wesley.

Date C.J. (1990a). Referential Integrity and Foreign Keys. Part I: Basic concepts; Part II: Further considerations. In *Relational Database Writings*. Wokingham: Addison-Wesley.

The discussion on referential integrity in Section 8.2.5 is based on this reference.

Date C.J. (1990b). *An Introduction to Database Systems*. Vol. I, 5th edn. Wokingham: Addison-Wesley.

Denning D.E. and Denning P.J. (1979). Data security. *ACM Computing Surveys*, **11**(3), 227–249.

Denning D.E., Denning P.J. and Schwartz M.D. (1979). The tracker: a threat to statistical DB security. *ACM TODS*, **4**(1).

Elmasri R.A. and Navathe S.B. (1989). *Fundamentals of Database Systems*. New York: Benjamin/Cummings.

Chapter 20 of this book contains a discussion on security issues for centralized DBs.

Fernández E.B., Summers R.C. and Wood C. (1981). *Database Security and Integrity*. Wokingham: Addison-Wesley.

Although this book was written several years ago, much of the material is still relevant. It provides a good basic coverage of integrity and security issues in DBs.

Garcia-Molina H. (1991). Global consistency constraints considered harmful for heterogeneous database systems. *Proc. 1st Int. Workshop on Interoperability in Multidatabase Systems*, Kyoto, Japan, 248–250.

This position paper argues that the existence of global integrity (consistency) constraints for MDBs, by definition, violates nodal autonomy and should therefore not be allowed. The implications of the absence of such constraints on support for concurrency control in MDBMSs is examined.

National Bureau of Standards (1977). *Data Encryption Standard*. Federal Information Processing Standards Publication 46, U.S. Department of Commerce, Washington, DC.

Describes the Data Encryption Standard referred to in Section 8.5.3.

Öszu M.T. and Valduriez P. (1991) *Principles of Distributed Database Systems*. New York: Prentice Hall.

Rivest R.L., Shamir A. and Adleman L. (1978). A method for obtaining digital signatures and public key cryptosystems. *CACM*, **21** (2), 120–126.

Sheth A.P. and Larson J.A. (1990). Federated database systems for managing distributed, heterogeneous and autonomous database systems. *ACM Computing Surveys*, **22** (3), 183–236.

SOLUTIONS TO EXERCISES

8.1

```
CREATE TABLE STUDENT      (student#   DOMAIN   (student#) NOT NULL,
                           name       DOMAIN   (name)     NOT NULL,
                           address    DOMAIN   (address)  NOT NULL,
              PRIMARY KEY  student#)  ;

CREATE DOMAIN student#    INTEGER
              student# > 0 AND student#  <  100000;
```

```
    CREATE DOMAIN name          VARCHAR (20);
    CREATE DOMAIN address       VARCHAR (20);
    CREATE TABLE  COURSE          (course#    DOMAIN   (course#)  NOT NULI
                                   title      DOMAIN   (title)    NOT NULI
                                   lecturer   DOMAIN   (name)
                  PRIMARY KEY      course#);
    CREATE DOMAIN course#       CHAR (6);
    CREATE DOMAIN title         CHAR (15);
    CREATE TABLE  RESULTS         (student#   DOMAIN   (student#) NOT NULI
                                   course#    DOMAIN   (course#)  NOT NULI
                                   grade      DOMAIN   (grade),
                  PRIMARY KEY     (course#,   student#)
                  FOREIGN KEY   student# REFERENCES student# OF TABLE
                                STUDENT,
                                NULLS NOT ALLOWED,
                                DELETION CASCADES,
                                UPDATE CASCADES
                  FOREIGN KEY   course# REFERENCES student# OF TABLE
                                COURSE,
                                NULLS NOT ALLOWED,
                                DELETION RESTRICTED,
                                UPDATE CASCADES);
CREATE DOMAIN         grade     CHAR (1);
```

8.2

```
DEFINE TRIGGER FAILURE-CONSTRAINT
ON RESULT:
grade='F'
ACTION NOTIFYSTUDENT-PROC (course#, student#);
```

8.5

Table 8.3 Authorisation matrix for Exercise 8.5.

DATA OBJECTS

USERS	Student	Course	Result
Jones	Select	None	Select Update
Smith	None	Update Delete Select	None
Brown	None	None	Select Update
Murphy	All	All	All

8.8

```
SELECT      COUNT (*)
FROM STATDB
WHERE       job='programmer';
```

Response: 4

```
SELECT      COUNT (*)
FROM STATDB
WHERE       job='programmer'
AND  NOT

            address='Dublin';
```

Response: 3

The user has now discovered that there can be only one programmer who lives in Dublin, who must therefore be Murphy. He can therefore issue the following queries to obtain Murphy's salary:

```
SELECT      SUM (salary)
FROM STATDB
where       job='programmer';
```

Response: 62900

```
SELECT      SUM (salary)
FROM STATDB
WHERE       job='programmer'
AND NOT
            (address='Dublin'):
```

Response: 42900

The user then just subtracts the answers to the two queries 62900 − 42900 = 20000
which is Murphy's salary. The predicate

```
job = 'programmer' AND NOT (address = 'Dublin')
```

is called a **single tracker**.

8.11

```
CREATE   VIEW     HAEMOPHILIACS
         AS       SELECT patient#, name, dob, gpn, telno
         FROM     PATIENT, GP
         WHERE    PATIENT.gpn = GP.gpname
         AND      sex='M'
         AND      diagnosis='haemophilia'.
```

9 Logical Distributed Database Design and Administration

9.1 Introduction

This chapter is divided into two separate, but related, parts. The first part deals with logical DDB design, while the second discusses the administration of a DDB. In Chapter 4, we examined the problems associated with physical DDB design (i.e. how best to distribute the data amongst the sites in order to improve overall performance). Of course, in the case of a multidatabase system, which integrates *pre-existing* DBs, the physical layout of the data is already fixed and cannot be altered. It is the job of the query optimizer alone to obtain the 'optimum' performance. The design of the global conceptual schema (logical DDB) design is by contrast applicable to both homogeneous DDBs and MDBs.

The role of the DDB administrator is to decide initially what data to include in the DDB, how to structure it and subsequently how to manage it. Hence logical design of a DDB is part of this remit. For simplicity, we will present the issues of DDB design and management separately.

We begin with an overview of the software life cycle to see where the DB and DDB design processes fit into the overall framework of systems development. We differentiate between DDB design for homogeneous and heterogeneous DDBs, since each presents quite separate problems. Homogeneous DDBs are designed top-down, while heterogeneous (in particular, multidatabases) are integrated ('designed') bottom-up. Also, homogeneous DDBs are installed in 'green fields' sites, whereas MDBs, by definition, are built on top of fixed, pre-existing local systems.

A similar distinction is made when we discuss database administration. Administration of a homogeneous DDB is not very much different from administration of a centralized DB, whereas administration of an MDB requires new skills. The local DBs, in the MDB are administered as standard independent, centralized DBs, to which a global administration layer is added, which is responsible for all the integration issues.

9.2 Software life cycle

A number of phases of development can be identified in the evolution of large software systems, whether centralized or distributed, starting with the initial feasibility study to decide whether the system is worth developing in the first place, to the final phase when the system is actually operational. This development cycle, referred to as the **software life cycle**, has six principal phases:

(1) During the feasibility study phase, a careful analysis of the feasibility and potential of the proposed software system is carried out;

(2) The requirements collection and analysis phase involves extensive discussion between system designer(s) and the end-users of the system. The objective of the designer is to gain a detailed understanding of what the proposed system is intended to do, what data is needed by the various applications of the system, and what processes are to be performed on the data;

(3) The design phase involves the detailed design of the system. In the case of (D)DB systems, it involves the design of the (D)DB itself and of the applications which access the (D)DB;

(4) During the implementation phase the system is fully implemented and tested; in a (D)DB system, this phase includes initial loading of the (D)DB;

(5) Phase 2 produces a detailed requirements specification for the system and phase 5, the validation and acceptance testing phase, is concerned with evaluating the newly developed system against those requirements. This evaluation includes both the functional and performance requirements;

(6) Operation is the final phase of the software life cycle when the system 'goes live'.

Although these phases are well defined and involve quite different processes, there are often feedback loops, especially between the earlier phases. However, if a problem is found during the operational phase, which requires a major change to the system because the requirements in stage 2 were not properly specified, the cost of rectifying the error can be very high. New applications will be developed during the operational phase and this is a normal part of the software life cycle. However, the system should be able to integrate these new applications smoothly, without requiring major restructuring of the system. In recent years, many tools have been developed to support various phases of the life cycle, in particular CASE (computer-assisted software engineering) tools, which are mainly aimed at phases 2 to 4. They often provide facilities for rapid prototyping which are very useful in the proper and accurate capture and specification of user requirements, which is a notoriously difficult task. In the context of this chapter, we are concerned with phase 3 of the life cycle, the design phase.

In Section 2.2.6, we introduced the process of normalization of relations. Normalization represents the final phase of the logical DB design process. It is preceded by the mapping of the enterprise data model onto relational tables. The **enterprise data model** is an abstract representation of the entities of interest in an organization, together with the relationships (1 : 1, reflexive, 1 : *n*, *m* : *n*, etc.) between those entities. The enterprise model is independent of any particular DBMS or DB model. One of the most common representation methods for enterprise models is based on the **entity-relationship (ER)** approach. Many CASE tools offer the possibility of converting the formalized enterprise model automatically into schema definitions for a target DBMS (centralized), without any 'human intervention'. If the functional dependencies are known, it is possible to ensure that only normalized tables are generated. Thus, in terms of the software life cycle, the output of phase 2 includes an enterprise model which can be converted relatively simply into a set of normalized tables. At this stage, the user views and applications which access the (D)DB through those views, are designed. The final design stage is then the physical DB or internal schema design. It is really only at this stage that distribution aspects should come in to the picture.

9.3 Logical design for distributed databases

In Section 2.4.1, an important distinction was made between homogeneous DDBMSs in which the DDB is designed top-down, and MDBMSs, which follow a bottom-up approach to the integration of a number of preexisting DBs. **Homogeneous DDB design** follows exactly the same stages

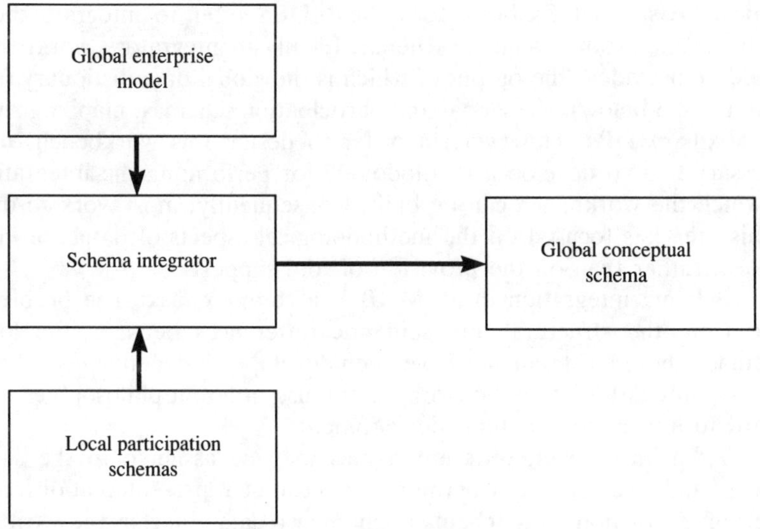

Figure 9.1 Schema integration.

of design as for a centralized DB; the distribution aspect only comes in at the final stage, when decisions have to be made about how to allocate the (fragments of) global relations to sites (see Chapter 4).

MDB design, on the other hand, presents a totally new problem, namely **schema integration**, and the remainder of this section will examine this issue. In this case, the local DBs are fully designed and implemented – they are at the operational phase of the software life cycle. The MDB design process should also follow the standard phases of the life cycle, focusing on the development of *global* applications. The output of the requirements collection and analysis phase should be a global enterprise model. It is at this point that pure DDB and MDB design processes diverge, since in the case of MDBs, we now have to consider pre-existing local conceptual schemas, or more correctly, the local participation schemas, since the local DBMSs may only contribute a subset of their data to the MDB. The objective then is to merge together the local participation schemas, with the help of the global enterprise model, to produce an integrated conceptual schema, as shown in Figure 9.1.

9.3.1 Schema integration

Most of the existing MDB prototypes have concentrated primarily on the technical means of providing the functionality of an MDBS. It is essential to examine the ways in which an organization would actually go about exploiting this technology. In particular, given a heterogeneous collection of local DBs, what facilities does the MDBS offer to integrate those databases and produce a global schema? Ideally an integrator's workbench should be provided, the output of which is the global data dictionary (see Section 9.6.3 below), the global and participation schemas, mapping rules and auxiliary DBs. However, in order to design this workbench, it is necessary first to develop a methodology for performing the integration on which the workbench can be built. Consequently, most work to date in this area has focused on the methodological aspects of database integration, rather than on the provision of tool support.

Schema integration in an MDB is a complex task. The problems arise from the structural and semantic differences between the local schemas. These local schemas have been developed independently following, not only different methodologies, but also different philosophies with regard to information systems development.

At a basic level, different names may be assigned to the same concept and vice versa. Furthermore, data can be represented at different levels of abstraction. One schema might view a data object as the attribute of an entity, whereas another might view it as an entity in its own right.

The problems associated with database integration and the stages required to produce an integrated global schema are best understood by working through an example. The example presented below in Figures 9.2(a) to (f) is very simple, but serves as a guide to the issues involved. There are two local schemas, Schema A, which is the schema for the outpatient department of a hospital and Schema B, which models a G.P.'s DB for these patients. Figure 9.2(a) shows the original schemas. The objective is to produce a single, integrated, uniform global schema from the two local schemas as shown in Figure 9.2(f). In Figure 9.2(b) we have identified that *result* in Schema B is a synonym for *diagnosis* in Schema A and we have chosen to use *diagnosis* at the global level and we must therefore replace *result* in Schema B with *diagnosis*. In Schema A, *consultant* is an attribute of the *Outpatient* entity, whereas in Schema B, the consultant is represented by the entity *Consultant Referral*. If we decide that it is more appropriate to make *consultant* an entity at the global level, then we must make *consultant* in Schema A into an entity as shown in Figure 9.2(c).

We are now ready to superimpose (merge) the two schemas using the *Consultant Referral* entity as the link between them, as shown in Figure 9.2(d). Next we recognize that the entity *Patient* is in fact a subset of the *Outpatient* entity and we can therefore create a subset relationship as shown in Figure 9.2(e). Finally, we note that there are certain properties in common between the *Patient* and *Outpatient* entities and since *Patient* is a subset of *Outpatient*, we can drop these common properties from *Patient*, leaving it with only the properties which are peculiar to it. The final integrated model of the global conceptual schema is shown in Figure 9.2(f).

Note that if the GP Patient DB (Schema B) included patients who were not outpatients, it would be necessary to define a new entity called *Person*, rather than adopting the approach above. This new entity would be the union of the two existing patient entities, *Outpatient* from Schema A and *Patient* from Schema B, which would then become subsets of the new *Person* entity as shown in Figure 9.3.

9.3.2 Approaches to schema integration

Schema integration is a relatively recent concept, relating specifically to the problems associated with DDBs, in particular the integration of a set of pre-existing local schemas into a single global schema. It represents a natural evolution of the **view integration** process which has been developed for centralized DBs, whereby application views are merged to produce a single, unified conceptual schema. Indeed the global schema is itself a 'superview' defined over all the underlying DBs. The methodologies associated with view integration are better developed than those for schema integration, although many of the problems are common to both.

Schema integration requires a semantically rich data model. It is too complex a task to be performed using the relational model or even the entity relationship model. Some way of expressing that an entity is a subset of another entity (as *Patient* is of *Outpatient* in the example above) is required. The ability to define subsets in this way is often referred to as **generalization**. Without generalization, we risk losing information as a result of the merge process. Thus, in our example above, we would lose the distinction between the *Patient* entity representing GP patients, and the *Outpatient* entity representing outpatients in a hospital if we merged them into a single entity. Alternatively, we could leave them as separate entities with the resulting semantic confusion and redundancy in common properties. A second advantage of generalization identified by Dayal and Hwang relates to the handling of null values. Consider our example again, but ignoring, for simplicity, the *consultant* attribute of *Outpatient* in Schema A and the *consultant* entity in Schema B:

- Entity *Outpatient* in Schema A has attributes *name*, *number*, *address* and *diagnosis*,
- Entity *Patient* in Schema B has attributes *name*, *address*, *married* and *children*.

We can model these two entities by a single global entity called *global-patient* which has all the attributes of both *Outpatient* and *Patient*, that is

- Entity *global-patient* has attributes *name*, *number*, *address*, *diagnosis*, *married* and *children*.

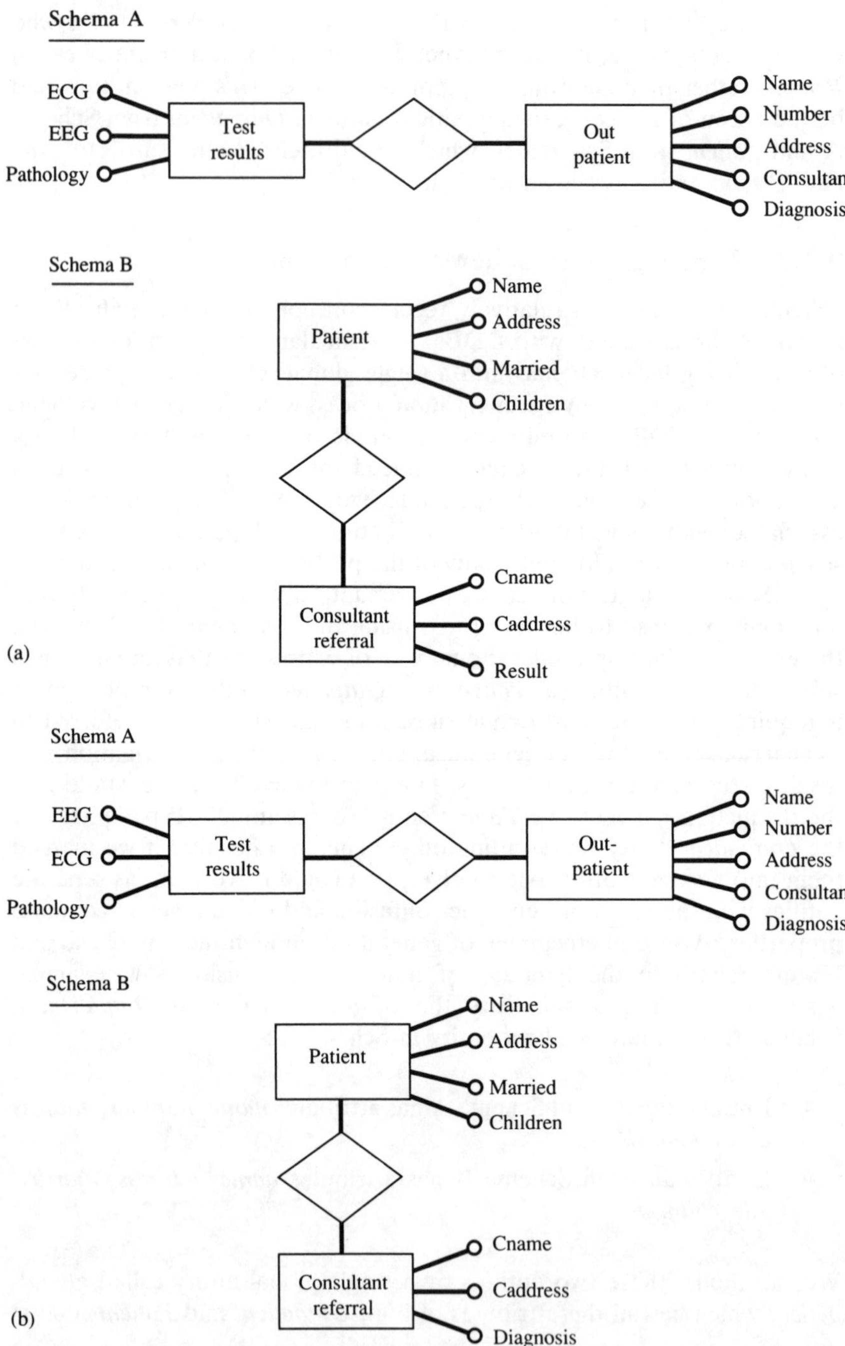

Figure 9.2 (a) Original schemas A and B before integration. (b) Choose *diagnosis* for *result* in B. (c) Make CONSULTANT REFERRAL into an ENTITY in A. (d) Superimposition of schemas. (e) Creation of a subset relationship. (f) Drop properties of PATIENT common to OUTPATIENT.

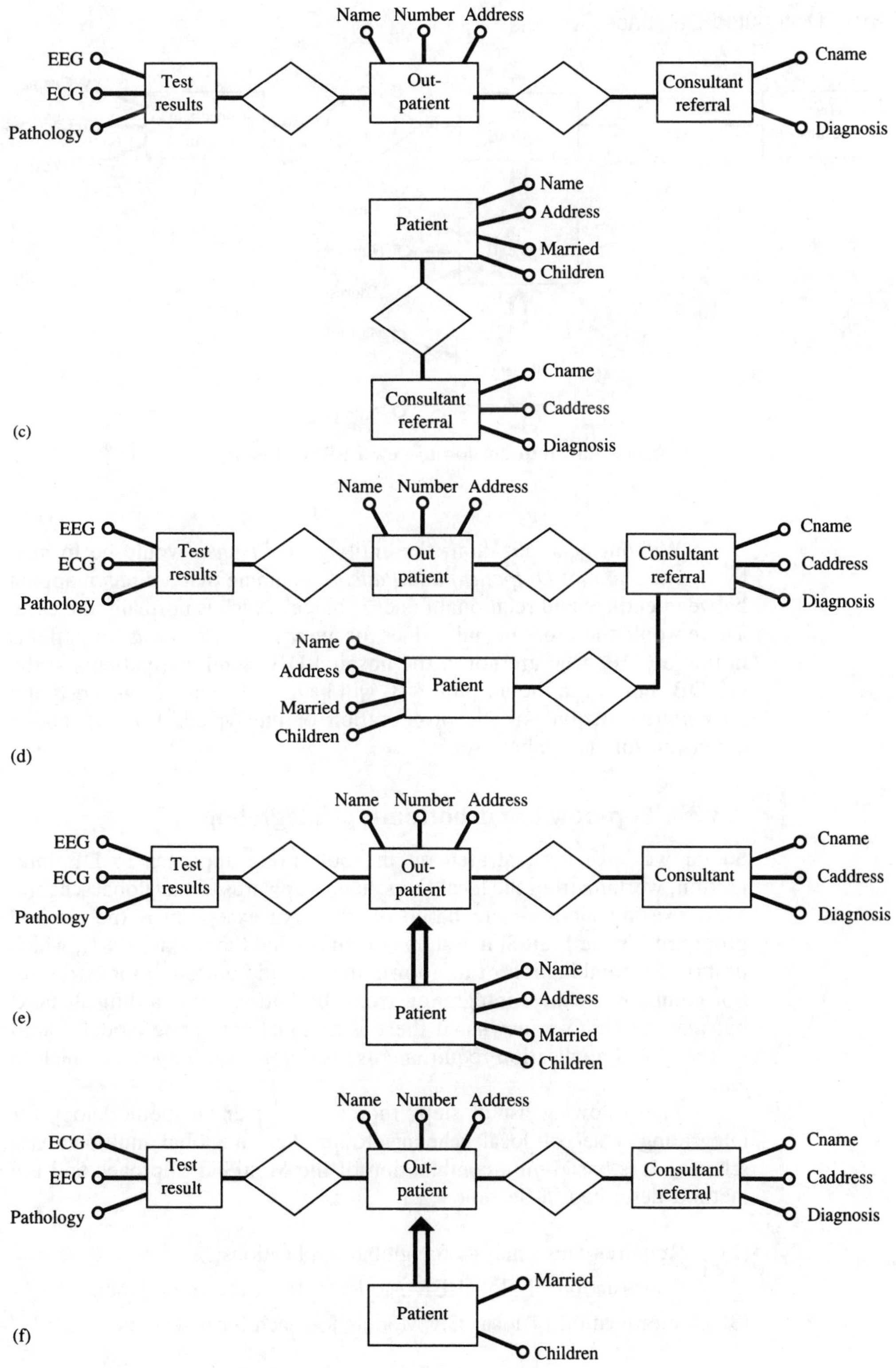
Name
Number
Address
EEG
ECG
Pathology
Test results
Out-patient
Consultant referral
Cname
Diagnosis
Patient
Name
Address
Married
Children
Consultant referral
Cname
Caddress
Diagnosis
(c)
Name
Number
Address
EEG
ECG
Pathology
Test results
Out patient
Consultant referral
Cname
Caddress
Diagnosis
Name
Address
Married
Children
Patient
(d)
Name
Number
Address
EEG
ECG
Pathology
Test results
Out-patient
Consultant
Cname
Caddress
Diagnosis
Patient
Name
Address
Married
Children
(e)
Name
Number
Address
ECG
EEG
Pathology
Test result
Out-patient
Consultant referral
Cname
Caddress
Diagnosis
Patient
Married
Children
(f)

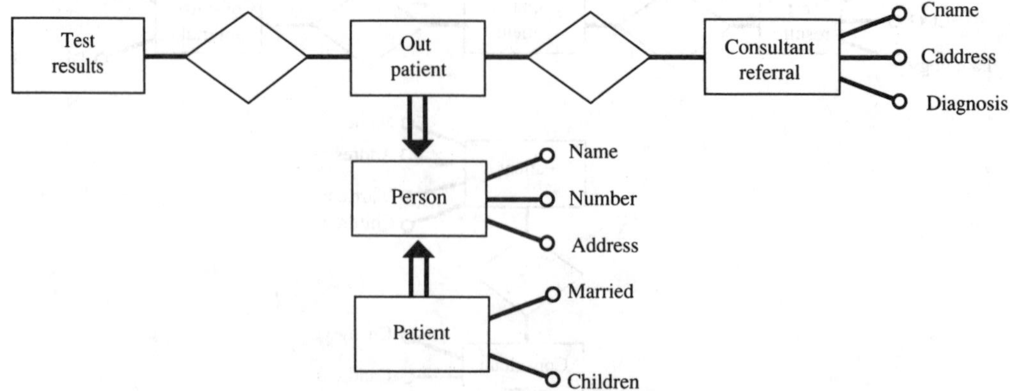

Figure 9.3 Introduction of new PERSON entity.

Without generalization, the entity *global-patient* would be formed by an outer join of *Outpatient* and *Patient*, assuming that a direct mapping between entities and relational tables is made, which is normally the case. There would therefore be null values for *number* and *diagnosis* for patients in the GP DB, who are not in the hospital DB. Similarly, patients in the GP DB, but not in the hospital DB, will have null values for *married* and *no children* attributes. The proliferation of null values leads to added confusion for the global user.

9.3.3 Top-down and bottom-up integration

So far we have concentrated on the bottom-up approach to DB integration, working from the local DB schemas upwards to the global schema. Most existing methods are based on this. An exception is the method proposed for the MultiStar system (Mostardi and Staniszkis, 1987), which proposes a combination of top-down analysis and bottom-up integration. For complex schemas, integration from the bottom-up is a difficult task, but may be eased somewhat if there is a global enterprise model, based on the global application requirements, available as a 'target' at which to aim.

The following list of steps represents a manual methodology for integrating a set of local schemas to produce a global multidatabase schema. It is based on a combination of the MultiStar approach and the method described in Section 9.2.1.

(1) Requirements analysis for global applications;
(2) Construction of global ER Model A from the requirements;
(3) Specification of local ER Models for each local schema.

At this point, it would be useful to enter the data into the dictionary, which would then form the basis for the global data dictionary (see Section 9.6.3) for the multidatabase. Where a local node already has a data dictionary and/or ER model, the process can clearly be speeded up and greatly simplified.

(4) Identification of synonyms between local schemas, renaming using standard terminology as required;
(5) Match entities and attributes across all schemas, converting attributes to entities or vice versa, if required. Each local entity/attribute should be matched with global entities/attributes;
(6) Combine modified local ER models by superimposition to form a draft global ER model. At this stage, all synonyms and homonyms should have been identified and catalogued in the dictionary;
(7) Identify any generalizations (subsets) of entities;
(8) Remove any common attributes between generalizations to produce global ER Model B;
(9) Compare the two global ER models, A and B, and adjust if necessary.

At all stages throughout this process, it will be necessary to keep comprehensive notes on the transformations (unit conversions, generalizations, etc.) applied for the subsequent construction of the auxiliary DB (see Section 2.4.2). It is quite possible for two DBs to record the same information but to represent it in a different way, so the identification of synonyms is not as simple as noticing that the same attribute is called two different names.

Consider, for example, two DBs, one in Dublin and the other in Cork, recording information about incoming and outgoing flights. For simplicity, we will assume that each DB consists of only one relation:

```
DUBLIN (flight_no, airport, arr/dep, date, dep_time,
        arrival_time)
```

at the DUBLIN site and

```
CORK   (flight_no, source, destination, date,
        dep_time, arrival_time)
```

at the CORK site.

In the DUBLIN DB, the arr/dep attribute indicates whether the plane is arriving in Dublin or departing from Dublin. Thus if arr/dep = 'arr' then the airport attribute records the source of the flight, the desti-

Table 9.1

DUBLIN

Flight_no.	Airport	Arr/dep	Date	Dep_time	Arrival_time
XY123	Charles de Gaulle	Dep	01.06.91	14:10	14:40
PQ781	Stanstead	Arr	05.07.91	10:50	12:05
XY492	Luton	Arr	30.06.91	15:35	16:40
AB936	Roissy	Dep	14.07.91	09:16	10:00
XY401	Heathrow	Dep	02.08.91	17:52	18:02
AN322	Cork	Arr	27.07.91	12:10	12:52

CORK

Flight_no.	Source	Destination	Date	Dep_time	Arrival_time
AN418	Cork	Luton	03.06.91	13:42	14:58
XY912	Roissy	Cork	19.07.91	10:10	10:05
AN326	Cork	Dublin	27.07.91	12:10	12:52

nation is Dublin. If arr/dep = 'dep' then the airport attribute records the destination of the flight, the source is Dublin. The CORK DB is much more straightforward, simply recording the source and destination for each flight. An example of the relations is given in Table 9.1 and the corresponding ER diagrams in Figure 9.4.

Assume that the global relation, FLIGHT_INFO, which is the view containing all the information from both the DUBLIN and CORK relations, has the same format as the CORK, relation,

```
FLIGHT_INFO (flight_no, source, destination, date,
             dep_time, arrival_time)
```

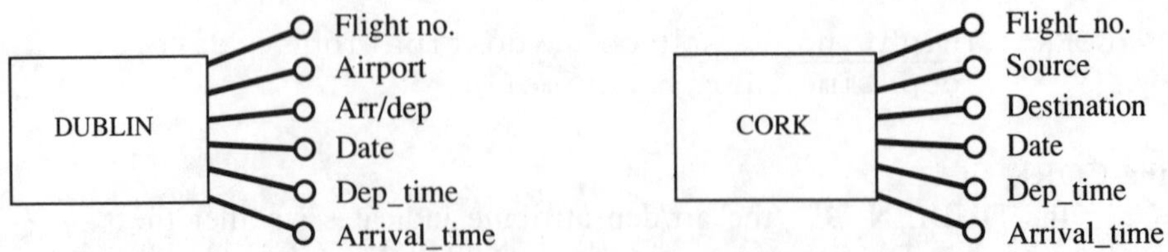

Figure 9.4 ER diagrams for DUBLIN and CORK.

Example 9.1 Procedure to materialize global relation.

```
begin
  do while not end-of-relation DUBLIN
    FLIGHT_INFO.flight_no=DUBLIN.flight_no
    FLIGHT_INFO.date = DUBLIN.date
    FLIGHT_INFO.dep_time = DUBLIN.dep_time
    FLIGHT_INFO.arrival_time = DUBLIN.arrival_time
    if DUBLIN.arr/dep='arr'
      then begin
        FLIGHT_INFO.Source = DUBLIN.airport
        FLIGHT_INFO.destination='Dublin'
      end
      else begin
        FLIGHT_INFO.source='Dublin'
        FLIGHT_INFO.destination = DUBLIN.airport
      end
    end-if
    next tuple
  end-do
  FLIGHT_INFO = FLIGHT_INFO UNION CORK
end
```

To create FLIGHT_INFO, we cannot simply take the UNION of the DUBLIN and CORK relations. Instead we have to specify rules to be stored in the auxiliary DB, for converting the DUBLIN relation into the global format. A procedure, in pseudo-code, for materializing FLIGHT_INFO is given in Example 9.1. Thus we can see that the conversion of relations into a consistent global format is by no means straightforward.

9.3.4 Interoperability without using global conceptual schema

In large, complex, heterogeneous environments, the construction of an integrated global conceptual schema can be too onerous a task. A global schema is essential where tight integration between member DBs is required, but where a more loosely constructed federation of DBs is envisaged, the effort of building a global schema may well not be worthwhile (see Section 2.4.1). Where such loosely-coupled MDBSs make use of export schemas (see Figure 2.23), the logical DDB design effort goes into the design of the export schemas. This effectively covers a somewhat slimmed down version of the first five steps in the manual integration process described above. The export schema represents a view defined over part of the DDB only. Where there are no export schemas (as in Figure 2.22), there is effectively no logical DDB design stage at all, and the federation is much more loosely coupled. Users define their own views at run-time using powerful query languages, such as MSQL developed by Litwin *et al*. There is also considerable interest in the development of standards for DBs which make them self-describing. Such standards would be of enormous benefit to such loosely-coupled database systems.

9.3.4 The object-oriented approach to schema integration

There is growing interest in the application of object-oriented techniques to schema integration. One of the fundamental aspects of the object-oriented approach to data modelling is that both data and the processes which operate on the data (known as **methods**) are modelled together. By contrast, conventional data modelling considers only the data; the processes (the application programs) are dealt with independently. This division is reflected in traditional DBMSs in which the data is stored in the DB, while the application programs are stored separately, often in a software library. The power of the object-oriented approach to data management is discussed in Section 11.4. The advantages of the object-oriented approach to schema integration can be summarized as follows:

(1) The object-oriented model is semantically rich;
(2) Methods can be used to provide powerful integration functions, for example to handle complex conversions and semantic conflicts between local and global levels as illustrated in Example 9.1;
(3) The object-oriented approach provides the possibility of reuse by global users of local application programs by exporting them to the global level as user-defined methods;
(4) The integration of multimedia DBs (relational tables, text, graphics, etc.) is feasible. Thus, for example, it would be possible to combine a map stored in an image DB with the details of various features represented on the map stored in a conventional RDB.

The object-oriented approach to schema integration is equally applicable whether or not a global conceptual schema is used. It is generally assumed that once the local schemas have been integrated, global users will view the DDB as an object-oriented DDB. In other words, the canonical data model is object-oriented, and users access the DB through object-oriented languages, such as object-oriented extensions to SQL, Smalltalk and C++.

9.4 Distributed database administration

As with most other aspects of distributed database technology, administration of the distributed data resource represents a more generalized, and therefore more complex, problem than in the centralized case. In centralized systems, the distinction is made between *database* administration and *data* administration. The former has now become regarded as largely a technical data processing function concerned with the day to day management of the physical database itself. Data administration, on the other hand, is concerned with a much broader view, which focuses principally on the management of the data resource of an entire corporation. Since the corporate data resource will normally be distributed, data administration is *de facto* concerned with distribution. In the remainder of this chapter we will review the centralized database administration function and examine its role in the distributed environment.

9.4.1 Local database administration

The database administration function grew up alongside the development of DB technology. Initially it was very broadly based and often ranged from the initial selection of the DBMS itself, through conceptual schema design, to physical implementation, performance monitoring and so on. In other words the **DB administrator (DBA)** was responsible for the management of the DB system throughout the entire software life cycle. The DBA belonged in the data processing department and, while the DBA had a liaison role between users and management, their function was primarily technical.

As the information systems within large organizations continued to expand and diversify, particularly with the advent of the mini- and microcomputers at the end of the 1970s, the clock almost turned full circle. The centralized corporate DB still existed under the control of the DBA, but alongside it a number of independent PC- and minicomputer-based systems evolved. The situation increasingly resembled the pre-database days of the 1960s and early 1970s, when many organizations were suffering problems associated with heterogeneous file systems (e.g. incompatibility, data redundancy, lack of security and integrity). The solution this time was not provided by centralization because the advantages of a more distributed approach to information systems were overwhelming (see Chapter 1). At the same time, it was essential, from a management point of view, to gain some measure of control over these diverse systems, if only to ensure integrity and also avoid unnecessary duplication of data and effort. Hence a level of administration, known as **data administration**, was introduced above DB administration, which encompassed the entire data resource from mainframe to micro. Thus some tasks, such as conceptual schema design which previously would have been performed by the DBA would now become the remit of the data administrator (DA). As indicated above, DB administration is increasingly a highly technical, specialist function related to the physical management of a single DB or group of DBs. Generally speaking, therefore, the administration of a DDB is more likely to be viewed as the function of a DA rather than a DBA. In this chapter, therefore, we will refer to administration of the local DBs as local **database** administration and administration at a global level as **data** administration.

9.4.2 The effect of distribution on database administration

The effect of distribution of the data resource on the administration function depends critically upon where control of the distributed database resides (i.e. the degree of nodal autonomy). In homogeneous DDBs, which are designed top-down, there is only one level of control – the global level – whereas in heterogeneous MDBs, both local and global control must co-exist. We will look at the implications of these two scenarios on the function of the local DBA.

In the homogeneous DDB approach, control is centralised in the DDBMS itself. Such systems can realistically be administered as a global extension to the centralized case with no separate local administration. Thus the DBA becomes effectively a **distributed DB administrator (DDBA)**. The role is therefore the same as for a DBA, but with increased complexity to handle the distribution of the data. Thus the DDBA will require tools to assist in the optimal allocation of base relation fragments to sites, of replication and so on. The DBA must be able to monitor performance in order to tune the system and, if appropriate, reorganize the layout of the data on physical storage so that the overall efficiency is improved. This may involve the migration of data from one site to another as well as physical reorganization of the data at a single site. As far as the function of the DA is concerned, the homogeneous DDB behaves like a centralized DB with a single administrator, the DDBA. Thus there is no distinction between global and local administration and all users are essentially global users of the DDB.

By contrast, in the MDB approach, there is a very clear and important distinction between the local and global administration. Local users are users of a local nodal DB under the control of the local DBMS and hence of the local DBA. In the face of nodal autonomy, it is the local DBA who decides what data to contribute to the global MDB, who should be allowed to read it, who should be allowed to update it. The local DBA also has the right to withdraw at any time some or all of the local data from participation in the MDB. Clearly, such potential anarchy, if carried to the ultimate extreme, would effectively be unworkable. Even for very loosely coupled systems, there must be a network manager, who is responsible for seeing that the MDB network functions reliably. Also, the notion that each local DB is completely and absolutely autonomous and independent is probably not a very common scenario. After all, if there are global users of the MDB, then there must be some organizational coupling, however loose, between the individual nodes. A common use for MDB technology would be in organizations with strong departmental or branch autonomy, where departments had invested in a variety of centralized DBMSs, but where there is a need to support some applications which cross organizational boundaries, as for example in the field of strategic planning. In such a situation, there is definitely a notion of control over the MDB as a whole (i.e. global control). This control would be vested in the hands of the DA, who would liaise with the local DBAs and would report to corporate senior management.

The only realistic application scenario where such a notion of overall control of the MDB appears absent is where the MDB is being used to assist in the provision of summary information from the local DBs to a third party. This situation could arise, for example, in the health field, where each hospital reports on a periodic basis to a regional health authority, giving statistical (depersonalized) information, such as number of inpatients, average length of stay, diagnosis, treatment required and so on. Each hospital will have its own independent, autonomous DB. There can be doubt that in such an application, confidentiality of medical data requires that nodal autonomy is supreme. It is most unlikely, given the nature of the interaction between the systems, that a global schema would be required in such a scenario. The various sites, including the regional site, would simply agree protocols amongst themselves, which would then allow them to cooperate together in a loosely-coupled federation.

9.4.3 Administration functions

In this section, we will look in more detail at the administration functions of the local DBA in conjunction with the DDBA for both homogeneous DDBs and the global DA for multidatabases.

The functions of the DBA of a *centralised* DB can be summarized as follows:

(1) Design and implementation of the local conceptual DB schema (logical DB design);

(2) Design and implementation of the local internal DB schema (physical DB design);

(3) Design and implementation of the external DB schemas (local user views) in consultation with the local users;

(4) Implementation of local security and integrity constraints (where these are not explicitly included in the local schemas);
(5) Local DB tuning and performance monitoring;
(6) Planning and implementation of local DB reorganization (as required);
(7) Documentation of the local DB and local schemas.

Where the DB is only a local node in a *distributed* environment, the following functions must be added:

(8) Definition of those portions of the local DB which are to be contributed to the global DB (i.e. local fragments of global relations),
(9) Mapping rules between those fragments and the local data,
(10) Conversion rules between local and global data (e.g. miles to kilometres);
(11) Specification of security and integrity constraints on the fragments which are peculiar to the global level – these will be in addition to those defined on the local DB itself.

Thus the functions of the DDBA incorporate all 11 of the items listed above and those of a DBA of a centralized DB only the first 7 items.

Since actual data does not reside at the global level – only meta-data – the global DA's role is quite different from that of the local DBA. The principal functions of the DA can be summarized as follows:

(1) Documentation of the global data resource;
(2) Establishment and monitoring of standards for data naming, ownership, and so on;
(3) Liaison with global end-users, management, data processing personnel, network administrators and local DBAs;
(4) Conflict resolution between different user/management groups;
(5) Definition of global security and integrity constraints;
(6) Development of a data resource plan;
(7) Definition of the global schema;
(8) Promotion of data sharing to avoid unnecessary duplication of data between local nodes and also to improve overall integrity.

Clearly, the most important role of the DA will be one of liaison with the local DBAs, since it is their data which is to be integrated into the global DDB. As in centralized DBSs, there is often a problem of conflicting requirements for data placement, data naming and so on among the different users of the DB. Indeed, in a distributed environment, this problem is exacerbated by the physical distribution of the data and by the degree of local autonomy granted to individual nodes.

9.5 Meta-data management

A DDB is a virtual entity consisting of a view across possibly heterogeneous underlying data collections. The *data* in the system resides in the DBs at the local nodes; everything else is *meta-data* – data about that data. In the remainder of this chapter, we will discuss the two principal tools for meta-data management, namely the system catalogue and the global data dictionary.

9.5.1 The local system catalogues

The principal role of the DA is to manage the corporate data resource. Hence the most important tools at the disposal of the DA to do this job are the local DBMSs themselves. A local DBMS incorporates, through its data definition language (DDL), functions for the definition of conceptual, internal and external schemas, together, in most systems, with facilities for the definition of security and integrity constraints. DBMSs provide powerful management tools for that part of the data resource stored in DBs. Once operational, the DBMS provides the DBA with performance monitoring tools together with utilities for the physical reorganization of the DB.

A local DBS consists of two quite separate parts: the data itself, stored in the DB, and the description of that data, or meta-data, stored in the system catalogue. The catalogue can be thought of as the run-time version of the schemas defined through the DDL.

There are three basic approaches to catalogue management in a distributed environment:

(1) **Centralized catalogue**: the catalogue is stored once at a single site. The disadvantages of such an approach are obvious – the site would immediately become a bottleneck as all global queries would have to be processed initially (decomposed and optimized) at that site. Furthermore, failure at that site would mean immediate and total failure of the whole DDBS;

(2) **Fully replicated catalogues**: the catalogue is fully replicated at each node. This is the approach taken in NDMS and has the advantage that it is easy to implement. However, update of the catalogue becomes difficult as the system must ensure that all updates are propagated to all sites immediately. There is a real danger here of

inconsistencies developing. Also, the fully replicated catalogue could be very wasteful if most of the accesses are local or to one or two sites only in the network;

(3) **Distributed catalogues**: this approach takes into account the fact that the catalogue is a DDB and hence can be subject to the same distribution rules (i.e. fragmentation, partitioning and replication) as the DDB itself.

There are a number of alternative strategies to implementing distributed catalogues. It is a widely accepted rule-of-thumb that a large proportion of the accesses will be to local data and only a small proportion to remote data. This in many ways constitutes the principal attraction of distributed systems. Hence the portion of the catalogue stored at an individual site will contain the meta-data for the local data at that site. This will then handle the majority of the requests. In addition, where replication of the meta-data is permitted, information pertaining to remote data can also be stored at a site. Of course some basic information, such as the names and probably also the attributes of all global relations in the system, must be replicated at all sites and a local site must know where to go to locate meta-data for non-local data. This approach was adopted by R*, which introduced the notion of a **birth-site** for each entity and which forms part of the identifier for that entity. SDD-1 and Distributed INGRES, which both support distributed catalogues, employ a **cache** to store remote portions of the catalogue. This cache is refreshed from time to time, but is not kept up to date automatically. While such an approach could give rise to inconsistencies, update of the catalogue (meta-data) is relatively rare, compared to update of the data itself, and therefore this approach represents a reasonable and practical alternative. A similar method has been adopted in the EDDS system, with the local portion of the global catalogue stored by the local DBMS. Built-in views on the local catalogue are provided to control access for the different users of the catalogue. For example, end-users can obtain information about the data available by querying the catalogue. Remote nodes can also access the catalogue to obtain the information necessary to process remote queries. Finally, the local DBA and global DA will require privileged access in order to update the catalogue.

9.5.2 Global data dictionary

It is now widely recognized that the facilities for management of meta-data provided by the system catalogues of centralized DBMSs are insufficient for the information processing needs of today. At best, they provide for the syntactic definition of the data in the DB, but little or no support is provided for recording the meaning of the data. Consider, for example, the term WAGE. To the employee, this means the amount they are paid every week, after tax, social insurance, health insurance, pension contribution and so on have been deducted. To the tax inspector, the WAGE is the gross pay before any deductions have been made. To the employer, on the other hand, the WAGE might mean the amount that has to be paid out each week to and on behalf of an employee. For example, it would include not only the gross wage of the employee prior to any deductions, but also any contributions made on the employee's behalf, such as employer's contributions to social welfare, pension schemes and so on. Hence there is plenty of room for confusion even with the relatively simple concept of a weekly WAGE. It was to overcome this type of problem and also to provide much more extensive and flexible management of meta-data that data dictionary systems (DDS) were developed. Note that some writers differentiate between the data dictionary (inventory) and data directory (location) aspects of this system, calling the combined system a data dictionary/directory system. However, in this chapter, we prefer to use the term data dictionary (DD) to encompass both these functions.

The principal aim of any DDS, whether in a centralized or distributed environment, is to document all aspects of the data resource. To perform this task successfully and also to ensure that the DD is regarded as the sole authority for the definition and description of meta-data within the organization, it must provide a number of facilities, which are summarized below. Note that the catalogues are effectively a subset of the DDS.

(1) Syntactic and semantic definitions of data, applications systems and programs, users and user views; thus, in addition to defining the data objects themselves, the DD also defines ownership and access rights to those objects and identifies which application programs use those objects;

(2) Retrieval capabilities from the DD itself, to assist in the development of application programs;

(3) Specification of security and integrity constraints on the data plus information for recovery;

(4) Statistical information on database access patterns, performance and so on (some of this information may be stored in the log);

(5) Functional interfaces to other software modules, in particular the provision of meta-data for DBMSs, application programs and so on.

In a distributed environment, the following functions must be added:

(6) Global, participation, fragmentation and allocation schema and global user view definitions;

(7) Local to global mappings, including rules for materialization of global relations (some of the details may be stored in the auxiliary DB, the contents of which should be defined in the DD);
(8) Networking information, including network topology, site addresses and so on;
(9) Global security (access) and integrity constraints;
(10) Statistical data to support query optimization (see Chapter 6).

The present generation of DDSs clearly do not provide all, if any, of the functions (6) to (10) above, which is not surprising since they were not designed with the problems of DDBSs in mind. However, it is generally agreed that an essential feature of a good DDS is **extensibility**, that is the ability to support the addition of new entities in the DD. With such a facility, it would be possible for the global DA to incorporate all the functions listed above. The life expectancy of a DDS in most organizations must be at least a decade, which is a relatively long time in computing terms. Hence the DDS must be able to respond to changing needs of the information systems environment in which it operates. Such changes are inevitably going to be more frequent in a distributed environment. From the global DA's point of view, the DD is the most important and fundamental management tool, without which it would be very difficult to build and maintain an efficient DDBMS.

DDSs have grown up alongside DBMSs and are variously interfaced to them. At one extreme, the DDS can be a totally free-standing, **independent** system (Figure 9.5(a)), which operates like a special purpose DBMS, except that instead of managing data, it manages meta-data. Such an approach offers a high degree of flexibility and enables the meta-data for new DB systems to be incorporated easily. Indeed, it can hold meta-data for non-DB systems. Independent DDSs generally provide utilities for the automatic generation of DDL from the DDS to load the catalogue for a variety of DB packages. This will help ensure consistency of meta-data between the DBMS and the DDS. Thus the independent DDS offers a high degree of independence of meta-data from the surrounding computing environment.

At the other extreme, the DDS can be totally **embedded** as an integral part of the DBMS itself, replacing the system catalogue (Figure 9.5(b)). All access to the data in the DB is via the DDS. Clearly, such an approach avoids the problems of inconsistency arising from the duplication of meta-data. It will also be cheaper since only one software package is required. However, such a system cannot generally be used to store meta-data for systems other than its own DBMS.

A compromise between these two approaches is offered by the **application** DDS (Figure 9.5(c)), which allows the DDS to run as a separate application under the control of the DBMS. The DBMS will still

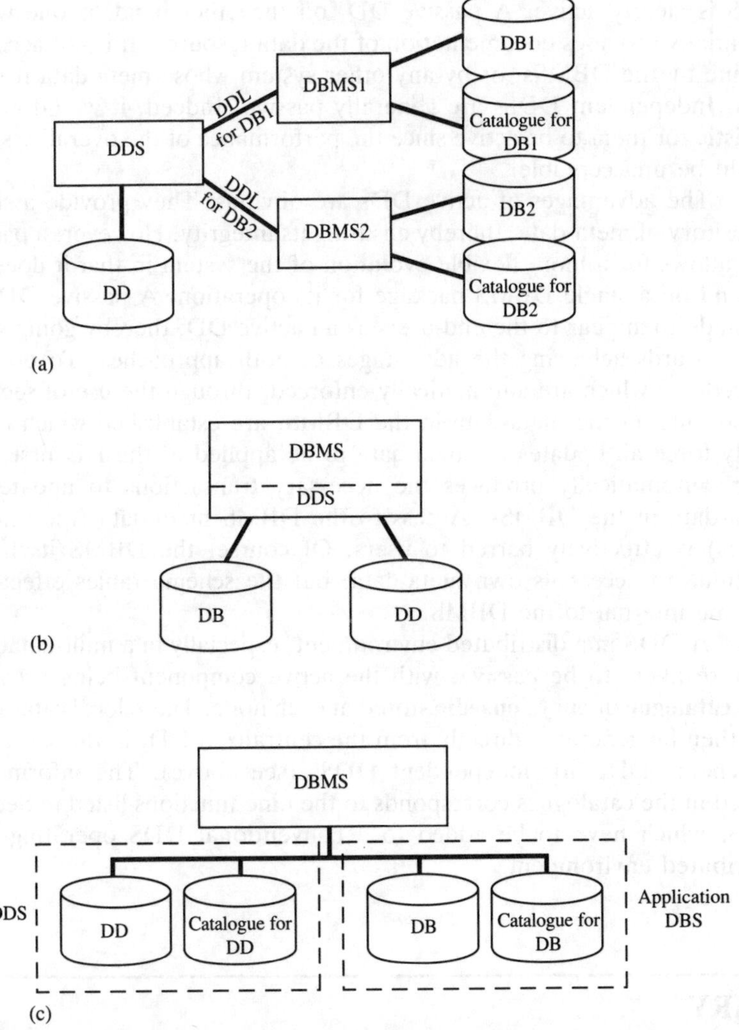

Figure 9.5 (a) Independent DDS. (b) Embedded DDS. (c) DB-application DDS.

need to maintain its own internal DDL tables, including meta-data for the meta-data which is stored in the data dictionary DB! Meta-data for non-DB systems can also be included. However, this approach suffers from the same drawback as the independent DDS, since once again meta-data is duplicated between the DD and the DBMS(s).

Such a classification of DDSs is helpful, but in recent years a distinction has been made which is more useful in the context of DDBMSs. DDs are classified as either **active** or **passive**. An active DD is one which is accessed by the DBMS in order to process a user query. An embedded

DDS is clearly active. A passive DD, on the other hand, is one which essentially provides documentation of the data resource. It is not accessed on-line by the DBMSs, or by any other system whose meta-data it manages. Independent DDSs are generally passive. Indeed, it would not be realistic for them to be active since the performance of the overall systems would be unacceptable.

The advantages of active DDs are obvious. They provide a single repository of meta-data, thereby ensuring its integrity. However, a passive DD allows for a more flexible evolution of the system in that it does not depend on a single DBMS package for its operation. A passive DD can be made to appear to the end-users as an active DD, thereby going some way towards achieving the advantages of both approaches. To do this, procedures which are automatically enforced, through the use of security constraints on the meta-data in the DBMS, are established which effectively force all updates on meta-data to be applied to the DD first. The DDS automatically produces the necessary transactions to update the meta-data in the DBMSs. Access to the DBMS meta-data (the schema tables) is effectively barred to users. Of course, the DBMS itself will continue to access its own meta-data, but the schema tables effectively become internal to the DBMS.

A DDS in a distributed environment, especially in a multidatabase, is more likely to be passive, with the active component being provided by a **catalogue** or **encyclopaedia** stored at each node. These local catalogues can then be generated directly from the centralized DD, in the same way as schema DDL for independent DDSs (see above). The information stored in the catalogues corresponds to the nine functions listed in Section 9.6.3, which have to be added to a conventional DDS operating in a distributed environment.

SUMMARY

This chapter has reviewed two different aspects of DDB management, namely logical DDB design and DDB administration. In both cases, we saw that it is important to distinguish between top-down homogeneous DDBs and heterogeneous bottom-up designed DDBSs such as multidatabases. In the case of the former, both design and administration are the same for the centralized case, with a few extra facilities to incorporate the distributed dimension. Multidatabases, on the other hand, offer a quite different challenge. The main problem for logical MDB design is DB integration (i.e. the integration of the local (participation) schemas into a single, uniform global schema). A manual methodology for performing DB integration was given. It is likely that schema integration methods of the future will be object-oriented, possibly augmented by rule-based techniques from artificial intelligence knowledge-based systems.

Under the heading of administration, we saw that MDB administration is complicated by the fact that there are two levels of control: local corresponding to the local database administrator and global corresponding to the data administrator. In a homogeneous DDB environment, there is really no local level of administration, but the function of the distributed database administrator corresponds more closely to that of a local database administrator than to that of a global data administrator. In other words, the distributed database administrator is responsible for the management of a single data resource, which just happens to be distributed.

Data is viewed today as an important corporate resource in just the same way as plant and personnel. A company would not attempt to manage its employees without knowing and recording a good deal of information about them. In the same way, it is impossible to manage data without a comprehensive inventory of that data indicating what it is, what it means, where it is stored and how it is used and by whom, and so on. This sort of data about data is called meta-data. Management of meta-data is a key concept in data administration. It is also relevant to the issues discussed in this chapter under logical DDB design. The schema integration process, for example, is concerned with the integration of meta-data, and this task will be made easier if an integrated global DD is available for the management of that meta-data. The final section of the chapter was devoted to examining the various ways in which meta-data can be managed, through system catalogues and data dictionaries, in a distributed environment.

EXERCISES

9.1 (a) If the information systems within an organization are managed by a heterogeneous collection of independent file systems and DBMSs, outline the problems which you would expect the organization to be facing which could be solved using a multidatabase approach.

(b) What is a data dictionary system (DDS) and what are its functions?

(c) If the organization mentioned in part (a) above purchased an independent, passive DDS, which supported all the functions you have listed in your answer to part (b), discuss in detail the effect this would have on the organization. You should explain how the DDS would or would not help the organization overcome the information processing problems you have identified in your answer to part (a).

9.2 A university has three separate DBs (A, B, C) containing information about full-time students, part-time students and staff. DB_A contains information about full-time students (name, address, degree for which they are registered and their overall result) together with the grades they have obtained in the various courses they have taken and the lecturer for each course is also recorded. DB_B contains the same information for part-time students, but with an additional attribute to indicate their full-time job (day-job). DB_C contains information about the lecturing staff and the courses which they teach; the number of hours per course and the rate per hour are also recorded. Figure 9.6. gives the ER model for the three DB schemas.
Integrate the three schemas to produce a global schema; show each step of the DB integration process, identifying the transformations performed at each stage.

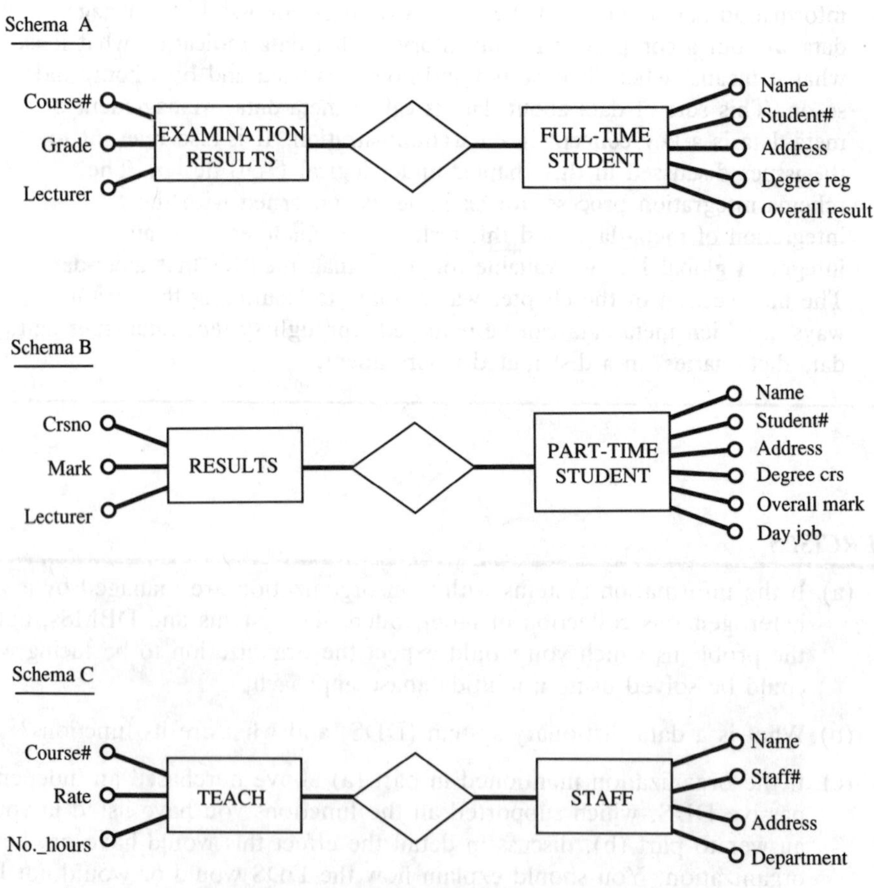

Figure 9.6 Local ER models for Exercise 9.2.

Bibliography

Allen F.W., Loomis M.E.S. and Mannino M.V. (1982). The integrated dictionary/directory system. *ACM Computing Surveys*, **14** (2), 245–86.

A good easy-to-follow introduction to the functions and facilities of data dictionary systems in a centralized DB environment.

Appleton D.S. (1986). Rule-based data resource management. *Datamation*, 86–99.

This paper presents a high level view of managing the data resource in which the vital role of meta-data is emphasized.

Batini C., Lenzerini M. and Navathe S.B. (1986). Comparative analysis of methodologies for database schema integration. *ACM Computing Surveys*, **18** (4), 323–64.

An excellent introduction to view and schema integration, on which much of the material presented in Section 9.3.1 is based.

Bell D.A., Fernández Pérez de Talens A., Gianotti N., Grimson J., Hutt A. and Turco G. (1986). *Functional Requirements for a Multidatabase System*. MAP Project 773, Report 04. Available from Institute of Informatics, Ulster University, N. Ireland.

Bertino E. (1991). Integration of heterogeneous data repositories by using object-oriented views. In *Proc. 1st Int. Workshop on Interoperability in Multidatabase Systems*, 22–9, Kyoto, Japan, April 1991.

This paper gives an overview of an object-oriented approach to schema integration. The approach involves building a local object-oriented view of each underlying heterogeneous data resource, which may optionally be combined into integrated object-oriented views. Views are defined using an object-oriented query language described by Bertino *et al.* (1989).

Bertino E., Negri M., Pelagatti G. and Sbattella L. (1989). Integration of heterogeneous database applications through an object-oriented interface. *Information Systems*, **14** (5).

Braithwaite K.S. (1985). *Data Administration: Selected Topics of Data Control*. New York: Wiley.

Ceri S. and Pelagatti G. (1984). *Distributed Databases: Principles and Systems*. New York: McGraw-Hill.

Chen P.P. (1976). The entity relationship model – towards a unified view of data. *ACM TODS*, **1** (1), 48–61.

The original paper on entity relationship modelling, one of the most widely used modelling techniques in the business world.

Czejdo B. and Taylor M. (1991). Integration of database systems using an object-oriented approach. In *Proc. 1st Int. Workshop on Interoperability in Multidatabase systems*, 30–7, Kyoto, Japan, April 1991.

This paper presents an interesting and fairly concrete approach to object-oriented schema integration. Global users access the underlying heterogeneous data collections through Smalltalk. The approach can be used for both tightly and loosely coupled MDBSs (i.e. with or without a global conceptual schema).

Dao S, Keirsey D.M., Williamson R., Goldman S. and Dolan C.P. (1991). Smart data dictionary: a knowledge-object-oriented approach for interoperability of heterogeneous information management systems. In *Proc. 1st Int. Workshop on Interoperability in Multidatabase Systems*, 88–91, Kyoto, Japan, April 1991.

This paper gives a brief overview of a method of schema integration which combines case-based reasoning with object-oriented techniques.

Database Architecture Framework Task Group (DAFTG) of the

ANSI/X3/SPARC Database System Study Group. (1986). Reference model for DBMS standardisation. *ACM SIGMOD*, **15** (1), 19–58.

This paper presents the final report on a reference model for DBMS standardization produced by DAFTG. The model proposed combines the standard ANSI–SPARC three-level architecture with an orthogonal intension–extension dimension, which incorporates the idea of self-describing databases.

Dayal U. and Hwang H. (1984). View definition and generalisation for database integration in a multidatabase. *IEEE Trans. on Software Engineering*, **10** (6), 628–44.

De Marco T. (1979). *Structured Analysis and System Specification*. New York: Yourdon Inc.

Durrell W.R. (1985). *Data Administration: a practical guide to successful data management*. New York: McGraw-Hill.

ElMasri R., Weeldryer J. and Hevner A. (1985). The category concept: an extension to the entity relationship model. *Data and Knowledge Engineering*, **1** (1), 75–116.

ElMasri R., Larson J. and Navathe S.B. (1986). *Schema Integration Algorithms for Federated Databases and Logical Database Design*. Technical Report, CSC–86–9: 8212, Honeywell Corporate Research Center.

Grimson J.B. (1986). Guidelines for data administration. In *Proc. IFIP 86*, Dublin, Ireland, 15–22, Amsterdam: North-Holland.

Litwin W., Abdellatif A., Nicolas B., Vigier P. and Zeroual A. (1987). *MSQL: A Multidatabase Language*. INRIA Research Report 695, Rocquencourt, France.

MSQL (see Section 9.3.3) is an extension of SQL which enables queries to be issued across multiple relational databases (i.e. loosely-coupled MDBs with no global schema).

Litwin W., Mark L. and Roussopoulos N. (1990). Interoperability of multiple autonomous databases. *ACM Computing Surveys*, **22** (3), 267–93.

A review of loosely-coupled multidatabase systems.

Mark L. and Roussopoulos N. (1986). Metadata management. *IEEE Computer*, **19** (12), 26–36.

This paper presents a self-describing database system based on an integrated, active data dictionary. Providing extensibility of the DD for effective management of meta-data is central to this design (see Section 9.6.3).

Lindsay B. (1980). *Object Naming and Catalog Management for a Distributed Database Manager*. IBM Research Report RJ2914, San Jose, CA.

Lindsay B. and Selinger P.G. (1980). *Site Autonomy Issues in R*: A Distributed Database Management System*. IBM Research Report RJ2927, San Jose, CA.

Mannino M.V. and Effelsberg W. (1984). *A Methodology for Global Schema Design*, UF-CIS Technical Report TR-84-1, University of Florida, Gainesville, Florida FL 32611.

Mostardi T. and Staniszkis W. (1987). *Multidatabase System Design Methodology*. Poland, MultiStar Project, Internal Report CRAI, Cosenza, Italy.

The DB methodology for the MultiStar MDBS is described in this paper.

Neuhold E. and Stonebraker M. (1977). A distributed version of INGRES. In *Proc. 2nd Berkeley Workshop on Distributed Data Management and Computer Networks*, Berkeley, California.

Rothnie J.B., Bernstein P.A., Fox N.*et al.* (1980). Introduction to a system for distributed databases (SDD-1), *ACM TODS*, **5** (1), 1–17.

Sheth A.P., Larson J.A., Cornelio A. and Navathe S.B. (1988). A tool for integrating conceptual schemas and user views. In *IEEE Conf. on Data*

Engineering, 176–183, Los Angeles, California.

The model used for integration is an extended ER model, called the entity–category–relationship model, which supports generalization and subclasses and also allows constraints to be defined on the relationships. The interactive tool described in the paper provides a graphical interface to the user and includes an integrated data dictionary.

Staniszkis W., Kaminski W., Kowalewski M., Krajewski K., Mezyk S. and Turco G. (1985). Architecture of the network data management system. In *Distributed Data Sharing Systems*. (Schreiber F.A. and Litwin W., eds., 57–76, Amsterdam: North-Holland.

Walker H.M. (1982). Administering a distributed data base management system. *ACM SIGMOD Record*, **12** (3), 86–99.

Whang W.K., Navathe S.B. and Chakvarthy S. (1991). Logic-based approach for realizing a federated information system. In *Proc. 1st International Workshop on Interoperability in Multidatabase Systems*, 92–100, Kyoto, Japan, April 1991.

This paper describes an approach to schema integration in which the rules for integration are defined in first-order logic. Logic programming (Prolog) is used for both integration and implementation.

Wilson T.B. and Larson J. (1975). Distribution of data administration authority. In *Proc. ACM Pacific NW Conf.*

SOLUTIONS TO EXERCISES

9.2

Step 1: Figure 9.7(a).
Choose *course#* for *crsno* in schema B.
Choose *grade* for *mark* in schema B.
Choose *ID#* for *student#* in schemas A and B and for *staff#* in schema C.
Choose *degree_reg* for *degree_crs* in schema B.
Choose *overall_result* for *overall_mark* in schema B.
Choose RESULTS for EXAMINATION RESULTS in schema A.

Step 2: Figure 9.7(b).
Make *lecturer* in TEACH an entity in schemas A and B.

Step 3: Figure 9.7(c).
Superimpose schemas, matching TEACH entities and RESULTS entities. Recognize that lecturer in schemas A and B is the same as name in schema C and can therefore be eliminated as an attribute of the TEACH entity.

Step 4: Figure 9.7(d).
Create new STUDENT entity and make FULL-TIME STUDENT and PART-TIME STUDENT subsets of STUDENT. Then create a new PERSON entity and make STUDENT and STAFF subsets of PERSON.

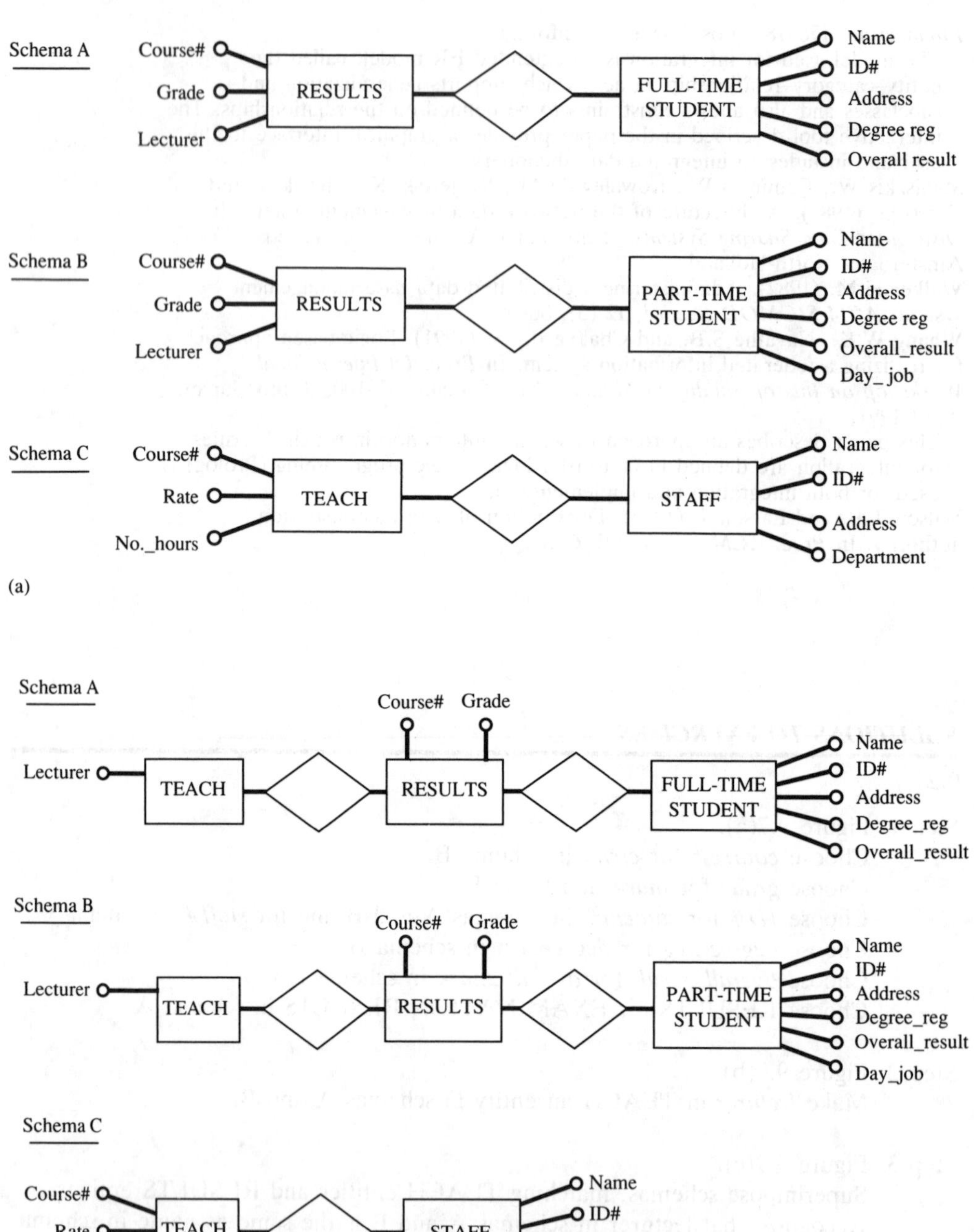

Figure 9.7 (a) Standardization of attribute names. (b) Make lecturer in TEACH into an entity in schemas A and B.

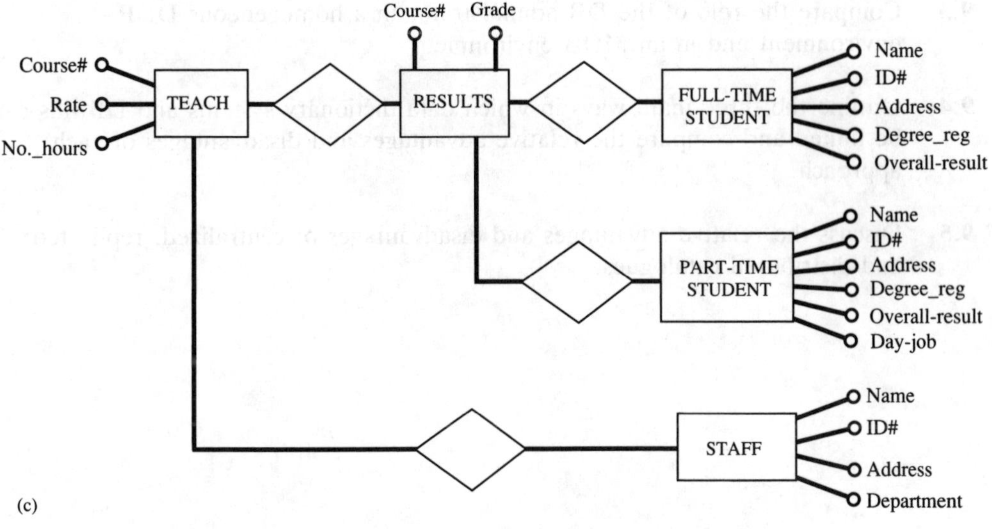

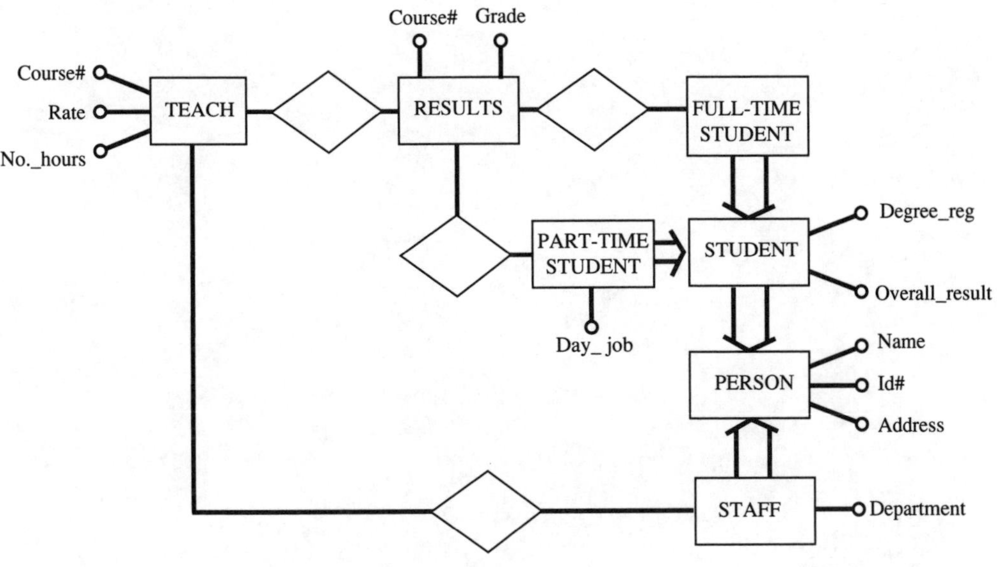

Figure 9.7 (c) Superposition of schemas. (d) Create new STUDENT and PERSON entities and subset relationships.

9.3 Compare the role of the DB administrator in a homogeneous DDB environment and in an MDB environment.

9.4 Outline the three main ways in which data dictionary systems and DBMSs can be linked and compare the relative advantages and disadvantages of each approach.

9.5 Discuss the relative advantages and disadvantages of centralized, replicated and distributed catalogues.

10 A Case Study – Multidatabases in Health Care Networks

10.1 Introduction

10.1.1 An overview of some problems in medical informatics

In health care networks computers are being used with increasing enthusiasm, although the exploitation of their capabilities still lags behind that of industry in general. The 'information technology revolution' has made a great impact on daily life in modern society, being used in familiar applications from high-street cash dispensers to children's education. Increasing exposure to computing tools and services has meant that much of the mystique surrounding the discipline is disappearing, and the next generation of medical professionals and other workers in the health sector can be expected to have a very positive approach to computing.

However, in the medical world the potential of this revolution in the information processing world is still largely untapped. For example, each hospital, or even each department in a hospital, keeps its own patient records and it is difficult to access them, even if they are computerized, from another care unit. This is made worse by the fact that access might perhaps be required years after the acquisition of the information. The patient's or relative's memory has still to be relied upon to an alarming and unnecessary extent. The challenge of computing is not receiving much enthusiasm in many cases. There is a general lack of coordination, integration and direction in current efforts to apply computing in health networks.

Having said this, there are many conspicuous successes in applying computers in medicine. Diagnostic imaging, laboratory analysis, intensive care monitoring, medical record keeping and statistical analysis, and numerous other organizational and basic operational functions have all been demonstrably enhanced by using computers in projects of various scales and scopes. But applications have generally been developed piecemeal with the result that something of an information archipelago has evolved. So while the information needed by a user may already be stored on a computer, often the user is unaware of the fact that it is accessible and that modern information handling tools are available to help in this. Clinical professionals in some disciplines have been slower than they should be to make direct use of the technology.

Some of this backwardness is undoubtedly a result of the traditional inertia of these particular professions. However, the major contributing factor is probably lack of awareness of what is realistically promised by the new tools to save time, improve care, carry out basic administration, assist in diagnosis and selectively assemble and recall patients' histories, and even keep the professional up to date with medical procedures, diseases and treatment. A system able to hold fuller patient details, perhaps ultimately a complete and comprehensive cradle-to-grave medical history, in a well-organized, selective and responsive manner would surely demand their attention on ethical grounds alone.

The aim of this chapter is to examine the potential of the distributed database approach to the rationalization and integration of information handling functions within health care networks and to help answer questions raised by potential users. The overriding purpose is, however, to provide a demanding application backdrop for the consideration of the computing functions and systems introduced in earlier chapters. The case study presented here should help make some of the concepts more concrete. Detailed assessment of the value of the systems discussed in this chapter, from both the medical and administration viewpoints, must be left to the professionals in the respective domains.

10.1.2 Some dichotomies of medical informatics

Various dichotomies which may require tradeoffs and compromise are detected when computerization in health information networks is contemplated. The balancing of these divisions presents exceedingly difficult problems, many of which remain challenges for researchers and systems developers. For example, the costs of an approach must always be compared with the value of applying it when considering innovations such as this. Also, any models used for the understanding or control of a real-world system must, by definition, lose information as detail is shed in a simplification process. To be humane as well as scientific a system must avoid being impersonal, and the art or craft side of medicine – dealing with 'the total person' – demands the management of a large amount of detailed information. The generalizations studied in textbooks are appropriate for objects, events and other entities of limited numbers of attributes. These pose few problems of representation in a computer, but care-oriented entities such as patients are extremely complex, demanding much more detailed representation than these. It is costly to obtain this added value.

It is a hypothesis worthy of consideration that the technological developments considered in earlier chapters contribute substantially to the handling of the cost-value dichotomy.

Top-down versus bottom-up is a dichotomy which is frequently encountered in computing. Given adequate resources and a 'green-fields' situation, a system can be created to exploit all possible aids for approximating the 'ideal' information system, which must of course be defined by medical rather than computer people or even philosophers. However, in reality account must be taken of the *status quo* and a bottom-up process iterating towards the logical ideal identified during the top-down design is likely to be more appropriate. Other dichotomies are those of data versus information (or even knowledge) and function versus performance.

The latter of tradeoff deserves further comment because of its ubiquity. The data collections for our applications can be understood as part of a communication process between physicians and other physicians, scientists and possibly educators. Because such communication is rarely synchronized and exclusive – one supplier communicating with only one user of data – buffers or databases are used in this communication process. These buffers must be flexible enough for the purpose, hence we really need knowledge and multimedia information as well as the structured data we usually consider for domains such as medicine. However, this functionality should not be provided without due consideration of its implications. For example, the performance of the system must be carefully considered. Does the system meet the responsiveness, throughput and device utilization index values required for it to be useful in the workplace for which it is designed? If not, it will not be a real solution to the users' problems.

The distributed versus centralized debate already hinted at has been considered by many authors for EDP in general and for medical systems in particular. The case for distribution has already been made in this book.

Finally, the dichotomy of 'paper tigers' versus products must be mentioned. Inexperienced readers of technical computing literature, particularly in the database and networking areas, may be misled into identifying concepts described in learned journals with those of the same name in vendors' literature. To exploit marketing opportunities – for modest products – vendors have been known to use terms associated with sophisticated and elegant techniques which may lead purchasers to be over-optimistic about their products.

Chapter 3 of this book has dealt with the capabilities of products and the features of architectures and prototypes which are likely to lead to products within some years.

10.2 The health information network

10.2.1 Objectives

The demands of computerized information systems in a health network with regard to hardware and software are rarely matched by industrial applications. The problems to be solved are therefore correspondingly diverse and require many innovative techniques.

The objectives of such computerization are to:

- Reduce the need for, and duration of, treatment of patients by good prevention methods and early diagnoses;
- Increase the effectiveness of treatment to the extent allowed by improved information;
- Relieve professionals and other workers in care units of information processing and documentation burdens, thereby freeing them for more direct care of the patient;
- Enhance the exploitation of resources available for health care by good management and administration;
- Archive clinical data, facilitate the compilation of medical statistics and otherwise support research for the diagnosis and treatment of disease.

10.2.2 Information flow in health care networks

Consider the information and data needs of typical primary health care networks within particular geographic regions each serving a population of a few million inhabitants. The pattern in most European countries (an example from Sweden is referenced at the end of this chapter) is that regions such as these are split for administrative purposes into a number of (essentially autonomous) subregions, coordinated by a central administration.

Usually each subregion is in turn divided into local areas or districts servicing populations bounded by rough geographic borders. For example, the Department of Health and Social Services in the United Kingdom splits up the Northern Ireland region which has a population of about 1.6 million into four Area Boards. The decomposition in the South of Ireland is slightly different in that the primary units for the decomposition are eight Health Boards and only in the areas of high population, such as the Dublin area, are these further subdivided into smaller districts.

This underlying pattern of decomposition into manageable administrative units or districts is repeated in many countries. A small number of general hospitals and various small hospitals, clinics, health centres and community care units providing district nursing and school nursing serve each district.

General hospitals have a great variety of specialist wards, laboratories and other such facilities. Specialist hospitals for psychiatry, maternity, paediatrics, geriatrics and orthopaedics at strategic sites supplement the general hospitals.

In a typical network composed of such a collection of care units, quite extensive collections of computerized information processing systems are to be found running on a variety of computer configurations with variations between their systems software: database management systems, file handling packages, operating systems and so on. Typically the challenge of computerization has been receiving rapidly increasing attention in recent years and on the ground the level of computerization is increasing.

Communication of clinically important information, but also administration or managerial information, is essential for continuing and improving patient care and operational efficiency. Current technology offers a lot of assistance here. For example, departments in large hospitals with local systems can link with central systems and this has presented a challenge to health information systems developers. Laboratory results can be communicated via telecommunication lines to a ward or other site. Patient administration data can be acquired at a series of workstations connected to a central computer by public telephone network or local area network within the hospital. This promises to remove some of the problems associated with manual records systems which suffer from disadvantages due to the difficulty of access to information, and in which vital information can be overlooked simply because of the inaccessibility of the data.

It has been recognized for some time that database systems offer potential solutions to these problems largely because of the features of flexibility of access and ease of modification to meet the various end users' specialized needs. Coupled with current and emerging telecommunications services and products, the management of data within hospitals and other health units can be greatly improved. Mobile populations and the 'centralized' nature of the specialist care units, for example, could mean that data in another subregion, or even region, might be required. Remote accesses such as these are likely to remain rare, and even accesses between neighbouring hospitals are comparatively rare, but current information technology now offers attractive alternatives to the traditional methods of meeting these remote access as well as internal accesses requirements.

10.3 Some sites and databases in health care networks

During the data analysis phase of a study of such a typical network, six important sites or functional area types were identified as providing a realistic and representative scenario for a case study. The sites were

(1) Community care units for schools and the community;

(2) General practitioner or health centre units providing a first contact point for patients with the health care network;

(3) Casualty units within hospitals for treating accidents or other emergencies requiring urgent responses;

(4) Laboratories, usually within hospitals, to provide analyses of samples from various other units;

(5) Patient records offices, for the administration of medical records within hospitals;

(6) Wards for the treatment of in-patients within hospitals.

The requirements of each of these sites were distilled from the output of the data analysis phase of the study, supplemented by data descriptions reported by other studies, and expressed as a collection of five descriptions: data objects handled, functions carried out, events triggering each function; constraints on the functions; and the distribution of the functions and the data around the network.

These are presented in Databases 10.1 to 10.6. It is clear that each of the objects of the static schema can be considered as a relation scheme of a database, although due to the piecemeal development of computer systems in the network observed earlier, these are likely to be implemented, if at all, as flat files, or using heterogeneous collections of database packages.

Database 10.1 DATABASE C: COMMUNITY CARE DATABASE

A STATIC SCHEMA

Objects related to care facilities

ØC1 Service (service #, Serve type, Serv description, authority required, cost)

ØC2 Professional (professional #, name, address, phone no, TU, car reg no, professional type, clinic/region, duties, grade [years qualified]).

ØC3 Clinic/unit (unit #, name, address, head, phone no, residential details)

Objects related to population

ØC4 Patient (patient #, DOB, address, job, next-of-kin, financial details)

ØC5 Ailment (ailment #, code, professional types needed)

ØC6 Household (house #, surname of head, address, phone no, no in household, shared accomodation?)

ØC7 School (school #, name, address, phone no, headmaster, no of children)

Objects related to administration of facilities

ØC8 Patient-Serv (patient #, service #, dates, problem, no of contacts/treatments, comments)

ØC9 Patient-Prof-Contact (patient #, professional #, date, reason, location, comments)

ØC10 Patient-Ailment (patient #, ailment #, date of diagnosis, date of discovery, symptoms/duration, comments)

ØC11 School-Service (school #, service #, date, comments)

ØC12 Patient-Clinic (patient #, clinic #, date, comments)

B DYNAMIC SCHEMA

Functions related to provision of a service

FC1 Service is requested at a school or home or clinic

FC2 Professional attendance is scheduled

FC3 Appointments are made

FC4 Services are rendered

FC5 Documentation is completed

FC6 Documentation is distributed/received by users

Functions related to administration and management

FC7	Financial and statistical reports are made
FC8	Allowance and welfare services are developed, refined or otherwise adjusted
FC9	Health professionals activities are monitored and manpower planned
FC10	Health professionals procedures are defined, developed and evaluated
FC11	Preventative services are defined, developed and evaluated
FC12	Clinic/Unit procedures are defined, developed and evaluated
FC13	Records are maintained
FC14	Details of patients records are accessed by interested parties if CC1
FC15	Details held at other sites are accessed by users if CC1

Events

EC1	Request for service is received
EC2	Appointment is agreed
EC3	Services are rendered
EC5	Documentation is completed

Conditions

CC1	Enquirer qualified

C DISTRIBUTION SCHEMA

(i) Sites where functions are performed

SC1	Admin Centre FC2, FC3, FC7–FC15
SC2	Clinic/Unit FC1, FC3, FC4, FC5, FC6, FC15
SC3	School/Home FC1, FC3, FC6
SC4	Professionals' Base (HQ) FC3, FC5, FC6, FC14
SC5	Other enquiry site FC14

(ii) Sites where objects are held

SC1	Admin Centre ØC1–ØC8, ØC11 and some others
SC2	Clinic/Unit ØC12
SC4	Professionals' Base ØC9, ØC10

Database 10.2 DATABASE G: GENERAL PRACTITIONER – HEALTH CENTRE DATABASE

A STATIC SCHEMA

Objects related to clinical activities

ØG1 Centre (centre #, address, phone no, no of doctors, no of treatment rooms, no of anxiliaries)

ØG2 Doctor (Dr #, name, address, phone no, room no, date of qualification, date of appointment here)

ØG3 Nurse-Auxiliary auxiliary #, name, address, phone no, grade, date of qualification, date of appointment here)

ØG4 Treatment Session (patient #, auxiliary #, treatment #, time, date, treatment code, comments)

ØG5 Receptionist (receptionist #, name, address, phone no, qualification, appointment date)

ØG6 Treatment Room (room #, type, equipment)

ØG7 Doctor-rota (Dr #, day-session)

ØG8 Patient (patient #, admin details, history, lab, previous diagnoses, treatment, free test)

ØG9 Dr-Patient-Encounter (Dr #, patient #, session, diagnosis, treatment, referral, comments)

ØG10 Lab-sample (request #, lab #, patient #, sample #, call time, priority collector, no of tests, volume, doctor #, specimen type, comments).

ØG11 Aux-Rota (auxiliary #, day-session)

ØG12 Prescription (Dr #, patient #, session, details)

ØG13 Appointment (Dr #, patient #, session, details)

ØG14 Ailment incidence (patient #, ailment #).

N.B. There are many other possible objects relating to practice management and epidemiology, screening etc.

B DYNAMIC SCHEMA

Functions related to clinical activities

FG1 Patient makes an appointment (for treatment or consultation)

FG2 Patient checks in at reception if CG1

FG3 Patient waits in Waiting Room

FG4 Patient details are sent to doctor
FG5 Patient is treated
FG6 Patient consults with doctor
FG7 Prescription is written
FG8 Patient is referred to hospital if CG2
FG9 Samples are taken
FG10 Doctor visits patient at home if not CG1
FG11 Discharge (from Hospital) information is added to patient's record if CG3
FG13 Consultant's opinion is added to patient's record if CG2

Events

EG1 Auxiliary becomes available
EG2 Doctor becomes available
EG3 Treatment/consultation is complete

Conditions

CG1 Patient is able to attend surgery
CG2 Doctor requires a specialist opinion
CG3 Patient has just undergone a period of hospitalization

C DISTRIBUTION SCHEMA

(i) Sites where functions are performed
All except FG11 are performed at Health Centre
FG11 is done at Lab (probably at Hospital)
FG8, 12 require communication with Hospital

(ii) Sites where data is stored
All at Health Centre except possibly ØG1

Database 10.3 DATABASE K: CASUALTY

A STATIC SCHEMA

Objects related to reception and dealing with patients in medical/surgicalemergencies

ØK1 Reception (receptionist #, date, transport means)

ØK2 Patient (patient #, s'name, xname, addr. DOB, job, next of kin)

ØK3 Doctor call (arrival #, hour called, n type doctor)

ØK4 Arrival Doctor (arrival Dr #, Dr #, nr arrival)

ØK5 Moving (patient #, date, place # (origin), place # (dest))

ØK6 Subregion (patient #, date, subregion #, result)

ØK7 Region (patient #, date, region #, result)

ØK8 Result (patient #, date, synthesis result)

ØK9 Diagnosis (patient #, date, Dr #, diagnosis #)

ØK10 Therapy-Med (patient #, date, Dr #, medicine #, text)

ØK11 Therapy-Sur (patient #, date, surgeon #, text)

Objects related to asking for test (maybe Lab or other)

ØK12 Lab-Request (test #, sample #)

ØK13 Sample (sample #, date of sample, sampler #, place #)

ØK14 Result (test #, date result, result #, checking)

ØK15 Res-Interpret (test #, date interpret, interpret #, interpreter #)

ØK16 Diagnosis-Res (test #, patient #, date, proposition #, person #)

ØK17 New-Sample (call #, test #)

Objects related to appointment in another dept

ØK18 Rendevous (appt #, call #, state of Rendezvous)

General objects

ØK19 Receptionist (receptionist #, name)

ØK20 Transportation (code #, means)

ØK21 Dr (type #, Dr #, name)

ØK22 Place (place #, place)

ØK23 Subregion (subregion #, wording)

ØK24 Region (region #, wording)

ØK25 Diagnosis (diagosis #, wording)

ØK26 Medicine (medicine #, wording)

B DYNAMIC SCHEMA

Functions

FK1 interview of patient

FK2 call Dr

FK3 wait for Dr

FK4 clinical exam (elementary)

FK5 clinical exam (regional)

FK6 determine destination in hospital if CK1

FK7 process clinical info
FK8 elaboration of a conclusion re diagnosis
FK9 write prescription if CK2
FK10 action for surgical therapy if CK3
FK11 call for test if CK4
FK12 conduct test
FK13 New global synthesis on patient return from test
FK14 New global synthesis after interpretation of result
FK15 New sample for lab
FK16 Ask for appointment

Events

EK1 Patient presents
EK2 Doctor is called
EK3 Doctor arrives
EK4 Patient is moved
EK5 Lab request sent
EK6 Test result received
EK7 Treatment is started

Conditions

CK1 Patient must be moved
CK2 Pharmacy services required
CK3 Surgery necessary
CK4 Lab test required

C DISTRIBUTION SCHEMA

Sites where functions are performed

SK1 Casualty Department FK1-5, FK7-11, FK13-15
SK2 Labs. FK12
SK3 Hospital records FK6, FK16
SK4 FC2

Database 10.4 DATABASE L: LABORATORY DATABASE

A STATIC SCHEMA

Objects relative to request for a test

ØL1 Patient (hospital #, name, DOB, ward/bed/clinic, class, sex, blood type, Dr code, next-of-kin, next-of-kin address, comments)

ØL2 Sample (request #, hospital #, sample #, coll time, receipt time, priority, collector ID, collector location, no of tests, volume, Dr code (ordering), specimen type, repeat?, comments)

ØL3 Test req (request #, hospital #, test #, type, test code)

Objects relative to receipt of sample at lab

ØL4 Receipt (request #, receipt #, receipt time, priority, receiver)

ØL5 Verification (request #, hospital #, comments)

Objects related to work-load scheduling

ØL6 Schedule (workstation #, technician #, test type, test #)

ØL7 Status (test #, patient #, priority, comments)

ØL8 Test-avail (test code, test type, measurement units, reference limits by age/sex expected values (qc), comments)

Objects related to dissemination of results

ØL9 Results (test #, result #, sample #, date and time)

ØL10 Result detail (test #, result #, sample #, feature #, result)

General aspects

ØL11 Lab-receptionist (receipt #, name)

ØL12 Doctor (Doctor #, name, speciality)

ØL13 Collector (collector #, name, site)

B DYNAMIC SCHEMA

Functions

FL1 Tests requested by doctor

FL2 Sample taken by collector

FL3 Request filed by collector

FL4 Sample and request transported to lab

FL5 Sample received by lab

FL6 Sample split up for various tests requested

FL7 Sub-samples scheduled by priority for workstations/technicians if CL1

FL8 Delay-waiting for workstation/technician

FL9 Delay-waiting for sub-result

FL10 Inquiries about status of each test (poss by patient) if CL3

FL11 Writing out sub-results/results

FL12 Quality control if CL1

FL13 Requests for repeats if CL2

FL14 Discrimination of results/receipt of results by user

FL15 Production of various (billing, workstation summary, technician summary) reports/receipt of some of these by hospital records department

FL16 Subsequent enquiry about test results (from perhaps remote sites) if CL3

Events

EL1 Sample is prepared

EL2 Sample arrives at lab reception

EL3 Sample is verified

EL4 Sample is split for tests and scheduled

EL5 Tests are completed

EL6 Results are completed

EL7 Results are received at patient location

Conditions

CL1 The results are within reference limits

CL2 Further tests are required

CL3 Enquirer is qualified

C DISTRIBUTION SCHEMA

(i) Sites where functions are performed

SL1 Lab FL1, FL2, FL3, FL10, FL14
FL4, FL5, FL6, FL7, FL8, FL9, FL11, FL12, FL13, FL14, FL15

SL2 Patient location (ward, clinic, other hospital etc) FL1, FL2, FL3, FL10, FL14, FL16

SL3 Hospital records FL15

SL4 Other enquiry site FL10, FL14, FL16

(ii) Sites where objects are held

SL1 ØL2 ØL3 ØL5 ØL9 ØL10 ØL12 ØL13

SL2 ØL1 ØL2 ØL3 ØL4 ØL5 ØL6 ØL7 ØL8 ØL9 ØL10 ØL11 ØL12

SL3 ØL1 ØL11 ØL12 ØL13

SL4 ØL9 ØL10 ØL12

Database 10.5 DATABASE R: HOSPITAL PATIENT RECORDS

A STATIC SCHEMA

A All objects are assumed to be related to patient records

ØR1 Patient (patient #, name, DOB, address, ward, bed, class, sex, blood type, doctor code, next-of-kin, next-of-kin address, comments)

ØR2 Appointment (Dr #, patient #, session #, location)

ØR3 Hospitalisation (patient #, patient name, patient DOB, time/date, doctor #, ailment, treatment (free format))

ØR4 Outpatient Encounter (patient #, patient name, address, DOB, time, date, treatment/diagnosis, comments)

ØR5 Index (patient #, patient name, address, DOB, chart location)

ØR6 Doctor (doctor #, name, address, phone no, office no, date of attendance?, specializing . . .)

ØR7 Nurse (nurse #, name, address, rank, years service, current ward, . . .)

ØR8 Bed (bed #, ward #, patient # (if occupied))

ØR9 Patient chart (patient #, treatment #, entry #, date, doctor #, . . .)

ØR10 Important ailment (ailment #, treatment #)

ØR11 Treatment (treatment #, ailment)

B DYNAMIC SCHEMA (only for patient oriented activities)

Functions

FR1 Receipt of referral from GP

FR2 Appointment made (I/P) with consultant (if CR2)

FR3 Appointment made (ØP) with consultant (if CR2)

FR4 Appointment made (ØP) with radiology if CR5

FR5 Appointment made (ØP) with other treatment centre if CR6

FR6	Make available previous records
FR7	Registration of patient as I/P if CR2
FR8	Discharged/death notes prepared if CR3
FR9	Letter to GP is prepared/sent if CR3
FR10	Patient chart is sent to/received from other hospital
FR11	Patient chart is received/sent to the hospital if CR4
FR12	Ward informed of admittance date if CR2

Events

ER1	Letter arrives from GP
ER2	Patient arrives at reception
ER3	Patient's previous hospitalization is acquired
ER4	Patient dies/is discharged
ER5	Patient admitted straight to ward

Conditions

CR1	Patient has been hospitalized here before
CR2	Patient is to be admitted
CR3	Patient dies or completes treatment
CR4	Patient sent to/admitted from other hospital
CR5	X-raying required
CR6	Other treatment required

C DISTRIBUTION SCHEMA

(i)	sites where functions are performed	SR1	Records office (FR1 FR2 . . . FR10)
		SR2	Other hospitals' records office (FR10 FR11 FR1 FR9)
		SR3	Patient's site (home ?) (FR2 FR3 FR4 FR5)
		SR4	Ward (FR12 FR8 FR10 FR11)
		SR5	Treatment centre (FR5)
			Radiology (FR5)
(ii)	sites where objects are held	SR1	(OR1-OR9)
		SR2	(OR9)
		SR3	-
		SR4	(OR9)
		SR5	(OR9)
		SR6	(OR9)

atabase 10.6 DATABASE W: WARD DATABASE

A STATIC SCHEMA

Objects related to ward facilities and patients

ØW1 Ward (ward #, sister, specialism, phone no, no of beds)

ØW2 Bed (bed #, patient)

ØW3 Ward-state (ward #, date, empty beds)

ØW4 Patient (patient #, name, DOB, address, problems/symptoms, consultant, GP, religion, care plan, transport, diet, prev ward, date admission to ward, date of discharge, comment)

ØW5 Physician (Dr #, name, address, specialism)

ØW6 Nurse (nurse #, name, address, grade, weeks schedule, date of joining ward, comment)

Objects related to ward functions

ØW7 Pat-examination (patient #, date, time, results) -measurements

ØW8 Pat-operation (patient #, date, time, theatre number, anaesthetist, surgeon, comments)

ØW9 Pat-medication (patient #, date, time, medication centre, quantity)

B DYNAMIC SCHEMA

Functions related to provision of service

FW1 Patient admitted to ward

FW2 Details are recorded by nurse

FW3 Patient discharged from ward

FW4 Anaesthetist visits patient

FW5 Patient prepared for treatment (eg x-ray)

FW6 Patient treated (surgically/physio/etc) if CW4

FW7 Dressings are done

FW8 Medication administered

FW9 Patient is examined (x-rays etc again)

FW10 Meals are ordered

FW11 Observations/measurements/samples are taken if CW3

FW12 Request for test is made

FW13 Rsults of tests are received/used

FW14 Nurse (etc) starts/ends work-shift

FW15 Nurse (etc) schedule is planned (also kitchen staff/cleaners)

FW16 HAA etc reports prepared

FW17 Meals are served

FW18 Stocks are ordered from pharmacy/stores, etc if CW7

FW19 Nursing care plans are formulated

FW20 Visitors (clergy, welfare, library, social worker, etc) are organized/interviewed

Functioning related to administration and management

FW21 Move patient to treatment unit if CW2

FW22 Details of patients released to interested parties if CW1

FW23 Patient death procedures performed if CW5

FW24 Clinician-on-call is called if CW6

FW25 Delay - waiting for doctor

FW26 Records of patient at other site (hospitals, labs, records etc) accessed if CW1

Events

EW1 Arrival of patient at ward

EW2 Calling for emergency doctor

EW3 Arrival of doctor

EW4 Examinations complete

EW5 Treatment complete (eg return from theatre)

EW6 Nurse/sister arrives on duty

EW7 Nurse leaves duty

EW8 Meals arrive

EW9 Patient leaves ward

EW10 Patient dies

EW11 Visitors arrive

EW12 Visitors depart

EW13 Discharge letter posted

EW14 Meal is served

Conditions

CW1 Enquirer is suitably qualified

CW2 Patient needs treatment elsewhere

CW3 Clinician request further info

CW4 Patient signs for treatment

CW5 Patient dies

CW6 Patient requires emergency treatment

CW7 Stock reminder point passed

```
C  DISTRIBUTION SCHEMA
 (i)      Sites where functions are performed
          all at ward/ward-office
 (ii)     Sites where data stored
            some of ØW1-ØW6, at least, stored at record office
            rest (+ possibly copies) stored at ward
N.        ØW4 might reasonably be assumed copied at ward - for active
B.        patients
```

10.4 The appropriateness of DDB technology for health applications

The exploitation of computing equipment to meet the data and information needs of a health provision network raises many exceedingly interesting and challenging problems. Consider some of the particular cases of the, possibly pre-existing, databases and distributed databases identified at network sites in the previous section as in Figure 10.1.

Health centre

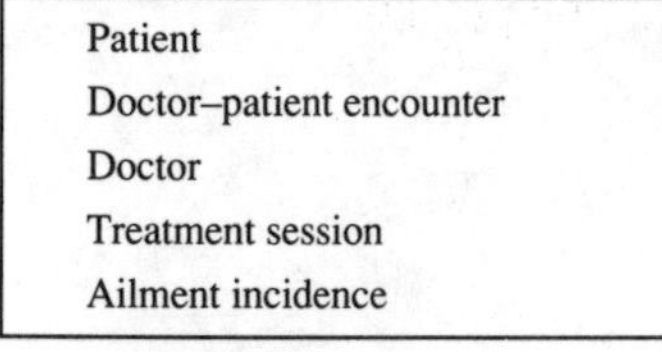

Stored using a simple file structure

Community care unit

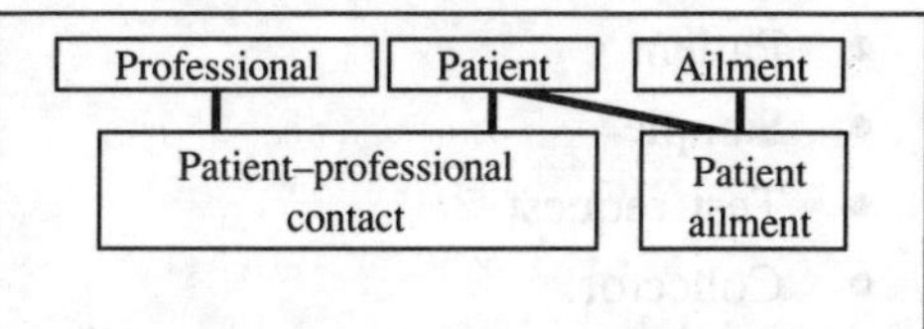

Stored as a CODASYL database

Hospital A

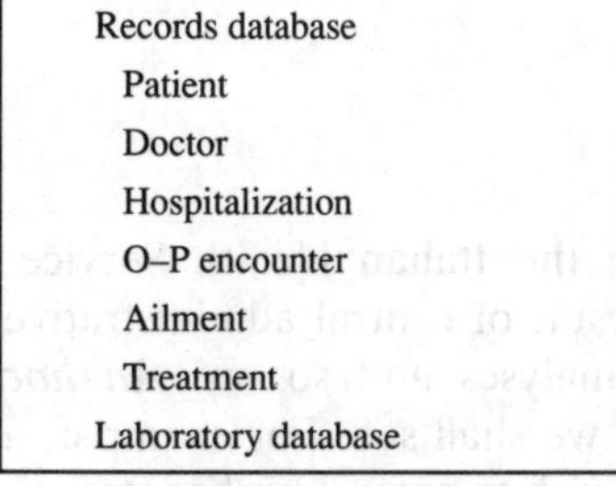

Stored as 2 relational databases

Hospital B

Records database
Patient
Doctor
Hospitalization
O–P encounter
Ailment
Treatment
Laboratory database

Stored using simple file structures

N.B there are 5 nodes here;
the 'records' objects are all described by the same attributes – but the names can change between sites.

Figure 10.1 A sample scenario.

In the community care database, we have several probable objects. The corresponding relations are taken from Bell (1990). For example:

- Professional
- Patient
- Ailment
- Patient–professional.

In the hospital records database, probable relations include:

- Patient
- Doctor
- Hospitalization
- Treatment
- Out-patient.

In the laboratory database, there are relations corresponding to such objects and events as

- Patient
- Sample
- Test request
- Collector.

At the health centre probable example relations are

- Patient
- Doctor
- Doctor–patient–encounter
- Treatment session.

As we will see in an example from the Italian Health Service, additional access traffic is generated as a result of central administrative activities, for global planning, statistical analyses and so on. *Ad hoc* queries can also arise from time to time, as we shall see. For example, a researcher into some obscure disease might wish to extend his/her statistical sample to a more significant size by concatenating it with data held at other sites.

In the case of health applications, the logical 'hub' of the enquiries relating to a particular patient is his/her local general practitioner's record system or the local health centre's filing system. Nearly every type of access based on an individual patient's identity involves this key site at some stage and to some degree. Evolutionary forces within the domain encouraged the development of the systems in this way, and these are unlikely to change much as a result of adopting a distributed database approach. So this characteristic will probably persist.

There is an interesting hierarchy or network of (distributed) databases within the distributed databases for this application. There are many (distributed) databases in the system which correspond to individual patients, doctors and many other objects. Some of these may appear as 'simple' entities in other distributed databases. Consider an extreme case of a patient who has some chronic condition such as asthma or hypertension, which may be particularly persistent. He or she could quite conceivably also be found, perhaps several years later, to be suffering from some other chronic condition, for example arthritis. A patient like this could, over a decade say, accumulate a sizeable collection of details resulting from frequent consultations, tests and treatments. Now all patients' records constitute a (distributed) database in a structural or intensional sense. However the physical size of the record of an individual chronically ill patient could mean that it qualifies as a database in the extensional sense also.

Suppose such a doubly-unfortunate patient has a bulky record of investigations for asthma and an extensive record of orthopaedic consultations over many years. Access to the record is triggered by events such as changes of consultants, or re-examinations of the original orthopaedic diagnosis and prognosis with hindsight. Or a search could be requested of the records to find when a new aspect of either condition, now clearly apparent, first started (albeit imperceptibly at the time). Searches such as these may demand the most efficient access techniques available to help the care professional to cope with the bulk of data. Database methods are attractive in that they provide such methods.

Databases may exist for a great variety of purposes, some of which can be rather unexpected. An example is of a database used by a clinical dermatologist to assist in the identification of where in a patient's environment a particular allergen exists. A database developed for this application uses a CODASYL-like network structure to find intersections of inverted lists which link articles and materials associated with allergies, jobs, hobbies associated with the patient and the site of the rash on the patient's body.

10.5 Queries on the databases

From the previous sections it is possible to classify activities using the databases into three categories as in Figure 10.2.

When the functions are centralized and local, a centralized local database is appropriate, and as indicated in Figure 10.3, there are many databases in existence for such activities.

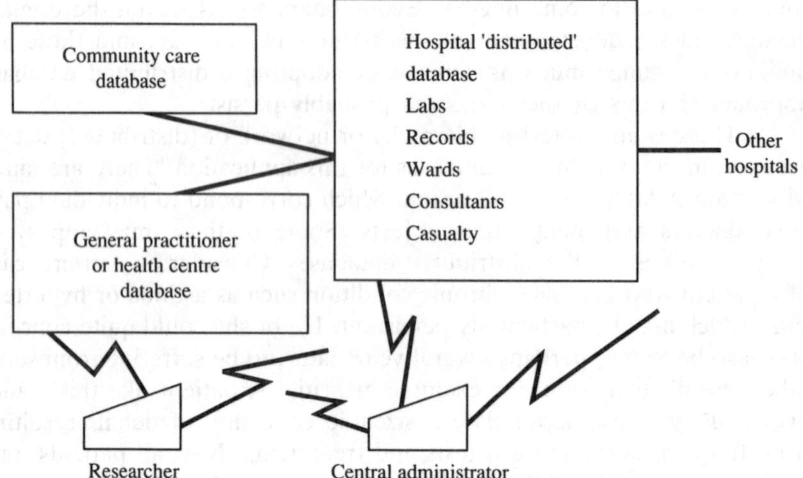

Figure 10.2 Sites and databases in a health care network.

For less localized applications, involving hospitals or other multisite sub-networks which do not have pre-existing databases, and essentially in a 'green-fields' situation as far as computing equipment is concerned, a homogeneous distributed database system, perhaps based on INGRES/STAR, or one of the other products listed in Chapter 3, may be suitable. Another possibility is to use a special-purpose product for the particular application and information network under consideration. Linking these products to other local data systems at the other sites can raise difficult heterogeneity problems, however.

Class of function	Type of database	Examples
Standard local	Centralized local	Community care, GP
Standard global	Homogeneous(?) distributed database	Records–wards DB Labs–wards DB
Ad hoc remote	Heterogeneous	Research GP–labs DB

Figure 10.3 Application classes.

The multidatabase approach is certainly attractive for networks exemplified by that in Figure 10.4. The feasibility of adoption of this approach is greatly enhanced by limiting the degree of heterogeneity if possible, as we shall see in Section 10.6.

So for health care networks in general, we require an architecture which will handle both 'local' distributed databases and 'global' distributed databases. This is provided to some degree by several of the systems described in Chapter 3.

Figure 10.1 illustrates a type of situation which often arises when computerization is carried out in a piecemeal way as described earlier. The case study here is taken from Bell (1990). Suppose that the four sites illustrated have developed computerized data collections independently to support their local functions, and that these collections are heterogeneous, perhaps simple files alongside CODASYL databases and relational databases.

The analysis that resulted in these schemata was carried out during a preliminary feasibility study and it would have to be carried out in a much more thorough manner if the databases for specific networks had to be identified. Various additional site types and sub-types (for different kinds of laboratory, for example) would also be present.

As a rule the 'databases' described here were created to meet the needs of patient care and to support day-to-day operations of the organization and planning exercises. They can also be used for research projects.

These intersite accesses, while they are not critical, would be very useful if available, as illustrated below.

10.5.1 Patient care queries

(a) An anaesthetist in hospital A wants to know all relevant details, especially recent ones, of a patient X, who resides in a regional area including hospital B and other health units, before administering anaesthetic.

(b) A laboratory analysis request is made

- From a GP to Hospital A
- Within Hospital A.

10.5.2 Administrative queries

(a) An administrator asks: 'which doctors are registered at both health centre, H, and community care unit, C?'

(b) Another administrator poses the question: 'Which doctors are registered at both hospitals A and B, work in orthopaedics, and earn more than £35,000 p.a.?'

10.5.3 Research query

Scenario: A consultant dermatologist has a hypothesis that there is a definite link between a patient's contracting ringworm and his or her subsequent (about five years later) contraction of a particular skin cancer. He wishes to gather all records of the incidence, severity, treatment and patient background for both diseases. Some of the required details are in hospital in-patient files, some in out-patient files, and some only in health centre files.

Access here could conceivably be via some date-related access path, for example, it could be expressed as a search for information on encounters in the past 12 months.

10.6 Two specific applications

10.6.1 National health care planning and control

An application of Multistar set in the Italian Health Service has been developed as a case study to exemplify the usability and functionality of multidatabases. It is referenced at the end of this chapter. There is a requirement for pertinent and timely information from the 700 local health units (LHUs) in districts, each serving 50–150 000 people. This is used for planning and management of the health service. The LHUs are partitioned into 21 regions, and the top level of the hierarchical reporting and management structure is a national coordination node where yearly budgeting and funds allocation takes place.

Each site in the network has its own information system and the idea is to make use of information gathered routinely in the daily working of the local units for the higher level functions carried out at the nodes further up the hierarchy. Information and raw data compiled according to both local and global standards is continuously examined so that the effects of management decisions can be monitored.

A large distributed heterogeneous information network is already in existence and so the multidatabase approach is appropriate here. At each site an information public view (IPV) is maintained. These views hold data that could be useful to other sites. Archives consisting of five years' data are maintained in these IPVs. Statistics for management, planning and control at all levels are made available through the maintenance of this collection of views.

As well as this key requirement for the information network, there is a list of secondary objectives for the system. It includes

- Provision of support for medical research,
- Support for the integration of care at the local level as well as the global level,

- Global *ad hoc* accesses to the data at the nodes,
- Maintenance of the pre-existing local autonomy.

To enhance the ease of integration, system-wide rules and procedures were instituted so that there would not be an imbalance towards the bottom-up approach (at the expense of the global organizational requirements).

The design of the test-bed system stipulated that there should be a central node (on a DEC VAX 11/750) in Rome at the Ministry of Health. Indices of population health and the profiles obtained from concatenated local information were to be held at this key node. This central node also maintains access to the whole database and so can test hypotheses and delineate scenarios for health planning and control at national level. At each local site a Honeywell PC under MSDOS using Oracle for local database functions was first suggested, but later Unix workstations were specified. A remote query facility from the Rome node was specified, for use with the ITAPAC communications package.

In summary, there are users at the three reporting levels of the hierarchy in Figure 10.4. At the top level, Ministry of Health personnel coordinate the plans in the regions and LHUs by compiling the data according to a predefined requirements list. This of course requires access to the IPVs for information. At this level there is also a transitive link

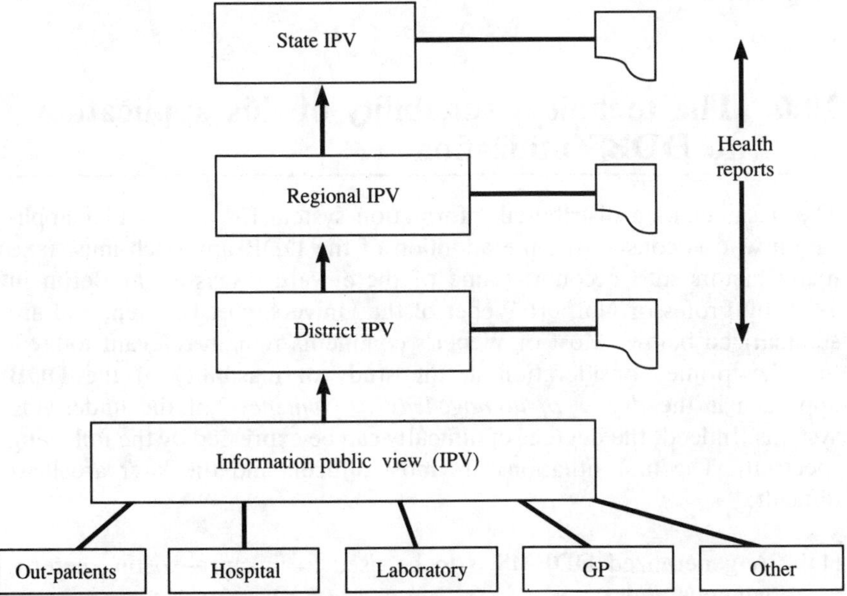

Figure 10.4 Connections between HIS and management information systems.

between LHUs so that the exchange of information between them is supported. At the next level down, regional users similarly plan and control operations at the LHUs, and monitor the results of decision making. Users at the local level are generally concerned with only a specialized information system and fall into the normal categories of users and suppliers of information and computing professionals.

10.5.2 Hospital information systems (HIS)

We have already considered some of the contributions that a multidatabase or other DDB system can make to the integration of distributed data collections in a hospital. If we consider a large teaching hospital of about 1000 beds, 25 000 in-patients per year, and 250 000 outpatients per year, information flow and processing efficiency are of prime importance. Resources must be used efficiently and information must be timely. In addition to the data needed for direct care of patients, data to support planning and management is again required. The hypothesis on which HIS is based is that both of these types of data can share data routinely collected as the results of care episodes.

The hub of the HIS wheel is a patient archive system (PAS) and other departmental systems, such as radiology, casualty and laboratory are at the ends of the spokes. Because of the piecemeal acquisition of computing systems likely to have preceded the call for integration, it is likely to be essential that the HIS be capable of dealing with heterogeneous local systems.

10.6 The technical suitability of this application to DDBS utilization

The designer of a distributed information system for a particular application who is considering the adoption of the DDB approach must take many factors into account. Some of these were discussed in Berlin in 1982, by Professor Norbert Weber of the University of Bremen, and are summarized below. Most of Weber's comments remain relevant today.

A prime consideration in the study of feasibility of the DDB approach is the *degree of homogeneity or 'sameness'* of the underlying systems. Indeed, the degrees of difficulty can be expressed by the following spectrum. The first situations are most difficult and the later are least difficult:

(1) A generalized DDBMS is to be used to link pre-existing heterogeneous nodes;

(2) A generalized DDBMS is to be used to link pre-existing homogeneous nodes;

(3) There are no systems in existence before the new system is to be developed and a generalized DDBMS is to be used;

(4) There are again no existing constraints, and an application specific (tailored) DDBMS is to be used.

Clearly there are situations which fall between these gradings, for example, varying levels of homogeneity of subcomponents further stratifies case 1.

Another important factor is that of the *localization of queries and updates*. The difficulty faced by allowing distributed updates as well as queries has a dramatic negative effect on the case for adoption of the approach. So, again ranking in descending order of attractiveness, we can categorize the degree of difficulty as follows:

(1) Fully distributed updates are permitted as well as queries.

(2) Only local updates are allowed, but queries can be distributed.

A further factor affecting the difficulty of adoption of the DDB approach is the *redundancy factor* of the data, and the need for consistency to be maintained. Here we have the following ranking:

(1) Multiple copies of certain sets of data must all be kept consistent;

(2) Multiple copies must be kept again, but with only the requirement that some single primary copy is kept fully correct;

(3) Only one version of each data object exists.

A related consideration is that of *how the data is partitioned for storage at different sites*, and the ranking in this case is as follows:

(1) Vertical and horizontal partitioning is required;

(2) Only one kind of partitioning is permitted;

(3) No partitioning is allowed.

Weber also gave some guidelines on the types of communications which are easiest to work with.

For the medical applications considered here, homogeneity is something which should probably be aimed at to some degree. There is a very delicate choice to be made when considering a level of standardization. Flexibility and both idiosyncrasies and preferences of the local users and their applications should be maintained. If harmonization can be achieved without necessarily imposing a grey 'sameness' throughout the network, it should be consciously pursued, and this is one of the most attractive features of providing transparent integration of local data systems.

It is therefore probable that all four of the degrees of homogeneity will be encountered within the subsystems of the network. Weber's guidelines indicate that the most homogeneous of these subsystems are likely to find distributed database systems most feasible.

By careful design of the network the problem of updatability will probably not be too important for most of the applications outlined in this chapter, or for those envisaged as *ad hoc* transactions. The updating of a particular relation, tuple or attribute is unlikely to demand a sophisticated scheduler to ensure the correctness, at high performance, of a set of interleaved transactions on the item at these granular levels. The simple reason for this is that the probability of two transactions sharing simultaneous access to any such item is very low and 'inconsistent' replicas may be tolerable. This is not to say that this aspect of transaction processing can be ignored, but rather that relatively simple mechanisms, such as keeping a 'primary copy' for conflict resolution and supporting locks, which can be fairly pessimistic in most cases because of the performance levels required and workload characteristics, are adequate. Moreover, it is expected that by far the greater proportion of the access traffic in general, and updates in particular, will be local.

The amount of redundant data will be high in this application, but the low required consistency level is likely to remove any problem here. All three kinds of partitioning of individual relations can be foreseen, and relatively modest query evaluation algorithms will probably be sufficient for the application's needs.

SUMMARY

In this chapter we have looked at the objectives of computerization of health care systems, and we have concentrated upon the information handling problems encountered when distributed computing facilities are used. In particular we have examined the suitability of the DDB approach to handling these problems. We have presented 'evidence' that several databases exist at various functionally and organizationally distributed sites in health care networks, and use the distributed nature of the information processing in this application to make some of the concepts dealt with in earlier chapters more concrete. We believe that the distributed database approach can help in making sense of several dichotomies in medical informatics.

We also provide an intuitively acceptable set of criteria to help determine if the DDB approach is appropriate for a particular application environment.

EXERCISES

10.1 Why are health care networks considered to be potentially excellent application domains for distributed database systems?

10.2 In a countrywide national health care system a choice is to be made between using a global schema or not when adopting the multidatabase approach to handling accesses to data between sites.

What factors would have led to the choice of the multidatabase approach, and what factors should be taken into consideration when choosing between the alternatives above?

10.3 The Department of Education in a country has decided to install distributed databases in the regions of the country (each of a few million inhabitants) in order to further their objective of increased sharing of teaching resources and also to help in the vertical reporting they require for regional administration purposes.

Sketch and explain a sample layout of an intraregional network which might be useful for this, indicating why pre-existing databases are likely to be available at the sites.

How would the multimedia aspects of the application be catered for? How would the interregional aspects of the application domain be handled?

10.4 Repeat Exercise 10.3 for the administrative and operational needs of a futuristic supermarket chain dealing with warehouses, retail stores and home-delivery services. Assume that the organization of the enterprise is based on a two-level geographical grouping of services (analogous to the regional and national levels of the previous question).

10.5 Repeat Exercise 10.4 for a group of future travel agents working at regional and national levels. (Multimedia data here could be the equivalent of current travel brochures, maps, railway networks, etc.).

10.6 Repeat Exercise 10.4 for a national police force seeking to integrate multimedia police files from various locally-autonomous sites.

10.7 Suggest how the relations of Section 10.4 would be supplemented if the radiology department of the hospital, which has to deal with collections of digitized X-ray images layered by age (e.g. there is a two-week file held on reasonably fast access storage, and a two-year file and a ten-year file which are less accessible, being required much less frequently). Assume that the images are represented by descriptions held on structured records in computer systems.

10.8 Suggest some further queries of each type in the example in Figure 10.1.

Bibliography

Bell D.A. (1985). The application of distributed database technology to health care networks. *Int. J. Biomedical Engineering*, **16**, 173–82.

Bell D.A. (1990). Multidatabases in health care. *Database Technology*, **3**(1), 31–9.

Bell D.A. and Carolan M. (1984). Data access techniques for diagnosis in clinical dermatology. In *Proc. 5th Int. Congress of EFMI*, Brussels, Belgium.

Bell D.A., Fernández Pérez de Talens A., Gianotti, N. *et al.* (1987). Multi-Star: A Multi-database system for health information systems. In *Proc. 7th Int. Congress of EFMI*, Rome, Italy.

Bell D.A., Grimson J.B., Ling D.H.O. and O'Sullivan D. (1987). EDDS – A system to harmonise access to databases on mainframes and micro. *J. Information and Software Technology*, **29**(7), 362–70.

Blois M.S. (1983). Information and computers in medicine. In *Proc. MEDINFO Conf. 83*, Amsterdam, Holland.

Bush I.E. (1981). Hospital computer systems – for medicine or money? In *Proc. Computer Applications in Medical Care.*

Fernández Pérez de Talens A. and Giovanne P.M. (1987). Use of a multidatabase management system MULTISTAR to obtain the centripetal information flows for the national health statistics. In *Proc. 7th Int. Congress of EFMI*, Rome, Italy.

Giere W. (1981). Foundations of clinical data automation in co-operative. programs. In *Proc. Computer Applications in Medical Care*, Washington DC, IEEE Computer Society Press.

Grimson J.B. (1982). Supporting hospital information systems. In *Proc. 4th Congress of European Federation of Medical Informatics (EFMI)*, Dublin, Ireland.

Huet B., Polland C. and Martin J. (1982). Information analysis of an emergency unit and a pre-diagnosis unit. In *Proc. 4th Int. Congress of EFMI*, Dublin, Ireland.

The conceptual schemas in Section 10.3 were modelled on a single-site schema given here.

Isaksson A.I., Gerdin-Jelger U., Lindelow B., Peterson H.E. and Sjöberg P. (1983). Communications network structure within the Stockholm county health care. In *Proc. 4th World Conf. on Medical Informatics*, Amsterdam, Holland.

Whiting-O'Keefe Q.E., Simborg D.W. and Tolchin S. (1981). The argument for distributed hospital information systems (HIS). In *Proc. Computer Applications in Medical Care.*

11 Future Developments in Distributed Databases

11.1 Introduction

In this chapter we will review technological developments in a number of areas, which are likely to impact on future generations of distributed database systems. There can be no doubt that distributed databases systems, especially in the form of multidatabase systems which allow integrated access to heterogeneous data collections, will grow in importance over the next few years. Most large organizations now take distribution for granted. The availability of reliable, standard data communications makes it possible for each user to have their own PC or workstation connected to the network. The network, in turns, provides a wide range of facilities to its users including printing, access to database servers and electronic mail.

Brodie (1989) has predicted that the information systems of the future will be based not simply on distributed database technology but rather on **intelligent interoperability**. Such systems will require not only the applications of techniques from the field of distributed databases to support interoperation of systems, but also the incorporation of techniques from artificial intelligence, in particular knowledge-based systems and natural language processing, to provide the intelligence. In addition to this, richer information retrieval techniques capable of handling multimedia data, as discussed briefly in Chapter 1, will be required by future applications. In the first part of this chapter we will review ways in which artificial intelligence and database technologies can be effectively integrated and we will also introduce the idea of distributed artificial intelligence.

The development of DBMS technology is generally regarded as having two distinct phases, or **generations**:

- First generation: hierarchical and network systems
- Second generation: relational systems.

First generation systems required the user to navigate across the DB to locate and retrieve the desired data, whereas those of the second generation allow users simply to state what data they want and leave the system to locate that data in the DB.

There appear to be two rival approaches to the next generation of the DBMS:

- Object-oriented DBMSs.
- Extended relational systems

Both approaches are relevant to DDB technology and it certainly seems likely that both will gain acceptance in the marketplace, although probably by different user communities. We will therefore discuss both in Sections 11.4 and 11.5.

New data modelling concepts are required for handling multimedia data collections. When these collections are also dispersed, it is clear that the problems of DDB are greatly intensified. In Section 11.6, we will review some of the recent contributions to this rapidly evolving area. However, we simplify the discussion somewhat by showing how multidatabase concepts and the relational model can provide a pragmatic way forward in handling distributed multimedia data.

11.2 Integrating artificial intelligence and databases

11.2.1 Introduction

The field of artificial intelligence (AI) is very broad and covers a wide range of disciplines including psychology, philosophy, linguistics and sociology, as well as computer science itself. The unifying aim of AI is to seek to develop computer systems which behave 'intelligently'. It would be inappropropriate in this book to even give a brief overview of AI, rather the objective of this section is to give the reader an indication, from the database perspective, of ways in which AI techniques could be effectively exploited by DBMSs.

We will look at two of the more important ways in which techniques from AI can provide DBMSs with enhanced functionality:

(1) Interoperability with knowledge-based systems
(2) Natural language query facility.

11.2.2 Interoperability with knowledge-based systems

There has been a major resurgence of interest in knowledge-based systems, particularly expert systems, in recent years and yet their commercial success has not matched the amount of research and development effort that has gone into them. Expert systems (ESs) attempt to capture the 'expertise' of human specialists in areas such as geological exploration, fault detection in electrical circuits, management of computer configurations and medical diagnosis. Impressive results have been obtained in a number of limited domains of expertise.

Medicine has traditionally provided a fertile source of ESs. One of the pioneering systems, MYCIN, was developed to recommend antibiotic therapy for bacterial infections of the blood. One of the reasons for the large number of medical ESs is that medicine is already divided into a number of specialities and expert systems are at their most successful when working in a narrow highly focused domain. Another important reason, however, has been the so-called 'demand-pull' from medicine. Clinicians suffer from 'data intoxication'. So much data on patients is generated by, for example, the modern laboratory, that clinicians can find it difficult to sift through it all and extract what is significant. By incorporating techniques from ESs, clinicians can be given assistance in separating the important from the less important.

Essentially, an ES has the component structure shown in Figure 11.1. The flow of information is from the human domain expert – the supplier – to the person seeking the advice – the user. The expertise is captured by means of a knowledge acquisition module. It is composed of logical rules or other material forming the basis of reasoning, backed up by hard facts and evidence from sensors and tests. The inference engine manipulates the information in the knowledge base using some control strategy (for example, forward chaining – linking the rules together on the basis of results found so far) to select rules to fire in particular circumstances. An explanation module is used so that the user or supplier can ask the system to justify its conclusions to date.

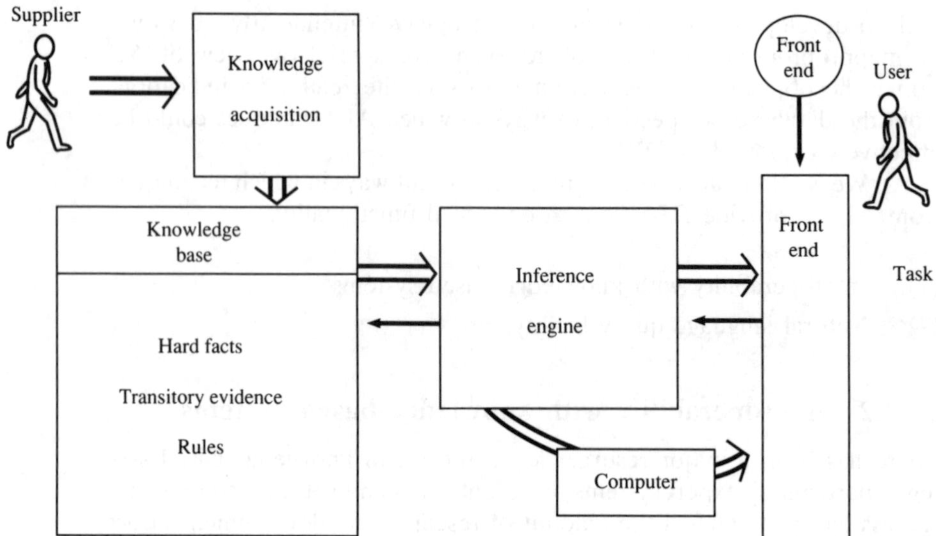

Figure 11.1 An expert system's components.

There are two main reasons for the lack of exploitation of the potential of this technology in practice:

- Restricted domain
- Lack of integration.

In cases where ESs have been applied, the domains considered are often too restricted and are too simplistically viewed to be of practical use.

Complex problems require more knowledge, of a 'deeper' kind, than is normally to be found in demonstrations of the expert systems approach to problem solving. We will return to this issue in Section 11.3.

ESs are generally developed as stand-alone systems which are not integrated into the general information processing environment. A busy hospital laboratory, for example, can make very effective use of ES technology by analysing patient test results to detect abnormal results, suggest possible diagnoses, automatically schedule further tests on the basis of the results obtained to date and so on. The potential for improving the efficiency and cost-effectiveness of the laboratory through the use of ES technology is there, but it can never be fully realized if it is not integrated into the routine laboratory system.

How can this integration be achieved? We can identify three main ways in which ESs and DBs can be coupled together:

(1) Enhanced expert system
(2) Intelligent DB
(3) Intersystem communication.

The resulting combined system is often referred to as an expert database system.

In the **enhanced expert system** approach (Figure 11.2(a)), the basic ES is augmented by special data management functions or is interfaced to a dedicated general purpose DBMS. With the former approach, the effort involved can be similar to writing a full-function DBMS, while the

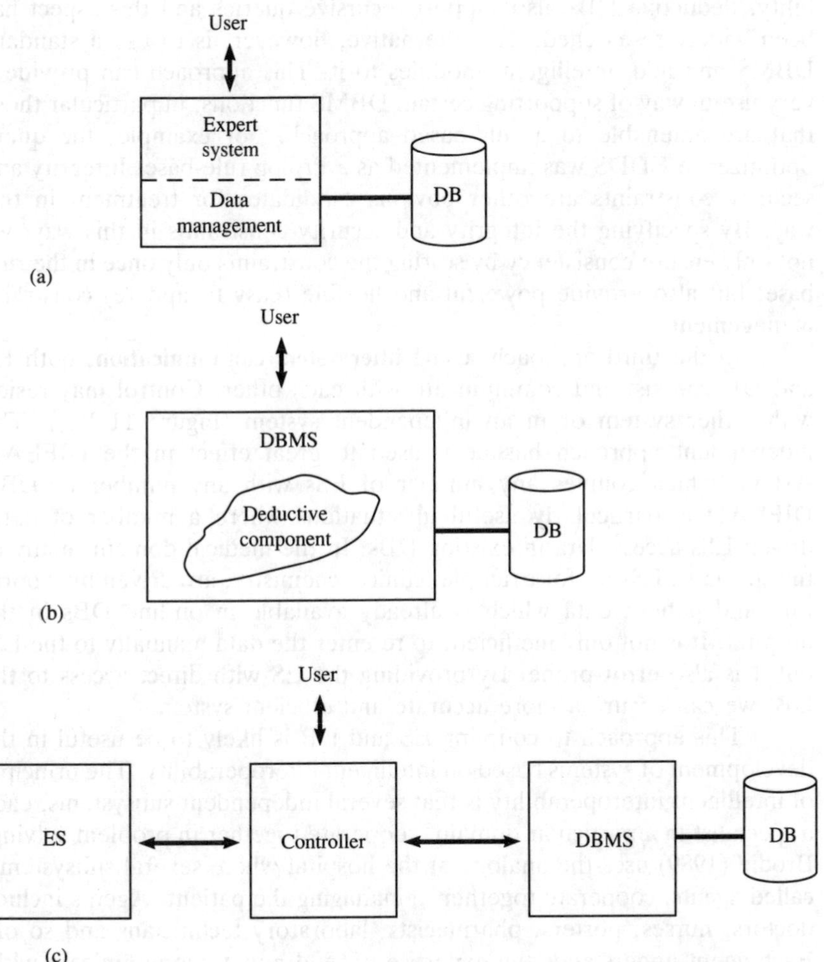

Figure 11.2 Coupling ES and DBs. (a) enhanced expert system, (b) intelligent DB, (c) intersystem communication.

latter approach effectively embeds the DBMS in the ES making the DB inaccessible to other applications.

In the **intelligent DB** approach (Figure 11.2(b)), a deductive component is embedded in the DBMS and this is the approach adopted in so-called **deductive databases**. However, deductive DBMSs never gained widespread acceptance and commercial systems are hard to find. A deductive DB is one which is capable of deducing additional facts, that is adding more data to the data by applying inference rules (deductive axioms) to the data. Prolog (often with extensions) is the preferred language for implementing the facts and rules. Moreover, the facts (referred to as **predicates** in Prolog) can be conveniently represented as relations and hence stored in an RDB. Apart from the inferencing capability, deductive DBs also support recursive queries and this aspect has been widely researched. The alternative, however, is to use a standard DBMS and add 'intelligent' modules to it. This approach can provide a very useful way of supporting certain DBMS functions, in particular those that are amenable to a rule-based approach. For example, the query optimizer in EDDS was implemented as a Prolog rule-base. Integrity and security constraints are other obvious candidates for treatment in this way. By specifying the integrity and security constraints in this way, we not only ensure consistency by storing the constraints only once in the rule base, but also provide powerful and flexible (easy to update) constraint management.

In the third approach, using **intersystem communication**, both ES and DB co-exist and communicate with each other. Control may reside with either system or in an independent system (Figure 11.2(c)). The independent approach has been used to great effect in the DIFEAD system, which couples any number of ESs with any number of DBs. DIFEAD is particularly useful in situations where a number of data-driven ESs access data in existing DBs. In the medical domain, many of the specialist ESs in, for example, clinical chemistry, are driven by laboratory and patient data which is already available in on-line DBs in the hospital. It is not only inefficient to re-enter the data manually to the ES, but it is also error-prone. By providing the ES with direct access to the DB, we can ensure a more accurate and efficient system.

This approach to coupling ES and DB is likely to be useful in the development of systems based on intelligent interoperability. The principle of intelligent interoperability is that several independent subsystems, each a specialist in a particular domain, cooperate together in problem solving. Brodie (1989) uses the analogy of the hospital where several subsystems, called **agents**, cooperate together in managing the patient. Agents include doctors, nurses, porters, pharmacists, laboratory technicians and so on. Each agent understands the expertise of, and how to communicate with, every other agent. The doctor knows how to write out a prescription which will be filled correctly by the pharmacist; the nurse knows how to call the porter and request that a patient be brought down to X-ray and so on.

The agents in the information systems based on intelligent interoperability correspond to various subsystems: one might be the hospital information system, based on conventional DB or DDB system, another might be an ES in a particular medical speciality and yet another an X-ray imaging system. Efficient management of the hospital – staff, patients and resources – requires a cooperative effort between all these subsystems. We discuss this in more detail in Section 11.3.

11.2.3 User interfaces

As information systems grow and increase in complexity, the problems faced by users in understanding the data content and in trying to retrieve relevant data quickly and easily become acute. Users often find themselves in the situation of knowing that the information they want is 'in there somewhere', but find it virtually impossible to formulate a query to extract it. The field of human–computer interaction/man–machine interfaces has become enormously important and nowhere more so than in the DB field. If end-users and organizations are going to be able to exploit their information resources to the full, then it is essential to provide easier and more user-friendly query methods and languages. There is growing interest in developing query languages based on iconic graphical user interfaces (GUIs) using standards such as OSF/Motif and OpenLook. These standards have the advantages that all applications can have the same look and feel.

For the end-user who is not a regular user of the system and who wishes to pose *ad hoc* queries, an interface based on natural language offers tremendous advantages. Indeed, such interfaces to DBs were one of the first applications of natural language (NL) processing techniques. It soon became apparent that a general purpose NL interface, which could cope with all the semantic richness and ambiguity of NL, was not feasible given the present state of NL processing technology. It was found necessary to limit severely the range of allowable NL queries. The subset of NL queries is often so restricted and artificial that such interfaces offer few advantages over conventional query languages. From a DDB point of view, the benefits of a general purpose, unconstrained NL query interface are considerable. For example, in a loosely coupled multidatabase system with no global schema, there would be no need for users to learn a new and complex query language to support interoperability. In fact, with full NL support, users would be able to move freely from one DBMS to another, without any need for retraining.

11.3 Distributed expert systems

11.3.1 Introduction

Extensive domains require larger knowledge bases of the conventional kind described above. One way of tackling this problem is to use groups of smaller expert systems, like those already in existence, in concert. So two prominent characteristics of 'second generation' expert systems are

(1) Including deeper knowledge – reasoning from first principles – in addition to the shallower 'compelled hindsight' stored typically as rules in conventional expert systems;

(2) Linking diverse expert systems which have been developed in isolation from one another, but which have overlapping domains.

It is this latter trend which is of interest here, because distributed expert systems (DESs) have a lot in common with distributed databases, and in certain quarters have actually been regarded as extensions of DDBs.

In the next subsection we look a little more closely at the motivations for the DES approach and this allows us to become more familiar with their requirements. This leads to a discussion of the different types of DES and we then focus on the particular modules one would expect them to have. We conclude this brief discussion of what is an exciting and challenging movement in computing by considering some specific problems raised when the development of a DES software system is contemplated, and a summary of the similarities and differences to be observed when we compare DESs and DDBs.

11.3.2 Motivation

There has been great interest in distributed artificial intelligence (DAI) in the last ten years or so. This turns out to be a very broad area and it is not easy to produce a definitive taxonomy of the efforts that have been made in it. We will attempt this task shortly, but in the meantime we content ourselves with looking at the forces which have led to it. The objective is to get individual problem-solving modules, or agents, to interact constructively in the solution of problems that are beyond the capability of any one of the agents by itself.

Two basic scenarios exist in DESs. As in DDBs, one is for use in a retrofit situation, where the individual expertise is already in existence, manifested by the regular work of the local agents, and their resources – reasoning methods and facts or evidence – are required to be collectively exploited to solve 'global' problems. The other is where the system developer wishes to distribute the expertise in a 'green fields' situation so as to enhance performance (by sharing workload), robustness (by replication of functionality among the agents), flexibility (by allowing alternative expertise to be added piecemeal to the global capability) or otherwise to improve the effectiveness or efficiency of problem solving. These objectives and motivations are clearly analogous to those for DDBs, but it can be seen that here the emphasis is on problem solving as a whole rather than simply on the data storage and access aspects of solution techniques. However these two activities are closely related, not least because the latter is a sub-activity of the former as we have already seen at various places in this book.

The problem-solving angle also accounts for another motivation which is not a primary consideration for DDBs. Having multiple points of view on a problem or sub-problem allows different types of expertise to be brought to bear on it. An example of this in human group-based problem solving is the 'second opinion syndrome' one encounters in medical consultations. Doctors dealing with rare or very complex diagnoses like to check their conclusions against those of other specialists, and perhaps discuss the discrepancies, before a final commitment is made. This can also add greatly to the peace of mind of the patient. So confidence, due to variety, is increased all round.

This really is important in the medical domain, and it is the common experience of problem-solvers in general that, when complex or unusual cases are met, two heads are better than one. It must be said, however, that a sort of 'law of diminishing returns' becomes operative in this process. So, although great benefits can potentially accrue from making full use of all the available expertise, there is no guarantee that increasing the number of experts will increase the quality of the advice. In fact, at some stage adding more agents could even decrease the response quality.

Another advantage of distributed information systems that is particularly important in the expert system world, although it is also evident to a lesser extent in the DB world as well, is the fact that information resources in general can be reusable. This is of major importance in ESs because of the fact that, at the present stage of evolution, ESs are exceedingly problem-specific and their development represents a large investment, not least in the knowledge acquisition tasks. So reuse would increase the economic as well as the usage advantages to be gained from the ES development.

Perhaps one of the most influential considerations for considering the DES approach is the need for straightforward concatenation of knowledge. In any local ES there could clearly be a lack of completeness in that only part of a global problem can be solved locally, because some of the skills required for the full solution are not present. This deficiency is compounded by the fact that not all the data – established facts and more transitory evidence – may be available at the local site.

11.3.3 Types of DES

We are talking about a system which is a network of agents such as rule-based expert systems. Questions will be asked of the system, either via a global module or via an individual agent, and strategies for distributed responses have to be devised. If we ignore the massively parallel (connectionist) approach to AI which is outside our scope here, it is possible to identify two different types of distributed problem-solvers in this context. These are decentralized problem-solvers and collaborative reasoners.

In the case of **decentralized problem-solvers** parts of the global system are distributed among the distributed agents. The agents pick up their sub-problems and solve them asynchronously. The partial solutions are returned to the requesting site where a global solution is synthesized from them.

It is possible to distinguish two sub-cases here, where the respective emphases are on solving the sub-tasks and on sharing or compounding the data from different nodes.

An example of the first kind is the hierarchically organized parallel expert system (HOPES), in which a global system is broken down into natural components, in this case for efficiency reasons to support real-time problem solving. This approach is useful in ill-structured domains, where the heuristic knowledge is scarcer than, for example, in medical diagnosis. It is well suited to domains such as signal processing, where the sensed data is usually 'noisy'.

As its name suggests, HOPES is hierarchically structured and parallelism can be exploited at the lower levels of the hierarchy. As in the well-known Hearsay II system, each of the loosely coupled agents contributes highly specialized knowledge for use on some sub-problem. The hierarchical structure is well suited to the multistage problem solving encountered in most engineering and similar systematic domains. Channelling the information flow between the agents is effected by having multiple 'blackboards' shared among agents at various levels.

For example in Figure 11.3, agent Ax will collect results of cooperation between agents Ax_1, . . ., Ax_4 from blackboard B. The results are displayed on the blackboard for Ax's use, but B is also used by the agents below it as they interoperate during the derivation of a collective response to a task. They use it as a channel during their intragroup communications.

Other agents at the same level as Ax might want to make use of this result as well, or they might want to work with Ax in some other way. They would use a higher level blackboard H for this purpose. This stratification can be repeated to give multiple levels.

A typical application of this system described by its designers would be in the interpretation of radar signals. The agents at the bottom level would have to carry out the following tasks:

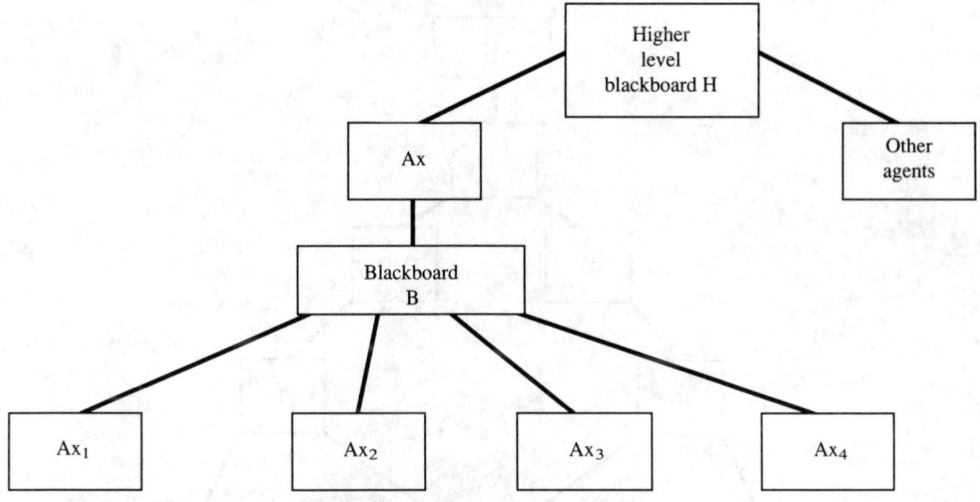

Figure 11.3 HOPES hierarchies.

(1) Extract relevant information from the sampled signals (C),
(2) Determine the velocity of the target (V),
(3) Determine the distance from the target (D).

Two blackboards B_1 and B_2 could be used for the extraction of the results from these agents and to allow them to be fed to higher level agents, which would then:

(4) Monitor velocities of the target over some period (MV),
(5) Monitor the distances from the receiver over a period (MD).

At the highest level another agent, H, would use the results from MV and MD via B_3, and summarize changes in velocity and distance, using them to determine, for example, if the target is human. The approach is illustrated in Figure 11.4.

An example of the second sub-type, which incidentally does decompositions as well if required, is the distant vehicle monitoring test-bed (DVTB) which is also used for target tracking. This time the application is to trace vehicles' histories in some domain of interest on the basis of signals it receives. We choose this system as our illustration of this sub-type because the emphasis is on the integration of signals coming from various sources, in order to get a holistic picture of the space being monitored, rather than on dividing a problem amongst different specialists. The idea is that if several, say four, overlapping subregions are monitored by pieces of equipment with different levels of reliability,

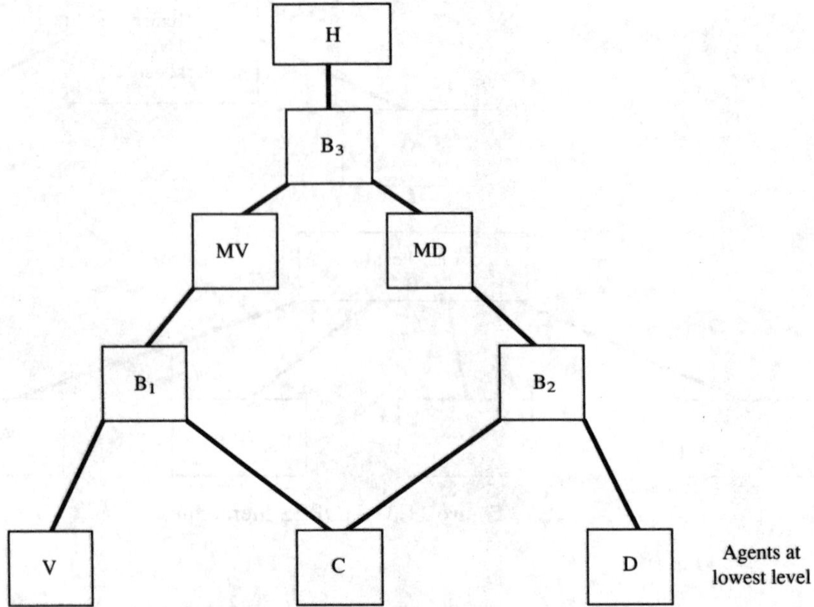

Figure 11.4 HOPES in radar signal interpretation.

then the picture of the real 'world' that is required can be built up from the different jigsaw pieces.

In the example in Figure 11.5, a sensing agent S would be assigned to each of the four overlapping subregions, $R_1, \ldots, R_4$. Corresponding to each region there would also be an interpreting agent I carrying out appropriate subtasks of interpretation for the local region. A further integrating agent could then be used at a level above these with the task of making gross sense of these local interpretations. Further levels can be envisaged in order to multiply the area being monitored. For example four regions the size of R can be monitored as a unit by incorporating another gross interpreter above them.

In the case of **collaborative reasoning** all the agents address the same problem. The problem is not normally decomposed in this case, but each agent uses its local knowledge to come up with a result in collaboration with the others. The agents can all be considered to be cooperating on the solution of one problem, although it is possible that the system as a whole will work on several problems concurrently. The idea here is that of horizontal collaboration such as can be found in the medical world. A consultant could confer with another kind of specialist in a complex case. A team of experts with different specialisms work together on a case. An example would be where a specialist orthopaedic surgeon requires the

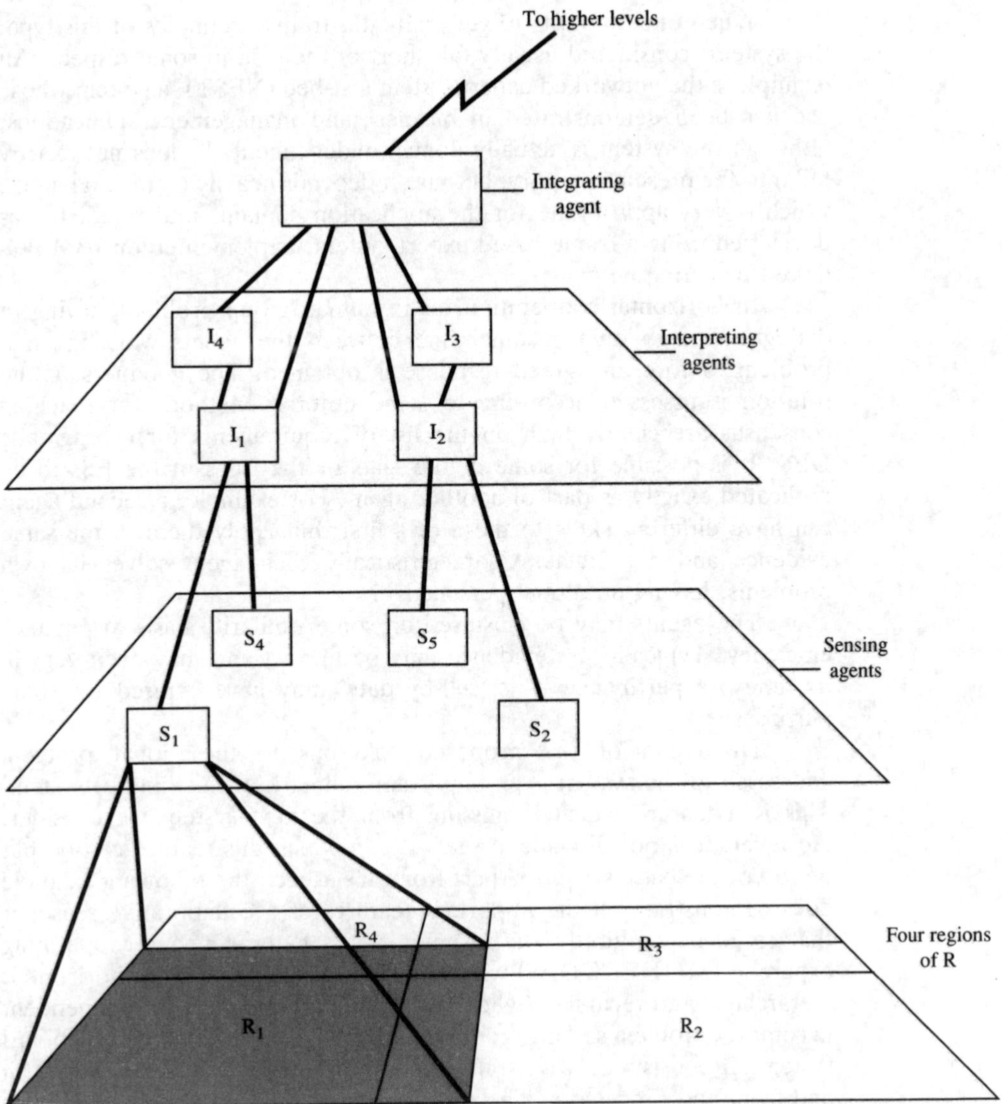

Figure 11.5 DVTB region monitoring.

advice of a radiologist and a cancer specialist for a particular diagnosis. To make the example a little more general we could include non-professional experts such as laboratory staff in the team as well as the clinicians.

Many systems like this are purpose-built and so are applicable to just one particular domain of knowledge, such as some branch of medicine. Other domains with tailored systems of this class are traffic control, speech recognition and industrial control.

When one attempts to get really illustrative examples of this type, the systems considered usually fall short of the goal in some respect. An example is the networked expert system test-bed (NEST), a system whose use has been demonstrated in business and management applications, although the system is actually domain-independent. It does not exactly fall into the present category, because it depends heavily on manual input, which is very appropriate for the application domains illustrated. It was developed using a frame-based expert system, implemented on IBM PCs linked by a ring network.

In horizontal cooperation, as in human group problem solving, a dialogue can go on for some time between the agents working on a problem, before an agreed response is obtained. The goodness of the solution is assessed according to some criteria. Methods for reaching consensus are clearly high on the list of requirements for a pragmatic DES. It is possible for some of the facts or the rules of the ESs to be replicated exactly as part of another agent. For example, a second agent can have different skills to those of a first, but apply them to the same evidence and hard facts. Characteristically each agent solves its own problems, having no global perspective.

The agents may be clustered on some similarity basis to enhance efficiency. Typically the evidence may be inexact and may even vary in its timewise pertinence – its 'sell-by date' may have expired for some purposes!

Discussion of the proposed solutions to the global problem addressed to the system is an important hallmark of this kind of system. This is a feature which is missing from the next system we consider. However, it is not difficult to see ways in which this feature can be put on top of the basic system. Apart from this aspect, the following example does demonstrate all the important features of a collaborative reasoner that could be required. The example is the heterogeneous cooperating expert system (HECODES) which is a framework suitable for horizontal, hierarchical and recursive (where the agents are mutually interdependent in complex problem solving) cooperation. It is again based on a blackboard system. It consists of a centralized control system, a blackboard system and front-end processors. The contributing agents can be heterogeneous with respect to control strategy, knowledge representation method and the program language used for implementation. A prototype of the system was implemented in 1988 on a network of DEC VAX machines, some of which are as much as 60 miles apart.

In Figure 11.6 the ESs, the control subsystem and the blackboard subsystem are nodes in a network, and the nodes are linked by telecommunications cables. Each ES can plan solutions and solve local problems independently, using domain-specific knowledge. Each has the additional ability to apply for assistance from, and offer assistance to, the others via the control subsystem. There are front-end processors to interface between

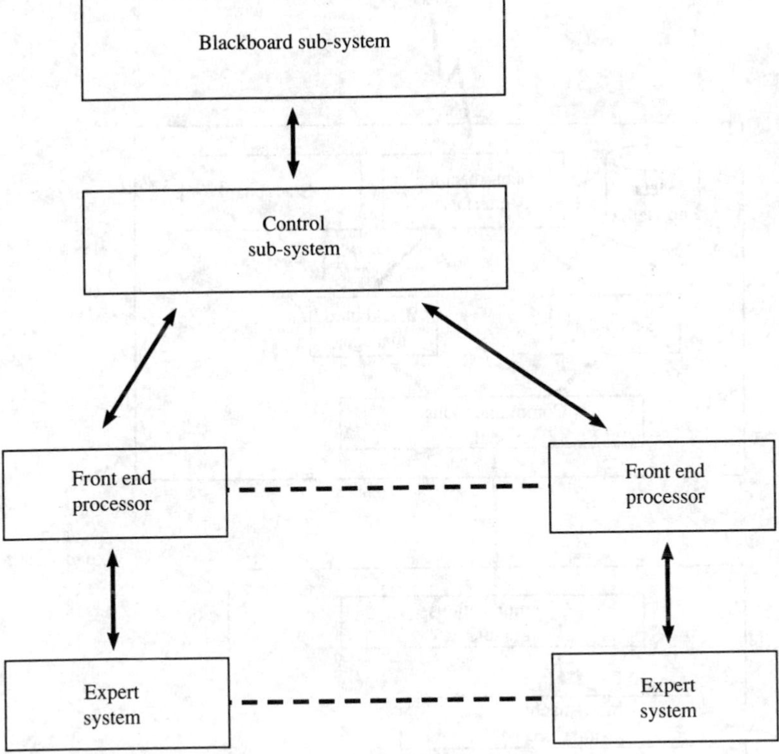

Figure 11.6 Overall HECODES architecture.

the node and the control subsystem. The blackboard subsystem stores shared information for the ESs and structured information for the control subsystem. The control subsystem is responsible for managing the cooperation and communications between the nodes and for the run-time management of HECODES. In practice the blackboard and control subsystems are stored at one (central) node to minimize communications.

If we now focus on the agent nodes in the system, we can identify three main functional modules: the management, communications and man–machine-interface modules. The modules are all designed to be domain-independent.

The scheduler module in the central (control) node is a key element of HECODES (see Figure 11.7). When it is fed meta-knowledge comprising the control information for all the ESs, it is able to schedule the whole system's operation and manage the cooperation between the agents. The blackboard manager carries out all operations involving the blackboard, which has its usual role for communications between the agents. The communications module has a self-evident role, and the front-end pro-

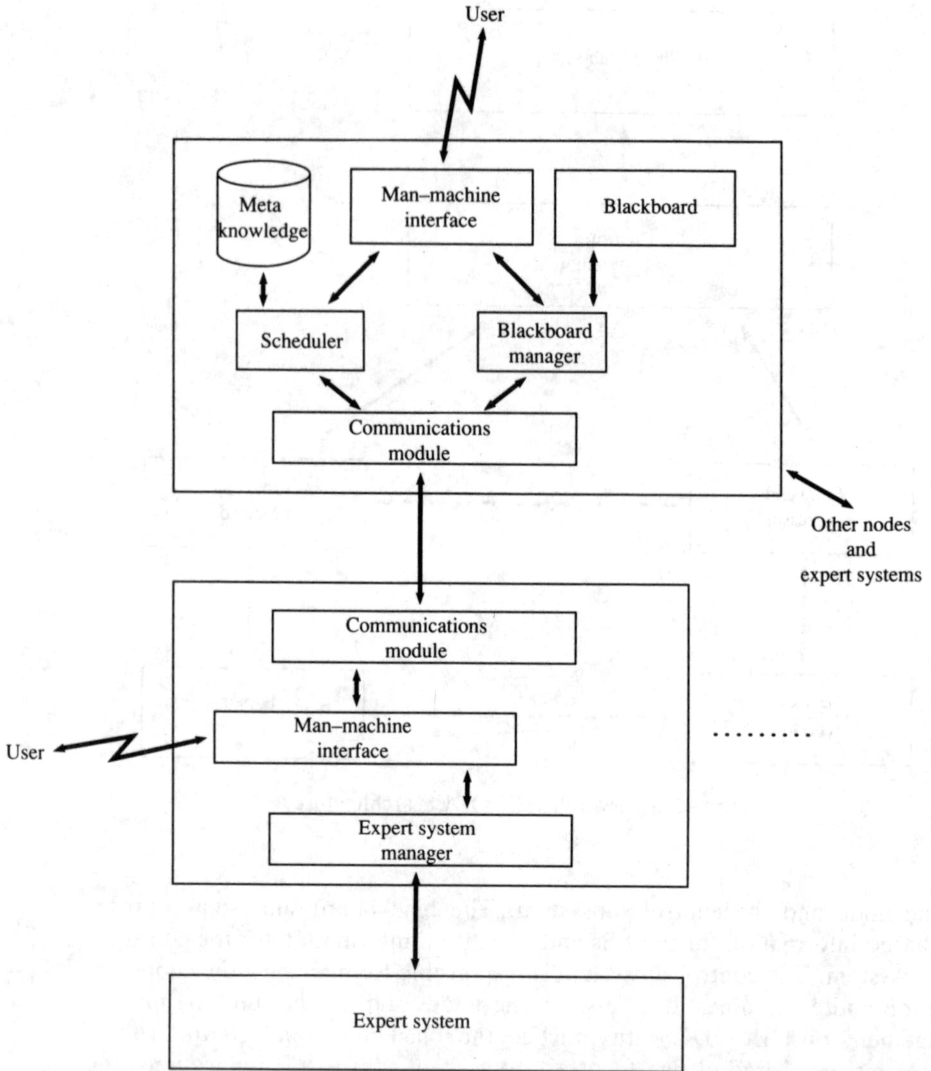

Figure 11.7 Detailed module structure of HECODES.

cessors in Figure 11.6 provide the interfacing between the ESs and the control node. Each of these modules can be very complex. For example, the scheduler must detect and remove, or better still avoid, deadlocks in the system, which can occur due to cyclic waiting loops, much as for DDBs. Another example is the interfacing that is required between different ESs, for example, where they use different methods of dealing with evidence or other knowledge which is inexact, as is usually the case.

the case. HECODES has proved to be an exceedingly useful vehicle for research into these and other important issues.

11.3.4 Modules of a DES

Certain essential modules of a DES can be distinguished from the example systems discussed above and others.

Task assignment can be approached in two ways, corresponding to the two types of system identified above. For the first type decomposition, assignment and solution, followed by synthesis of solutions, is the pattern. In the case of collaborative reasoning systems, 'collective deliberation' best describes the approach taken. The group identifies which issues are most important, proposes alternative solutions, exposes these to detailed discussion, and then prioritizes the solutions before presenting a final response.

Organization also corresponds to the two types of DES. Centralized control is hierarchical, using decomposition of the task at a control node as a preliminary to solving the problem. Decentralized control is based on what resembles a committee structure and is more appropriate for horizontal collaboration. Even in systems where the group is less 'consciously' solving one problem, such as when HECODES is being used, this is an important feature in collaboration.

Other general architectural issues such as which languages to use, what levels of abstraction to allow or which detailed system modules to include in a system, must also be considered.

In considering **coordination**, we follow the terminology of Huhns by calling the planning of solutions 'coordination' and the execution of the solutions 'collaboration'. There are a large variety of reasoning methods, complex domain models and parallelism that could be encountered in the general case. How are conflicts to be handled? Who does the coordination? Who chooses partners, considers compatibility and conducts the liaison? How is integrity maintained, both of communicated knowledge and of local knowledge? How is heterogeneity dealt with, and uncertainty and differences of scales and scopes handled? What about the management of availability? In the user interface, what vocabulary do we support at the global level?

How do we coordinate **learning**, the exchange of evidence, hard facts and methods? Do we allow the control modules to learn from their experiences?

For **communications**, do we use blackboards and if so what is their design? How do we keep the costs down? What recovery, security and correctness features do we need/provide? Recovering from real-time control systems problems is difficult because a commitment often cannot be undone – how do you call a launched rocket back? The interactions between nodes can cause increased uncertainty by delays as well as by introducing errors.

All of these architectural and organizational features require further attention from researchers and we can expect significant progress in this field for some time into the future.

11.3.5 DDBs versus DESs

There are many similarities between DDBs and DESs, even leaving aside the more obvious ones due purely to distribution. These have been indicated in the preceding subsections. An obvious example is that both have private information as well as shared information.

However, we want to focus here on the differences between the two types of system. There are three clear distinguishing features based on the capabilities of the nodes, which reflect the *differences* between ESs and DBs in general.

(1) The first of the differences that we consider is that of repositories versus agents. Whilst it is not easy to clearly define the differences between the capabilities of the nodes in the two types of system, it is evident that there is such a distinction and that it goes a long way towards defining the boundary between the systems.

DDBs are data and factual knowledge stores only. There are in fact some systems such as D-POREL which incorporate some deductive capability, and there are some systems commercially available which encapsulate methods with data in the stores, such as ONTOS. However these are considered as out-liers as far as DDBs are concerned and serve to show that we are really talking about a continuum rather than two clearly partitioned system classes.

In DESs the agents are, by definition, composed of factual knowledge sources supplemented by reasoning capabilities.

(2) In a DDB there is a single answer to a query. On the other hand, in DESs there may be no unique solution to a given problem.

These distinctions are supplemented by a number of less universally manifested differences.

(3) Database systems tend to neglect incompleteness problems in data, or try to get away with a minimum of effort in this respect. The same is generally true for the handling of the time domain. There are exceptions, for example EDDS pays particular attention to both of these issues, but these are not considered to be mainstream features of DDBs in the way they are for DESs.

(4) In DDBs it is unusual to find significant or extensive data replication. On the other hand, in type 2 DESs in particular, either

rules or facts might appear at several places in the network. It is still unusual, however, to find both rules and facts replicated.

(5) In spite of the recent increase of interest in loosely-integrated federated DDB systems, it is still the norm to have a global schema in a DDB. This is not the case in DESs, which have a local perspective only. In DESs, if a problem cannot be solved locally it is passed to a 'neighbour'.

(6) In type 2 DESs, dialogue can take place between agents. The rate of convergence to a solution depends heavily on the organization of this feature, for example in the choice of criteria to measure this rate.

11.4 Object-oriented databases

Although the object-oriented approach to programming has been around since the 1960s in the form of the Simula programming language, the ideas have remained largely unexploited by the DB world until well into the 1980s. To date the main impetus for the development of object-oriented techniques has been in the area of graphical user interfaces (GUIs). Many of the GUIs which are so popular today, such as the Macintosh, Microsoft Windows, OSF Motif and Open Look, are object-based.

A number of factors have triggered interest in the application of object-oriented techniques to DBs as a means of overcoming many of the perceived shortcomings of the RDB approach. These include

- Lack of DB support for non-business applications,
- The impedance mismatch between procedural and DB query languages,
- The need to develop better computer models of the real world.

The object-oriented approach appears to provide a solution to these problems.

11.4.2 Characteristics of non-business type applications

Non-business applications are characterized by two principal attributes which distinguish them from business applications. These are

- Complex objects
- Long-lived transactions.

RDB technology is ideally suited to the needs of business type applications. Such applications are reasonably modelled using the flat two-dimensional structure of RDBs. Engineering applications such as computer-aided design and manufacturing (CAD/CAM) systems require support for much more complex objects than the relation. In particular, the requirement that attributes in relations contain atomic values (i.e. in first normal form) adds considerable complexity for applications which are trying to model complex hierarchical data structures. For example, a GP DB could be structured hierarchically by grouping patients by family and recording details of each visit by a family member and any tests performed in a tree, as shown in Figure 11.8. To model this situation using an RDB, we have to store each relationship as a separate relation and build up composite primary keys, as shown in Figure 11.9. This approach clearly adds complexity for the user and also imposes a perform-

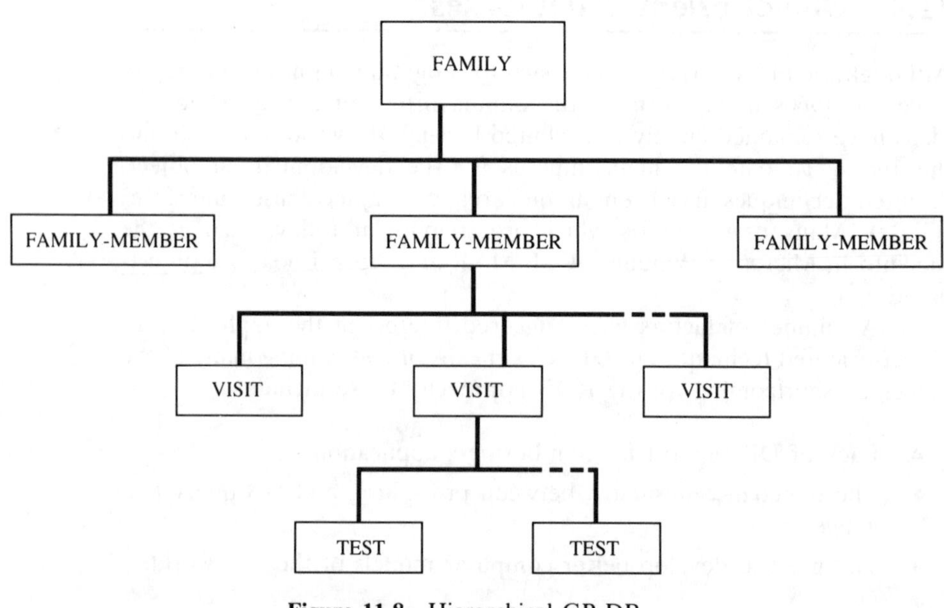

Figure 11.8 Hierarchical GP DB.

FAMILY (*Family-name*, ...)

FAMILY-MEMBER (*Family-name*, *patient-name*, ...)

VISIT (*Family-name*, *patient-name*, *date*, ...)

TEST(*Family-name*, *patient-name*, *date*, *testid*, ...)

Figure 11.9 Relational representation of hierarchical GP DB.

ance penalty. If the GP wants to display all the data relating to one patient, such a simple request would involve three JOINs!

Another important characteristic of many non-business applications is their use of long-lived transactions. For example, in an engineering design system, it is quite common for a design engineer to check a component out of the DB, work on it over several days, or even weeks and then check it back in. The recovery managers of RDBMSs are not designed to handle such long-lived transactions.

Finally, conventional RDBMSs restrict users to a finite set of predefined data types such as string, integer and real. Many are not suited to the storage of arbitrary strings of text and very few can handle the enormous bitmaps generated by imaging systems. There is a need in many applications to handle multimedia information – conventional data, images, graphics, text, even voice. Users need to be able to define abstract data types and operations on these types. For example, we might wish to search for a particular word in a text string or to rotate a graphical image through a certain angle.

11.4.3 The impedance mismatch

Apart from the obvious needs of non-business applications, the DB community is turning to the object-oriented paradigm to provide a solution to the so-called **impedance mismatch** problem. In order to develop applications using conventional DB technology, two programming languages are required – a query language, such as SQL, and a procedural language such as COBOL or C. These two languages do not fit together well. SQL is a set-at-a-time language; in other words it operates on entire relations and the result of an SQL operation is itself a relation. Procedural languages cannot handle whole relations; they can only handle a single tuple at a time. This problem is referred to as the impedance mismatch between the two programming languages.

Fourth generation languages (4GLs) represent an attempt to overcome this impedance mismatch problem, and have achieved varying degrees of success. The object-oriented approach attempts to remove the problem altogether; the object-oriented programming language and object-oriented DBMS types are one and the same.

11.4.4 Basic object-oriented concepts

The basic idea underlying the object-oriented model is quite simple. An **object** is any real-world entity (e.g. a car, a patient). Associated with every object is a set of **attributes** (e.g. name, address, telephone number of the patient object). For every object, there is a set of operations, called **methods**, which can be performed on the object (e.g. admit a patient, discharge a patient). Methods and attributes are stored together (i.e. they are **encapsulated** in the object). This is quite different from the way relations and procedures which operate on those relations are handled in RDBs. Relations (the attributes) are stored in the DB and procedures (the methods) are stored separately in a software library. An important advantage of encapsulation is that it facilitates reuse of code. Most large software projects start coding from scratch, making little if any use of existing and possibly similar code. Compare this to hardware projects, where most of a new machine could be made up of components of an existing design. Some of these components may not require any modification whatsoever for use in the new machine, whereas others might require only minor modifications. Very few components would have to be built totally from scratch.

Objects which share the same methods and attributes can be grouped together into a **class** (e.g. the class of patients). Classes themselves can be organised into a hierarchy such that subclasses **inherit** attributes and methods from superclasses. For example, the patient class could be divided into two subclasses – in-patients and out-patients – as shown in Figure 11.10. Both in-patients and out-patients share some methods and attributes with either parent class, but each has some additional features which are peculiar to themselves. For example, an in-patient will have a ward number and a bed number, whereas an out-patient will have an appointment date and so on. Inheritance provides a powerful tool for modelling and also facilitates code reuse since the code for registering a new patient can be shared by both in-patients and out-patients.

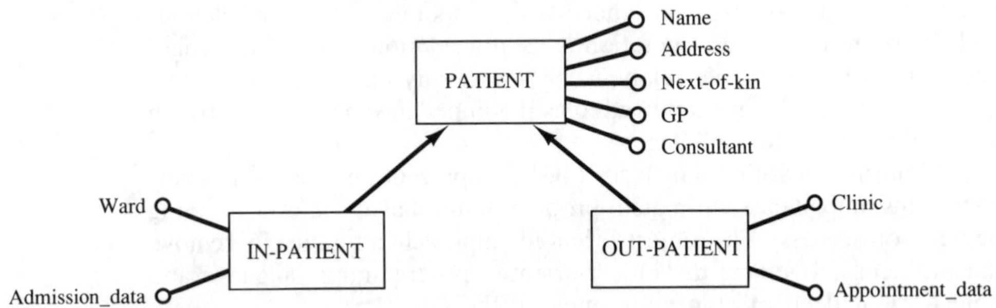

Figure 11.10 Class inheritance in an OODB.

11.4.5 Distributed object-oriented DBMSs

The first commercial object-oriented DBMSs (OODBMSs) have only emerged quite recently and so very little thought has been given to the development of distributed versions of these products. However, the need for inheritance in DDBs has already been shown in the schema integration problem discussed in Chapter 9. This has led people to suggest that object-oriented techniques could provide a powerful 'glue' for integrating heterogeneous systems.

The canonical model for the global system would be object-oriented, rather than relational. However, while this approach has many attractions, the absence of a standard object model and associated query language makes such a solution to integrating heterogeneous systems today less generally applicable. A common approach today is to design systems using the object-oriented model and then map the model onto a relational DB during the implementation. The disadvantage of this is that the materialization of 'object-oriented' views can require the construction of multiple JOINs across several relations.

11.5 Extended relational systems

It seems very unlikely that OODBMS will replace RDBMS in all application areas. RDBMS and SQL are now an accepted industry DB standard and many organizations have invested a lot in the technology through their use in complex applications. Moreover, for many organizations, the relational approach is perfectly satisfactory. They do not need complex objects, long-lived transactions or abstract data types, so there is no incentive whatsoever for them to change. It is probable therefore that OODBMS will co-exist with extended relational systems.

The basic idea behind the development of extended RDBMSs is to extend the relational model to overcome some of its present shortcomings, that is to adopt an evolutionary approach rather than the revolutionary approach of OODBMS. Advocates of the extended relational approach to third generation DBMS, the Committee for Advanced DBMS Function, have issued a manifesto (CADF, 1990) analogous to the object-oriented database system manifesto (Atkinson *et al.*, 1989). In particular, the Committee propose three tenets which third generation DBMSs must follow and which the authors state can be met by extending the current relational model:

(1) In addition to standard data management functions, third generation DBMSs must support complex objects (including text, graphics, images, etc.) and rules (not just relational integrity);

(2) Third generation DBMSs must provide all the capabilities of second generation systems, including in particular, non-procedural access through query languages such as SQL and data independence;

(3) Third generation DBMSs must be open to other subsystems; this requirement is particularly important in relation to DDBMS.

Under each of the three tenets, the Committee also put forward a number of more detailed propositions. In particular, there is agreement between them and the OODBMS proponents that third generation DBMSs must support complex objects, functions (DB procedures and methods), inheritance and encapsulation. A number of research prototypes have been developed which explore various issues in the evolutionary step towards third generation DBMS through the extended relational approach. There is also considerable interest in the development of relational systems which allow non-first normal form relations, the so-called NF^2 relations, which allow attributes of relations to be relations themselves. Several researchers have proposed extensions to SQL to support objects.

11.6 Multimedia databases

11.6.1 Introduction

In Chapter 1 of this book we pointed out that information systems which deal with only structured text (i.e. using record-based databases), even if they are supplemented by techniques for reasoning from AI (such as expert systems), can provide only imperfect models of the real world. Information can be communicated to users from suppliers using images (including graphics, pictures and diagrams), voice, unstructured text and even video, and in certain situations, it is impossible to dispense with these. Modelling the real world as, for example, 2-D tables and communicating on this basis is bound to fall short of the ideal.

Applications which demand the use of 'non-structured media' include office information systems, geographical information systems, engineering design systems, medical information systems and military command and control systems. For some time database researchers have been endeavouring to address the additional issues this raises for generalized database management systems.

The issues include modelling the part of the world of interest, interrogating the database, presentation of results and ensuring acceptable performance – problems which present a higher level of challenge than the corresponding problems for conventional databases. When the systems are distributed as well, clearly each of these problems is aggravated and, of course, additional harmonization and integration difficulties are met as well.

Interestingly, the ideas of multidatabases give us a hint as to a possible approach to this problem. If the heterogeneity we dealt with in previous chapters is extended to include multiple media, we can use some of the solutions to MDB problems as a starting point for addressing the distributed multimedia problems.

In the next subsection we rehearse the arguments for multimedia databases in a little more detail, and from this get a clear picture of the requirements. Following this we survey some of the previous work aimed at getting insights into multimedia database problems and trying out some of the proposed solutions. Insights pertinent to our study come from a variety of different sources, such as papers, books and reports on applications like the office information systems and medical information systems listed above. However we restrict our attention here to looking at some examples of reasonably generic approaches to the problems. Then we consider the modules or organization one would expect to find in a multimedia database system, and consider how we could 'grow' multimedia DBSs (MMDBSs) from MDBs.

11.6.2 Motivation

Multimedia data can be defined for our purposes as data in the form of computerized text (structured and unstructured), sound and/or images. If computers are to be exploited fully in the communication process described in Chapter 1 (Figure 1.2), they must be able to handle information of the type that applications end-users normally handle. This 'handling' must include basic information processing for storing and accessing information and also some more complex and specialized information processing for identifying material of interest – matching, clustering, retrieving on the basis of content, to list just a few examples.

A multimedia database management system (MMDBMS) is a software system which manages the data in the same manner as conventional DBMSs. For structured data alone such DBMSs do a fine job. For unstructured text, such as in office documents and bibliographic systems, a variety of tools can be found for most computers and workstations. These include electronic mail services, text editors and formatters and information retrieval system 'databases' (see Chapter 1).

However, in non-computer systems, users and suppliers of information communicate using a rich variety of media and language elements. An obvious example is where they talk directly to each other. A dialogue of verbal questions and answers is a particularly venerable mode of communication. Using maps, diagrams and little sketches, the communication process can be greatly expedited. Examples of this are when computer experts are designing new applications, and this is a reflection of the methods of communication methods used commonly in society at large – for giving directions to someone from out of town, or instructing an architect on your proposed new house. Pointing to objects or following the course of a circuit diagram with a pencil and suchlike 'body language' certainly helps in clarifying concepts which are difficult to articulate verbally or in text.

So we can say that if computers are to be applied in any way optimally to communications between people, the goal must be to store and utilize information recorded using the kinds of media with which the people are familiar. Clearly a very high-level means of addressing queries to the system must be provided and it should include, at the minimum, the use of voice and image.

When responses are returned, further refinement, for example by browsing, of the information may have to be carried out before usable output is obtained. Some sort of clever presentation device is needed for this.

When it is considered that medical images, for example, take up several megabits of storage, it becomes clear that efficiency of both data storage and transfer is of paramount importance. Moreover, given the diversity of the data objects in a system like this, an obvious problem of heterogeneity and data modelling is encountered. So information representation and information integration (or harmonization) are needed as well.

The climate is now right for developments of MMDBMSs because of the familiar pattern of various technological advances to match these user demands. The powerful workstations with the capacity and power needed to accommodate multimedia data collections, and with the screen technology and data handling software to match, are now on the market. Communications links with sufficient bandwidth for much of the job, backed up by appropriate standards, are in place in many organizations. Storage technology, optical and otherwise, provides the empty information reservoir of a size which can take this bulk. Data representation advances allow data modelling with higher fidelity to reality.

11.6.3 Where we are now

Multimedia data is a naturally occurring phenomenon. The main aim of a MMDBMS is to provide system support in the form of uniform representation, storage, manipulation and retrieval facilities for heterogeneous data on multiple media. Several survey papers can be found among those listed in the references, but in this subsection we present a brief overview of the current status of the evolution of DBMSs in this direction.

There are three major approaches to the problem of handling multimedia data. The first is to use a bottom-up philosophy. Starting with conventional databases systems, usually relational, successive adaptations have been made in order to make the systems capable of handling different types of media. Examples are the REMINDS system which uses a relation-based approach to image and text integration and the POSTGRES system which is a close descendant of INGRES handling at least some of the unstructured data arising in applications.

It has been suggested that the RDM needs to be extended in several ways to accommodate multimedia objects. The extensions include: variable-length fields for flexible object-sizing (e.g. large text documents can be accommodated using this feature), abstract data typing (with a hierarchy of types, for example) and non-first normal forms (where entities can have other entities as their attributes). Most commentators agree that some sort of object-orientation is needed.

Handling complex interobject relationships, permanent (system-defined) identifiers or surrogates, property inheritance, allowing objects to have procedures as attributes and allowing users to define data types of their own are required. There are various difficulties which still retard the development of this approach, such as how to incorporate the new data types and functions into query languages, how to implement the functions and how to exploit novel system features during query optimization.

An alternative to this bottom-up approach is to make a fresh start and develop a MMDBMS which from the outset is geared to integrating multimedia data. Typical of the research that has been going on in this area is the work carried out at the University of Waterloo in Canada on the MINOS project. The researchers aim to handle compound documents using a variety of media. The documents are subdivided into pages or screenfulls of visual information and fixed lengths of audio information. Browsing capabilities for both voice and text are provided by the system which is designed *ab initio* for multimedia data handling. The system architecture of MINOS, implemented on Sun workstations, consists of a multimedia object server and numerous networked work stations. The server subsystem is backed by high-speed magnetic disks and optical disks. It provides performance-oriented features such as physical access methods, recovery subsystems, caches and schedulers.

A query-trace for MINOS is instructive. Object-oriented queries are addressed to it by users at work stations, and evaluation is carried out at the server. Visual indexing cues (arrays of miniature images, for example) can be provided to help navigation and in the clearer formulation of fuzzy queries. A presentation manager in the work station is used to help the user carry out a browse-mode perusal of data objects related to his/her enquiry.

The third approach is to develop a multimedia database for some application as a one-off exercise. This was a common pattern in the early days of conventional databases. A specific data management system is designed and bespoke-tailored to some very specific environment. In fact this produces an elaborate, one-off, application system rather than the generalized system support we are looking for here.

So while we can learn a lot from the experiences gained developing these systems, they are outside the scope of our treatment of the subject. We are considering the multimedia equivalent of the conventional DBMS. The applications could be any of those listed above, or any other applications which require minimum cost, maximum flexibility and other, often conflicting, characteristics of its accesses to multimedia data in a 'corporate' data reservoir.

11.6.4 Module architecture – evolving from multidatabase systems

We base our model architecture on that of a system called medical image data access method (MIDAM). This is a system designed specifically for integrating text and images in a hospital environment, but it really is a particular customization of a more general architecture which could be applied just as well to any, possibly distributed, multimedia data environment.

This system is interesting in that it is a hybrid, 'bred' from a DDBMS and individual media-handling systems such as image processing or information retrieval packages. It is based on the RDM, so conventional MDBMS techniques can handle the multisite indexing aspects of the operations. The multimedia aspects are handled in a rather crude, but effective, way.

If we focus on text and images only for the purposes of this discussion, it is interesting to note that the local medium-handling software systems are likely to provide analogous functionality. Some sort of pattern recognition capability is provided in each case for abstracting features and indexing objects. In both cases it is no longer novel to use the RDM to handle the resulting abstracts. The RDM can also handle, at a crude level, the basic gross document-matching functions: 'given image 1 get me the images that are similar to it'.

In the MIDAM system, the EDDS system is used on top of local RDBMSs to provide the integration capability. Additional code is included to cover for the inadequacies of the RDM. The architecture is shown in Figure 11.11.

Consider the operation of the system as it handles image queries. Image queries address an image descriptor database (IDD) and when matches are made, entire documents are pulled from the raw database and routed to the presentation manager (PM) at the user's site, where editing, browsing and so on can be carried out. When a request for an image is received, an EDDS query is generated, and the global image director (GI) logs this. EDDS deals with the query in the usual way, but when the IDD is accessed pointers to the image are sent, along with navigational information, to the local image handler (LIH), via the local image pointer handler (LI). The retrieved image is routed via the network components and the GI to the PM.

In hospital applications the network for images has to be of much greater bandwidth than for text. It makes sense to have different networks for text and images. The local network component (LNC) has to make sure that the responses go to the right networks. Also, in this environment the request site and the site to which the response has to be delivered are often different. This is not illustrated in Figure 11.11. Pre-fetching of bulky data with respect to predicted usage patterns is highly desirable here as well, and this capability is sewn into the fabric of the system.

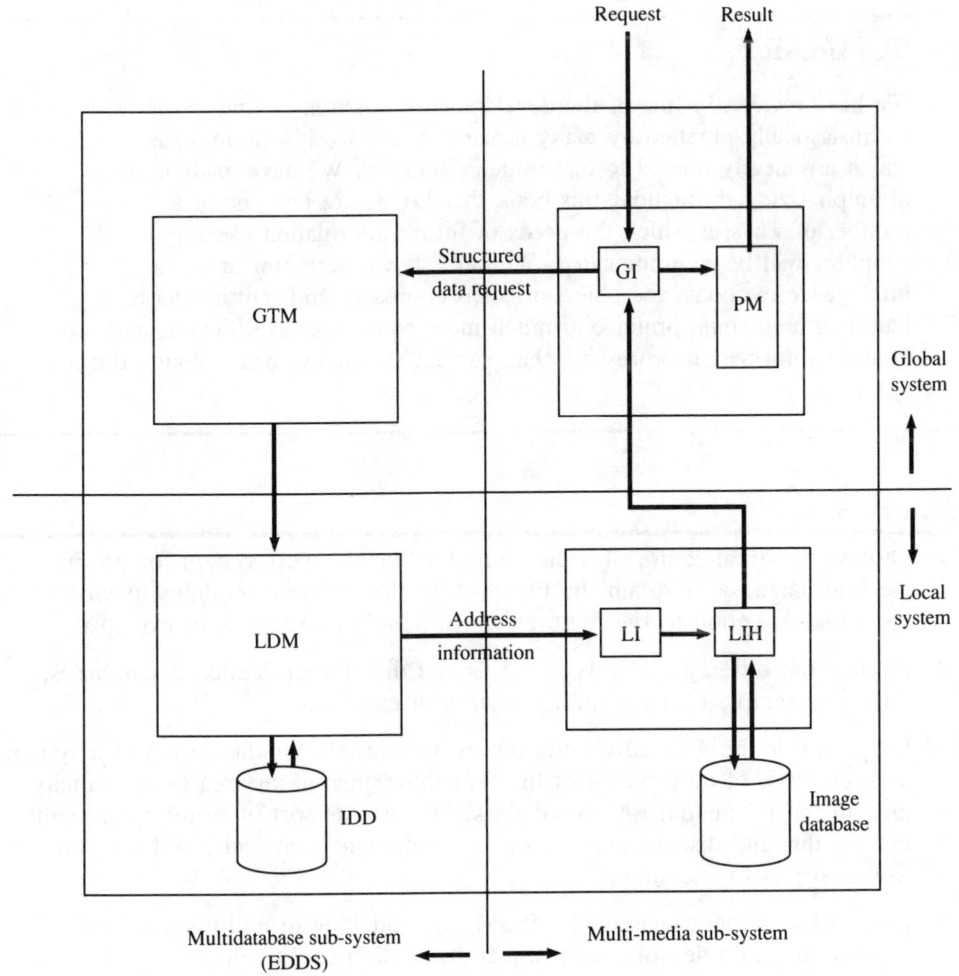

Figure 11.11 MIDAM architecture.

When the bulk objects have been delivered to the workstations, local image processing and other manipulations can be carried out to suit the application.

We believe that these sorts of considerations will be important in other application domains as well. However, each domain will have some idiosyncratic problems, so the highly flexible, customizable MIDAM approach can be used, where the fixed part of the system is EDDS and the rest can be tailored given some important set-in-concrete system support.

SUMMARY

We have reviewed some of the developments which are being enthusiastically pursued by many research teams worldwide in areas which are clearly related to distributed databases. We have made a point of emphasizing throughout this book that DDBs are just one of a number of ways in which the needs of future information users and suppliers will be communicated. We have shown here how artificial intelligence methods, the object-oriented approach, and multimedia data handling hold some promise of much more comprehensive, flexible and efficient information processing than current systems provide. Watch this space!

EXERCISES

11.1 Outline the architecture of a distributed artificial expert system for use in medical diagnosis. Explain the functions of the different modules, paying particular attention to the features which handle inexactness of evidence.

11.2 Explain the differences between DESs and distributed deductive databases. Give an example of a typical application of each class.

11.3 Suppose it is the year 2010 and you are responsible for the design of a system to keep track of movements of the remaining gnus in an area of one square mile in the Kilimanjaro National Park. Discuss the sort of system you might use for this and discuss some of the more difficult technical problems you would expect to encounter.

11.4 Discuss the inadequacies of the RDM for modelling in multimedia applications, and describe how object-orientation could help.

11.5 What sort of effect do you think object-orientation would have on the system architecture of MIDAM?

11.6 Drawing illustrations from a variety of applications areas, discuss the motivations for having multimedia databases.

11.7 (a) What are the three main approaches to coupling databases and expert systems?
(b) Discuss the relative advantages and disadvantages of each approach.

11.8 What are the characteristics of the object-oriented approach which make it a particularly suitable choice for the canonical model for interoperable DBMSs?

11.9 (a) What are the two rival contenders for the title 'third generation DBMS'?
(b) Which contender is described as evolutionary and why?
(c) Which contender is described as revolutionary and why?

Bibliography

Abul-Huda B. and Bell D.A. (1988). An overview of a distributed multimedia DBMS (KALEID). In *Proc. EURINFO Conf. on Information Technology for Organisational Systems*, Athens, Greece.

This paper presents an overview of the problems of integrating distributed multimedia data. KALEID was an early implementation of a system like the MIDAM system, but it was not restricted to medical applications or restricted to text and images only.

Alexander D., Grimson J., O'Moore R. and Brosnan P. (1990). *Analysis of Decision Support Requirements for Laboratory Medicine*. Eolas Strategic Research Programme Project on Integrating Knowledge and Data in Laboratory Medicine, Deliverables D1, D2, D3 Department of Computer Science, Trinity College, Dublin, Ireland.

This report gives a comprehensive review of computerized decision support techniques in laboratory medicine from instrumentation through to patient management systems.

Al-Zobaidie A. and Grimson J.B. (1988). Use of metadata to drive the interaction between databases and expert systems. *Information and Software Technology*, **30**(8), 484–96.

The taxonomy for coupling ESs and DBs presented in Section 11.2.1 is based on this paper, which also describes the DIFEAD System mentioned in Section 11.2.1.

Atkinson M., Bancilhon F., De Witt D., Dittrich K., Maier D. and Zdonik S. (1989). The object-oriented database system manifesto. In *Proc. Deductive and Object-oriented Databases*, Kyoto, December 1989. Amsterdam: Elsevier-Science.

This much publicized paper presents the ingredients which the authors feel should go into a system for it to be called an OODBMS. They divide features into those which they consider mandatory (complex objects, object identity, encapsulation, types or classes, inheritance, overriding combined with late binding, extensibility, computational completeness, persistence, secondary storage management, concurrency, recovery and *ad hoc* query support) and those which are optional (multiple inheritance, type checking, inferencing, distribution, design transactions and versions).

Bancilhon F. and Ramakrishnan R. (1986). An amateur's introduction to recursive query processing strategies. In *Proc. ACM SIGMOD Conf.*, 16–52, Washington, D.C.

This paper gives an easy-to-follow overview of recursive query processing strategies, which form an important part of the research on deductive DBs.

Beech D. (1988). A foundation for evolution from relational to object databases. In *Proc. EDBT 88, Advances in Database Technology*, Venice, Italy, March 1988. Also in *Lecture Notes in Computer Science* Vol. 303 (Schmidt J.W., Ceri S. and Missikoff M., eds.), 251–70. Berlin: Springer-Verlag.

This is an interesting proposal for an object-oriented extension to SQL, called OSQL.

Bell D.A., Grimson J.B. and Ling D.H.O. (1989). Implementation of an integrated multidatabase-PROLOG system. *Information and Software Technology*, **31**(1), 29–38.

Bell D.A. and Zhang C. (1990). Description and treatment of dead-locks in the HECODES distributed expert system. *IEEE Trans. on Systems, Man and Cybernetics*, **20**(3), 645–64.

The causes of deadlocks in distributed expert systems in general are examined and classified and methods of avoid them are put forward.

Particular attention is paid to the design of features for deadlock resolution in HECODES. Experimental results are used to distinguish between the alternative strategies.

Bell D.A., Shao J. and Hull M.E.C. (1990). Integrated deductive database system implementation: a systematic study. *Computer J.* **33**(1), 40–8.

This paper provides a comparison between the various approaches to incorporating a deductive component into a relational DBMS.

Bell D.A., Ling D.H.O. and Kofakis P. (1991). *Interoperability of Distributed Text and Image Databases in a Medical Environment*. Internal Report, University of Ulster, N. Ireland.

This paper describes the MIDAM system, based on using EDDS to integrate the distributed relations describing the images and text stored around a hospital. The application requirements are clearly spelt out to justify the customizing carried out.

Brodie M.L. (1989). Future intelligent information systems: AI and database technologies working together. In *Readings in Artificial Intelligence and Databases* (Mylopoulos J. and Brodie M.L., eds.), 623–73. Morgan Kaufmann.

This is an interesting paper in which the author proposes that the next generation of information systems will be based on intelligent interoperability requiring the effective integration of techniques from (D)DB to support information management and interoperability and AI to provide the intelligence.

Committee for Advanced DBMS Function (1990). Third generation database system manifesto. In *Proc. IFIP WG2.6 Conference on Object Oriented Databases*. Windermere, England, July 1990.

This is the alternative proposal to that of Atkinson *et al.* (1989) for the third generation of DBMSs.

Christodoulakis S., Ho F. and Theodoridou M. (1986). The multi-media object presentation manager of MINOS: a symmetric approach. In *Proc. ACM SIGMOD Conference*, 295–310, Washington DC.

A useful introduction to MINOS.

Copestake A. and Sparck Jones K. (1990). Natural language interfaces to databases. *Knowledge Engineering Review*, **5**(4), 225–49.

An excellent review of the issues involved in the provision of natural language interfaces to DBs.

Dadam P., Kuespert K., Anderson F. *et al.* (1986). A DBMS prototype to support extended NF^2 relations: an integrated view of flat tables and hierarchies. In *Proc. 1986 ACM-SIGMOD Conference on Management of Data*, 356–67, Washington DC.

Dahl O. and Nygaard K. (1966). Simula, an Algol-based simulation language. *CACM*, **9**(9), 671–8.

Simula is regarded as the first object-oriented programming language.

Dai H., Anderson T.J. and Monds F.C. (1990). A framework for real-time problem solving. In *Proc. 19th European Conf. on AI*, Stockholm, Sweden.

This paper gives an account of the philosophy behind the HOPES system and outlines the architecture.

Deen S.M. *et al.* (1990). *Proc. International Working Conf. on Cooperating Knowledge Based Systems*, Keele, England, October 1990 (to be published).

This is an excellent volume to look out for. Most of the DES issues raised in Section 11.3 are dealt with to some extent.

Durfee E.H., Lesser V.R. and Corkill D.D. (1987). Cooperation through communication in a distributed problem solving network. In *Distributed Artificial Intelligence* (Huhns M.N., ed.), 29–58. Morgan Kaufmann.

This is one of many excellent papers describing the DVMT system.

Gardarin G. and Valduriez P. (1989). *Relational Databases and Knowledge Bases*. Wokingham: Addison-Wesley.

Guan J.W. and Bell D.A. (1991). *Evidence Theory and its Applications*, Vol. 1, Amsterdam: North Holland.

Guan J.W., Bell D.A. and Lesser V.R. (1990). Evidential reasoning and strength in expert systems. In *Proc. 3rd Irish Conference on AI and Cognitive Science*, Belfast, September 1990.

Hughes J.G. (1991). *Object-oriented databases*. New York: Prentice-Hall.

Huhns M.N., Mukhopadhyay U., Stephens L.M. and Bonnell R.D. (1987). DAI for document retrieval: the MINDS Project. In *Distributed Artificial Intelligence* (Huhns M.N., ed.), 249–84. Morgan Kaufmann.

One of many excellent papers in this volume.

Lu R. and Zhou L. (1990). The architecture and user languages of D-POREL*. *Database Technology*, **3**(1), 1–9.

One way of distributing intelligence around a network is to use the distributed deductive database approach which is adopted for D-POREL*.

Matsuo F., Futamura S. and Shinohara T. (1986). Efficient storage and retrieval of very large document databases. In *Proc. IEEE Int. Conf. on Data Engineering*.

A good summary of the problems of multimedia data and proposed solutions in the mid-1980s. Many of these are still pertinent.

Minker J., ed. (1988). *Foundations of Deductive Databases and Logic Programming*. Morgan Kaufmann.

O'Moore R.R. (1988). Decision support based on laboratory data. *Methods of Information in Medicine*, **27**, 187–90.

This paper explains the need for and advantages of decision-support systems in laboratory medicine.

Parsaye K., Chignell M., Khoshafian W. and Wong H. (1989). *Intelligent Databases, Object-oriented, deductive hypermedia technologies*. New York: Wiley.

Poggio A., Garcia Luna Aceves J.J., Craighill E.J. *et al.* (1985). CCWS: A computer-based multimedia information system. *IEEE Computer*, **18**(10), 92–103.

CCWS, a multimedia system for military command and control activities, is described.

Shaw M.J., Harrow B. and Herman S. (1990). NEST: a networked expert systems testbed for cooperative problem solving. In *Proc. Int. Working Conf. on Cooperating Knowledge Based Systems*, 11–17. Keele, England, October 1990 (to be published).

The NEST framework for designing group problem-solving systems is presented. Particular attention is paid to the coordination mechanisms and learning schemes.

Shao J., Bell D.A. and Hull M.E.C. (1990). An experimental performance study of a pipelined recursive query processing strategy. In *Proc. DPDS 90*, 30–43 July 1990. Dublin, Ireland.

Shortcliffe E.H. (1976). *MYCIN: Computer Based Medical Consultation*. New York: Elsevier.

MYCIN was one of the pioneering rule-based decision support systems.

Stonebraker M. (1990). The implementation of POSTGRES. *IEEE Trans. on Knowledge and Data Engineering*. **2**(1), 125–142.

POSTGRES is one of the best known and most developed examples of the extended relational approach to third generation DBMSs.

Woelk D. and Kim W. (1987). Multi-media information management in an object-oriented database system. In *Proc. 13th Int. Conf. on VLDB*, 319–330.

Brighton, England.

This paper advocates the use of object-oriented data modelling concepts for multimedia databases. It is well worth a read as an introduction to multimedia databases.

Woelk D., Kim W. and Luther W. (1986). An object-oriented approach to multimedia databases. In *Proc. 1986 ACM SIGMOD Conf.*, 311–325, Washington DC. May 1986.

Zhang C. and Bell D.A. Some aspects of second generation expert systems. In *Proc. 1st Irish Conf. on Artificial Intelligence*, Dublin, Ireland.

An account of some of the issues which expert systems in the next few years will address.

Zhang C. and Bell D.A. (1991). HECODES: a framework for heterogeneous cooperative distributed expert systems. *Data and Knowledge Engineering*, **6**, 251–73.

This paper describes the architecture of HECODES in minute detail.

Glossary/Acronyms

2PC	Two Phase Commit - a recovery protocol	247ff
2PL	Two Phase Locking - a concurrency control method	181ff
3GL	Third Generation Language - e.g. COBOL, C	15
3PC	Three Phase Commit - a recovery protocol	256ff
4GL	Fourth Generation Language - e.g. FOCUS, RAMIS	15
ACF/VTAM	Telecommunications software from IBM	69
ADABAS	A DBMS from Software AG	72
ADDS	Another Distributed Database System	89
ADR	Applied Data Research, Inc	69
ADR/D-NET	A DDBMS	69
AI	Artificial Intelligence	364ff
ANSI	American National Standards Institute	16
ANSI-SPARC	The Americal National Standards Institute-Standards Planning and Requirements Committee - responsible for the standard 3-layer reference architecture for DBMS	16
ARPA	A North-American scientific and academic computer network	91
AVG	"Average" in SQL	155
BCNF	Boyce Codd Normal Form	32
BDAM	Basic Direct Access Method - a file access method	78
BSAM	Basic Sequential Access Method - a file access method	78
B(R)	Number of bytes per tuple in R	141
B-tree	A data storage and access structure (index)	67
B(X)	Number of bytes in attribute collection X	141
C	A programming language	79
c	Cost of joining two tuples	127
C_c	Cost per tuple concatenation	139
C_{cpu}	Importance weight of CPU	144, 147
C_m	Importance weight of messages	144
C_{mb}	Cost per message byte	147
C_p	Importance weight of I/O	147

C_{pm}	Cost per message weight	147
C_t	Cost per tuple comparison	139
C(R)	Cardinality of R	141
C(RA)	Inverse selectivity of attribute A in R	141
CA-DB/PC	A personal computing element of the CA database environment	72
CA-DB:STAR	A DDB system product from Computer Associates	69
CARD(R)	Cardinality of R	139
CASE	Computer-aided software engineering	12
CCA	Computer Corporation of America, Inc	73, 158
CCITT	Comitié Consultatif International de Télégraphique et Téléphonique - the international committee of national PTTs	43
CCR	Commitment, Concurrency and Recovery - part of the RDAP protocol aimed at providing support for 2PC	43
CEIL(X)	The next whole number greater than X	148
CICS	Customer Information Control System	79, 82
CICS/ISC	CICS/Intersite communications	82
CLAN 6	An ICL computer	79
COBOL	Common Business-oriented Language	76
CODASYL	Conference on Data Systems Languages - the organisation responsible for maintaining COBOL standards	28
CPU	Central Processing Unit	126, 127
CRAI	Consorzio per la Ricerca e le Applicazioni di Informatica	78
CSA	Cooperative Systems Architecture	67
DA	Data Administrator	316
DAI	Distributed Artificial Intelligence	370ff
DAPLEX	The programming language of Multibase	73, 112
DATACOMM/DB	A DBMS from ADR	69
DB	Database	7
DBMS	Database Management System	7
DBA	Database Administrator	71, 315
DBase III	A micro DBMS	86
DB2	A relational DBMS from IBM	68
DBTG	Database Task Group - a subcommittee of CODASYL responsible for the original definition of network DB model	28
DC*	The data communications module of R*	82
DD	Data Dictionary/Directory	321
DDB	Distributed Database	6, 44ff
DDBA	Distributed Database Administrator	316
DDBMS	Distributed Database Management System	6, 44ff
DDL	Data Definition Language	93, 107
DDS	Data Dictionary/Directory System	321
DES	Data Encryption Standard	294
DES	Distributed Expert System	370ff
DML	Data Manipulation Language	93, 107
D-POREL	A deductive version of POREL	380
DQ	The query language for DATACOMM/DB	71
DQS	Distributed Query System - an MDBMS	73, 77
DVTB	Distant Vehicle Monitoring Test-bed	373ff

EC	European Commission	64
EDDS	Experimental Distributed Database Management System	83, 362
EDP	Electronic Data Processing	335
ER	Entity-relationship - an approach to data modelling	304
ES	Expert System	365
FAP	File Allocation Problem	102ff
FLOOR(X)	The next whole number less than X	148
FOCUS	A 4GL	15
GCA	Global Communications Architecture (Ingres)	67
GDD	Global Data Dictionary	84, 320ff
GDM	Global Data Manager	76
GI	Global Image Director	390
GTM	Global Transaction Manager	83
GUI	Graphical User Interface	381
HEARSAY II	A blackboard-based system	372
HECODES	Heterogeneous cooperating distributed expert system - a distributed expert system prototype	376ff
HIS	Hospital Information System	358
HOPES	Hierarchically organised parallel expert system - a distributed expert system prototype	372ff
IDD	Image descriptor database	390
IDMS	A network DBMS	71
IDMS DB/DC	IDMS geared up for communications	77
IDMS/R	IDMS with a relational front-end	72
INGRES	A relational DBMS from ASK/Ingres	66ff
INGRES/NET	A network protocol for INGRES/STAR	67
INGRES/STAR	A distributed version of INGRES	65, 354
I/O	Input/output	125, 144
IPV	Information Public View	356
ISAM	Indexed Sequential Access Method	67
ISO/OSI	International Standards Organisation/Open Systems Interconnection - a standard 7 layer protocol for data communication	40–43
ITAPAC	An Italian communications package	357
$J_c(R^*)$	JOIN cost for R*	147
$J_{css}(R^*)$	Single site JOIN cost for R*	147
KP	Knapsack Problem	103, 127
L_i	Length of inner record	148
L_{max}	Maximum message length	148
L_{ok}	Length of outer key	148
L_r	Average message length	148
LAN	Local area network	38–39
LDI	Local Data Interface	76
LDM	Local Data Manger	83
LHU	Local Health Unit	356–358
LI	Local Image Pointer Handler	390

LIH	Local Image Handler	390
LINDA	A MDBMS	91
LNC	Local network component	390
M_c	Message cost	147
MAX	"Maximum" in SQL	135
MDB	Multidatabase	48ff
MDBMS	Multidatabase Management System	48ff
MIDAM	Medical image data access method	390ff
MINOS	A multimedia data system	389ff
MMDBMS	Multimedia database management system	387ff
MRSDM	A MDBMS	90, 91
MSDOS	The Operating System of some micro-computers	67, 357
Multibase	A MMDBMS	73, 121, 153, 160
MultiStar	A MMDBMS	78, 356
NDMS	Network Data Management System - a MDBMS	77
NEST	Networked Expert System Test-bed	376
NF^2	Non-first normal form - nested relation	386, 389
NL	Natural Language	369
NOMAD	A 4GL	15
O_{css}	Single site cost of accessing the outer table	147
ONTOS	An OODBMS	380
OODBMS	Object-oriented DBMS	318ff
OpenLook	Sun Microsystems GUI standard	381
ORACLE	A relational DBMS	72, 357
OS	Operating System	77
OSF/Motif	Open Software Foundation's GUI standard	381
P_{io}	Average number of inner relation pages fetched/outer relation tuple	147
PC	Personal computer	72
PM	Presentation Manager	390
POREL	A heterogeneous DDBMS	88, 90
POSTGRES	An extended version of INGRES having richer modelling capability	388
PRECI*	A distributed relation-based DDBMS	83, 89
PSE	Packet-switch exchanges - nodes in a network responsible for temporary storage of messages and for routing of messages in a network	38
PTT	National Post and Telegraph Organisation	43
QSAM	Queued Sequential Access Method - a file access method	78
Query-by-Forms	A user-interface for INGRES	67
QUIST	A semantic query optimisation system	160
R_{io}	Number of matching tuples in inner relation	147
R_o	Cardinality of outer relation	147
R*	An IBM DDBMS prototype	80, 124
RAMIS	A 4GL	15

RDAP	Remote Database Access Protocol - part of the ISO/OSI application layer	43
Rdb	A relational DBMS	68
RDB	Relational Database	20ff
RDBMS	Relational Database Management System	20ff
RDM	Relational data model	390
REMINDS	A relation-based image and text system	388
RDS*	Relational Data System*, part of R*	81
RMS	A relational DBMS	68
RODAN	A Polish DBMS	77
RPG	Report Program Generator - a programming language from IBM	71
RSS*	Relational Storage System*, part of R*	81
Sc(R,Lr)	Number of messages × C_{pm} + size of table × C_{mb}	147
SDD-1	A System of Distributed Databases	88, 124, 136ff
Sirius-Delta	An early DDBMS	83, 90
SNA	Systems Network Architecture for data communications	79, 82
SQL	Structured Query Language	34ff
SQL/DS	A DBMS based on SQL from IBM	68
STAR*VIEW	A DDB monitor	68
SUM	"Sum" in SQL	135
System/R	An IBM prototype relational DBMS	129, 135ff
t	Transmission cost/tuple	27
t_a	Transmission cost/attribute	139
TCP/IP	A networking system for connecting processors	68
TM*	Transaction Manager for R*	81
UCDM	Unifying Conceptual Data Model	109, 120
VDR	Ventorial Data representation	78
VSAM	Virtual Storage Access Method	71, 78
VTAM	Virtual Telecommunication Access Method	82
WAN	Wide area network	38
X.25	CCITT and ISO standard to provide basic data communications; it covers the bottom three layers of the ISO/OSI architecture	43

Author Index

Subject Index